THE Battle FOR THE Ashes

Editor: Norman Barrett
Designer: Martin Bronkhorst
Photographs by: Adrian Murrell

Published by the Daily Telegraph
135 Fleet Street, London EC4P 4BL

First published 1985
© Daily Telegraph 1985
Statistics © Bill Frindall 1985

British Library Cataloguing in
Publication Data
Carey, Michael,
The battle for the Ashes.
1. Ashes (Cricket trophy)
I. Title   II. Frindall, Bill
794.35'865   GV928.G7

ISBN 0-86367-078-4
ISBN 0-86367-073-3 Pbk

Printed and bound in Great Britain
by Garden City Press
Typeset by
Thomas/Weintroub Associates

THE Battle FOR THE Ashes

The Daily Telegraph Story of the 1985
England v Australia Test Series

MICHAEL CAREY
MATCH REPORTS & REVIEWS

BILL FRINDALL
STATISTICS & SCORING SHEETS

ALAN SHIELL
AN AUSTRALIAN VIEW

𝔇aily 𝔗elegraph

Editor's note

The Battle for the Ashes is the day-by-day record of the 1985 Test series between England and Australia as reported in the columns of the *Daily Telegraph*. The previews and reports are by Michael Carey, the chief cricket correspondent of the *Daily Telegraph*, with the Australian viewpoint contributed by Alan Shiell of the *Adelaide Advertiser*, who is also the Australian cricket correspondent of the *Daily Telegraph*.

Bill Frindall, in addition to supplying detailed scorecards and ball-by-ball scoresheets, provides a statistical preview for each Test and his special radial charts for individual hundreds. There is an explanation of his scoring method on pages 9-10, with a list of symbols used.

Contents

Interest running high

E ven before a ball was bowled in the 1985 Cornhill Test series, public interest was running higher than usual for the visit of an Australian side. All the encouraging signs were that, by the end of the six-match battle for the Ashes, financial records would be broken whether or not their cricketing counterparts were threatened.

It was not difficult to pinpoint sundry reasons for this. England, for the first time for three years, could pick their strongest side; Ian Botham was due to return after a winter's break from the game; and, not least, the achievement of David Gower and his team in winning in India in an era where success abroad was becoming notoriously difficult, perhaps led to hopes of a bright new dawn for the game in this country.

Ironically, just as the English cricketing public prepared to welcome back the likes of Graham Gooch, John Emburey and Peter Willey, who had all served three-year suspensions for taking part in the unofficial tour to South Africa in March 1982, the Australians encountered similar problems just before their own tour began.

Their party, under the leadership of Allan Border, had already been named when news broke of an impending pirate tour to South Africa later in the year. Three players were replaced. Others who were said to be involved in the South African trip later changed their minds and continued in the touring party when it became clear that their international careers might otherwise be in jeopardy.

The public's appetite was possibly also whetted by the prospect of a return to more 'normal' cricket after the often dubious tactics employed by the West Indies fast bowlers in triumphing by 5–0 the previous summer. The Australians, too, had suffered during the previous winter, the nadir of that series coming when Kim Hughes broke down while announcing his resignation of the captaincy at a press conference.

Their was also the intriguing side-issue of the England captaincy. David Gower had taken over from Bob Willis at the start of the West Indies series and, after a lack of success which had not been difficult for anyone to predict, took England to India where their arrival in Delhi coincided with the assassination of the Prime Minister, Mrs Indira Gandhi.

Later, on the eve of the first Test in Bombay, the deputy British High Commissioner was also murdered by a gunman. But Gower and his team took the ensuing problems in their stride and, after losing the first Test, won the series by two games to one, the first visiting side to come from behind and win on the subcontinent.

Gower suddenly found his name bracketed with Douglas Jardine and Tony Greig, the only England captains to win in India, and J.W.H.T. Douglas, F.T. Mann and Leonard Hutton, the only ones to triumph overseas after losing the first match of a series. But there was still the delicate problem of his individual form.

He had struggled against the West Indies and then again in India, until playing his one influential innings at a time when it was most needed, in the last Test in Kanpur. Though he would never say as much publicly, it seemed that the demands of captaincy were taking their toll of Gower's gifts as a batsman.

At the start of the new English season, his day-to-day fortunes were put under the closest scrutiny, much as, for totally different reasons, the progress of Donald Bradman used to be. The selectors, in a difficult position, fuelled the speculation by appointing Gower for only the first two Tests, though the inference was that it was only his form – rather than any aspect of his leadership – that was causing them concern.

Gower, meanwhile, had to lead England in the three one-day internationals, which preceded the Tests. When he made modest scores in the first two, it led to the splendidly ironic sight of Gower being advised to resign by Jim Laker in the newspaper that employed them both! Laker, however, based his argument on Gower's leadership rather than his form.

Then, in the third game, Gower made a century at Lord's. It was by no means flawless and, with England already two down, it could be said that the Australian bowling was not what it might have been. It was, though, Gower's first three-figure score in some 40 innings in all forms of cricket since becoming captain. When he followed it with one for Leicestershire against the tourists, which was described by reliable local judges as one of the finest exhibitions of batting they had seen, it looked as though Gower was coming to terms with himself at exactly the right time.

Meanwhile, Botham, after his winter's rest, had started the season by twice making the fastest hundred (each off 76 deliveries), and the Australians arrived, determined, well-organised on and off the field, and doubtless irked by suggestions that the last-minute upheavals in their party would have an adverse effect on either their playing strength or their collective morale.

Oddly enough, it seemed that just the opposite might happen. In Australia in 1982–83, England were undone by sheer pace after injuries to Terry Alderman and Dennis Lillee in the first Test had forced Australia to make changes. Now, with Alderman and the still unproved Rod McCurdy opting for South Africa, they brought back Jeff Thomson and added to their party Dave Gilbert, a promising but virtually unknown fast bowler who had the twin merits of not employing an over-long run and using the bouncer sparingly.

Thomson, though now 34, was said to have bowled at times as fast as anyone (West Indians apart) in Australia the previous winter. Additionally, he had learned from his brief but impressive period with Middlesex the need, on English pitches, to bowl length and line and to conserve energy.

With the admirable Geoff Lawson expected to be an influential figure and Craig McDermott, at 20, a bowler of genuine pace, as emphasised by his ten wickets in his first two Tests, it looked as though this would be where Australia's strength would lie in the series, in contrast to England who, with worries about their seam attack, had a strong hand of stroke-playing batsmen.

If a further aperitif were needed, it was provided by Border himself, who, in a series of classy and near-flawless displays, made centuries in his first four innings of the tour, a feat previously achieved only by Charlie Macartney. Additionally, Border and his team did much to restore the status of tourists matches against the counties, by playing as much positive cricket as the weather permitted and striving for a result when practical.

It was gratifying, too, that most of the counties played fair, not only by the Australians but by their own members, and reverted to the policy of fielding their strongest side. And so to Headingley . . .

Bill Frindall's scoring method

To enable readers to reconstruct every moment of the series, my detailed scoring sheets are reproduced in full for each Test. It is possible to completely reconstruct a match ball-by-ball from these sheets, and to tell exactly what happened to each delivery; who bowled it to whom, from which end, at what time, how the batsman reacted, what he was wearing on his head, and who was umpiring at each end.

Unless a wicket falls, each line across the various columns contains a full record of one over. The time at which the bowler commenced his run to deliver the first ball is recorded in the first column (TIME). The bowlers' columns are divided into the two ends of the ground and the bowler's name and the number of his over in that innings are entered in the appropriate spaces. Each ball is recorded in the columns of the batsman facing it. At the end of each over all the cumulative totals columns are updated (or left blank if they have not changed). These comprise the six columns on the extreme right of the sheet, and the number of balls faced and boundaries hit by each of the two batsmen.

If a wicket falls, the four columns for the dismissed batsman are ruled off, and the rest of the over is recorded two lines below to allow for the incoming batsman's name to be entered.

The NOTES column is used for detailing extras and recording times for partnerships and individual scores when they reach multiples of fifty. I also note outstanding fielding, dropped catches, confident appeals that have been unsuccessful, injuries and various other data which may be required to satisfy commentators' enquiries later in the match. I also keep a running total of maidens (M 23) and no balls (NB 10) to cross-check my bowling figures and total number of balls faced (no balls are included as they can be scored off, but wides are ignored as they cannot). Alongside each batsman's name on the ball-by-ball sheet I note his head-gear, abbreviating helmet as H. If he bats left-handed I also note LHB.

I also employ a cryptic method to chart the scoring strokes of each individual innings. It is based on the following key, which is reversed for left-handed batsmen. Although this method is only approximate, it does show if a player has a favourite scoring area or if a bowler tends to concede runs to a particular stroke. It is also possible to reconstruct a scoring chart of a batsman's innings. To make the symbols more exact, I annotate 3/4 above a shot which bisects those two areas (cover and extra-cover). Straightish on-drives are represented by 5/6 and a straight drive which passes the bowler's stumps on the leg-side is shown as 5(6).

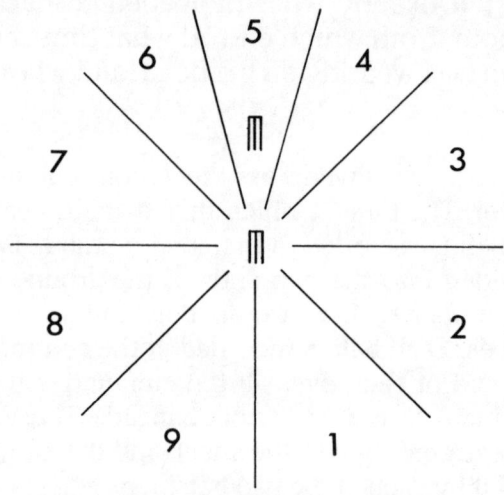

I also use these symbols when a batsman's intended scoring strokes are fielded and no runs accrue. Balls played defensively have a dot above the normal dot, and those which the batsman ignores have no symbol above the dot. Other symbols which I use are:

B	Bye	S	Sharp (quick) run
E	Edged stroke	X	Played and missed on off-side
EP	Edged ball into pads	X^L	Played and missed on leg-side
F	Full toss	Y	Yorker
G	Hit on glove	↑	Bouncer
L	LBW appeal	↓	Shooter
LB	Leg bye	∩	Bowler used shortened run-up
P	Hit on pad (no appeal)		

No balls (⊙ or ④, etc) and wides (⊹ or ⸬, etc.) are recorded in the conventional way. Each bowler's figures are annotated in his column at the end of his spell or at a major interval in the play.

First Test

HEADINGLEY

JUNE 13, 14, 15, 17, 18

ENGLAND

D.I. Gower (captain), G.A. Gooch, R.T. Robinson, M.W. Gatting,
A.J. Lamb, I.T. Botham, P. Willey, P.R. Downton, J.E. Emburey,
N.G. Cowans, P.W.J. Allott

AUSTRALIA

A.R. Border (captain), A.M.J. Hilditch, G.M. Wood, K.C. Wessels,
D.C. Boon, G.M. Ritchie, W.B. Phillips, S.P. O'Donnell,
G.F. Lawson, C.J. McDermott, J.R. Thomson

Botham's role as bowler may be key

While Australia seem prepared to take a chance on the fitness of Geoff Lawson, England are as usual holding their team selection cards close to their chest for today's first Cornhill Test at Headingley. It marks the start of a long awaited six-match Ashes series which has already gripped the country's imagination, and the choice of Leeds as the opening venue, for the first time, merely adds to the flavour and intrigue of the contest.

Not only do both sides have their memories – and survivors – of the epic of 1981 when England became only the second side to triumph after following on, but there is extra spice in the knowledge that this game will be played on the same pitch. If it favours the fast bowlers, as it did four years ago, only the weather – it was dry but cold and blustery yesterday – seems likely to prevent the series starting with an outright result.

It would also lay greater emphasis on the way England approach their task with both bat and ball. Patience and discipline with the one, control and accuracy with the other, are the watchwords, as emphasised by Peter May, chairman of selectors. In fact, the final make-up of England's side could well depend to a certain extent on some aspects of this, particularly in what role as a bowler David Gower envisages Ian Botham playing on his return to the Test arena. After his winter's rest and recuperation, he may well come back as an out-and-out strike bowler, as he was when taking 6–95 in the first innings in 1981, along with a little matter of an unbeaten 149 which turned the match upside-down.

In the intervening years, however, Botham has not been the same bowler at this level, so much depends on whether the selectors feel they need to go into the game with three other recognised seam bowlers in support. This would give them a similar balance to four years ago, when Willey played in support of Botham, Old, Willis and Dilley, although there was a time, Mike Brearley has since admitted, when he thought he would regret omitting Emburey.

Gower may face a similar dilemma this morning, for although in the last

10 Tests at Leeds the quicker bowlers have taken 262 wickets – compared with a modest 32 by the spinners – Emburey, because of his accuracy and ability to drift the ball, can also be effective in seam bowling conditions. Thus it would be desirable to have him in the side, not least because he is a specialist, and in any case there seems certain to be some moisture in the pitch which might be exploited if England bowl first. The qualities of Willey, who is a particularly courageous player of fast bowling, need no re-emphasising here, but both he and Emburey could play only if it were thought that Gooch was capable of filling a bowling role on a ground where the ball has a reputation for swinging, whatever else it may do.

Lawson looked pale and drawn after his throat infection when he appeared at the nets yesterday, but his presence would probably be of in-estimable psychological value to Australia, and the word is that he will play. In any case, Thomson and McDermott and Co ought to enjoy bowling here, even though, after producing an unacceptable number of no-balls in their last match, they have the problem of finding someone to come down the slope at the Kirkstall Lane end.

This may only be a little local difficulty for a side who under Allan Border have been exemplary on and off the field. They are no doubt as aware as the rest of us of the importance of this series to those following it at home after an endless stodgy diet of moderate one-day stuff.

AUSTRALIAN VIEWPOINT

Border seeks sixth win in 40 on tour

Australian cricket sees this 53rd Ashes series as the launching pad for a new, successful era for itself. Obviously, English cricket has similar thoughts about its future following the meritorious 2-1 victory in India. The Australians, motivated and inspired by Allan Border's strong leadership, have made an auspicious start to their tour, not losing a first class match and winning the Texaco Trophy series 2-1.

But the merry-go-round that is an 18-week, 29-match England tour, has not been an easy ride, nor has it been totally convincing over the past six weeks. The Australians have had an unsettling run of injuries and illnesses, with the usual frustrations and delays because of the weather, to the extent that many players, particularly the bowlers, are 'underdone'.

Importantly for Australia, the 17 players and team manager, Bob Merriman, an Arbitration Commissioner from Geelong, have forged a warm, united team spirit that even they might not have believed was possible in the wake of the original defections to the 'rebel' tour of South Africa. They have been bonded together by the obvious common cause of wanting to beat the Old Enemy and, in doing so, prove to sceptical English critics that they do not form a second-class colonial XI.

Team spirit is one thing, winning Test matches is quite a different matter, and, in this regard, Australia's dismal overseas record needs to be corrected urgently. Since early 1977, Australia have won only five (and lost 19 and drawn 15) of the 39 Tests they have played outside Australia. Twelve of those have been in England, where Australia's only success came at Trent Bridge in the first match of the 1981 series. But history will have no bearing on what transpires this time at Headingley, where Australia have won only twice in 10 Tests since World War II. It merely helps illustrate the enormity of the task confronting them.

STATISTICAL PREVIEW

Spinners' unhappy run

For the first time Headingley has the honour of staging the opening match of an Ashes series. Only three of the 47 Tests played on that ground since 1899 have been the first of a summer: v New Zealand in 1949, and v India in 1952 and 1967.

Slow bowlers have taken only 32 of the 305 wickets to fall in the last ten Leeds Tests (10.5%). That figure is inflated by the 1975 match against Australia when spin accounted for 11 out of 33, the now exiled Edmonds taking six of them on his debut.

The Australians have had to endure 21 one-day internationals since they last played Test cricket on January 2. Of the 61 limited-over 'Tests' played during the winter, 31 were held in Australia.

Imminent Test career highlights involve Lamb (45 for 2,000 runs), Willey (77 for 1,000 runs), Cowans (1 for 50 wickets), and Gower (1 for 50 catches).

Australians take toll of slack bowling

Australia launched their defence of the Ashes by making 284 for six in the first Cornhill Test at Headingley yesterday, due in part to Andrew Hilditch's admirable innings of 119 but also to much indifferent bowling by England.

Most sides would settle for scoring the best part of 300 on the first day of a Test anywhere in the world, let alone at Leeds, where, as expected, the ball moved around all day, albeit not at any great pace.

As it happened, Australia obtained no fewer than 176 of their runs in boundaries, testimony to the way in which Hilditch, particularly, took toll of the generous supply of loose deliveries in making the highest score of his Test career.

Ironically, England were more successful later in the day, when Gooch bowled a valuable spell, than when the ball was new, and their efforts may be put into perspective when the Australian fast bowlers explore this pitch's possibilities.

England omitted Foster from their 12, so Emburey joined Gooch and Willey in returning to Test cricket after a three-year exile. Australia, in contrast, opted for an attack with four fast bowlers and no recognised spinner.

Border also chose to bat after winning the toss, although on an overcast morning England might have wanted to bowl first anyway, unless they harboured understandable worries about the possible difficulties of batting fourth here.

Not suprisingly the ball moved about, with occasional variations in bounce, but the morning was rather less profitable than England might have expected, partly because Hilditch, especially, proved adept at dealing effectively with the loose delivery.

Of these, there were rather more than any side would want to bowl in helpful conditions and ironically it was also a session when the good ball tended to beat the bat rather than find the edge.

Wood, having started with two fours in Cowan's wayward first over, was leg before to Allott, who quickly settled into a groove which made the batsmen play more often, though overall neither Hilditch nor Wessels, while having some problems, had to work as hard as they might have expected.

Elegant, Hilditch is not, but in these conditions his dogged approach, based on getting forward as far and as often as possible and with no risk taken, served his side highly effectively.

But he also missed little when the bowlers strayed, and when Botham appeared, he was able to hook him comfortably for six. Botham, beating the bat one minute but varying wildly the next, seemed to epitomise England's inconsistencies.

With usually at least one inviting ball an over, Hilditch and Wessels did not need to look elsewhere in adding 132 in 38 overs before Wessels, slashing hard at Emburey, was brilliantly caught by Botham at slip.

Emburey was not seen again until 40 overs later, which, while on the one hand understandable in these conditions, was hardly a reflection of the way the attack as a whole was functioning. He had, in any case, managed to straighten the ball.

By now Hilditch had gone past his previous best score of the tour, a modest 60, with increasingly confident strokes. He hooked Cowans for a second six and moved to three figures soon afterwards off only 140 balls.

Border, meanwhile, needed some luck against Botham and Cowans, but hereabouts it was Gooch, finding the ball would swing from a full length, who did a valuable and much needed stabilizing job.

Eventually, Hilditch, pushing forward to a widish outswinger, was caught behind, and this led to the most convincing period of ascendancy England's bowlers had enjoyed all day.

Boon, ill at ease against the moving ball, became Gooch's second victim when, shaping for a lavish stroke on the back foot, he was totally flummoxed and palpably leg before to a ball that came back at him and did not bounce much.

Cowans, now running in well and producing some very testing deliveries, then had Border well caught low down at slip by Botham from a ball angled across him, but this was followed by a partnership of 55 in only 12 overs by Phillips and Ritchie.

Phillips found plenty of bowling which could be forced with power and timing off the back foot, and it needed the return of Emburey to remove him with the aid of Gower's left-handed catch off a mixture of bat and pad.

AUSTRALIAN VIEWPOINT

'Digger' removes 'Who?' tag

A ndrew 'Digger' Hilditch is renowned for his addiction to practice and his total dedicated, disciplined approach to the game. But his style of batting often is more in the ugly-duckling than elegant-swan mould, and this may have something to do with the long struggle he has had to gain the recognition and acclaim he so richly earned yesterday.

The Adelaide solicitor, 29, who is married to Bobby Simpson's younger daughter, Kim, was a national hero last Christmas when his four-hour 70 and 5½-hour 113 enabled Australia to draw the fourth Test and deny the West Indies their 12th consecutive Test victory.

Yet Hilditch's detractors emerged again following his unsuccessful start to this England tour – 250 runs in 10 first-class innings.

Yesterday, in a courageous, uncharacteristically aggressive innings he surely dispensed with his 'Andrew Who?' tag and identified himself as an authentic Test cricketer.

Overnight
Australia 284 – 6 (A.M.J. Hilditch 119)

England given fluent start by Robinson

Though rain and bad light permitted only 36 overs at Headingley yesterday, the first Cornhill Test lost little else in entertainment value, especially when England were making 134 for two off only 24.4 overs after dismissing Australia for 331.

Ian Botham's feat of three wickets in four balls precipitated the end of Australia's innings, after which it was England's turn to be confronted with more wayward bowling than they could have dared hope for on a pitch which still had its complications.

The opportunity was not missed, particularly by Tim Robinson who, though originally cast in the role of anchorman, was able to make a fluent, unbeaten 66 by punishing the bad ball much as Hilditch had done the previous day.

He and Mike Gatting added an unbroken 84 in only 15 overs after Craig McDermott's breakthrough. Later there were signs, notably during one over from Simon O'Donnell, that such comfortable progress may not continue if and when Australia manage to bowl with the straightness the conditions demand.

Australia lost their last four wickets for five runs after a lengthy stoppage for rain, largely due to Botham, and it was a huge bonus after the way England had started the day.

Though the ball was new, both McDermott and Ritchie were given the encouragement of near-half volleys, which were driven comfortably for four, and momentarily it looked as if England were about to repeat their flawed performance with the ball.

On the resumption, however, Ritchie was persuaded to try to pull Botham from outside his off stump and played emphatically on, and from the next ball, which nipped back, O'Donnell was adjudged lbw.

Lawson played and missed at the next, and after he had edged Allott to Downton, Botham rounded this eventual phase off by finding a gap between McDermott's bat and pad. So, much potential damage by the lower order had been averted.

When England batted, Lawson was not at his best after his illness, but it was all so clear that the pitch still offered plenty to the bowlers when length and line were right.

This, as on the previous day, was not as often as desirable, which enabled Robinson to begin with some excellent strokes from bowling that fed his strength on the back foot.

But Gooch was quickly lbw to McDermott and Gower had not scored when he narrowly escaped a similar fate, perhaps because umpire Meyer considered the ball had pitched fractionally outside leg stump.

As expected, the extra pace of the Australian bowlers emphasised variations in bounce, and Robinson, at 22, was missed at third slip off McDermott, who has suffered more than most from fielding lapses on this tour. Perhaps his colleagues have a form of McDermottitis.

With Robinson missing little that could be cut or forced, England rattled up 50 in 10 overs, whereupon Gower, who had also profited from the bowlers' variations, was caught behind from a ball angled across him and perhaps going on off the seam.

Robinson then took three fours off one over from Lawson, and moved past 50 from only 58 balls with his ninth boundary. Australia were spared more punishment only by a decision to go off for bad light.

A brief resumption permitted O'Donnell, in his first over, to hint that he might have the right pace and length to be Australia's most effective bowler on this pitch. Both Robinson and Gatting took blows from balls that bounced and when bad light again intervened, Australia were much less pleased than earlier.

AUSTRALIAN VIEWPOINT

Victims of great talent

Craig McDermott yesterday added two more illustrious names to his imposing list of 12 victims in only three Test appearances. In disposing of Graham Gooch and David Gower in his first five overs, McDermott, 20, polished his reputation as the most exciting fast bowler in the world.

Clive Lloyd and Wes Hall said in Australia six months ago that McDermott had the potential to be 'great' after he dismissed West Indians Larry Gomes (twice), Richie Richardson, Jeff Dujon, Desmond Haynes, and Viv Richards in the fourth Test in Melbourne. He also claimed the wickets of Gordon Greenidge, Richardson, Haynes and Lloyd in the fifth Test in Sydney.

A tall, powerfully built athlete and a champion all-round sportsman as a Brisbane schoolboy, McDermott has altered his bowling action to put less strain on his left side, which troubled him earlier on this tour. He used to have quite an upright approach to the wicket; now he bustles in much lower in the manner of Dennis Lillee and Rodney Hogg.

Thanks to McDermott, Australia's new-ball attack yesterday looked more hostile than England's had been on Thursday, but Tim Robinson appreciated the variations in line and length just as much as Andrew Hilditch enjoyed the wayward offerings of England's quick bowlers.

Geoff Lawson's six overs for 45 runs suggested he was still feeling the effects of the viral throat infection that weakened him earlier in the week. This was another reason for Allan Border to be pleased about winning the toss, for Lawson could have struggled even more on Thursday.

Overnight
Australia 331 (A.M.J. Hilditch 119, G.M. Ritchie 46)
England 134 – 2 (R.T. Robinson 66 not out)

Robinson 175 gives England winning hope

A day of uninhibited aggression, built around Tim Robinson's memorable innings of 175 and Ian Botham's devastating half-century, left England with a lead of 153 with their last pair together after the third day of the opening Cornhill Test at Headingley.

A capacity crowd of some 18,000, behind whom the gates were closed before lunch, relished the sight of Australia's bowlers being savaged for four runs an over for most of the day.

Robinson's innings – exceeded only by R.E. Foster's 287 at Sydney in 1903-04 as the highest by an Englishman on debut against Australia – gave appreciative Yorkshire eyes their first glimpse of the qualities he had shown in India.

Nothing was more certain than that his aptitude for playing lengthy innings would punish Australia for the lapse in the slips which allowed him to escape at 22 when the going was infinitely harder the previous evening. And his presence for almost seven hours ensured that at the other end one stroke player after another could indulge himself.

The main difference between Delhi in December and Leeds in June (apart from the temperature!) was probably that Robinson, owing to the length bowled by all the Australian attack, was able to operate with great success on the back foot, although he missed little that could be stroked through mid-

wicket off his legs when they over-pitched.

Mostly in this manner he moved to his second Test century from only 143 balls, and then gradually overtook W.G. Grace, Ranjitsinhji, Duleepsinhji, and his Nottinghamshire colleague Derek Randall, all of whom had reached three figures on their first appearance against Australia.

Throughout all this, Australia's decision to go into the match with only four recognised bowlers rebounded on them. Lawson, though later said to be fully fit by his captain, was below his best until late in the day, and McDermott's lack of experience showed, though he also seemed to be troubled by a niggling injury.

So Australia could have done with a greater contribution from their most experienced bowler, Thomson, but not surprisingly he was unable to fulfil the unfamiliar role of stock bowler, and it was O'Donnell, in his first Test, who went closest to providing the control of length and line required.

Against the current England middle-order, it was not enough. The shape of things to come was set by Gatting, with some characteristic strokes off the back foot in a partnership of 136 in only 33 overs before, pulling, he was possibly undone by McDermott's extra bounce.

Lamb, dropped at cover by Wood when 14, then played a remarkable innings of 38 which contained no fewer than eight fours. He showed that even on a pitch where the ball was apt to bounce variably, he could hit through the line with great power, and at one point took 21 from three overs from Lawson before he was bowled through a considerable gap between bat and pad.

Yet even that was only the entrée to Botham's main course. He and Robinson complemented each other perfectly, with the opener quickly sensing that he needed only to push the singles while Botham, playing reassuringly straight from the start, made it virtually impossible to bowl at him.

It was glorious stuff and, with many runs coming in the arc between mid-on and mid-off, it was a controlled, calculated and clinical assault. Even David Hookes, the Australian batsman with the world's fastest century (from 34 balls) to his name, was left in awe as he watched.

When Border put himself on – which was by no means an unwise or necessarily desperate move – Botham struck him for a straight six into the top deck of the football stand. But the sight of Thomson being hit ferociously back over his head for four will be remembered longer, especially by those who were in Australia in 1974-75 or, come to that, three years ago.

Botham also picked up Thomson quite superbly for six, and at one point Australia had four men on the boundary to him. His control and selectivity were such that he perhaps played and missed only once in making 60 out of 80 added for the fifth wicket in 13 overs.

Eventually Thomson had the last word (and gesture, which we could have done without), when Botham played on to a ball slanted in at him from the edge of the return crease. He had faced only 51 balls, hitting ten fours and two sixes, and left to an ovation on a par with the one accorded his unbeaten 149 on the same ground four years earlier.

England's only worry then was to ensure they obtained a lead in keeping with the ascendancy of their batting. Not surprisingly, a relatively calm period of consolidation followed, during which Willey also fired off some strokes of quality, through the covers and square off the back foot, which brought up the 400, the last hundred having occupied only 16 overs.

By now Lawson was becoming more recognisable as Lawson and managing to bowl the odd delivery that showed there was still something in the pitch. In successive overs with the new ball, both Robinson and Willey fell to him, the latter mistiming an attempted stroke through mid-wicket, but Downton, with assistance from Emburey and Allott, maintained the tempo till the end.

The final word, however, went to Border who, in lamenting what he described as the worst Australian bowling performance for years, agreed with assessments that both sides had so far not made the most of the pitch and commented: 'I would love to have seen Dennis Lillee bowling on it.'

AUSTRALIAN VIEWPOINT

O'Donnell ends long search

Allan Border was concerned last week that his bowlers were 'underdone' going into the first Test at Headingley. So it was with some reluctance that the Australian captain rightly blamed them, along with two dropped catches, for England's 153-run lead.

While it is difficult to excuse the Australians' looseness – they often bowled too wide, too short or too full – it is worth noting the work they have been called to do in first class matches during the six weeks preceding the first Test.

Geoff Lawson (60), Craig McDermott (81), Jeff Thomson (89.3), and Simon O'Donnell (44) had delivered only 274.3 overs between them, collecting 30 wickets – Lawson five, McDermott eight, Thomson fifteen, and O'Donnell two.

In comparison, England's opening pair, Norman Cowans (183.2) and Paul Allott (245.4) had bowled 429 overs (and taken 68 wickets) in first-class matches before Headingley.

From any viewpoint, short-term or long, all-rounder O'Donnell's accuracy and economy at a slower pace than his three other colleagues were encouraging and significant.

The big, strong Victorian, still only 22 and a former prominent Australian rules football player with St Kilda (the old club of Keith Miller and Sam Loxton), should continue to blossom as the all-rounder for whom Australian cricket has been searching for years.

Overnight
Australia 331
England 484 – 9 (R.T. Robinson 175, I.T. Botham 60, M.W. Gatting 53)

Emburey's 3–12 spell opens up Australia

E ngland's bowlers, notably John Emburey and Ian Botham, left their side formidably placed in the first Cornhill Test at Headingley yesterday, Australia finishing still 12 runs behind with five wickets left when bad light caused a halt.

The pitch's increased eccentricity in bounce was England's main ally, and after Hilditch and Wessels had each made a tenacious half-century Australia's fortunes changed abruptly, four wickets going down for 16 runs.

A new ball becomes available to England after nine overs this morning, though, as the low bounce may continue to pose the greater problems, to take it or not may well be an intriguing decision.

England's total of 533 was their highest against Australia at Leeds and their best anywhere against them for 20 years, but after the events here of 1981, no one will be taking anything for granted.

Before all this, Downton and Cowans both played with much aplomb in adding 49 for England's last wicket, though the ease with which they did so might have given their side misgivings about the task ahead, the quality of the bowling notwithstanding.

Downton achieved his fourth Test half-century and Cowans, once finding he could pull Thomson comfortably for four, ensured that every Englishman except Gooch had reached double figures, a statistical quirk few would

have forecast.

By the time Australia batted, the early sun had conveniently disappeared behind cloud, and the new ball, in the hands of Botham and Allott, moved enough from a full length to pass the bat at encouraging intervals, sometimes at varying heights.

Botham, however, engineered the initial breakthrough with a much shorter delivery which may have bounced more than Wood expected, and from his hook he was superbly caught by Lamb covering a lot of ground from deep square leg.

Another 43 overs elapsed before England struck again, though Australia had reached only 20 when Wessels, at 11, might have been caught behind down the leg side off Botham, Downton getting a glove to the ball.

After that Hilditch and Wessels played with due deference to their side's position and the pitch, though, as in the first innings, the good ball again tended to beat the bat rather than find the edge.

Allott bowled particularly well at Wessels, allowing him no room outside the off-stump, but when Cowans appeared Hilditch hooked and slashed his first two deliveries for six and four, and at first was able to cut Emburey rather more often than the off-spinner would have desired.

Emburey, though, soon turned one ball enough to disconcert both Wessels and Downton, but otherwise at this stage the most likely-looking bowler was Gooch, moving the ball either way and beating the bat with negligible luck.

So Hilditch and Wessels were able to

inch their way along and had put on 139 when Wessels played back rather than forward to Emburey, who had switched ends, and was bowled off his pads when the ball drifted in.

This error at last gave England a new batsman to bowl at, which on this pitch was even more important than usual, and soon afterwards they had two, when Hilditch, sweeping, was caught by Robinson who had been moved to short fine leg for the stroke.

Botham, meanwhile, was wheeling through 15 successive overs at the other end, looking much more effective when he found a full length, and from

AUSTRALIAN VIEWPOINT

Border remains key to tourists' success

Australia's reliance on their captain, Allan Border, was illustrated again at Headingley yesterday when Ian Botham and John Emburey thrust England into a winning position in the first Test.

The cry is likely to be heard often this summer – when Border succeeds, Australia succeed; when Border fails, Australia fail.

While that may embarrass him and displease his team-mates, the simple truth is that if Border does not make a significant contribution with the bat in

there or thereabouts he produced a beautiful ball, lifting and leaving Border, who was unavoidably caught behind off a glove.

If Australia needed another example of the pitch's tendencies, it came in the next over when Ritchie met one from Emburey which hardly bounced and crept under his bat to hit the base of the off stump.

After that, England's successes were only moral ones. Twice Phillips and Boon were glad to accept the umpire's offer of the light, the second occasion when Gower was poised to introduce Willey to the attack.

each of the remaining five Tests, Australia really will struggle to keep the Ashes.

It is a huge responsibility, but Border's Test batting record indicates he is equipped to handle it, even with the additional strains of captaincy.

In this Test, in which he made 32 and eight, Border moved above Ian Redpath (by 38 runs) into eighth position on Australia's all-time Test run list.

The dismissals of Border and Greg Ritchie yesterday hardly could have come off more contrasting deliveries, Border caught at the wicket off an awkward lifter from Botham, Ritchie bowled by a lousy grubber from Emburey.

Overnight
Australia 331 and 190 – 5 (A.M.J. Hilditch 80, K.C. Wessels 64)
England 533 (R.T. Robinson 175, I.T. Botham 60, P.R. Downton 54,
M.W. Gatting 53; C.J. McDermott 4 – 134)

England one up but still have problems

E ngland took their first, often faltering, steps towards regaining the Ashes by winning the opening Cornhill Test by five wickets at Headingley yesterday to go one up in the six-match series.

Not surprisingly, the final phase was far from straightforward on this pitch, and England had reason to be thankful they needed no more than 123 in the fourth innings against bowling that was much improved.

These were duly obtained with 13 of the 50 overs in hand, though there were a series of mishaps against Lawson and O'Donnell, who, bowling straight and allowing the pitch to do the rest, illustrated that the eventual margin might well have been much tighter.

Both sides, indeed, would have reflected last night on what might have been, for there was a time when Wayne Phillips, assaulting some undemanding England bowling with the second new ball, threatened to do for Australia what Botham had done for England in 1981.

He fell nine short of what would have been an admirable century, however, and the curious approach of most of the other Australians, who perished with bats flailing when occupation of the crease was paramount, spared England possible embarrassment.

Not since 1905 have England taken the first Test against Australia and gone on to win the series. Whatever the worth of that particular statistic, it is now up to England to build on the considerable advantage of going ahead on the one ground where an outright result was almost guaranteed.

This may mean ignoring the facile adage that a winning team should not be changed and taking a close look at their bowling, not only in the light of what happened here but what will be required for the rest of the series, starting on a better pitch at Lord's.

So the return of Edmonds to partner Emburey, who emerged yesterday with five for 82, would make much sense. There must, too, be concern about seam bowling which allowed Australia to reach 200 for two in helpful conditions on the first day and was again variable in their second innings.

There was a time when Phillips looked as though he was batting back home on Adelaide's beautiful, true surface rather than this unpredictable one as he laid into some lamentably short-pitched bowling.

This was after England had made the best possible start when Boon was bowled off a boot by Cowans aiming across the line of a ball that would have otherwise missed his leg stump. And this in only the first over.

The new ball was delayed three overs while Emburey explored the possibilities of the old one. When it was taken, Allott immediately produced a delivery that climbed from just short of a length and flew to safety off the shoulder of O'Donnell's bat.

Despite this encouraging portent, the ball was dropped short by both Allott and Botham, and Phillips, pulling Allott for three successive fours, took Australia's lead past the psychologically crucial 100 mark.

By then, O'Donnell had been caught behind off Botham, but there was no reason why those that remained should not have made England work much harder. Instead, even though the later batsmen were not oppressed by close fielders, the last three wickets lasted only five overs.

This tilted the time-runs equation more England's way than might have been the case, and Gooch, especially, enjoyed a period of reconnaissance needed on this pitch after his earlier failure.

Robinson, however, was bowled between bat and pad by Lawson, whose convalescence seems to be coming along well, but his 175 in the first innings was enough to earn him the Man of the Match award from Bob Willis, a choice beyond argument.

By now, England were in a position where, as individuals, batsmen had much to lose and little to gain, and Australia reduced them to 83 for four when Gower, Gooch and Gatting all disappeared in quick succession.

Lamb timed the ball better than most in passing his 2,000th run in Test cricket, but there was a wretched episode at the end when the crowd swarmed on to the outfield as he made the winning hit.

But for this invasion, Lawson, running back towards the long-leg boundary, might have held a difficult catch off a steepling top edge.

In the context of the game, it meant nothing, but unless cricket heeds this and sundry other warnings, the day will surely arrive when an unsavoury episode of this sort will not only leave the result of a match in considerable doubt, but, worse, put a player's physical well-being at unnecessary risk.

AUSTRALIAN VIEWPOINT

Border puts blame on bowlers

So much-maligned Headingley has hosted another memorable Test match and England have beaten Australia there for the fourth time in their last five meetings.

This time, on a wicket both teams initially feared and never trusted throughout the five eventful days, England made fewer mistakes, particularly in bowling and catching.

They ultimately enjoyed a five-wicket margin after Australia had salvaged some pride and respect with their sturdy last-day fight with bat and ball.

The captains, David Gower and Allan Border, agreed last night that England's first innings score of 533 had sealed the result.

Gower said: 'A lead of 200 was fairly vital, and extraordinary to have under the circumstances (of the pitch). It was the biggest contributing factor to the result coming our way.'

Border reacted: 'I don't think England should have got 500 and, to be fair, I don't think they'd get 500 again. If they had to get 200 in their second innings, it would have been very interesting.

'To score two lots of 300 on this wicket, I thought our batsmen did their job. I didn't think there was that much difference between the teams, apart from some shoddy bowling.

'I don't think our bowlers will bowl that badly again. I'm very disappointed, but it's not the end of the world. We're still good enough to win a couple of Tests.'

Border, like Gower, said it was 'hard to have a "go" at the wicket' because of the number of runs scored (1,311 for 35 wickets – an average of 37 a wicket), but he added: 'They were difficult conditions the whole time to bat in, but the bowling was not as good as it could have been.'

The big bonus for England, apart from the outstanding comebacks by Ian Botham and John Emburey, was Tim Robinson's Man of the Match-winning 175, for which he should be eternally grateful to Greg Ritchie, who dropped him at third slip when 22.

For Australia, vice-captain and opener Andrew Hilditch, with 119 and 80, more than justified the tour selectors' faith in him.

Wicketkeeper-batsman Wayne Phillips proved he is one of the best strikers of the ball in the world and young all-rounder Simon O'Donnell recovered from the trauma of his first-ball dismissal to make an auspicious debut.

Result: England beat Australia by 5 wickets.
Australia 331 and 324
(W.B. Phillips 91, A.M.J. Hilditch 80, K.C. Wessels 64; J.E. Emburey 5 – 82)
England 533 and 123 – 5

AUSTRALIA 1ST INNINGS v. ENGLAND (1ST TEST) at HEADINGLEY, LEEDS on 13,14,15,17,18 JUNE, 1985.   TOSS: AUSTRALIA.

IN	OUT	MINS	No.	BATSMAN	HOW OUT	BOWLER	RUNS	WKT	TOTAL	6s	4s	BALLS	NOTES ON DISMISSAL
11.00	11.26	26	1	G.M.WOOD	LBW	ALLOTT	14	1	23	-	3	22	Pushed half forward - beaten by break back.
11.00	4.21	249	2	A.M.J.HILDITCH	c DOWNTON	GOOCH	119	3	201	2	17	182	2nd HS in Tests. Pushed at outswinger. 80 in boundaries.
11.28	2.38	151	3	K.C.WESSELS	c BOTHAM	EMBUREY	36	2	155	·	4	103	Edged cut to slip — sharp head-high catch.
2.40	5.10	117	4	A.R.BORDER*	c BOTHAM	COWANS	32	5	229	·	5	94	Edged low to 2nd slip — in front of his left shin.
4.23	5.05	42	5	D.C.BOON	LBW	GOOCH	14	4	229	·	1	45	Attempted to cut short ball that cut back and kept low.
5.07	2.15	93	6	G.M.RITCHIE	BOWLED	BOTHAM	46	7	326	·	8	64	Under-edged pull at long-hop into leg stump.
5.12	5.56	44	7	W.B.PHILLIPS†	c GOWER	EMBUREY	30	6	284	·	6	35	Inside edge to silly point via pad - left-handed catch (low).
5.58	2.26	53	8	C.J.McDERMOTT	BOWLED	BOTHAM	18	10	331	·	4	38	HS in Tests. Ball kept low. BOTHAM 3 WKTS in 4 BALLS
2.16	2.17	·	9	S.P.O'DONNELL	LBW	BOTHAM	0	8	326	·	·	1	Out 1st ball in Test cricket. Late on stroke. First dismissal (g.c.) on last tour
2.19	2.22	3	10	G.F.LAWSON	c DOWNTON	ALLOTT	0	9	327	·	·	3	His first first-class innings of the tour. Edged drive.
2.23	2.25	3	11	J.R.THOMSON	NOT OUT		4			·	1	3	
				EXTRAS	b - 1b 13	w 4 nb 1	18			2b	4s 1nb	590 balls (including 1 no-ball)	
				TOTAL	(98.1 OVERS - 399 MINUTES)		331					all out at 2.26 on the 2nd day.	

*CAPTAIN †WICKET-KEEPER

UMPIRES: B.J.MEYER and K.E.PALMER

```
14 OVERS   4 BALLS/HOUR
           3.37 RUNS/OVER
           56 RUNS/100 BALLS
```

WKT	PARTNERSHIP		RUNS	MINS
1st	Wood	Hilditch	23	26
2nd	Hilditch	Wessels	132	151
3rd	Hilditch	Border	46	68
4th	Border	Boon	28	42
5th	Border	Ritchie	0	3
6th	Ritchie	Phillips	55	44
7th	Ritchie	McDermott	42	42
8th	McDermott	O'Donnell	0	1
9th	McDermott	Lawson	1	3
10th	McDermott	Thomson	4	3
			331	

```
LUNCH: 96-1 (30 OVERS)(122 MIN.)   HILDITCH 61 (112)  WESSELS 19 (94)
TEA: 194-2 (58.1 OVERS)(13's lost)  HILDITCH 115 (238)  BORDER 19 (57)
      BAD LIGHT at 3.37pm (238 MIN.)
STUMPS: 284-6 (87 OVERS)   RITCHIE 22 (56)   McDERMOTT 0 (5)
(1st DAY)        (351 MIN.)
RAIN STOPPED PLAY at 11.25 am - resumed at 2.03 pm
LUNCH: 307-6 (93.2 OVERS)  RITCHIE 36 (81)   McDERMOTT 8 (30)
                 (376 MIN.)
```

FIRST TEST INNINGS in ENGLAND to DEBIT WIDES AND NO-BALLS to BOWLERS' ANALYSES.

RUNS	MINS	OVERS	LAST 50 (in mins)
50	72	16.1	72
100	133	32.3	61
150	173	42.1	40
200	247	60.5	74
250	318	78.5	71
300	364	90.1	46

HRS	OVERS	RUNS
1	13	48
2	17	48
3	14	59
4	15	39
5	16	40
6	14	55

BOWLER	O	M	R	W	
COWANS	20	4	78	1	-
ALLOTT	22	3	74	2	-
BOTHAM	29.1	8	86	3	3/-
GOOCH	21	4	57	2	3/4
EMBUREY	6	1	23	2	-
			13		
	98.1	20	331	10	

2nd NEW BALL taken at 6.00pm 1st day
- AUSTRALIA 284-6 after 86 overs

© BILL FRINDALL 1985

ENGLAND 1st INNINGS (IN REPLY TO AUSTRALIA'S 331 ALL OUT)

IN	OUT	MINS	No.	BATSMAN	HOW OUT	BOWLER	RUNS	WKT	TOTAL	6s	4s	BALLS	NOTES ON DISMISSAL
2:36	3:15	14	1	G.A. GOOCH	LBW	McDERMOTT	5	1	14	·	1	11	Missed backfoot defensive stroke - ball came back.
2:36	4:55	413	2	R.T. ROBINSON	C' BOON	LAWSON	175	6	417	·	27	270	100 on debut v AUS. Edged low to 1st slip. HS in Tests.
3:17	3:45	28	3	D.I. GOWER *	C' PHILLIPS	McDERMOTT	17	2	50	·	2	22	Edged firm-footed off-side push.
3:47	12:15	143	4	M.W. GATTING	C' HILDITCH	McDERMOTT	53	3	186	·	7	109	Mistimed hook - gentle skier to wide mid-on.
12:17	2:18	83	5	A.J. LAMB	BOWLED	O'DONNELL	38	4	264	·	8	64	Through 'gate' - ball cut back - faint inside edge.
2:20	3:20	60	6	I.T. BOTHAM	BOWLED	THOMSON	60	5	344	2	10	51	Played on - edged cut at ball that cut back. 50 off 45 balls
3:21	5:07	88	7	P. WILLEY	C' HILDITCH	LAWSON	36	7	422	·	5	67	Deceived by slower ball - flicked simple catch to wide mid-on.
4:57	5:42	128	8	P.R. DOWNTON †	C' BORDER	McDERMOTT	54	10	533	·	9	98	Miscued offside steer - high catch to cover-point.
5:09	5:42	33	9	J.E. EMBUREY	BOWLED	LAWSON	21	8	462	·	4	22	Beaten by low breakback.
5:44	6:19	35	10	P.J.W. ALLOTT	C' BOON	THOMSON	12	9	484	·	2	34	Edged to 1st slip - two-handed catch to his left.
6:21	(11:41)	44	11	N.G. COWANS	NOT OUT		22			·	5	28	
				EXTRAS		b 5 lb 16 w 5 nb 14	40						

TOTAL **533** (125 OVERS - 543 MINUTES) all out at 11.41 am on the fourth day. 776 balls (including 26 no balls).

(LEAD: 202)

* CAPTAIN † WICKET-KEEPER

BOWLER	O	M	R	W	
LAWSON	26	4	117	3	
McDERMOTT	32	2	134	4	
THOMSON	34	3	166	2	
O'DONNELL	27	8	77	1	
BORDER	3	0	16	0	
WESSELS	3	2	2	0	
			21		
	125	19	533	10	

© BILL FRINDALL 1985

2nd NEW BALL taken at 4.15pm on 3rd day.
ENGLAND 381-5 after 85 overs.

HRS	OVERS	RUNS
1	13	70
2	13	65
3	14	45
4	15	57
5	13	40
6	14	84
7	13	57
8	13	48
9	16	65

RUNS	MINS	OVERS	LAST 50
50	43	9.2	43
100	83	18.4	40
150	144	32.1	61
200	210	47.2	66
250	248	56.5	38
300	315	71.5	67
350	348	79.4	33
400	382	87.1	34
450	450	102	68
500	513	118	63

TEA: **81-2** (15 OVERS) ROBINSON 39 (69'), GATTING 7 (23') [69 MIN.]

STUMPS: **134-2** (24.4 OVERS) ROBINSON 66 (114'), GATTING 31 (58') (2nd DAY) [114 MIN.] (188 MIN LOST 2nd DAY) [197 BEHIND]

LUNCH: **229-3** (54 OVERS) ROBINSON 111 (236'), LAMB 20 (45') [236 MIN.]

TEA: **361-5** (82 OVERS) ROBINSON 144 (359'), WILLEY 10 (22') [359 MIN.]

STUMPS: **484-9** (115 OVERS) DOWNTON 28 (87'), COWANS 0 (3') (3rd DAY) [502 MIN.] (LEAD: 153)

ENGLAND'S TOTAL OF 533:-
THEIR TWELFTH-HIGHEST v. AUSTRALIA
THEIR HIGHEST v AUSTRALIA SINCE 1965-66 (558 at Melbourne)
THEIR HIGHEST v AUSTRALIA at HEADINGLEY

WKT	PARTNERSHIP		RUNS	MINS
1st	Gooch	Robinson	14	14
2nd	Robinson	Gower	36	28
3rd	Robinson	Gatting	136	143
4th	Robinson	Lamb	78	83
5th	Robinson	Botham	80	60
6th	Robinson	Willey	73	76
7th	Willey	Downton	5	10
8th	Downton	Emburey	40	33
9th	Downton	Allott	22	35
10th	Downton	Cowans	49	44
			533	

13 OVERS 5 BALLS/HOUR
4·26 RUNS/OVER
69 RUNS/100 BALLS

AUSTRALIA 2ND INNINGS

(202 RUNS BEHIND ON FIRST INNINGS)

IN	OUT	MINS	No.	BATSMAN	HOW OUT	BOWLER	RUNS	WKT	TOTAL	6s	4s	BALLS	NOTES ON DISMISSAL
11.52	4.06	196	1	A.M.J. HILDITCH	c Robinson	Emburey	80	3	151	1	13	155	Top-edged sweep to backward square-leg.
11.52	12.03	11	2	G.M. WOOD	c Lamb	Botham	3	1	5	-	-	12	Hooked long-hop to long-leg – running two-handed catch.
12.05	3.18	154	3	K.C. WESSELS	Bowled	Emburey	64	2	144	-	10	128	Bowled via pads by ball that kept low.
3.20	4.16	37	4	A.R. BORDER*	c Downton	Botham	8	4	159	-	-	35	Failed to avoid ball that lifted and left him.
4.08	11.04	78	5	D.C. BOON	Bowled	Cowans	22	6	192	-	2	69	Played across line of yorker.
4.18	4.21	3	6	G.M. RITCHIE	Bowled	Emburey	1	5	160	-	-		Played back to ball that hit stumps near base.
4.23	1.49	190	7	W.B. PHILLIPS †	c Lamb	Botham	91	8	307	-	12	171	Mistimed pull – skier to wide mid-on.
11.06	12.43	97	8	S.P. O'DONNELL	c Downton	Botham	24	7	272	-	3	73	Edged ball that lifted and left him.
12.45	2.01	38	9	G.F. LAWSON	c Downton	Emburey	15	9	318	-	3	20	Skied slog.
1.51	2.10	19	10	C.J. McDERMOTT	c Gooch	Emburey	6	10	324	-	-	20	Superbly judged running catch on long-on boundary.
2.03	(2.10)	7	11	J.R. THOMSON	not out		2			-	-	5	
				EXTRAS	b 4 lb 3 w 1 nb -		8			1	43	694 balls (no balls)	

TOTAL 324 all out at 2.10 pm on the fifth day.
(115.4 overs - 424 minutes)

* CAPTAIN † WICKET-KEEPER

16 OVERS 2 BALLS/HOUR
2.80 RUNS/OVER
47 RUNS/100 BALLS

WKT	PARTNERSHIP		RUNS	MINS
1st	Hilditch	Wood	5	11
2nd	Hilditch	Wessels	139	154
3rd	Hilditch	Border	7	27
4th	Border	Boon	8	8
5th	Boon	Ritchie	1	3
6th	Boon	Phillips	32	63
7th	Phillips	O'Donnell	80	97
8th	Phillips	Lawson	35	26
9th	Lawson	McDermott	11	10
10th	McDermott	Thomson	6	7
			324	

LUNCH: 50-1 (16 OVERS) (69 MIN.) HILDITCH 26 (69), WESSELS 20 (56)

TEA: 151-2 (52 OVERS) (190 MIN.) HILDITCH 80 (196), BORDER 2 (21)

STUMPS: 190-5 (76 OVERS) (272 MIN.) (4TH DAY) (12 BEHIND) BOON 20 (74), PHILLIPS 11 (59) (38 MIN. LOST ON 4TH DAY)

LUNCH: 291-7 (108 OVERS) (394 MIN.) (89 AHEAD) PHILLIPS 76 (181), LAWSON 6 (17)

HRS	OVERS	RUNS
1	13	43
2	18	60
3	18	44
4	17	31
5	17	21
6	15	65
7	17	58

RUNS	MINS	OVERS	LAST 50 (in mins)
50	69	15.5	69
100	115	30.2	46
150	188	51.3	73
200	302	84	114
250	342	93.4	40
300	401	110.1	59

BOWLER	O	M	R	W
BOTHAM	33	7	107	4
ALLOTT	17	4	57	0
EMBUREY	43.4	14	82	5
COWANS	13	2	50	1
GOOCH	9	3	21	0
	115.4	30	324	10

© BILL FRINDALL

2ND NEW BALL taken at 11.45 am 5th day - AUSTRALIA 211-6 after 88 overs.

ENGLAND 2ND INNINGS   (REQUIRING 123 RUNS TO WIN IN A MINIMUM OF 200 MINUTES)

IN	OUT	MINS	No.	BATSMAN	HOW OUT	BOWLER	RUNS	WKT	TOTAL	6s	4s	BALLS	NOTES ON DISMISSAL
2·20	4·08	88	1	G.A.GOOCH	LBW	O'DONNELL	28	3	71	-	3	65	Beaten by breakback – played back.
2·20	3·08	48	2	R.T.ROBINSON	BOWLED	LAWSON	21	1	44	-	4	30	off stump – through bat/pad gap pushing forward.
3·10	3·32	22	3	D.I.GOWER*	C° BORDER	O'DONNELL	5	2	59	-	1	18	Eager drive low to 2nd slip – two-handed, driving forward.
3·34	4·24	30	4	M.W.GATTING	C° PHILLIPS	LAWSON	12	4	83	-	2	20	Edged push at offside ball to keeper's right – two-handed, low.
4·10	(5·31)	81	5	A.J.LAMB	NOT OUT		31			-	5	63	Made winning hit.
4·26	5·05	39	6	I.T.BOTHAM	BOWLED	O'DONNELL	12	5	110	-	1	23	Played across ball that kept low and hit off stump.
5·07	(5·31)	24	7	P.WILLEY	NOT OUT		3			-	-	16	
			8	P.R.DOWNTON†									
			9	J.E.EMBUREY									
			10	P.J.W.ALLOTT									
			11	N.G.COWANS									
				EXTRAS	b - lb 7 w 1 nb 3		11			0⁶ 16⁴			235 balls (including 3 no-balls)

TOTAL   (38.4 OVERS – 171 MINUTES)   123-5

*CAPTAIN   †WICKET-KEEPER

© BILL FRINDALL

BOWLER	O	M	R	W	W	HRS	OVERS	RUNS	RUNS	MINS	OVERS	LAST 50 (in mins)
McDERMOTT	4	0	20	0	0/1	1	13	44	50	61	14	61
LAWSON	16	4	51	2	2/1	2	14	56	100	120	27	59
O'DONNELL	15.4	5	37	3	-/1							
THOMSON	3	0	8	0	0/1							
			7									
	38.4	9	123	5								

13 OVERS 3 BALLS/HOUR
3·18 RUNS/OVER
52 RUNS/100 BALLS

WKT	PARTNERSHIP		RUNS	MINS
1st	Gooch	Robinson	44	48
2nd	Gooch	Gower	15	22
3rd	Gooch	Gatting	12	14
4th	Gatting	Lamb	12	14
5th	Lamb	Botham	27	39
6th	Lamb	Willey	13*	24
			123	

TEA: 62-2 (18 OVERS) GOOCH 27 (86')
     (80 MIN.) GATTING 0 (6')
NEEDING 61 IN 60 MINUTES PLUS 20 OVERS

ENGLAND WON BY 5 WICKETS
WITH 15·2 OVERS TO SPARE

MAN OF THE MATCH: R.T.ROBINSON
(Adjudicator: R.G.D.WILLIS)

ATTENDANCE: 54,018
RECEIPTS: £301,000

1ST DAY TIME	BOWLERS MAIN STAND END (B.J.MEYER) BOWLER	O.	BOWLERS KIRKSTALL L. END (K.E.PALMER) BOWLER	O.	BATSMEN SCOREBOARD LEFT SCORING	BALLS	6s/4s	SCOREBOARD RIGHT SCORING	BALLS	6s/4s	NOTES	O.	RUNS	W.	L BAT	R BAT	EXTRAS
					WOOD			(LHB) HILDITCH									
11·00			COWANS	1	::.4.4.	6	2					1	8		8		
05	ALLOTT	1			..PL	11		2E 1	1			2	9			1	
09/11	— " —		— " —	2				x 1E 3/88 .422..	7	1	sawdust - 2 min delay	3	17			9	
15½	— " —	2			::P7/8.	17						4	19		10		
20			— · —	3				..x..	13		M1	5					
24	— " —	3			x:.½EL:.4W	22	3					5(5)	23	1	14	9	–
26					WESSELS			(LHB)							0		
28	— · —	3			L	1						6					
29			— " —	4				L:29.4..	19	2		7	27			13	
33½	— · —	4			2E 3 3 7E ::.!	5		! EP	21		Hit in ribs.	8	28		1		
38			— · —	5	:3:.x5(6)!	11						9	29		2		
43	— · —	5			P.2:.	15		.2St	23		Ro appeal (LAMB).	10	31		3	14	
47			— · —	6				:: 1E3/32 .44.	29	4		11	39			22	
50½	— · —	6			7E	17		2/3 EP.8 4.:2	33	5		12	46		4	28	
56			BOTHAM	1	7! L:	20		.!!	36		1HR	13	48		5	29	
12·00	— · —	7						:P:...	42		M2	14					
05			— · —	2	:::x!:	26					t thigh M3	15					
08	— · —	8			::.	29		:x7 .!	45			16	49			30	
12			— · —	3	.2 P	32		48 49 6.1	48	1/5		17	58		7	37	
16½	— · —	9						...2/1 L	54		M4	18					
20½			— · —	4	x.P 3.3	38					M5	19					
24½	GOOCH	1						PE!6..	60		t nw. played on. M6	20					
27			— · —	5	x7 .!	40		:::.7 4	64	1/6		21	63		8	41	
31	— · —	2			62 :.!	42		:::..	68			22	64		9		
34½			— · —	6	:..2.8	48					M7	23					
37½	— · —	3						L:.44..	74	1/8		24	72			49	
41			— · —	7	::4:.:	54	1				50 p'ship: 74 min.	25	76		13		
45	— · —	4			!.x2	57		..2	77		HILDITCH 50: 106' t Round wkt.	26	77			50	
48			— · —	8	2 :.	58		:x EP L 8	82			27	78			51	
52	— · —	5			x.9 :.	61		72 LB .2	85		(LB)	28	82		14	53	1
55			— · —	9	32/39 4.1 x	65	2	½2 LB 4.	87	1/9	(LB)	29	92		19	57	2
59	— · —	6				65	2	:!:..3 4	93	1/10	t Round wkt 2HR	30	96	1	19	61	2
1·02	LUNCH										M7 NB-				L U N C H		
1·41			COWANS	7	:::.x!9	70		.	94			31	97		20		
45	ALLOTT	10			P8/7 L EP x .2:.	76						32	99		22		
50			— · —	8	.Px	79		P LB	97		(LB) M8	33	100				3
55	— · —	11			PP9 :.2	82		+37	100			34	103		24	62	
59			— · —	9				PT½8.3 23 .4.4.	106	1/12	t over w/k.	35	111			70	
2·04	— · —	12			4 5(4) !	84	2	5(6)8/7.. 44.	110	1/14	M8 NB-	36	120	1	25	78	3

31

FIRST TEST
SHEET 2

1ST DAY TIME	MAIN STAND BOWLER (MEYER)	O.	END	KIRKSTALL L. BOWLER (PALMER)	O.	END	SCOREBOARD LEFT SCORING	BALLS	6s/4s	SCOREBOARD RIGHT SCORING	BALLS	6s/4s	NOTES	O.	RUNS	W.	L BAT	R BAT	EXTRAS
							WESSELS	84	2	HILDITCH	110	1/14	M8 NB-	36	120	1	25	78	3
2·08				COWANS	10		·¼·· :·6	90					M9	37					
13	EMBUREY	1					9/4	91	3	6:P:3LB	115		3LB 100 p'shp 128'	38	127		29		6
16½ Round wkt to LHB.				—··—	11					:7 P ::2	121			39	129			80	
20½	—··—	2					8:2: 4·	94	4	:41	124	1/15		40	139		34	85	
24½				—··—	12		2 1	95		2 9x½ 1 2·	129			41	143		35	88	
29	—·—·	3					33 Px4 ···1	100		6··1	130			42	145		36	89	
32				—·—·	13		:1	101		8/73 EP75 6··1	135	2/15		43	152			96	
37	—·—·	4					·W	103	4	88/7 2 1	138			43⁵	155	2	36	99	6
38							BORDER		LHB										
40	—·—·	4					P 1						3HR	44			0		
41				BOTHAM	10		7P·1	3		3 2 :1	142		HILDITCH'S (2nd 184'	45	157		1	100	
46	ALLOTT	13					5/6 7 ·4·+	8	1	L	143			46	162		6		
50				—·—·	11		x 1E7 ·4·+	14	2				(W)	47	167		10		7
55	—·—·	14					8 x ·2·	19		3 1	144			48	170		12	101	
59				—·—·	12		E6	20		3: 8 7 ·2·1	149			49	173			104	
3·03	—·—·	15					:1	21		3x ·x7 ·3	154			50	176			107	
07				—·—·	13		↑····1	26		2E 1	155			51	177			108	
11	—·—·	16					7 ·4··	29	3	:P·1	158			52	182		16	109	
15				—·—·	14					·····22	164		M10	53					
19½	GOOCH	7					3 ↑·4·: ···	35					(W)	54	183				8
23				—··—	15		LB 9 ·1	37		8 ↑9 2 8EP 1 4·1	168	2/16	(LB)	55	191		17	115	9
27	—·—·	8					:↑·P·:7	43					↑Round wkt to LHB.	56	192		18		
29½				—·—·	16		:↑↑·E2	49					↑Hip. 6-nr played on. ‡Round wkt. M11	57					
33	—·—·	9					8 ·1	50		:··LB	173		(LB)	58	194		19	115	10
36				—··—	17		↑1 ·1	51	3		173	2/16	↑BAD LIGHT	58¹	194	2	19	115	10
3·37	TEA												M11 NB-		T E A				
4·10				BOTHAM	17		↑···3	56					M12 4HR	59					
13	GOOCH	10								:+ r 4···	179	2/17	(W)	60	199			119	11
17				—··—	18		2 ··8·	62						61	201		21		
20	—··—	11								:EP 61 ·W	182	2/17		61³	201	3	21	119	11
21										BOON							0		
23	—·—·	11					·1	63		:6/5 3	2			62	204			3	
25				—··—	19					L8 3·P ·2····	8			63	206			5	
29	—·—·	12					·4 3·x ·4·	69	4					64	210		25		
31½				—·—·	20		x ·1	71		6 7· E½	12			65	211			6	
35	—·—·	13								·3 P x ··1	18		M13	66					
38				—·—·	21		8	72		:P½ 26· ·2	23			67	214		26	8	
42	—·—·	14					+·L···1	78					(W)	68	215				12
44				—··—	22		2 2	79	4	F8/7L·7 ·4··1	28	1	M13 NB-	69	222	3	28	13	12

First-Test centurions, England's Tim Robinson (above, driving Simon O'Donnell during his match-winning innings of 175) and Australia's vice-captain Andrew Hilditch (left). Robinson went on to average over 60, but Hilditch, who scored 119 and 80 in the first Test, failed to live up to this bright start thanks largely to his penchant for suicidal hook strokes.

Everything's under control on the first day at
Headingley as a policeman guards the wicket,
enjoying his lunch by kind permission of
Australian TV.

Above: Unfortunately there were not enough police on hand to prevent the inexcusable pitch invasion at the end of the match, as Lamb and McDermott make for the pavilion. Although England's victory was assured, Lamb, who made the winning hit off a steepling top edge, might have been caught by Lawson had not the crowd swarmed onto the outfield while the ball was still in the air.

Left: The two captains David Gower (right) and Allan Border share a joke after the match. The series continued to be played in a cheerful and sporting spirit.

Geoff Lawson gets in a tangle as he tries to avoid a
bumper from a belligerent Botham, who took
seven wickets in the Headingley Test.

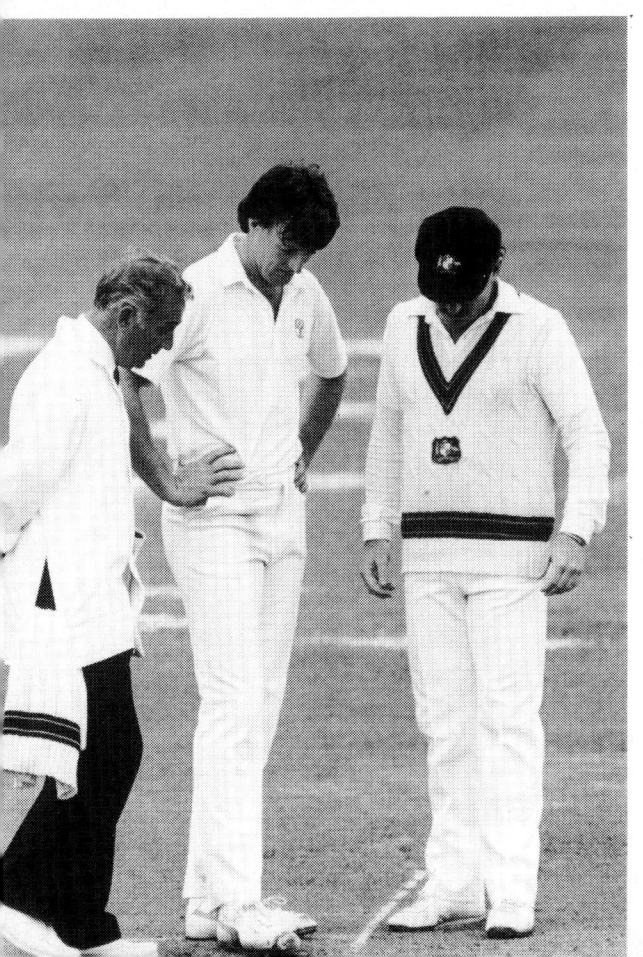

Above: Her Majesty the Queen, shaking hands with David Gower, is introduced to the two teams at Lord's during the second Test.

Left: Umpire David Evans, who no-balled Geoff Lawson 20 times, discusses the problem with the errant bowler and his captain, Allan Border.

The incident that swung the second Test Australia's way, as Allan Border is 'caught' and then dropped by Mike Gatting at 87 in Australia's first innings. In the top picture Gower looks on anxiously as Gatting stops the ball, and then (second picture) seems to have it safely cushioned between hands and thighs. In the bottom two pictures, as Gatting throws the ball up in jubilation, Border begins to walk and Gower to smile.

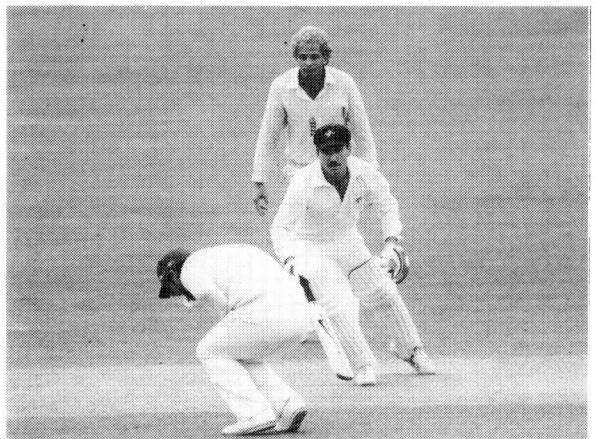

The smile begins to fade from
Gower's face (top two pictures)
as Gatting loses control and,
perhaps ill-advisedly, dives
after the ball. Border,
meanwhile, oblivious to this
sensational development,
continues on his way to the
pavilion. Downton joins in the
despairing scramble for the ball
(second from bottom), and
(bottom) Border finally turns
round to observe the chaos and
receive a reprieve, as the
umpire, no doubt persuaded by
the frantic efforts of the
England fielders, judged that
Gatting had not got 'complete
control' of the ball at any stage.
Border went on to make a
match-winning 196.

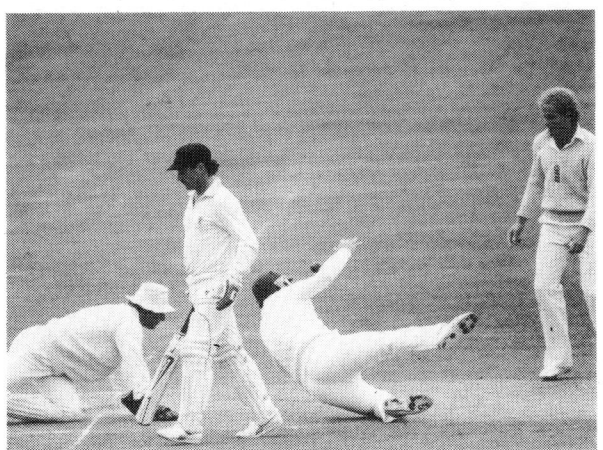

The Australian players cheer on the Lord's balcony as Simon O'Donnell hits the winning run. Thereafter in the series, Australia were always fighting a rearguard action and had very little else to cheer about.

1ST DAY TIME	BOWLERS (MEYER) MAIN STAND END BOWLER	O.	(PALMER) KIRKSTALL L. END BOWLER	O.	BATSMEN SCOREBOARD LEFT SCORING	BALLS	6³/4	SCOREBOARD RIGHT SCORING	BALLS	6³/4	NOTES	END-OF-OVER TOTALS O.	RUNS	W.	L BAT	R BAT	EXTRAS
					BORDER	79	4	BOON	28	1	M13 NB-	69	222	3	28	13	12
4.48	GOOCH	15			:	80		:O. †.² . ¹	34		† Round wkt. NB (NB) 1	70	224			14	13
52			COWANS	14				E†×× 4 ·	40		† nr. played on. M14	71					
56½	- · -	16			. . × P L † . .	86					† over wkt M15	72					
5·00			- · -	15	. × 2 3 . . 4	91	5	.	41		(LB)	73	229		32		14
04	- · · -	17						. . P L W	45	1		73³	229	4	32	14	14
05			}					RITCHIE								0	
07	- · · -	17	}					. . P	2		M16	74					
09			- · -	16	3 E1 . W	94	5					74³	229	5	32	0	14
10					PHILLIPS		LHB								0		
12			- · -	16,	† 2 LB . 4 .	3	1				† Thigh. (LB) 5HR	75	234		4		15
15	- · -	18			E1 4/ S P .† . E2 4 4	9	3				† Round wkt	76	242		12		
18½			- · -	17	3 × LB . . .	12		P E7 . ¹ .	5		(LB)	77	244			1	16
24	- · · -	19			: 4 4	15		. . . :	8			78	245		13		
27			- · -	18	4/ 7 9 E1	17		: 3 3 76 . 4 1	12	1	† nr. played on.	79	251		14	6	
31	- · · -	20			. 7 . 4 . . ×	22	4	8/ 7	13			80	256		18	7	
35			- · -	19	L . × 4 . . 4	26	5	. 1E . 1	15			81	261		22	8	
39	- · · -	21						4 7 4 . × 7 . 4	21	3		82	269			16	
42½			- · -	20	× 2 2/3 . 1 . 4	29	6	7 3 LB 2 . .	24		(LB)	83	277		27	18	17
48	EMBUREY	5						. . . ³ . 4 .	30	4	50 p'ship: 38min.	84	281			22	
51			BOTHAM	23	3 6 2/3 . 2 . 1	33		. 2E .	32			85	284		30		
55	- · -	6	}		P E7 . W	35	6					85²	284	6	30	22	17
56			}		McDERMOTT										0		
58	- · -	6			. . . P	4					M17	86					
6·00			- · -	24	4 -	4	-	† 7 . P † ×	38	4	† NEW BALL M18 NB1	87	284	6	0	22	17
6·03	STUMPS	-	1ST DAY										S	T	U	M	P S
2ND DAY 11·00	ALLOTT	17			6 · 7 5 P .	10					M19	88					
04			BOTHAM	25	. . 6 3 4 . 7 . 4 . . 1	44	5				6HR	89	289			27	
08	- · -	18			5(6) 6 4 4 .	13	2	. 7 9 . 1	47		* Lamb misfielded	90	298		8	28	
12			- · -	26	† . . .	16		4 6 1 4 . 1	50	6		91	303		33		
16	- · -	19			. . .	19		8 P 8 2 . 1	53			92	306		36		
21			- · -	27	. × ×	24		LB . 1 .	54		(LB) M20	93	307				18
24	- · · -	20			. .	24	2	† . 7	56	6	† RAIN. M20 NB1	93²	307	6	8	36	18
11·25	RAIN STOPPED PLAY													R	S	P	
1·00	LUNCH													L	U	N	C H
2·03	ALLOTT	20						7 × 46 . . 4 .	60	7		94	311			40	
05			BOTHAM	28	L . . . × × 4	30	3					95	315		12		
09	- · -	21			P . . . 5 . 4	35	4	¹ 1	61			96	320		16	41	
13			- · -	29	4 1	36	4	4 4 EX 4 1 W	64	8		96⁴	326	7	17	46	18
15											M 20 NB1						

2ND DAY TIME	BOWLERS (MEYER) MAIN STAND END BOWLER	O.	(PALMER) KIRKSTALL L. END BOWLER	O.	BATSMEN SCOREBOARD LEFT SCORING	BALLS	6s/4s	SCOREBOARD RIGHT SCORING	BALLS	6s/4s	AUSTRALIA 1ST INNINGS NOTES	O.	RUNS	W.	'L' BAT	'R' BAT	EXTRAS
					McDERMOTT 36		4	O'DONNELL	-	-	M 20 NB1	96⁴	326	7	17	0	18
2·16			BOTHAM	29				W	1	-	First ball in Tests	96⁵	326	8	17	0	18
17								LAWSON								0	
19				29				, 1				97				0	
20	ALLOTT	22			½1	37		E1 · W	3	-		97³	327	9	18	0	18
22																	
23		22						:4³4	3	1		98	331			4	
26			--·--	30	x W	38	4		3	1		98	331	10	18	4	18
2·26	ALL OUT										M20 NB1 / 590 balls		ALL OUT				

34

2ND DAY TIME	BOWLERS (MEYER) MAIN STAND END BOWLER	O.	(PALMER) KIRKSTALL L.END BOWLER	O.	BATSMEN SCOREBOARD LEFT SCORING	BALLS	6s 4s	SCOREBOARD RIGHT SCORING	BALLS	6s 4s	ENGLAND 1ST INNINGS NOTES	END-OF-OVER TOTALS O.	RUNS	W.	'L' BAT	'R' BAT	EXTRAS
					GOOCH			ROBINSON			Light poor - drizzle.						
2.36			LAWSON	1	.4 .8/9	4	1				† umpires consulted.	0⁴	5	-	5	0	-
39	RAIN and BAD LIGHT														R S P		
3.04			LAWSON	1				. .	2			1					
06	McDERMOTT	1			. . 9/7.4 . .:3	10					(W)	2	6				1
10	- . -		- . -	2				.:.. 3 .7/8 3 E1 224	8	1		3	14			8	
14½	- . -	2			W	11	1					3¹	14	1	5	8	1
15					GOWER		LHB								0		
17	- . -	2			LB L.	3		E1 3 . 1	10		(LB)	4	16			9	2
21			- . -	3				2 4	17	2	NB 1	5	22			15	
26	- . -	3			9 2 9/ (3)	6		x 8 .3 .7	21		NB 2	6	29		4	18	
31			- . -	4	3 4 . . L. .	12	1					7	33		8		
35	- . -	4						5(6) . 63 15 4	27	3	* Dropped 3RD slip (RITCHIE)	8	37			22	
39			- . -	5	8 16 8/ .7 3 242 .:1	18	2					9	46		17		
43	- . -	5			x 4B E1 W	22	2				(4B)	9⁴	50	2	17	22	6
45					GATTING										0		
47	- . -	5			.:.v	2					M 1	10					
48½			- . -	6				. . 8/7 3 3 ⊙4.4.4	34	6	(NB) NB 3	11	63			34	7
54	- . -	6			6 . . 19 .:. 1	8						12	64		1		
58			THOMSON	1	3 . 1	10		. 2/3 6 .:2 . 3	38			13	70		2	39	
4.02	- . -	7			7 . 1	11		EP . 4LB 1 LB	43		(4LB) (LB)	14	76		3		12
07			- . -	2	. . ⊙ (4)	19	1		43	6	(NB) NB 5	15	81	2	7	39	13
4.10	TEA										M 1 NB 5				T E A		
4.30	McDERMOTT	8			x . 7 .:. 1	23		LB	45		(LB)	16	83		8		14
35			THOMSON	3	8/7 . 3	25		3 7 .:2 ..	49			17	88		11	41	
38	- . -	9			4 6† 2 1	27		2/3 . 7 4 .:..	53	7	† Good stop (Thomson)	18	95		14	45	
42			- . -	4	: . 3	30		3 . 1 2 . 1	56		50 p'ship : 38 min.	19	101		17	48	
46	- . -	10			7 2 x .:.	34		4 8 2 (4) 1	59	8	ROBINSON'S 50: 86' NB 6	20	106			53	
52			- . -	5				6. . 2 7 . 2 . 1	65			21	108			55	
55	- . -	11			4 . 8† (4) . 4 . .:c.	42	3				(NB) NB 8	22	117		25		15
5.01			- . -	6	8 4	43	4	. .:. 3 6†8 (4)1	71	9	NB 9	23	126	2	29	60	15
5.05	BLSP - RAIN														B L S P - RAIN		
5.49	O'DONNELL	1			3†	45		2 4 G9† . 2 2 1	75		† Repairs to Robinson's right hand. † Groin	24	131			65	
57			THOMSON	7	3 2 . .	48	4	†2 1	76	9		24⁴	134	2	31	66	15
5.59	BLSP										M 1 NB 9				B L S P		
6.50	PLAY ABANDONED														S T U M P S		

3RD DAY	BOWLERS (MEYER) MAIN STAND END	O.	(PALMER) KIRKSTALL L.END	O.	BATSMEN SCOREBOARD LEFT SCORING	BALLS	6s/4s	SCOREBOARD RIGHT SCORING	BALLS	6s/4s	ENGLAND 1ST INNINGS NOTES	O.	RUNS	W.	'L' BAT	'R' BAT	EXTRAS
TIME					GATTING	48	4	ROBINSON	76	9	M1 NB9	24⁴	134	2	31	66	15
11·00			THOMSON	7	·.:	50						25					
02	O'DONNELL	2			P ·.·.. L	55		LB	77		(LB) M2 2HR	26	135				16
06	— · —		— · —	8	4 2 ·.: 1	57		.: 5/65 .: 9/9	81			27	138		32	68	
09	— · —	3			L ·.· 1	58		P ·.·.·8	86			28	139			69	
14			— · —	9	5/4 9/12 ·.: 1	61		3 8 4 ·. 4 1	89	10		29	144			74	
17½	— · —	4						4/5 · 7 P : ·.· 2 :	95			30	146			76	
21			— · —	10	·.: 3S 1	64		3 3 7 ·.:	98			31	147		33		
24	— · —	5			·.: 6 7 ·.· 4 6	70						32	148		34		
29			McDERMOTT	12	2 4·④ 1	74	6	2 4 ·.· 2 :	101		100 p'ship: 98 min NB 10	33	159		43	78	
34	— · —	6			· L PP½ ·: 1	80	7					34	163		47		
38			— · —	13	3 4 ·.: 1	83		·.: 86P 5(4) ·.· ①	105		• Nr. played on. NB 11	35	166		48	80	
42½	— · —	7			·.· 6 ·: 1	85		·.: P 6 ·.: 3	109			36	170		49	83	
46			— · —	14	2 7 ·: P ·.· 1 :	90		LB	110		(LB) GATTING's 50: 115	37	172		50		17
50½	— · —	8						·. L 6 4⅔ ·.· 4	116	11		38	176			87	
55			— · —	15	·① P PF · 4S	97					(NB) • Appeal ct wkt. NB 12	39	177				18
12·00	— · —	9			2 ·: 1 ·.·	100		·.· 4 2/3 ·: 1	119		3HR	40	180		51	89	
04			— · —	16	·.: 8 1	102		1/X 6 3S ·.·.· 1 8	123			41	183		52	91	
08	THOMSON	11			3S ·.· 1	103		2 2 ·: 1 ·.· :	128			42	185		53	92	
11			— · —	17	·.·.· ①W 7/6	109	7				(NB) NB 13	42⁵	186	3	53	92	19
15					LAMB										0		
17	·		— · —	17	/			·:	129			43					
17½	— · —	12			2 L L · P S 7 ·.· 4	6	1					44	190		4		
21			— · —	18	·.· 4 1	9		3 6 2 ·.: :	132			45	191			93	
26/27	— · —	13						4 7 × × 3 4 ·.·.·. :	138		McDermott boot trouble. M3	46					
30			— · —	19	X 3 P ·.· 4 ·①·: :	16	2				(NB) NB 14	47	196		8		20
35	— · —	14						6 19 3 4 ·.· 4 ④ ·.·	145	13	NB15 ROBINSON's 100: 211	48	204			101	
40			LAWSON	7	2LB 7 4 ·.· 4 ·.·	22	3				(2LB)	49	210		12		22
44	— · —	15						5 2 4 ·.· :	151		M4	50					
47			— · —	8	X S 30 ·.· 2 · :	28					• Dropped cover (WOOD).	51	212		14		
51	— · —	16						3 4/9 3 7 ·.·.· 4 4 2	157	15		52	222			111	
55			— · —	9	·: + · 5(6) 7 4 1	32	4	4 4 ·.· :	159		(W)	53	228		19		23
59½	BORDER	1			9/7 2/7 ·.· 8S ·.·.· 1	37	4	·:	160	15		54	229	3	20	111	23
1·02	LUNCH										M4 NB 15			LUNCH			
1·40			LAWSON	10	4 2 3 6 ·.· 4 4 ·.· :	43	6				50 p'ship: 46' 4HR	55	237		28		
44½	O'DONNELL	10			9 ·.· 4	44	7	·.·.· 5(4) 6 ·: 4	165	16		56	246		32	116	
49			— · —	11				8/6 2 7 · 4 7 ·: 4	171	17		57	250			120	
53	— · —	11			·: 8 1	47		·: 5 P :	174			58	251		33		
57			— · —	12	·.: 3 4 ·.·	53	8					59	255		37		
2·01	— · —	12			·.·.· 1	57	8	·.· 9 1	176	17	M4 NB 15	60	256	3	37	121	23

36

3RD DAY TIME	BOWLERS (MEYER) MAIN STAND END — BOWLER	O.	(PALMER) KIRKSTALL L. END — BOWLER	O.	BATSMEN SCOREBOARD LEFT SCORING	BALLS	6s/4s	SCOREBOARD RIGHT SCORING	BALLS	6s/4s	ENGLAND 1ST INNINGS NOTES	END-OF-OVER TOTALS O.	RUNS	W.	'L' BAT	'R' BAT	EXTRAS
					LAMB	57	8	ROBINSON	176	17	M4 NB15	60	256	3	37	121	23
2·05			McDERMOTT	20	∴ . ∴	61		1E LB 4 ∙	178	18	(LB)	61	261			125	24
10	O'DONNELL	13						∴ . ∴ 5P	184		M5	62					
14			— " —	21	9 LB ∙ 1	63		∙9/8 × 7	188		(LB)	63	264		38	126	25
18	— ∙ — —	14			×W	64	8					63¹	264	4	38	126	25
					BOTHAM										0		
20	— ∙ —	14			∙ × LB	3		∴ ∙	190		(LB) M6	64	265				26
24			— ∙ —	22	∴ ∙ 1	6		∴ ∴ ∙	193			65	266		1		
28	— ∙ — —	15			∙ 4 ∴ ∴ 4 8	12	1					66	270		5		
31½			— ∙ —	23	7 7 ∙ 4 ∙	15	2	∙ Y 6 ∙ 3	196			67	277		9	129	
37	— ∙ —	16						∴ . ∴ 3 6	202		BALL CHANGED M7 5HR	68					
42			— ∙ —	24	5(4) 1 4 6 4 76× ④ + ∙ 4 ∙ 4	22	5				(W) NB 16	69	290		21		27
47	— ∙ —	17			3 ∙ 1	23		7 7 5P 2/3 6 ∙ 1	207			70	292		22	130	
52			THOMSON	17	∙ 9 ∴ × 8 1	28		9 1	208			71	295		24	131	
56	— ∙ —	18			∴ ∙ 4 5+ 1 6 ∙ 4 ∙ 44	34	8				† Good Stop (McDermott)	72	307		36		
3·01			— ∙ —	18				7 ∴ ∙ 4 5 ∙	214	19		73	311			135	
05	BORDER (Round wkt)	2			LB ∙	35		∴ 7 ∙ 4 7 ∙ 4	219	20	(LB) So P'ship: 47'	74	316			139	28
08			— ∙ —	19	(4B) ∙ 7 ∙ 5(B) L ① ∙ 2 4 ④ ∙	43	9				(4NB) NB 18	75	327		43		32
13	— ∙ —	3			9 5 4 4 6 1	46	1/10	∴ ∙ 5	222		BOTHAM'S 50: 55'	76	338		54		
17			— ∙ —	20	7 8 ∙ EX 6 ∙ ∙ W	51	2/10					76⁵	344	5	60	139	32
20					WILLEY										0		
21			— ∙ —	20	∙ 1	1						77					
22	LAWSON	13						∴ ∙ ∙ 3	228		M8	78					
26			— ∙ —	21	∴ ∙ LB	4		6 ∙ 44 ∙ 4	231	21	(LB)	79	349			143	33
30	— ∙ —	14			3 ∙ ∙ 3 4 ④ 1E	11	1				NB 19	80	355		6		
35			— ∙ —	22	8 ∙ ∙ 3	13		4 ∙ M9 4 7 ∙ 1	235		(W)	81	360		9	144	34
39½	— ∙ —	15			7 ∙ ∴ ∙ 8P	18	1	∙	236	21	*Mr. played on 6HR	82	361	5	10	144	34
3·43	TEA										M8 NB 19			T E A			
4·01			THOMSON	23	2 ∙ 4 4 8 2 ∙ 44	24	3					83	371		20		
05	O'DONNELL	19						3 4 ∙ 5(6) × L 4 ∙ ∙	242	22		84	375			148	
09			McDERMOTT	25	6 ∙ ∙ ∴ 00	30		∙ 4 ∙ 4	244	23	(NB) ROBINSON'S 150: 372 min. NB.21	85	381		21	152	35
15	— ∙ —	20			† ∙ 2 4 + ∙ ∙ ∙ 1	36					†NEW BALL (W)	86	382				36
19			— ∙ —	26				8 5 1 1 5(6) 4 2④ ∙ 4 ∙	251	26	So P'ship: 44 min.	87	396			166	
24	— ∙ —	21			3 ∙ ∙ 8/9 4 ∙ ∙ 1	40	4	∙ 7 ∙ 1	253			88	402		26	167	
28	— ∙ —			27	6 ∙ 1	41		× ∙ 4/5 6 6 ∙ 4 ∙ 3	258	27		89	409			174	
33	— ∙ —	22						∙ 6 ∙ 3 ∴ ∙	264		M9	90					
37			LAWSON	16	3 ∙ 7 5 5 7 2 ∴ ∙ 3	47						91	414		31		
41	— ∙ —	23			∴ . ∙ 4	53					M10	92					
45			— ∙ —	17	∙ 3 8 ∙ ∙ 1	56		4 9 ∙ 1 ○ ∙	268		(NB) NB 23	93	417		32	175	37
49½	— ∙ —	24			∴ ∙ † ∙ 2 P	62	4		268	27	M11 NB 23	94	417	5	32	175	37

3RD DAY	BOWLERS (MEYER) MAIN STAND END		BOWLERS (PALMER) KIRKSTALL L. END		BATSMEN SCOREBOARD LEFT			BATSMEN SCOREBOARD RIGHT			ENGLAND 1ST INNINGS NOTES	END-OF-OVER TOTALS					
TIME	BOWLER	O.	BOWLER	O.	SCORING	BALLS	6s/4s	SCORING	BALLS	6s/4s	NOTES	O.	RUNS	W.	L BAT	R BAT	EXTRAS
					WILLEY	62	4	ROBINSON	268	27	M 11 NB 23	94	417	5	32	175	37
4.54			LAWSON	18				W	270	27		94²	417	6	32	175	37
55								DOWNTON							0		
57			— · —	18	:	63		P : ○	4		NB 24 7HR	95	418			1	
5.01	O'DONNELL	25						P · · ·	10		M 12	96					
05			— · —	19	4 ! · W	67	5					96⁴	422	7	36	1	37
07			EMBUREY												0		
09			— · —	19	· 2	2						97	424			2	
10½	— · —	26			· 3	3		P 4 · 1	15	1		98	429			6	
15			— · —	20				· · · ! !	21		Appeal ct wkt. M 13	99					
19	— · —	27			· · 44 · ·	9	2					100	437			10	
23			— · —	21				· · · 4 ·	27	2	be-flagged streaker	101	441			10	
28	THOMSON	24			· · · 1	13		44	29	4		102	450			11	18
32			— · —	22	· 4	16	3	· 4 ·	32		Lobbed between bowler & mid-off	103	455			16	
37	— · —	25			· 4 1	19	4	· · 2	35			104	462			21	20
41			— · —	23	P · W	22	4					104³	462	8	21	20	37
42			ALLOTT												0		
44			— · —	23	· · ·	3					M 14	105					
46	— · —	26			· · ·	6		2 · 1	38			106	465			23	
50			— · —	24				· 7 8	44		M 15	107					
55	— · —	27			4 · · · 1	11		· 7	45		8 HR	108	466			1	
59			— · —	25	· ?	13		· · 4 ·	49	5		109	471			2	27
6.04	— · —	28			4 · ○ · ·	20	1				NB NB 25	110	476			6	38
08			WESSELS	1				· · · · ·	55		M 16	111					
10½	— · —	29			· · 4 1	24	2	! ·	57			112	481			11	
14			— · —	2	· ! · · 6 B	29		· ? 1	58		B	113	484			12	28	39
17	— · —	30			· 7 · 2 W	34	2					113⁵	484	9	12	28	39
19					COWANS										0		
21	— · · ·	30			· 1	1					M 17	114					
22			— · —	3	· 1	1		· · · · ·	64	5	M 18 NB 25	115	484	9	0	28	39
6.24	STUMPS	—	3RD DAY								STUMPS						
3RD DAY 11.00	THOMSON	31			· · 4 · 1	7	1					116	489		5		
04			MCDERMOTT	28		13					M 19	117					
08	— · —	32			· 4	14	2	· 24 ·	69	6	Run refused. Holland sub for Wood	118	500		· 9	35	
12			— · —	29				24	75	7	Runs refused.	119	506			41	
16½	— · —	33			7 · 1	18		· 4 ·	77			120	508			10	42
21			— · —	30	· 4	19	3	· ·	82		Run refused.	121	513			14	43
25	— · · ·	34			○ · 2	22		4 · ·	86	8	Runs refused. ct O'Donnell NB	122	519			48	40
29½			— · —	31	· · 4 ·	92	9				Runs refused. Downton ct b: 119'	123	523			52	
34	LAWSON	26			· · 44 ·	28	5				9 HR	124	531		22		
38			— · —	32		28	5	2 · · · · W	98	9	Runs refused. M 19 NB 26	125	533	10	22	54	40
11.41	ALL OUT										776 balls		ALL OUT				

4TH DAY	BOWLERS				BATSMEN				AUSTRALIA 2ND INNINGS					
	MAIN STAND END (PALMER)		KIRKSTALL L. END (MEYER)		SCOREBOARD LEFT			SCOREBOARD RIGHT		NOTES	END-OF-OVER TOTALS				
TIME	BOWLER	O.	BOWLER	O.	SCORING	BALLS	6s/4s	SCORING	BALLS	6s/4s		O.	RUNS	W.	'L' BAT	'R' BAT	EXTRAS

TIME	BOWLER	O.	BOWLER	O.	SCORING	BALLS	6/4	SCORING	BALLS	6/4	NOTES	O.	RUNS	W.	L BAT	R BAT	EXTRAS
					HILDITCH			WOOD		1HB							
11.52			BOTHAM	1	:·8/:1	2		↑·×··4	4			1	1	1			
56½	ALLOTT	1			LB·:·	3		↑··9·18/·2·1	9		(LB)	2	5			3	1
12.02			—·—	2				··8/6·W	12	-		2³	5	1	1	3	1
03					⌐			WESSELS								0	
05			—·—	2	4:·:19/4	6	1				† Hit on 'box'.	3	9		5		
07½	—·—	2			::·8/8·:·:	11		9·:	1		• Mr. played on.	4	10			1	
12			—·—	3				2·2·×·9/·4·	7	1		5	14			5	
15	—·—	3			·:·P··G	17					M1	6					
19½			—·—	4	·s(4)/s(4)4·P·2/·4·2·:·:	13	2				† Round wkt.	7	20			11	
23	—·—	4			2·26··2/3·×/2·2·:·2··	23						8	26		11		
27			—·—	5	×·:·	26		·:·2	16			9	27			12	
31½	—·—	5						P··3·:·:·	22		M2	10					
36			—·—	6	8/1·P·4/7·2·4··	31	2	2/3	23			11	33		16	13	
39½	—·—	6						L·×·:·67/·:·1	29			12	34			14	
43½			—·—	7	·1/2·4··	34	3	×·×/3·9/·4·1	32	3	1HR	13	43		20	19	
47½	—·—	7						GTL··6	38		† Repairs to finger. M3	14					
54			EMBUREY	1	×·:·4/·1	37		·:·3/·1	41		† Turned sharply. Round wkt to LHB.	15	44		21		
57½	—·—	8			7/1·:·4·4/·4	42	4	7/1	42	3		16	50	1	26	20	1
1.01	LUNCH										M3 NB-			LUNCH			
1.40			EMBUREY	2				·:·:·3/·4	48	4		17	54			24	
43	COWANS	1			↑8·1/2·/2·6·4·1	46	1/5	·:·7/·1	50		50 p'ship: 59 min.	18	66		37	25	
49			—·—	3	2·:·:·6/	50		·:·8/·1	52			19	67			26	
52	—·—	2			7	51		L·×·3·4··2/·:·:	57			20	69		38	27	
56			—·—	4	4·:·:·:·:	57					M4	21					
58	—·—	3						·4·:·:·13	63		M5	22					
2.03			—·—	5	4/4·4/·:·:·	63	1/6					23	73		42		
05½	—·—	4			·6/4	64		·3·:·×·4/·3	68			24	76			30	
10			—·—	6				·:·:·9·46/·4·	74	5		25	80			34	
13	GOOCH	1			·:·:·×	70					M6	26					
16			—·—	7				2/3·×·2/1··L·/4·4·:·	80	7		27	88			42	
19	—·—	2			·×·9E/·:·1	75		·:·2/1	81		• Mr. played on.	28	90		43	43	
22			—·—	8				2/1·4·:·	87	8		29	94			47	
25	—·—	3			8/1·3/1	77		†·:·4/·3·:	91		† Round wkt WESSELS 50: 102'	30	99		45	50	
29			—·—	9	·:·4/2·:·×·:	83	1/7				2HR	31	103		49		
31½	—·—	4			4/×·:·	86		4··2/·:·1	94			32	104			51	
34			—·—	10				·:·:·:·:·P·2/·1	100		100 p'ship • 112'	33	105			52	
37	—·—	5						P··:·×·:	106		M7	34					
39½			—·—	11	·:·:·6/·:·4/·4	92	1/8				HILDITCH'S 50: 130'	35	109		53		
42	—·—	6			P·P·:	95	1/8	3/6··1/2/·4·:·1	109	9	M7 NB-	36	114	1	53	57	1

FIRST TEST
SHEET 10

4TH DAY TIME	BOWLERS (PALMER) MAIN STAND END	O.	(MEYER) KIRKSTALL L.END	O.	BATSMEN SCOREBOARD LEFT	BALLS	6s/4s	SCOREBOARD RIGHT	BALLS	6s/4s	NOTES	O.	RUNS	W.	L BAT	R BAT	EXTRAS
					HILDITCH	95	1/8	WESSELS	109	9	M7 NB–	36	114	1	53	57	1
2.45			EMBUREY	12	. 8 . 1	97		: : 7 . 1 2	113			37	116		54	58	
48½	GOOCH	7			. : 4 x 5/6 . 4	103	1/9					38	120		58		
51½			BOTHAM	8	: : : 2 4 P . 4	108		1/3 1	114		Ⓦ	39	122			59	2
55	– . –	8						. 2 x : : :	120		M8	40					
58			– . –	9	2 : 3 1 : 1	113		9 1	121			41	124		59	60	
3.02	– . –	9						. E1 : : . 5/6 4	127	10	† over wkt.	42	128			64	
05			– . –	10	3. 7 . . 2/3/8 2 4 . 4	119	1/11				* dropped cover (ROBINSON)	43	139		70		
10	EMBUREY	13	round wkt.		: . 4 . 4/3 8 . 1	125						44	140		71		
14			– . –	11	1 . 1 x . 1 9 . 4	131	1/12				† over wkt	45	144		75		
18	– . –	14						x W	128	10		45	144	2	75	64	2
								BORDER		LHB	I.G. SWALLOW sub for ROBINSON (bruised finger – LH)					0	
20	– . –	14			. 8 . 1	132		: : 9/8 . 1	4			46	146		76	1	
23			– . –	12	: : : : . 1	138					M9	47					
26	– . –	15			:	139		: 5 : . 1	9			48	147			2	
29			– . –	13				. 2 : : :	15		M10 3HR	49					
33	– . –	16			: : : . 8 P	145					M11	50					
36			– . –	14				: x : . :	21		M12	51					
39	– . –	17			: : 9 4 : : :	151	1/13		21	–		52	151	2	80	2	2
3.41	TEA										M12 NB–		T	E	A		
4.00			BOTHAM	15				. . 8 : . :	27		ROBINSON back M13	53					
04	EMBUREY	18			: : : W	155	1/13					53	151	3	80	2	2
06					BOON										0		
08	– . –	18			. :	2					M14	54					
09			– . –	16	: 8 . 1 6/5 :	6		2 . 1 6	29			55	154		1	4	
12½	– . –	19			2 . 1 : :	9		: 3 . 9 1 8	32			56	159		2	8	
15			– . –	17				: . E1 . W	35	–		56	159	4	2	8	2
16								RITCHIE							0		
18			– . –	17				: . . 2 . 1	3			57	160			1	
20	– . –	20						: . x W	6	–		57	160	5	2	1	2
21								PHILLIPS		LHB					0		
23	– . –	20						. : . x	3		M15	58					
25			– . –	18	1 x : . : . 7	15					M16	59					
28	– . –	21						: : : 4 . 4	9		M17	60					
30			– . –	19	8 . 1 : 8 . 1	18		4 . L x . 1	12			61	163		4	1	
34	– . –	22			: : : 4 4 .	24	2		24			62	171		12		
37			– . –	20	:	25		3 . . . 2 1	17			63	172			2	
40	– . –	23			. 8 2 : : :	30		9 1	18			64	175		14	3	
43			– . –	21	:	31		1/2 . 2/3 2 . 1	23			65	178			6	
46	– . –	24				31	2	: : : : : :	29	–	M18 NB–4HR	66	178	5	14	6	2

40

4TH DAY TIME	BOWLERS MAIN STAND END (PALMER) BOWLER	O.	KIRKSTALL L. END (MEYER) BOWLER	O.	BATSMEN SCOREBOARD LEFT SCORING	BALLS	6s/4s	SCOREBOARD RIGHT SCORING	BALLS	6s/4s	AUSTRALIA 2ND INNINGS NOTES	END-OF-OVER TOTALS O.	RUNS	W.	'L' BAT	'R' BAT	EXTRAS
					BOON	31	2	PHILLIPS	29	–	M18 NB–	66	178	5	14	6	2
4·48½			BOTHAM	22	9	32		· · · 6 ·7	34			67	179		15		
52	EMBUREY	25			: : : : :7/8 1	38						68	180		16		
55			ALLOTT	9	· · LB	42		··	36		LB M19	69	181				3
5·00	– · –	26			3 : : : : P	48					M 20	70					
02			– · –	10	6 :	50		: 4 · 1	40	1		71	186			11	
06	– · –	27				50	2	4 : : : : 1	46	1	Round wkt to LHB M21	72	186	5	16	11	3
08	BLSP										Drizzle	BLSP					
5·31			ALLOTT	11	9	51		: : : : x	51			73	187		17		
35½	EMBUREY	28			7 : : : 4 L8	57						74	188		18		
38			– · –	12	: L8 : : 2	63						75	190		20		
42	– · –	29				63	2	3† : : : : 1	57	1	† Gower (s.point) hit on knee. M22	76	190	5	20	11	3
5·45	BLSP/STUMPS – 4TH DAY											BLSP/STUMPS					
5TH DAY 11·00			COWANS	5	8 : L : 7 YX W 69	69	2				overcast. SWALLOW subs MILLEY (bruised finger).	77	192	6	22	11	3
04					O'DONNELL										O		
06	EMBUREY	30			: : : : ·	5		8	58		Round wkt to LHB	78	193			12	
09			– · –	6				3 : x · 3 · 2 · · · 1	64			79	196			15	
14	– · –	31			: :	7		· 6 · 8 : 1	68			80	197			16	
17			– · –	7	: :	9		x : · 9 1	72			81	198			17	
21½	– · –	32			: : :	12		: 4 8 1	75			82	199			18	
24			– · –	8				4 : · L4 : 1	81		M23 5HR	83					
28	– · –	33			: : 7 2 7 · 2 1	18						84	201		2		
31			– · –	9				: : : 3 3 4 · ·	87	2		85	205			22	
35	– · –	34			· P · · P 1	24					M24	86					
38			– · –	10	½ 1	25		5/6 : · 2 7 4 · 1 ·	92	3		87	211		3	27	
42	– · –	35			7 P x : 1	31					M25	88					
45			– · –	11	3 : x 3/6 : : · 4	35	1	†4 1E : 1	94		† NEW BALL	89	216		7	28	
50	ALLOTT	13			G : · 2 1	38		P · 2 : 1	97			90	218		8	29	
54			– · –	12	3/4 4 x 8 1 4 · · 2 1	43	2	x : · 1	98			91	225		15		
59	– · –	14			1	44		7 x 78 P 4 · 44 ·	103	6	x over stumps.	92	238		16	41	
12·04			– · –	13	: : 1 18 28 4 · 1	50	3				50 p'ship : 60 min.	93	243		21		
08	– · –	15			· 9/8 1	52		½ 2/6 87. 2 4 2 ·	107	7		94	252		22	49	
13			BOTHAM	23	: P : P x : 1	58					M26	95					
16½	– · –	16			:	59		: x 3 x 2 : 1	112		MILLEY back PHILLIPS 50 : 138'	96	253			50	
20			– · –	24				3/4 P 73 · 2 4 · ·	118	8		97	257			54	
24	– · –	17			½E 1	60		: : 4 4/5 4/2 · · · 42 1	123	9	6HR	98	264		23	60	
28			– · –	25	: : x x : L 1	66					M27	99					
32	EMBUREY	36						4 · · · · 7† 1	129		Round wkt. M28 † Gatting hit (ch.leg)	100					
35			– · –	26	x · ½/2 1	68		3 6 4 2 4 · · 1	133	10	Downton nearly ct rebound.	101	270		24	65	
38	– · –	37			: : : : 1	72	3	· 8 1	135	10	over wkt to RHB M28 NB–	102	271	6	24	66	3

5TH DAY TIME	BOWLERS MAINSTAND END (PALMER) BOWLER	O.	KIRKSTALL L. END (MEYER) BOWLER	O.	BATSMEN SCOREBOARD LEFT SCORING	BALLS	6s/4s	SCOREBOARD RIGHT SCORING	BALLS	6s/4s	AUSTRALIA 2ND INNINGS NOTES	O.	RUNS	W.	'L' BAT	'R' BAT	EXTRAS
					O'DONNELL	72	3	PHILLIPS	135	10	M 28 NB -	102	271	6	24	66	3
12.42			BOTHAM	27	E1 W	73	3	: 2S 1	137			102³	272	7	24	67	3
43					LAWSON										0		
45			- · -	27	7 1	1		· 2	139		M29	103	274		1	68	
47	EMBUREY	38						· 4B 3† · 2	145		(4B) † Grower (s.pt) Hit on leg	104	278				7
50			- · -	28	†x : 8 1	5		2 5 21	147			105	282		2	71	
53	- · -	39						3 3 · 3 8 2 · · : 1	153			106	285			74	
56½			- · -	29	: 2 1	7		2/3 · 3 3 · · : 1	157		umpires discussed light.	107	286			75	
59	- · -	40			: P 3 4	10	1	· † 2 1	160	10	† Run refused.	108	291	7	6	76	7
1.02	LUNCH										M 29 NB -		L U N C H				
1.40			BOTHAM	30	8 1	11		1 6 2† · 8 22 : 1	165		† Alott misfielded.	109	298		7	82	
44	EMBUREY	41			: · : P 1	15		: 2 1	167			110	299			83	
47			- · -	31	}			9/1 1 6/7 44 · W	171	12	Round wkt.	110⁴	307	8	7	91	7
49					}			McDERMOTT			(crossed)				0		
51			- · -	31	} E1 4 44	17	3					111	315		15		
53	- · -	42			: 1	18		6 · · : LB 1	5		(LB) M 30	112	316				8
56			- · -	32	: 1	19		· † x x/3 6S 1	10			113	317			1	
2.00	- · -	43	}		3S W	20	3	: : : 7 1	14			113³	318	9	15	2	8
01½			}		THOMSON						(crossed)				0		
03½	- · -	43	}					6F 1	15			114	319			3	
04			- · -	33	1/2 xx 3 · · · 1	4		4 6 1 1	17		7 HR	115	322		1	5	
07	- · -	44			8 1	5	-	4/8) P 6 · W	20	-		115⁴	324	10	2	6	8
2.10	AUSTRALIA		ALL OUT								M 30 NB - 694 balls		ALL OUT				

ENGLAND 2ND INNINGS

5TH DAY	BOWLERS MAIN STAND END (PALMER)	O.	BOWLERS KIRKSTALL L.END (MEYER)	O.	BATSMEN SCOREBOARD LEFT SCORING	BALLS	6s/4s	SCOREBOARD RIGHT SCORING	BALLS	6s/4s	NOTES	END-OF-OVER TOTALS O.	RUNS	W.	'L' BAT	'R' BAT	EXTRAS
TIME	BOWLER	O.	BOWLER	O.													
					GOOCH			ROBINSON			WELLHAM sub (WOOD)						
2.20			McDERMOTT	1	·x·5(6)·LB 4 ·O1	5	1	·3 ·1 ··	2		(LB)(NB) NB1	1	8		5	1	2
25	LAWSON	1			·7 ··.·1	9		·L·· 4	4			2	9		6		
30			- · -	2	2·4··1P·	15	2	·				3	13		10		
34	- · -	2						·2 8 P· 2/36 ··4·	10	1		4	17			5	
38			- · -	3	2·6F 3 6 x1 2·· 2··	21						5	21		14		
42	- · -	3						·3 ·7 ·5(6) 4·· 2	16	2		6	27			11	
46			- · -	4	·7 ·7 ·1 ·1	25		6P 8/7 ··4	18	3		7	32		15	15	
51	- · -	4			8/7 LB	27		6 1x · x	22		(LB) M1	8	33				3
55			O'DONNELL	1	··· 2LB 8 6 ·2·	33					(2LB)	9	37		17		5
59	- · -	5						·3 7 7/8· 4 6 ·2·7··O4	29	4	(NB) NB 2	10	44			21	6
3.04			- · -	2	·3 6F 5 6·	39					M2	11					
08	- · -	6						W	30	4		11'	44	1	17	21	6
								GOWER	LHB							0	
10	- · -	6						·2 ·6·1	5		M3	12					
13½			- · -	3	7 8/7 ··· 8	45					M4 1HR	13					
17	- · -	7			·· 2LB 3 ·4	48	3	·P 9	8		(2LB)	14	51		21	1	8
22			- · -	4				x ·4 ·4 ·	14		M5	15					
26	- · -	8			·· 7 ··· 6 ·2	54						16	55		25		
30			- · -	5				·· 3 E1 4 W	18	1		16⁴	59	2	25	5	8
32								GATTING								0	
34			- · -	5				P·	2			17					
35½	- · -	9			·x 3 ·4·x 2· 2	60	3	··	2	-	(W)	18	62	2	27	0	9
3.40 TEA											M5 NB2			T E A		
4.00			O'DONNELL	6	7 8 6 4 ·1 ··	64		½ 1 1 ·1	4			19	65		28	2	
03	LAWSON	10						2/3 3 x· 2··4··	10	1	x over stumps.	20	71			8	
08			- · -	7	L W	65	3					20'	71	3	28	8	9
					LAMB											0	
10			- · -	7	x ·x 8 ····	5					M6	21					
14	- · -	11						·3 ··6· ·4··	16	2		22	75			12	
17½			- · -	8	···· 7 1 44	11	2				LAMB 2000 RUNS.	23	83		8		
22	- · -	12						E1 ··· W	20	2		23⁴	83	4	8	12	9
24								BOTHAM								0	
26	- · -	12						L 3 ··	2		M7	24					
27½			- · -	9	8/7 6 7 · 6· 4·1	17	3					25	87		12		
31	- · -	13			4 1	19	4	··· 3 1 2 ·	6		· in air - near mid-off.	26	94		17	2	
36			- · -	10	·1 9	21		4x· 71 ··41	10	1	2HR	27	100		18	7	
40	- · -	14			P· ·9/8	25		··	12			28	101		19		
45			- · -	11	··· xP ·5(6)	31					M8	29					
49½	- · -	15			8 1	32	4	·1 7 E8 x 2/3 ·1 ··1	17	1	· nr. played on. M8 NB 2	30	104	4	20	9	9

| 5TH DAY | BOWLERS (PALMER) MAIN STAND END | O. | (MEYER) KIRKSTALL L. END | O. | BATSMEN SCOREBOARD LEFT SCORING | BALLS | 6s/4s | SCOREBOARD RIGHT SCORING | BALLS | 6s/4s | ENGLAND 2ND INNINGS NOTES | O. | RUNS | W. | 'L' BAT | 'R' BAT | EXTRAS |
TIME	BOWLER		BOWLER								END-OF-OVER TOTALS					
					LAMB	32	4	BOTHAM	17	1	M8 NB 2	30	104	4	20	9	9
4·55			D'DONNELL	12	×2/·3	34		3L:8/2:·1	21			31	110		23	12	
59½	LAWSON	16			··3··†	40					†Lawson fell. M9	32					
5·04			–·–	13	7			·W	23	1	20 OVERS→	32²	110	5	23	12	9
05					{			WILLEY							0		
07			–·–	13	{8/7·1	41		:3 LB	3		(LB) 19	33	112		24		10
10	THOMSON	1			853·P·2···	47					18	34	114		26		
14			–·–	14	6··72····	52		3	4		17	35	115			1	
17	–·–	2	·		:·6··6/·4···	57	5	4s	5		16	36	120		30	2	
22			–·–	15	64	59		:·6·2/3	9		NB3	37	121			3	
25	–·–	3						×Y.·P·67s/:··Ọ··	16		(NB) °Dropped mid-wkt (BORDER)	38²	122				11
29			–·–	16	:·2·9/8·1	63	5		16	–	°chance to 14 Lawson-running	38+	123	5	31	3	11
5·31	ENGLAND		WON BY	5	WICKETS						back–impeded by invading crowd.						
											M 9 NB 3						
											235 balls						

KIRKSTALL LANE END

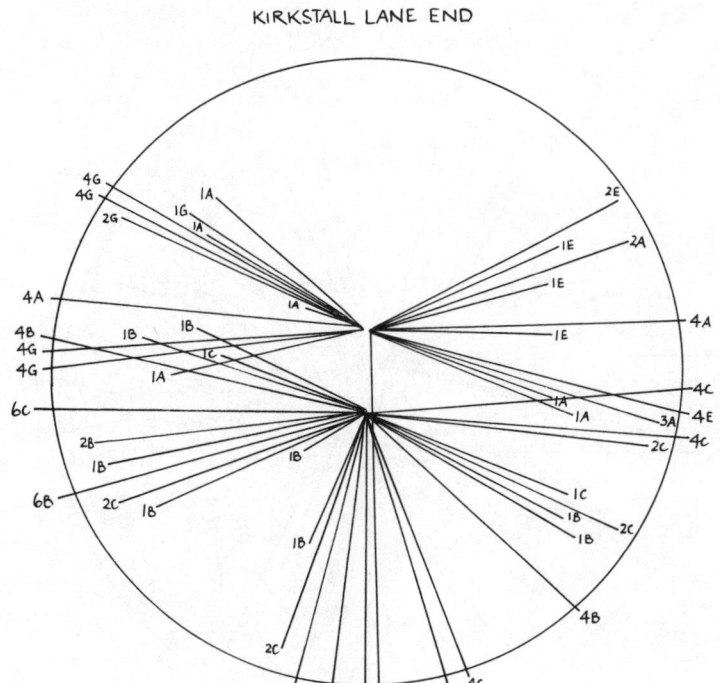

MAIN STAND END

BOWLER	SYMBOL	R U N S					TOTAL
		1	2	3	4	6	
ALLOTT	A	6	1	1	3	-	23
BOTHAM	B	8	1	-	3	1	28
COWANS	C	2	4	-	6	1	40
EMBUREY	E	3	1	-	1	-	9
GOOCH	G	1	1	-	4	-	19
TOTALS		20	8	1	17	2	119

A.M.J. HILDITCH at Headingley

119 RUNS
182 BALLS
249 MINUTES

© BILL FRINDALL 1985

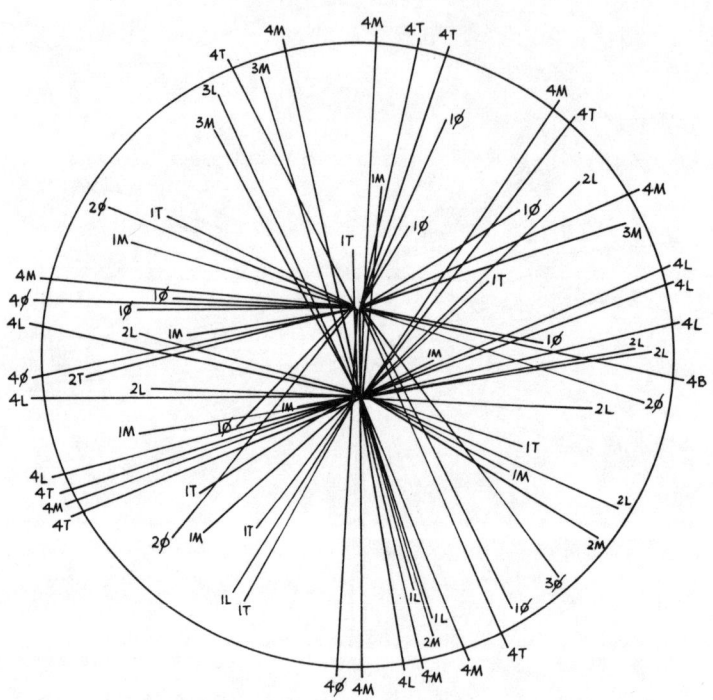

KIRKSTALL LANE END

MAIN STAND END

BOWLER	SYMBOL	R U N S				
		1	2	3	4	6	TOTAL
BORDER	B	.	.	.	1	.	4
LAWSON	L	3	7	1	7	.	48
McDERMOTT	M	8	2	3	9	.	57
O'DONNELL	Ø	8	3	1	3	.	29
THOMSON	T	7	1	.	7	.	37
TOTALS		26	13	5	27	.	175

R.T. ROBINSON at Headingley

175 RUNS
270 BALLS
413 MINUTES

© BILL FRINDALL 1985

46

SECOND TEST
LORD'S

JUNE 27, 28, 29, July 1, 2

ENGLAND

D.I. Gower (captain), G.A. Gooch, R.T. Robinson, M.W. Gatting,
A.J. Lamb, I.T. Botham, P.R. Downton, J.E. Emburey,
P.H. Edmonds, N.A. Foster, P.J.W. Allott

AUSTRALIA

A.R. Border (captain), G.M. Wood, A.M.J. Hilditch, K.C. Wessels,
D.C. Boon, G.M. Ritchie, W.B. Phillips, S.P. O'Donnell,
G.F. Lawson, C.J. McDermott, R.G. Holland

Victory may not suffice for Gower

As the Lord's groundstaff worked through the night in the hope of ensuring a prompt start to today's second Cornhill Test, England's captain, David Gower, might also have had a few uneasy moments while he pondered his immediate future. Gower finds himself in the unenviable position of leading his side against Australia, one up in the six-match series but knowing that even a second successive victory might not be enough to secure his hold on the captaincy.

Incongruous though that may seem, the selectors, in reappointing Gower for only the first two Tests of the series, made it clear that his lack of consistent form since taking over the role was uppermost in their minds.

Thus, while appreciative of his part in England's success in India last winter, they were concerned that he made runs only – albeit crucially – in the last Test, and hinted that they were looking for a greater contribution from him.

But he failed twice in the first Test at Headingley, as any batsman might have done on that particular pitch, even though England managed to amass their highest score against Australia for a decade.

Now he leads England on a ground where they have not beaten Australia for more than 50 years, outwardly trying to be as phlegmatic as possible but inwardly doubtless aware that a good ball here, an unlucky decision there, might be decisive.

In the past, England have retained captains – like Brearley and Illingworth – because of their flair for leadership when form deserted them. But another, Denness, felt obliged to stand down for one Test in Australia when the pressures mounted. Gower is still serving his apprenticeship as a captain, which is hardly his fault, and I suppose he would have to do everything wonderfully well and stage-manage an England win to counteract the effect of more failures with the bat.

On the other hand were England to take a 2-0 lead, the selectors might well be magnanimous enough to acknowledge Gower's part in it and, if so, make a stay of execution in the hope that in a successful side tensions might ease and runs flow. He has scored only 415 in 20 innings as captain.

At the moment though, all that is flowing at Lord's is water. In the past five days, one and a half inches of rain has fallen there and more than four inches in this merry month of June alone.

It rose above the welts of my shoes on a stroll over the outfield yesterday. It was hard to recall a more waterlogged playing area on the eve of a recent Test; hence the need for Mike Hunt, the new groundsman, and his staff to burn the midnight oil.

With the help of floodlights, they planned to spike and mop the playing area, all the time grimly aware that little more rain was needed to disrupt today's proceedings, though spectators can now obtain a refund if not a ball is bowled.

Throughout all that, Mr Hunt's first Test pitch remained covered as it has been all too often lately. So, though it is said to be firm, it will be a surprise if there is nothing in it for the bowlers at the start. England, I imagine, will want to play both their spinners, Emburey and Edmonds, in the knowledge that it should be a 'flat 'un' by the fourth or fifth day, if we ever get that far, and that its lack of preparation might also be a factor.

Australia have left out Thomson, after his efforts at Leeds, and have named two spinners, Holland and Bennett, in their squad.

But they are not blessed with England's all-round strength and may not want to omit a batsman to allow both to play.

As for England's last place, that may go to the newly selected Yorkshire seam bowler Arnie Sidebottom at the expense of Allott. At their best, there is perhaps not a lot between them, but the timing is right for the introduction of a new face.

AUSTRALIAN VIEWPOINT
Chappell boost for morale

I an Chappell, Australia's last winning captain in a Lord's Test, has been assisting the Australian cricketers' preparations this week for the key second Test duel with England.

Chappell coached and coaxed Australia's youngest batsmen, Greg Ritchie and David Boon, at the Waldorf Hotel on Wednesday evening after they had arrived from Southampton.

He also talked to the team's youngest players, all-rounder Simon O'Donnell, 22, and fast-bowler Craig McDermott, 20.

The invitation for Chappell to have a long talk with Ritchie, 25, and Boon, 24, came from the Australian's assistant team-manager Geoff Dymock, 38, who wanted Chappell to advise them about their confidence, attitude and general approach to cricket.

With Richie Benaud, 54, the 'old smoothie' hosting for the B.B.C., Chappell, 41, is in England as the front man for Channel 9's (Kerry Packer's) live television coverage of the Ashes series.

Chappell led Australia to an eight-wicket win at Lord's in 1972, when his younger brother Gregg, now 36, scored 131 – a classic innings that he rates as probably the finest of his career – and swing bowler Bob Massie took 16 for 137 off 60·1 overs in his Test debut to dismiss England for 272 and 116, to Australia's 308 and 81 for 2.

Australia need to win or draw this Test to keep alive their chances of retaining the Ashes. It is extremely doubtful whether they are good enough and experienced enough to come back from two down.

STATISTICAL PREVIEW

Australia lead 8–1

In 21 Tests at Lord's since 1896, England have beaten Australia only once but suffered eight defeats, their solitary victory being gained in Verity's Match in 1934. Six of the last seven Lord's Tests against Australia have been drawn, the only decisive result occurring in 1972 (Massie's Match).

England's win at Headingley was only their second in the opening match of an Ashes series in 13 attempts since 1930, their last success being in 1972.

Although Edmonds and Emburey have played a combined total of 51 Tests, they have appeared together for England only once. That occasion was also at Lord's, on Emburey's debut, against New Zealand in 1978. when they claimed a collective analysis of 2 for 59 in 41·1 overs.

If Sidebottom makes his Test debut, he will be the first Yorkshire player to appear for England since Boycott ended his career at Calcutta in January 1982, some 36 matches ago.

England and Australia share honours

England made 273 for eight after being put in by Australia on the first day of the second Cornhill Test at Lord's yesterday and probably both sides were left reflecting that they might well have achieved more.

David Gower's innings of 86, his highest as captain and made when the going was at its most awkward, led his side to 179 for three after initial difficulties against the moving ball.

From that point, however, Gower, Lamb and Botham all fell in quick succession, largely by their own hand, and Australia were spared what might have been a more difficult final session for wearying bowlers using an old ball.

Though the persistent McDermott and Lawson shared seven wickets, Australia also had their problems, notably when Lawson bowled an excessive number of no-balls, while they may take some convincing that they were apportioned their fair share of good fortune.

Miraculously, play started on time, which was a relief to those who had queued from an early hour and no little tribute to the stalwart efforts of the groundsmen, Mike Hunt and his staff.

England omitted Sidebottom, Australia opted for Holland as their solitary spinner, and it came as no surprise when Border preferred to bowl first after winning the toss.

As expected, the ball soon began to move off the seam, but the overall dampness – the square was liberally sprinkled with sawdust – produced problems not only for the batsmen but for the bowlers with their run-ups.

Lawson, especially, experienced trouble which made him tentative, but McDermott, moving the ball down the slope and occasionally making it bounce, was able to confirm his captain's judgement by removing Robinson and Gooch in his first spell.

Robinson had time to play only one good-looking drive before he was lbw and departed looking gloomily at his bat. Gooch, having missed little that was variable in length and line, must have narrowly failed to get the benefit of any doubt that he was outside off stump when struck on the pad.

Between times, the ball continued to thud regularly against the pads, possibly at times doing a shade too much, and in these conditions Gower was probably grateful to locate early on several near half-volleys from O'Donnell which he tucked away comfortably.

With his timing, the ball sped over the outfield more profitably than might have been expected. He also illustrated to O'Donnell that, at his pace on this pitch, the ball did not have to be all that short to be clinically dealt with off the back foot.

Thus was launched an important chapter in Gower's career. Gatting, meanwhile, began with a flourish he quickly realised could not be maintained against the moving ball, and he wisely settled for acclimatisation and accumulation.

By now Lawson had switched ends, only to encounter more problems with his rhythm. Having bowled half-a-dozen no-balls earlier, he now produced 13 in only four overs, to his and his captain's dismay. As often happens, he found that when he did get everything right he was unrewarded. Gatting, when 10, was, for instance, totally beaten by a ball that cut back sharply, narrowly missing both inside edge and perhaps leg stump.

This should have been indication enough of the need for care, but soon afterwards Gatting inexplicably offered no stroke to a ball that was scarcely outside off-stump and did not need to come back much to have him lbw.

What made this mode of dismissal all the more remarkable, not to say disappointing, was the memory of Gatting's two similar experiences on the same ground last year.

Fortunately, Gower was still batting with largely untroubled fluency, which was much needed during an

uncomfortable start by Lamb who found the middle of the bat elusive and, at six, all but edged Lawson to slip.

Eventually Lamb, encouraged by the odd half-volley, settled and worked out what was practical, and all was well until on the stroke of tea Gower was caught at slip driving at McDermott without – it has to be said – much movement of the feet.

Botham then did not bother to play himself in, and from only his eighth ball – in the first over after tea – drove powerfully on the rise and was caught on the cover boundary by Ritchie, who appeared to have been placed there for just such a stroke.

Lamb, having grafted for 36 overs, was caught behind driving at a very wide ball from Lawson, leaving Downton, Emburey and Edmonds to consolidate as best they could, with an unavoidable loss of entertainment to the crowd of 18,500.

AUSTRALIAN VIEWPOINT

Gamble is justified

Australia's hard-working fast bowlers, Craig McDermott and Geoff Lawson, justified Allan Border's gamble in sending England in at Lord's yesterday. Apart from David Gower, who played beautifully on a sluggish pitch, England's batting fell well short of expectations, even allowing for the quality of some of the wicket-taking balls.

Border really had no other option than to bowl first because of doubts

about the state of the under-prepared pitch and the overcast conditions.

The pity of it was that Australia again had only four bowlers and would have to bat last against England's crack spin pair, John Emburey and Phil Edmonds.

Border reasoned that the pitch would be at its best for batting today and tomorrow, so why not bat then?

It was believed Murray Bennett's left-arm orthodox style of bowling would be better suited to the conditions than Bob Holland's leg spinners.

Holland's inclusion was a more

attacking move and, statistically, the logical one, for he had taken 18 wickets in six first-class tour matches compared with Bennett's four in five.

While Holland bowled tidily and was never collared, the pitch played much too slowly for him to gain the necessary bounce or zip off it.

Surprisingly, only four times since the Second World War – in 1948, 1961, 1980, and 1981 – have Australia not had someone bowling leg spinners in a Lord's Test.

Those who did were Doug Ring and Richie Benaud (1953), Benaud (1956), Bob Simpson (1964), John Gleeson (1968 and 1972), Ian Chappell (1975) and Kerry O'Keeffe (1977). Benaud missed the 1961 Test with a shoulder injury.

There was a vast, much-needed improvement in the Australians' fielding and catching yesterday, and wicketkeeper Wayne Phillips, who has his critics, gloved the ball more consistently, despite a cracked left thumb and sore hands.

Overnight
England 273 – 8 (D.I. Gower 86, A.J. Lamb 47; C.J. McDermott 4 – 62)

Border takes advantage of Gatting slip

An incident-packed day in the second Cornhill Test ended in the gloom at Lord's last night with Australia's captain, Allan Border, holding his side together at 183 for four in reply to England's 290 all out.

Border's unbeaten 92, begun in more awkward conditions against demanding English seam bowling, was another timely contribution after Craig McDermott had finished with six for 70 in only his fourth Test.

Yet Border remains only by courtesy of an escape perhaps unprecedented in recent history, when at 87 (ironically the Australian unlucky number) he was 'caught' by Mike Gatting, who then lost control of the ball as he tried to toss it into the air to celebrate.

Thus encouraged, Border and Greg Ritchie had added an unbeaten 72 before the day's fifth and longest stoppage brought a premature end to the day's play.

The umpires, who had also had their share of problems, ruled that, even with the spinners operating, the light was too poor to continue.

On days like these, the umpires have a thankless task. They must try to be fair to both sides, recognise the needs of the paying customer, have to live with themselves and often end up satisfying nobody entirely.

Nor are they allowed to explain their actions, which might spare them the sort of abuse directed at them on one occasion yesterday. It has long been a source of irritation among the first-class umpires that, though they are vested with huge responsibilities, they still cannot be trusted to make a public utterance on the subject of playing conditions.

In this highly communicative era, would not a public address announcement offering an explanation for a stoppage, which may often not be as straightforward as it might seem, do much to ease frustrations all round?

Thus we all might have learned that the first stoppage, at the end of England's innings, was in deference to two tail-enders facing fast bowlers with the new ball. Having accepted the light then, England could hardly complain when it was twice later offered to Australia, although Gower had a lengthy discussion with the umpires on one occasion.

What did remain unclear, and led to much debate, was how much the umpires had paid heed to the TCCB ruling which states that play should be suspended only when there is 'a risk of serious injury to the batsmen'.

So much, I promise you, on that subject. The cricket, when it got going, was never without interest, notably once McDermott had finished England off and enjoyed the privilege of leading his side in on his first Test appearance at Lord's.

Two stoppages then helped to keep the bowlers fresh, and Allott found the new ball would bounce and move awkwardly from the Pavilion end, though his dismissal of Wood in his second over owed rather more to the batsman's penchant for the pick-up, from which he was caught at deep square leg.

Foster, meanwhile, also passed the bat, but, in a week where the catches have not been sticking for him, was denied Hilditch's wicket with 16 scored when Botham for once, could not react quickly enough at second slip.

This mattered little for soon afterwards Foster found a gap between Hilditch's bat and pad with what looked a quicker ball, while Allott continued to pose problems for Wessels and, initially Border.

It was Wessels, though, who lived most dangerously, notably when, with 44 scored, he received the benefit of the doubt for a catch behind down the leg side off Allott just as he seemed ready to walk.

Wessels had still not reached double figures when he had another near thing against Edmonds, before Botham ended his unconvincing stay by having him lbw with a ball which must have marginally avoided pitching outside the left-hander's leg stump.

While Border used his feet well to Edmonds, avoiding the problem of the rough around off stump, Botham struck again with an excellent bouncer from which Boon, unable to take evasive action, was caught by Downton off a glove or thereabouts.

A similar ball almost accounted for Ritchie, the ball this time flying over the wicketkeeper's head, and gradually the two Queenslanders began to restore order until Border's remarkable escape.

Going down the pitch to Edmonds, he played a firm stroke, which Gatting at short leg, clutched into his midriff. Border turned to go, but checked his stride when Gatting, in his exuberance, tried to throw the ball up only to lose it.

Both he and Downton unavailingly tried to retrieve the error, but the ball fell to earth. Under Law 32, it had never been in Gatting's complete control and so Border lived on – after, to coin a phrase, a Catch 32 situation which both batsman and fielder will long remember.

AUSTRALIAN VIEWPOINT

Umpire correct over 'catch decision'

There have been border incidents and more border incidents, but the extraordinary Border incident at Lord's yesterday has joined the list of those that will be talked about for as long as cricket is played.

Poor Mike Gatting! On his home ground, he failed to play a shot at an inswinger which trapped him leg before for only 14 on the first day of the Test; then, yesterday, he threw away the Australian captain's offer of a catch which might ultimately cost England victory and even lead to their defeat.

Gatting did not want to talk publicly last night about the incident, presumably for fear of saying anything that could be misconstrued as criticism of Dickie Bird, the umpire, who seems to have a unique flair for getting into a match.

Bird made the correct decision in not allowing the 'catch' for there was a real doubt whether Gatting actually had 'complete control' of the ball at any stage – as he and wicketkeeper Paul Downton could have unwittingly indicated by lunging so desperately to retrieve it before it fell onto the pitch.

Allan Border started to walk off (fortunately from the Pavilion end, where he was still behind the crease) believing Gatting had held the ball long enough – between his thighs – until he saw it tumble out, via Gatting's frantic hands.

It must have been one of the better sights an Australian captain, or any player for that matter, could see at the home of cricket.

Border said last night 'If he had held it any longer between his legs, I would have been out. But either in jubilation or to get control of the ball, he threw it up and the umpire made the right decision. My initial worry was that I might have been run out.'

Overnight
England 290 (C.J. McDermott 6 – 70)
Australia 183 – 4 (A.R. Border 92 not out, G.M. Ritchie 46 not out)

Border and Botham share the honours

Allan Border's innings of 196, his highest in Test cricket, and Ian Botham's achievement of taking five wickets in an innings for a record-breaking 25th time, combined to give Lord's its most memorable Test match Saturday for some time as the second Cornhill Test maintained its absorbing progress.

Border's 7½ hour stay and his partnership of 216 with his Queensland colleague Greg Ritchie tilted the match Australia's way after their early problems, and their satisfaction was complete when they took the prized wickets of Gooch and Robinson as England ended 98 behind.

The game had not been without incident or controversy on the first two days and this pattern continued, with England ending the day with not one but two nightwatchmen (Emburey and Allott), while earlier the lengthy absence from the England attack – uncommon in recent years – of Ian Botham had also been a talking point.

He had bowled only nine overs, and Australia had eased their way past England's 290 with Border and Ritchie together, when he appeared. He then performed with more pace and hostility than at any time in recent Test series, hustled all the batsmen and contributed to Australia's losing their last four wickets for only 27 runs.

Hindsight is a quality no captain has yet discovered how to use, and it was ironic that Gower, who, like his predecessor Willis, had so often been accused of over-bowling Botham to little purpose, now faced the other extreme, though I suggest the charge is not entirely proven.

Botham had an injured ankle strapped up, and while Gower admitted later that he might have erred on the side of caution, he could not have been certain. In any case, Botham later had the use of a ball only six overs old which probably bounced more than the old one in the morning.

Whatever the pros and cons, it may be that Gower, by keeping his dynamic all-rounder in fetters, has inadvertently discovered the best way, nowadays, of extracting the maximum from him. There was little doubt that Botham ran in with a vigour not seen for some time.

By then Border and Ritchie had got through the morning together, which was probably their first aim, though not without some luck. At 99 Border almost played on to Foster, and if England had possessed the nerve to support their bowlers with slightly more attacking fields, either Allott or Edmonds might have broken through.

As it was, a few near things escaped when Border, unusually for him, erred around off stump, while Ritchie, at 51, survived a concerted appeal for a catch behind which umpire Evans seemed to have got right without the aid of a slow-motion replay.

This and other episodes probably did much to convince England it was not their day, which is often the case when a side is spurning genuine chances by their inefficiency in the field, and Border went on to his thirteenth Test hundred with many strokes of quality.

An excellent judge of length and width, he cut and drove firmly, and with good footwork never allowed the spinners to dominate him. He also found time to encourage his less experienced partner, and before Botham appeared they had fewer problems than earlier against Allott and Foster, who had switched ends to take the new ball.

Ritchie had batted with growing confidence, finding a freedom he had rarely shown at this level, but as soon as Botham appeared he was unsettled by an extremely rapid bouncer, which left him sprawling on his backside.

Perhaps expecting another, he shuffled across his stumps and was palpably lbw to a ball of much fuller length, cruelly only six short of a century on the ground where it matters most. But importantly he had stayed with his captain for more than four hours.

Border now concentrated on weathering this period and hoping to blunt Botham, which perhaps contributed to a few more tentative moments, including inside edges against both Allott and Botham in quick succession, as he made his way past the 150 mark.

Phillips, once lifting Edmonds for six from a ball pitching in the rough around off stump, looked capable of playing a dangerously violent innings, but Botham, now operating mostly at a full length, had him well caught in the gully by Edmonds as he drove.

But Border went on, passing his previous best Test score of 162 (made against India in Madras five years earlier) and having become only the fifth Australian captain to reach three figures at Lord's – after Trott, Woodfull, Bradman and Hassett – before he was caught at slip by Gooch off Botham when poised to become the first to make a double century there.

The bowler was the first to shake his hand and Border departed to a wonderful ovation, in which the entire England team joined. He had lifted his side from 24 for two and, as the crowd rose, there was an agreeably nostalgic touch when Border doffed a traditional baggy green cap, rather than a functional modern helmet, in acknowledgment.

O'Donnell then offered more proof of his potential by firing off several strokes of power and timing, though between them he was dropped in the deep by Allott off Botham, who soon afterwards led England in after his unparalleled feat of taking five wickets in an innings on 25 occasions, eight of them at Lord's, in 75 Tests.

After all that, an uneventful climax was England's main requirement. But Gooch, having played several well-timed strokes off his legs, was perhaps undone by McDermott's extra bounce and caught behind down the legside in the ninth over.

Holland's leg-spin was then produced, possibly mainly in the hope of dislodging Emburey, the first of the nightwatchmen, and Australia had a real bonus when Robinson, his bat slightly tangled with a pad, was bowled by a flighted delivery with 34 scored.

Allott then appeared, although not until after a delay long enough to have Border jocularly discussing Law 31 (timed out), which hinted at much confusion in the England dressing room. He looked as if he had already showered, doubtless innocently believing his part in the day's proceedings was over, but did the job required of him.

AUSTRALIAN VIEWPOINT

Modern players rank with the all-time greats

Cricketers of the 1980's maintain that they can never appear in the pitiless glare of today's media the equal of their predecessors. They are probably correct.

Television shows all of us – from Sydney to London – exactly how so-and-so played and how he got out.

Players' styles, and the good and bad things about their batting, bowling and fielding, are beamed into almost every home, so that even Auntie Mabel has seen enough to argue about whether junior is this or that.

The great players of the past are not so indelibly recorded on colour television tape as are the Bothams, Chappells and Richards.

I love watching cricket's old black-and-white films, for the sheer fascination of it all, and because it proves to me, as a man of 40, that yesterday's heroes were no better than today's despite the eloquent, extravagant and often quaint prose written about them.

Those of us born during and after World War II could be excused for having an inferiority complex about the doyens of the past.

But cricketers of the world need feel inferior to only one man – Sir Donald Bradman, who attained standards of excellence that will probably never be equalled.

Sir Donald will be 77 on August 27. As our most successful sportsman and the greatest living Australian, he will always be a source of immense national pride.

He still has a computer for a brain and, significantly, he has always been a staunch advocate of the present-day players, believing, rightly, that a champion in one era would be a champion in any era.

Incidentally, if it is not telling tales out of school, Sir Donald was asked a year ago in my Adelaide newspaper's boardroom what he thought of the television version of the Bodyline series. He replied: 'Ten per cent. fact, 90 per cent. pantomime.'

The point of all this is that in Allan Border and Ian Botham we have been privileged to see at Lord's over the past three days two giants of cricket – in this or any other era.

Border has a batting average of 50·21 from 68 Tests, and Botham is just 32 wickets away from breaking Dennis Lillee's world record of 355.

Overnight
England 290 and 37 – 2
Australia 425 (A.R. Border 196, G.M. Ritchie 94, S.P. O'Donnell 48;
I.T. Botham 5 – 109)

Botham and Gatting offer gleam of hope

A ustralia were left needing 81 for victory with seven wickets standing in the second Test at Lord's yesterday after a disappointing England batting performance had been followed by another stirring exhibition of new-ball bowling by Ian Botham.

Running in if anything more impressively than in the first innings, despite an injured toe, Botham quickly reduced Australia to nine for two when they embarked on the task of making 127 after dismissing England for 261, with leg-spinner Bob Holland taking five for 68.

Botham removed both openers, Wood and Hilditch, in his first three overs, taking his tally of Test wickets to an England record of 326, and with the hitherto luckless Allott bowling Ritchie, Australia found themselves, with every nerve showing, at 22 for three.

As Botham inevitably tired, Wessels and Border carefully saw this epic day out, but the prospect of another England breakthrough this morning – when spectators will be admitted for £3 – keeps this compelling Test very much alive.

Botham had earlier made England's top score of 85, but neither this nor Gatting's unbeaten 75 could compensate for more failings in the middle order, this time by Gower and Lamb, which left England needing something miraculous from their bowlers. But who, after last night's final session, is to say they cannot do it?

Another near capacity crowd had assembled by lunch, at which time England were still three runs behind and had lost not only their two nightwatchmen but also Gower and Lamb.

Lawson clipped Allott's off stump with the fourth ball of the day, and four overs later Emburey played on to him, so Australia had the encouragement of two new batsmen to bowl at with the scoreboard reading 57 for four.

As if this were not, as foreshadowed, a considerable psychological boost for them, there was another scare for England when Gatting unaccountably and apparently belatedly offered no stroke to his first ball.

It cut back and hit the pads, though it would clearly have missed leg stump. Even so, it was a heart-stopping moment after which Gatting thankfully settled down to supply some of the application and occupation of the crease his side badly needed.

Gower, meanwhile, began in a manner so carefree that the uninformed spectator might have imagined England were some 200 ahead instead of battling, in the first instance, to try to save the match.

He timed several glorious strokes and once took three successive fours off Lawson. It was fine while it lasted; the question was how long could it last.

In fact, Gower had needed only 21 balls to make 22 with five boundaries when he was caught behind in a manner not dissimilar to his first innings dismissal.

He gets weary, I know, of reading

that he has not moved his feet, but equally there seems no need for a player of his talent to keep repeating the error, especially in these circumstances.

Lamb also failed to establish himself, perhaps misjudging the length of a slower ball from Lawson which he lofted comfortably to cover. And so Botham and Gatting found themselves cast as the last recognised batsmen, thanks to the change in the batting order, with much still to be done.

In the next 35 overs they did some of it, with Gatting sensibly and unselfishly adopting a secondary role, while Botham, after a circumspect start in deference to the situation, began to play his strokes.

They also did not neglect the push for one, which is not always the case when England's middle order is operating, and cleared the arrears soon after lunch, whereupon Botham hooked McDermott for a six which carried a long way into the Mound Stand.

By now, Holland had embarked on his influential spell of 30 successive overs. Though he found the ball would turn only when bowled very slowly, he exerted the restraint his side was seeking by going round the wicket to exploit the rough and, for one of his type, was extremely accurate.

This enabled Border to use his quicker bowlers from the Pavilion end, where they could exploit occasional variations in bounce, and such was the context of a gripping afternoon as Botham and Gatting completed a partnership of 131 priceless runs.

Without attempting anything too exotic, Botham still made 50 out of 73 in 61 balls. He played Holland mainly from the crease until he went down the pitch to attack a leg-break and lifted a comfortable catch to cover.

His disgust was self-evident, and thoroughly justified considering England's parlous position. This was emphasised when Downton was caught at slip off the next ball which, turning out of the rough, was a handy delivery to a new batsman.

Holland mopped up the tail, as leg-spinners are wont to do. Gatting made 25 of the last 26 from the bat despite having negligible support, and, after everything that has happened to him in this match, might have guessed he would be the one left high and dry.

AUSTRALIAN VIEWPOINT

Headingley scars are ready to be healed

Australia's scars from Headingley, 1981, finally will be healed at Lord's today – if Ian Botham stops walking on water.

What a cricketer! Is he really the same fellow who struggled through a Victorian District season with the university club in Melbourne in 1976-77?

Or the same one who scored 25 and took five Australian wickets in the Trent Bridge Test of 1977, and was promptly dismissed by some critics as just another player?

There are days when the incomparable Botham appears bigger than the game itself, and yesterday was another of those momentous days.

Inevitably, he will be criticised for getting out to such a hefty swipe when he had his 14th Test century at his mercy.

But is it fair to query the manner of dismissal of a player who has just blazed 85 off 117 balls to force his game back into contention?

Botham is Botham, and England should be grateful he is. His friendship with the Australians – he has entertained them at his Somerset and Yorkshire homes, and partnered Allan Border in a round of golf at Wentworth on Sunday, when a ball damaged his left instep – led to a former Australia captain saying during his innings yesterday: 'I wish they'd stop talking to him out there.'

Andrew Hilditch even applauded one of Botham's scorching cover drives. Isn't this supposed to be war? Whatever happened to 'sledging'? Perhaps cricket is reverting to its old gentlemanly ways after all.

Bob 'Dutchy' Holland, 38, the father of three sons, paid for his long-awaited trip to England by taking his five wickets yesterday. As he said last night: 'Leg-spinners are not obsolete.'

Holland played for Northern New South Wales against Mike Smith's MCC team in his home town of Newcastle in 1965-66.

Nearly 20 years later he is poised to be a member of the 10th Australian team to win a Lord's Test, and one that needs just 81 runs to achieve only Australia's sixth victory in 41 overseas Tests since early in 1977.

Overnight
England 290 and
261 (I.T. Botham 85, M.W. Gatting 75 not out; R.G. Holland 5 – 68)
Australia 425 and 46 – 3

Border the key as Australia level series

Though they were made to fight every inch of the way, Australia won the second Cornhill Test by four wickets before lunch at Lord's yesterday to level the six-match series at one-all.

Some Test it was . . . some series, too, it looks like being, and whatever happens next David Gower will be the man leading England. He was reappointed yesterday before the outcome of the game was known.

That was always likely once he had made runs and although England eventually lost a game of many twists and turns, the selectors clearly feel that one hiccough does not mar a summer.

As I suggested before this game, Gower, through no fault of his own, is still in the apprentice stage as a leader. But the selectors have never publicly voiced any doubts about him on that particular score.

Even if he had failed abysmally with the bat here, which he did not, it would have been harsh to remove the captaincy from him immediately after winning the first Test, and with the memory still fresh of England's success in India last winter.

He has not got everything right – as he would probably admit – but the hope must now be that, without the pressure of having to look over his shoulder, he can build upon what he has learnt and thus give the England side the continuity it needs at the top.

Nor, I would think, is it likely that any changes are contemplated for next week's third Test at Trent Bridge. Just as it often makes sense to change a winning team, as England did after the first test, it does not always follow that a losing team should be disturbed.

Oddly enough, it was England's batting which contributed much to their downfall here, on a better pitch than the one on which they laid the foundations of victory at Leeds, and there would be several moments on the last day or so when they would regret the absence of just one more lengthy innings.

This has much to do, as I have emphasised before, with the make-up of the English middle order, who are all stroke players, so the selectors have to accept that when they are good they are very very good, but this usually requires some form of ballast at the other end.

Robinson provided this at Leeds but he could not do so here, and the role of anchor-man belatedly fell to Gatting, who did the job well for four hours in the second innings before, because of the decision to use two nightwatchmen, he ran out of support.

Otherwise, the batting tends to have a wishy-washy appearance, which is out of keeping with the requirements of Test cricket. Even Gower and Botham, who each played one admirable innings, sacrificed their wickets, and it is no coincidence that the first two Tests have each been won by a side possessing a batsman with the ability to spend a long time in the middle.

After Robinson at Headingley, it was

Border at Lord's. His first innings 196 earned him the Man of the Match award from Ted Dexter, and his was the wicket England so badly needed yesterday but failed to obtain.

Otherwise, with Australia and perhaps even Border himself still jittery, anything could have happened, especially when England took wickets in the seventh and ninth overs of a blissfully warm morning.

Wisely, Gower used Edmonds to try to exploit the footmarks at the Pavilion end, while Botham, though he passed the bat, could not generate the sense of expectation of the previous evening

Even so, the ground was heavy with tension, which was heightened by the reading-room silence of the crowd, who erupted when, as Wessels played the ball firmly down, Gower grasped the ball left-handed and flicked it back into the stumps before Wessels, perhaps thinking of a single, could regain his ground.

Edmonds then produced a beauty for Boon, the ball turning a long way out of the rough to hit the off stump, and he went on to bowl superbly for the rest of the innings.

Ball after ball landed on the spot, giving England the control they needed if they were to pull off something remarkable, and if Phillips had not narrowly avoided midwicket with his first aggressive stroke, against Botham, Australia would have been 70 for six.

That was possibly a little watershed for both sides. When Emburey replaced Botham, he was cut for fours by both batsmen before he found his rhythm, strokes which eased the pressure and brought the psychologically vital sight of three figures on the scoreboard.

Border then nudged Edmonds agonisingly close to Gatting at short leg and the pair had put on 51 in 11 overs when Phillips, cutting at Emburey, was well caught by Edmonds by his ankles at backward point.

Gower then made a valiant effort to catch an improbable bat and pad chance offered by O'Donnell off Emburey, and hereabouts Australia's nerves were not helped, according to Border afterwards, by a long public address announcement requesting the crowd not to invade the playing area at the end. (They didn't.)

By now Border had become the seventh Australian batsman to pass 5,000 runs in Tests, and after O'Donnell had driven Edmonds for a straight six, Australia's 10th triumph in 28 Tests at Lord's was duly completed, conveniently just before closing time for those following the game on television and radio Down Under.

AUSTRALIAN VIEWPOINT

For once, Australians have reason to chant

Rod Marsh, the former Australian wicketkeeper, would have been proud of Allan Border yesterday, although some MCC members were not amused by the Australians' immediate vocal reaction to their four-wicket triumph over England in the second Test at Lord's.

In Marsh's time, when Australia won a Test match, he would lead the victory chant in the team's dressing room.

When Marsh retired at the end of the 1983-84 Australian season, he entrusted the responsibility to Border, who deservedly was in fine voice yesterday after his second win in five Tests, as the Australian captain, as well as his £500 Man-of-the-Match cheque from Cornhill.

Border and his jubilant team-mates duly chanted their victory anthem . . .

'Under the Southern Cross I stand, a sprig of wattle in my hand.

'A native of my native land Australia . . . you effing beauty!'

It was the 'effing' bit roaring across the hallowed turf of the home of cricket that startled (and, yes, probably disgusted) some MCC members and provoked guffaws from spectators walking across the ground towards the members' pavilion for the presentation.

Later, a few of the Australians gathered on the pavilion balcony and sprayed some of the crowd below them with their sponsor's cans of beer.

It was all good-natured stuff, and few took exception to the chanting, because Australian cricketers have not had much to crow about for a long time, and, anyway, their behaviour and general conduct have been exemplary over the first half of this 18-week tour of England.

The Australians' victory celebrations will assume a more domestic flavour this week, as several of them have their wives and children here. Border's wife, Jane, and their baby son, Dene, arrived from Brisbane yesterday.

The cricket? Border described it as 'fantastic' at his after-match Press conference.

'It has set the series alight,' he said. 'You couldn't have asked for more. I still think it will be a keen, closely fought series. These first two Tests have shown how evenly matched the teams are.'

Result: Australia won by 4 wickets
England 290 and 261
Australia 425 and 127 – 6 (A.R. Border 41 not out)

ENGLAND 1ST INNINGS v. AUSTRALIA (2ND TEST) at LORD'S, LONDON on 27, 28, 29 JUNE, 1, 2 JULY, 1985.   TOSS: AUSTRALIA

IN	OUT	MINS	No.	BATSMAN	HOW OUT	BOWLER	RUNS	WKT	TOTAL	6ˢ	4ˢ	BALLS	NOTES ON DISMISSAL
11-00	12-11	71	1	G.A. GOOCH	LBW	McDERMOTT	30	2	51	·	2	46	Breakback beat off-drive.
11-00	11-37	37	2	R.T. ROBINSON	LBW	McDERMOTT	6	1	26	·	·	23	Breakback beat defensive push.
11-39	3-36	197	3	D.I. GOWER *	C' BORDER	McDERMOTT	86	4	179	·	12	146	Edged drive to second slip.
12-13	1-50	57	4	M.W. GATTING	LBW	LAWSON	14	3	99	·	2	32	Padded up to breakback (cf 1984 v West Indies at Lord's - twice).
1-52	4-49	156	5	A.J. LAMB	C' PHILLIPS	LAWSON	47	6	211	·	4	119	Driving on the up - two-handed catch towards slip.
3-38	4-04	5	6	I.T. BOTHAM	C' RITCHIE	LAWSON	5	5	184	·	1	8	Skied drive to deep backward point.
4-06	5-35	89	7	P.R. DOWNTON †	C' WESSELS	McDERMOTT	21	7	241	·	1	71	Gentle skier to short cover - leading edge - short ball (leg side).
4-51	6-25	94	8	J.E. EMBUREY	LBW	O'DONNELL	33	8	273	·	4	74	Pushed outside breakback.
5-37	12-06	93	9	P.H. EDMONDS	C' BORDER	McDERMOTT	21	10	290	·	2	78	Edged push to second slip.
6-27	11-40	31	10	N.A. FOSTER	C' WESSELS	McDERMOTT	3	9	283	·	·	16	Edged drive to deep gully.
11-42	(12-06)	10	11	P.J.W. ALLOTT	NOT OUT		1			·	·	6	
				EXTRAS	b1 lb4 w1 nb17		23			0	28		619 balls (including 23 no balls).
				TOTAL	(99·2 OVERS; 429 MINUTES)		290						all out at 12-06 pm on 2nd day.

* CAPTAIN   † WICKET-KEEPER
UMPIRES: H.D. BIRD & D.G.L. EVANS

© BILL FRINDALL 1985

BOWLER	O	M	R	W	NB
LAWSON	25	2	91	3	7
McDERMOTT	29·2	5	70	6	7½
O'DONNELL	22	3	82	1	1½
HOLLAND	23	6	42	0	-
				5	
	99·2	16	290	10	

2ND NEW BALL taken at 11-10 am 2nd day.
- ENGLAND 273-8 after 90 overs.

HRS	OVERS	RUNS
1	13	43
2	13	45
3	10	42
4	16	50
5	14	35
6	16	48
7	15	20

RUNS	MINS	OVERS	LAST 50 (in mins)
50	68	15·0	68
100	135	28·1	67
150	207	43·5	72
200	274	59·3	67
250	351	79·3	77

LUNCH: 88-2
TEA: 180-4
STUMPS (1ST DAY): 273-8

26 OVERS [121 MIN.]	GOWER 38* (82)	GATTING 10* (48)
52 OVERS [240 MIN]	LAMB 28* (108)	BOTHAM 1* (2)
90 OVERS [387 MIN]	EDMONDS 9* (51)	FOSTER 0* (1)

13 OVERS 5 BALLS/HOUR
2.92 RUNS/OVER
47 RUNS/100 BALLS

WKT	PARTNERSHIP		RUNS	MINS
1st	Gooch	Robinson	26	37
2nd	Gooch	Gower	25	32
3rd	Gower	Gatting	48	57
4th	Gower	Lamb	80	104
5th	Gower	Botham	5	5
6th	Lamb	Downton	27	43
7th	Downton	Emburey	30	44
8th	Emburey	Edmonds	32	48
9th	Edmonds	Foster	10	31
10th	Edmonds	Allott	7	10
			290	

SECOND TEST
AUSTRALIA 1ST INNGS

AUSTRALIA 1ST INNINGS (IN REPLY TO ENGLAND'S 290 ALL OUT)

IN	OUT	MINS	No.	BATSMAN	HOW OUT	BOWLER	RUNS	WKT	TOTAL	6s	4s	BALLS	NOTES ON DISMISSAL
12·18	12·34	16	1	G.M.WOOD	C'EMBUREY	ALLOTT	8	1	11	·	1	17	Hooked directly to deep fine leg.
12·18	2·08	41	2	A.M.J.HILDITCH	BOWLED	FOSTER	14	2	24	·	2	25	Off stump out – bowled between bat and pad (driving).
12·36	3·18	93	3	K.C.WESSELS	LBW	BOTHAM	11	3	80	·	1	41	Delayed decision. Leg-stump delivery.
2·10	4·27	450	4	A.R.BORDER*	C'GOOCH	BOTHAM	196	7	398	·	22	318	Edged drive to second slip. (13 x H5 in Tests.) [THIRD-HIGHEST SCORE FOR AUSTRALIA AT LEEDS]
3·20	3·41	21	5	D.C.BOON	C'DOWNTON	BOTHAM	4	4	101	·	1	20	Failed to avoid bouncer (glove) – penultimate ball before tea.
4·05	2·37	269	6	G.M.RITCHIE	LBW	BOTHAM	94	5	317	1	10	212	Played across breakback.
2·39	3·13	34	7	W.B.PHILLIPS†	C'EDMONDS	BOTHAM	21	6	347	1	3	22	Sliced drive to gully.
3·15	4·41	66	8	S.P.O'DONNELL	C'LAMB	EDMONDS	48	8	414	1	6	69	Edged drive at leg-break to backward-point (driving).
4·29	(4·58)	29	9	G.F.LAWSON	NOT OUT		5			·	·	16	
4·43	4·55	12	10	C.J.McDERMOTT	RUN OUT [BORDER/O'DONNELL]		9	9	425	·	·	11	Responded slowly to Lawson's call for single to mid-wicket.
4·57	4·58	1	11	R.G.HOLLAND	BOWLED	EDMONDS	0	10	425	·	·	1	Attempted to pull a six off his first ball.

EXTRAS: b – lb 10 w 1 nb 4 = 15 — 752 balls (including 4 no-balls).

TOTAL 425 all out at 4·58 pm on 3rd day. (124·4 overs; 524 minutes) (LEAD: 135)

14 OVERS 1 BALLS/HOUR
3·41 RUNS/OVER
57 RUNS/100 BALLS

*CAPTAIN †WICKET-KEEPER

WKT	PARTNERSHIP		RUNS	MINS
1st	Wood	Hilditch	11	16
2nd	Hilditch	Wessels	13	23
3rd	Wessels	Border	56	68
4th	Border	Boon	21	21
5th	Border	Ritchie	216	269
6th	Border	Phillips	30	34
7th	Border	O'Donnell	51	52
8th	O'Donnell	Lawson	16	12
9th	Lawson	McDermott	11	12
10th	Lawson	Holland	0	1
			425	

LUNCH: 16-1 [5·4 OVERS, 28 MINUTES] — HILDITCH 7* (21'), WESSELS 0* (10')
TEA: 101-4 [29·5 OVERS, 134 MINUTES] — BORDER 58* (91')
STUMPS: 183-4 (2ND DAY) [52 OVERS, 228 MINUTES] [26 OVERS LOST] — BORDER 92* (185), RITCHIE 46* (94)
LUNCH: 261-4 [82·2 OVERS, 343 MIN.] — BORDER 144* (300), RITCHIE 69* (205)
TEA: 371-6 [110 OVERS, 466 MIN.] — BORDER 184* (413), O'DONNELL 20* (25)

BOTHAM'S 25TH INSTANCE OF FIVE OR MORE WICKETS IN A TEST INNINGS (WORLD RECORD).

Bowling

BOWLER	O	M	R	W
FOSTER	23	1	83	1
ALLOTT	30	4	70	1
BOTHAM	24	2	109	5
EDMONDS	25·4	5	85	2
GOOCH	3	1	11	0
EMBUREY	19	3	57	0
			10	1
	124·4	16	425	10

HRS	W	OVERS	RUNS
1	1/-	12	36
2	-	14	52
3	1/4	14	56
4	-	14	44
5	-	15	40
6	-	17	55
7	1	13	41
8	-	15	57

RUNS	MINS	OVERS	LAST 50 (in mins)
50	81	17·2	81
100	130	28·3	49
150	184	41·0	54
200	258	58·4	74
250	332	79·4	74
300	377	89·5	45
350	446	104·4	69
400	498	118·4	52

2ND NEW BALL taken at 1·51 pm 3rd day.
– AUSTRALIA 281-4 after 85·3 overs.

© BILL FRINDALL 1985

ENGLAND 2ND INNINGS

(135 RUNS BEHIND ON FIRST INNINGS)

IN	OUT	MINS	No.	BATSMAN	HOW OUT	BOWLER	RUNS	WKT	TOTAL	6s	4s	BALLS	NOTES ON DISMISSAL
5.11	5.49	38	1	G.A.GOOCH	c' PHILLIPS	McDERMOTT	17	1	32	-	1	29	Legside catch - missed leg glance.
5.11	5.55	44	2	R.T.ROBINSON	BOWLED	HOLLAND	12	2	34	-	.	29	Misjudged flight - played round straight ball.
5.51	11.22	41	3	J.E.EMBUREY	BOWLED	LAWSON	20	4	57	-	2	31	Played on - under edged chop at short ball.
5.57	11.03	16	4	P.J.W.ALLOTT	BOWLED	LAWSON	0	3	38	-	.	7	off stump out - late on ball angled in to him.
11.05	11.37	32	5	D.I.GOWER*	c' PHILLIPS	McDERMOTT	22	5	77	-	5	21	Edged firm-footed drive at ball angled across him.
11.24	(4.27)	246	6	M.W.GATTING	NOT OUT		75			-	6	181	
11.39	12.20	41	7	A.J.LAMB	c' HOLLAND	LAWSON	9	6	98	-	1	32	Deceived by slower ball - spooned catch to mid-off.
12.22	3.15	135	8	I.T.BOTHAM	c' BORDER	HOLLAND	85	7	229	1	12	116	Skied drive to cover.
3.17	3.18	1	9	P.R.DOWNTON†	c' BOON	HOLLAND	0	8	229	-	.	.	Edged leg-break low to slip - first ball (walked).
3.20	4.24	45	10	P.H.EDMONDS	c' BOON	HOLLAND	1	9	261	-	.	34	Edged cut to slip.
4.26	4.27	1	11	N.A.FOSTER	c' BORDER	HOLLAND	0	10	261	-	.	3	Pushed forward to silly point.

EXTRAS b 1 lb 12 w 4 nb 3 — 20

TOTAL (80 OVERS; 329 MINUTES) 261 all out at 4.27 pm on 4th day

6s 1 4s 27 484 balls (including 4 no-balls)

* CAPTAIN † WICKET-KEEPER

14 OVERS 3 BALLS/HOUR
3.26 RUNS/OVER
54 RUNS/100 BALLS

BOWLER	O	M	R	W
McDERMOTT	20	2	84	2
LAWSON	23	0	86	3
HOLLAND	32	12	68	5
O'DONNELL	5	0	10	0
	80	14	261	10

HRS	OVERS	RUNS
1	13	37
2	13	56
3	16	39
4	15	76
5	15	35

RUNS	MINS	OVERS	LAST 50 (in mins)
50	79	17.1	79
100	149	33.1	70
150	197	46.3	48
200	229	54.2	32
250	310	75.0	81

STUMPS: 37-2 (3rd day)	13 OVERS 59 MINUTES	EMBUREY 4* (5'), ALLOTT 0* (2')
LUNCH: 132-6	42 OVERS 181 MINUTES	GATTING 20* (98'), BOTHAM 23* (46')
TEA: 244-8	73 OVERS 305 MINUTES	GATTING 64* (22b), EDMONDS 0* (22')

WKT	PARTNERSHIP		RUNS	MINS
1st	Gooch	Robinson	32	38
2nd	Robinson	Emburey	2	4
3rd	Emburey	Allott	4	16
4th	Emburey	Gower	19	15
5th	Gower	Gatting	20	13
6th	Gatting	Lamb	21	41
7th	Gatting	Botham	131	135
8th	Gatting	Downton	0	1
9th	Gatting	Edmonds	32	45
10th	Gatting	Foster	0	1
			261	

© BILL FRINDALL 1985

AUSTRALIA 2ND INNINGS — REQUIRING 127 TO WIN IN A MINIMUM OF 441 MINUTES.

IN	OUT	MINS	No.	BATSMAN	HOW OUT	BOWLER	RUNS	WKT	TOTAL	6s	4s	BALLS	NOTES ON DISMISSAL
4.39	4.41	2	1	A.M.J.HILDITCH	c LAMB	BOTHAM	0	1	0	-	.	4	Hooked short ball to deep backward square-leg.
4.39	5.01	22	2	G.M.WOOD	c LAMB	BOTHAM	6	2	9	-	.	17	Fended short ball to gully via bat shoulder.
4.43	11.21	109	3	K.C.WESSELS	RUN OUT (GOWER)		28	4	63	.	3	86	Underarm throw from silly point.
5.03	5.27	24	4	G.M.RITCHIE	BOWLED	ALLOTT	2	3	22	.	.	16	Off stump out - drove across line off back-foot.
5.29	(12:32)	134	5	A.R.BORDER*	NOT OUT		41		89	.	6	89	Completed 5000 runs in Tests
11.23	11.31	8	6	D.C.BOON	BOWLED	EDMONDS	1	5	65	-	.	8	off stump - beaten by quicker leg-break.
11.33	12.13	40	7	W.B.PHILLIPS†	c EDMONDS	EMBUREY	29	6	116	-	4	32	Walk-away cut - point awed to right - superb low catch.
12.15	(12:32)	17	8	S.P.O'DONNELL	NOT OUT		9			.	1	24	Made winning hit off Edmonds.
			9	G.F.LAWSON									
			10	C.J.McDERMOTT									
			11	R.G.HOLLAND									

EXTRAS b - lb 11 w - nb - = 11

TOTAL (46 OVERS; 184 MINUTES) **127-6**

1⁶ 13⁴   276 balls (0 no-balls)

15 OVERS 0 BALLS/HOUR
2.76 RUNS/OVER
46 RUNS/100 BALLS

* CAPTAIN † WICKET-KEEPER

© BILL FRINDALL 1985

BOWLER	O	M	R	W	nb/w	HRS	OVERS	RUNS	RUNS	MINS	OVERS	LAST 50 (in mins)
BOTHAM	15	0	49	2	-	1	12	28	50	93	21.2	93
ALLOTT	7	4	8	1	-	2	17	37	100	156	37.5	63
EDMONDS	16	5	35	1	-	3	15	54				
EMBUREY	8	4	24	1	-							
		11		-								
	46	13	127	6								

WKT	PARTNERSHIP		RUNS	MINS
1st	Hilditch	Wood	0	2
2nd	Wood	Wessels	9	18
3rd	Wessels	Ritchie	13	24
4th	Wessels	Border	41	63
5th	Border	Boon	2	8
6th	Border	Phillips	51	40
7th	Border	O'Donnell	11*	17
			127	

STUMPS: 46-3 (4TH DAY) (81 REQUIRED)
21 OVERS [92 MINUTES]
WESSELS 25*(86') BORDER 12*(42')

AUSTRALIA WON BY 4 WICKETS at 12.32pm on fifth day

MATCH AWARD: A.R.BORDER (Adjudicator: E.R.Dexter)

SECOND TEST
SHEET 1

1ST DAY TIME	BOWLERS (D.G.L. EVANS) PAVILION END BOWLER	O.	(H.D. BIRD) NURSERY END BOWLER	O.	BATSMEN SCOREBOARD LEFT SCORING	BALLS	6s/4s	SCOREBOARD RIGHT SCORING	BALLS	6s/4s	ENGLAND 1ST INNINGS NOTES	O.	RUNS	W.	'L' BAT	'R' BAT	EXTRAS
					GOOCH			ROBINSON			overcast, humid. sawdust used.						
11·00			LAWSON	1	6 7 7 9/8 · 1 4 1	4	1	7Y 1 :	2			1	7		6	1	
05	MᶜDERMOTT	1			7&5 1	5		8 6 9 7 · · · · ·	7			2	8		7		
10	— · —		— · —	2	6 8P5 8/7 · 1 2 ·	10		7 1	8		WELLHAM sub (WOOD) (1 over)	3	12		10	2	
15	— · —	2			L 6F·7 · ·4·3	15	2	9 1	9			4	20		17	3	
20			— · —	3	L · · 2 6	21					M1	5					
24½	— · —	3						LP 8 3 L · · · ·	15		M2	6					
28½			— · —	4	8P 7 7S · 2 · 1	25		: 4 · 3	17			7	26		20	6	
33	— · —	4						· · · 7 8 L W	23	–	M3	8	26	1	20	6	–
37								GOWER		LHB						0	
39			O'DONNELL	1	7 1	26		· · 4 3 3 · 2 · 4	5	1		9	33		21	6	
43	— · —	5			7 1	27		6 L 3 3 1	10			10	34		22		
48			— · —	2	2/1 P 74 ·	31		· 7S 1	12			11	36		23	7	
52	— · —	6						7 4 · 6 · · ·	18	2		12	40			11	
56½			— · —	3	X · 4/3	34		XP6 · 2	21		1HR	13	43		24	13	
12·00	— · —	7			6 · 8 · · 9 · 1	40						14	44		25		
05			— · —	4	· 3 6 · 2 3	43		· · 8 · 2	24			15	51		30	15	
09	— · —	8	⎰		4 8 L · · W	46	2					15³	51	2	30	15	–
11			⎱		GATTING										0		
13	— · —	8	⎰		P 7 · 4 ·	3	1					16	55		4		
15½			— · —	5				2 8 · 2 · · · ·	30			17	57			17	
19	— · —	9			6 · · · · ·	9					M4	18					
23			— · —	6				7 7 4 4 · · · ·	36	4		19	65			25	
27½	LAWSON	5			8 X 8 2 · Ⓞ 1 ·	14		7 · · Ⓞ	39		NB NB 2 ✝ all run.	20	70		7	26	1
34			— · —	7	:	15		4 ✝7 · · · 4 1	44	5		21	75			31	
37	— · —	6			9Ⓞ · Ⓞ	17		3 P · L8 · ·	49		LB NB 3 ✝ Round wkt to LHB.	22	78		8	32	2
43			— · —	8	:	18		✝4 5(6) L 8 · 2 · 1	54			23	81			35	
47½	— · —	7						· 8 4 9 · · · Ⓞ 2 ·	61		NB NB 4	24	84			37	3
52			— · —	9	2/3 · 1	20		X 5 P ·	65			25	85		9		
54	— · —	8			8 1 · · P	24	1	4 ✝9 · Ⓞ1	68	5	NB NB 5 2HR	26	88	2	10	38	4
1·01	LUNCH										M4 NB5				LUNCH		
1·41			O'DONNELL	10				3 · · · · 7 · 4 ·	74	6		27	92			42	
45	LAWSON	9	⎰		2 X 2/3 L Ⓞ · · · 4 Ⓞ Ⓞ W 32	2					NB NB NB NB8	27³	99	3	14	42	7
50			⎱		LAMB							28			0		
52	— · —	9	⎰		✝ 1							28					
53			— · —	11	8 2 4 · · 6			4 3	75			29	102			45	
59	— · —	10			P 8 3E Ⓞ · 1	9		8 4 4 2✝ (2) · 1 ·	80		7 VESSELS misfielded. NB NB 10	30	107		1	48	8
2·05			MᶜDERMOTT	10	8 L 3 · ·	15						31	109		3		
10	— · —	11			4 · 8 · · 7 2 Ⓞ · Ⓞ · 1	21		4 · 1 3 LB	84		NB NB NB14 LB	32	116		6	49	11
18			— · —	11	· 4E · · · 7	26	–	4/3	85	6	GOWER's 50: 119 min M4 NB 14	33	119	3	6	52	11

71

1ST DAY TIME	BOWLERS (EVANS) PAVILION END BOWLER	O.	(BIRD) NURSERY END BOWLER	O.	SCOREBOARD LEFT SCORING	BALLS	6s/4s	SCOREBOARD RIGHT SCORING	BALLS	6s/4s	ENGLAND 1ST INNINGS NOTES	END-OF-OVER TOTALS O.	RUNS	W.	L BAT	R BAT	EXTRAS
					LAMB	26	–	GOWER	85	6	M4 NB 14	33	119	3	6	52	11
2.23½	LAWSON	12			0 · · 11 0 · 1	31		· · 0 22 0 ·	90		NB NB NB NB12	34	124		7	53	14
31½			McDERMOTT	12	· · 4 3 · 3/4 2	37						35	126		9		
36	O'DONNELL	12						7 4 · · · ·	96	7	3HR	36	130			57	
40			– · –	13	4 6 · 9 · 01	41		· · ·	99		NB NB 19	37	132		10		15
45	– · –	13			4 · 6 · P · 4 · · ·	47	1					38	136		14		
48½			HOLLAND	1				· · 7 7+P 6 · · 2 ·	105		Misfield (Hilditch & O'Donnell).	39	138			59	
52	– · –	14		·	· · · L P	53					M5	40					
55½			– · –	2				x 5/4 P · 4 7 · · 4	111	8		41	142			63	
58½	– · –	15			· · · x 7 P 2 ·	59						42	144		16		
3.02			– · –	3				· · · 6 · 4 3P	117		M6	43					
05	– · –	16			· 6 L 7½ P 4 4	65	3				50 p'ship · 75 min.	44	152		24		
09			– · –	4		· · · P ·	69		· 3 ·	119			45	155	/		66	
12	– · –	17						2 3/4 3 · 4 · 4 ·	125	10		46	163			74	
17			– · –	5	L · 7 P 7 2 ·	75						47	165		26		
19	McDERMOTT	14						· · · 4 3 3 2	131			48	166			75	
24			– · –	6				· · 2/3 9 4 · · 2	137	11		49	172			81	
27	– · –	15			· · 8/9 ·	78		3 · ·	140			50	173		27		
30½	·		– · –	7	· 6 9 · 1	81		7 · · 8 · 1	143		† Round wkt.	51	175		28	82	
34	– · · ·	16 }						4 3 6 1 · 4 W	146	12		51³	179	4	28	86	15
36				{				BOTHAM								0	
38	– · –	16 }				81	3	L 9 8 · · 1	3	–	4HR	52	180	4	28	1	15
3.40	TEA										M6 NB 19		T	E	A		
4.01			LAWSON	13				· · 4 · W	8	1		52⁵	184	5	28	5	15
04				{				DOWNTON								0	
06				13				· · 1	1			53					
07	McDERMOTT	17			P · 1E · L · 2 · ·	87						54	186		30		
12			– · –	14	· · 0 6²/³ 1	92		9 · · ↑ · 3	3		NB NB 20	55	189		31	1	16
17	– · · –	18			· 6† x · 8 · · 1	97		3/9	4		† Drinks stop (Ritchie) McDermott leg cramp.	56	191		32	2	
21			– · –	15				· · · · ↑ 1	10		M7	57					
26	– · –	19			· 3 7	99		4 1ss ↑ · 14	14			58	194		35		
30½			HOLLAND	8	2 3 · · 6 · 1	105						59	196		37		
33	– · –	20			6 4 · 3	107		2 1 ↑ · · 18	18			60	200		40	3	
37			– · –	9	· 6 · 7/6 7 · 2 ·	113					WELLHAM sub (McDermott)	61	202		42		
40	LAWSON	16			· 9 5/6 · 4 1	117	4	B · · 3 2 3 · · 20	20		B	62	211		47	6	17
45			– · –	10				· · 3 · · · 26	26		M8	63					
48	– · –	17 }			· E1 W	119	4					63²	211	6	47	6	17
49				{	EMBUREY										0		
51	– · –	17 }			· 3 2 · ·	4					McDermott back.	64	213		2		
53			– · –	11		4	–	· · · L 8 · 1 · 32	32	–	M8 NB 20	65	214	6	2	7	17

1ST DAY TIME	BOWLER (EVANS) PAVILION END	O.	BOWLER (BIRD) NURSERY END	O.	SCOREBOARD LEFT SCORING	BALLS	6s/4s	SCOREBOARD RIGHT SCORING	BALLS	6s/4s	NOTES	O.	RUNS	W.	L BAT	R BAT	EXTRAS
					EMBUREY	4	-	DOWNTON	32	-	M 8 NB 20	65	214	6	2	7	17
4·57	LAWSON	18			. : . 7	7		x . 4 4	35		5HR	66	215			8	
5·01½			HOLLAND	12	8 1	8		. : . 2 P	40			67	217		3	9	
04	- · -	19			6 ↑4 . ○3	12		↑4 3 . :	43		(NB) NB 21	68	221		6		18
09			- · -	13	. : . L . :	18					M 9	69					
12	- · -	20						8/ 7 6 7 4 ↑ 2 2 . 2 . 0 . 1	50		(NB) NB 22	70	227			14	19
17			- · -	14				. : 7 2 . :	56			71	229			16	
20	McDERMOTT	21		·	2 1	19		7/8 6 . 3 6	61			72	230		7		
24½			- · -	15	. : . : . 3 . 4	25	1					73	234		11		
27	- · -	22						P . 8 7/8 x 7 ↑ . 4 . :	67	1	X Appeal c wk (legside)	74	238			20	
31½			- · -	16	. 8 8 : 1 :	29		. 8/ . :	69			75	240		12	21	
34	- · -	23	⌐					○ W	71	1	(NB) NB 23	75¹	241	7	12	21	20
35		|⌐|					EDMONDS								0	
37	- · -	23	⌐		9G 1	30		9 2 . 1 .	4			76	243		13	1	
40½			- · -	17	1G 1	31		. : . + . :	9			77	244		14		
43	- · -	24			1 P P 6 4 . 2 . .	37						78	246		16		
48			- · -	18				P . : . : . :	15		M 10	79					
50	- · -	25			Y P 3/2 . x 7/8 . 4 . . 4	43	3					80	254		24		
55			- · -	19				8 8 f 3 . P . 4 . : . :	21	1		81	258			5	
58	O'DONNELL	18			. : . 4 . : 4 . :	49	4				(W) 6HR	82	263		28		21
6·02			- · -	20				. : . : . 4/3 3 . 2	27			83	265		7		
05	- · -	19			. : . : . 8/7 7 . 2	55						84	267		30		
08			- · -	21	. : . 9 . : . :	60		8 1	28			85	268			8	
10	- · -	20						4 3 . . . :	34		M 11	86					
14½			- · -	22	. : . : . :	66					M 12	87					
17	- · -	21			2 16 3 3 1 . 2 .	70		LB1 2 . 1	36		(B)	88	273		33	9	22
21			- · -	23				P 3 P . 4 . .	42		M 13	89					
23½	- · -	22	⌐		. : . L W	74	4					89⁴	273	8	33	9	22
25			⌐		FOSTER										0		
27	- · -	22	⌐		P . :	2	-		42	1	M 14 NB 23	90	273	8	0	9	22
6·28	STUMPS	-	1ST DAY								(2 OVERS LOST) DELAY (LIGHT - DRIZZLE)		STUMPS				
2ND DAY 11·10			LAWSON	21	x . 3	3		2 . . 9 . : . 1	47		† NEW BALL	91	274			10	
15	McDERMOTT	26						. x . : ↑	53		M 15	92					
19			- · -	22	8/15 . :	5		. x LB	57		(LB)	93	276		1		23
23	- · -	27			x L 1 2 . : . :	9		. 2/3	59			94	277			11	
27½			- · -	23				. . x x 1 3	65			95	278			12	
32	- · -	28			2 1	10		. : . 2 5 . 2 . 1 . : 2	70			96	282		2	15	
36			- · -	24	4 ↑ Y 1 . . 1 .	15		. 71			7HR	97	283		3		
40	- · -	29			2 W	16	-		71	1		97¹	283	9	3	15	23
											M 15 NB 23						

73

2ND DAY	BOWLERS (EVANS) PAVILION END		(BIRD) NURSERY END		BATSMEN SCOREBOARD LEFT			SCOREBOARD RIGHT			ENGLAND NOTES	1ST INNINGS END-OF-OVER TOTALS					
TIME	BOWLER	O.	BOWLER	O.	SCORING	BALLS	6s/4s	SCORING	BALLS	6s/4s	NOTES	O.	RUNS	W.	'L' BAT	'R' BAT	EXTRAS
					ALLOTT	.	-	EDMONDS	71	1	M15 NB 23	97⁵	283	9	0	15	23
11.42	McDERMOTT	29	⎫		×⁺. ¹⁺	3	-		71	1	⁺ umpires discussed light.	97⁶	283	9	0	15	23
46	BAD LIGHT		⎬								3 OVERS LOST		B	L	S	P	
12·00	– · –	29	⎭		∴∴	5					M16	98					
·01			LAWSON	25				⁴.²..!	77	2		99	289			21	
05	– · –	30			⁺⁸₁	6	-	W	78	2		99²	290	10	1	21	23
12·06	ENGLAND		ALL OUT								M16 NB 23		ALL		OUT		
											619 balls						

2ND DAY TIME	BOWLERS (EVANS) PAVILION END — BOWLER	O.	(BIRD) NURSERY END — BOWLER	O.	BATSMEN SCOREBOARD LEFT — SCORING	BALLS	6S/4S	SCOREBOARD RIGHT — SCORING	BALLS	6S/4S	AUSTRALIA 1ST INNINGS — NOTES	O.	RUNS	W.	'L' BAT	'R' BAT	EXTRAS
					HILDITCH			WOOD		LHB	71 overs						
12·18			FOSTER	1				3 · · · P	6		M1	1					
22	ALLOTT	1			↑8 1	1		P : · P 4↑ · 4	11	1	† All run.	2	5		1	4	
27	— · —		— · —	2	P ↑9↑ · 1	4		P ↑4↑9	14		† Almost played on.	3	7		2	5	
31	— · —	2			LB	5		² P↑²4↑ 3 · W	17	1	(LB) †4+8 disallowed	3⁴	11	1	2	8	1
34								WESSELS		LHB	(crossed)					0	
36	— · —	2			× 2 · 1	7						4	12		3		
38			— · —	3	: : 4 ×↑¹4 : ↑	13	1				° Dropped 2nd slip (BOTHAM) † Bo appeal (Edmonds)	5	16		7		
42½	— · —	3				13	1	² ↑4 L 2 · · · ·	4	−	M1 NB·	5⁴	16	1	7	0	1
12·46	BAD LIGHT	/	LUNCH								(1 over lost)		B	L	S	P/LUNCH	
1·31	ALLOTT	3			² · 1	14		² 1	5			6	18		8	1	
32½			FOSTER	4	× : · ¹ ² ↑ 2 ↑	19		: 6	6			7	19		9		
37	— · —	4			· 6S · 1	21		P P · ·	8			7²	20	1	10	1	1
40	BAD LIGHT												B	L	S	P	
2·04	ALLOTT	4						× · · 1	10		× appeal ct w/k Sidebottom sub (BOTHAM)	8					
06			— · —	5	↑1 : 3 × × · 4 W	25	2					8⁴	24	2	14	1	1
08					BORDER		LHB									0	
10			— · —	5	⁹ · 1	1		· 11				9	25		1		
12	— · —	5			¹ 9 · 1	3		: : : × 15				10	26		2		
16½			— · —	6	² ³ · 4 · 1	6	1	· · · 18				11	31		7		
21	— · —	6			· 8/1 · 8 4 · 1	11	2	· 19			1HR	12	36		12		
25			— · —	7	P · · 4 · ·7S 17							13	37		13		
29	— · —	7			· × · · P · 23						M2	14					
34			— · —	8	: : · 4 · 3	27		⁹↑ · ³ 1	21			15	41		16	2	
37½	— · —	8			· 5(6) · 3	29		³ × · ×↑ · · · ·	25		† Appeal ct w/k (legside)	16	44		19		
42			— · —	9	· · · 1 ↑ 1	34		⁴ 4	26	1		17	49		20	6	
46	— · —	9			5(6) · 7 · 2 · 3	38		ES · ·	28			18	54		25		
50			BOTHAM	1	6/7 3 : : · 4	42		: ² 1	30			19	58		28	7	
55	— · —	10			L · LB · 46			⁹ LB 1	32		(LB) (LB)	20	61			8	3
3·00			EDMONDS	1	· 4F · · 4 · 50			E↑ 8/↑↑ ·	34		° dropped w/k †Gatting hit (shoulder)	21	62		9		
05	— · —	11	over w/kt		2LB 51			· P × · ² · 1	39		× appeal ct w/k (2LB)	22	65		10	5	
10			— · —	2	4 · 6 9 5(6)/8 4 · 2 4↑1 56	4		⁸ 1	40		50 p'ship : 61 min.	23	77		39	11	
15	BOTHAM	2			: : 2/1 · 2 1 60			L W 41		1		23⁵	80	3	·42	11	5
18								BOON								0	
20	— · —	2						: · 1			HM The Queen arrived Over w/kt to RHB.	24					
21			— · —	3	· 86 · 1	62		: : : P · 5				25	81		43		
24½	— · —	3			P · 3 2↑74↑ 0 : · 2 4 : 69	5					(NB) NB 1 2HR	26	88		49		6
29				4				4 · · · P · 11			M3	27					
31	— · —	4			·1 8/7 · 72			P S(6) · 4 : 14			† Round w/kt to LHB. BORDER's 50: 83'	28	93		50	4	
36			— · —	5	7 9 6 2 4 1 75	6		· · · 17		1	M3 NB1	29	100	3	57	4	6

75

2ND DAY TIME	BOWLERS (EVANS) PAVILION END BOWLER	O.	(BIRD) NURSERY END BOWLER	O.	BATSMEN SCOREBOARD LEFT SCORING	BALLS	6s/4s	SCOREBOARD RIGHT SCORING	BALLS	6s/4s	NOTES	O.	RUNS	W.	'L' BAT	'R' BAT	EXTRAS
					BORDER	75	6	BOON	17	1	M3 NB1	29	100	3	57	4	6
3.39	BOTHAM	5			P 2 . . 1	77	6	. . TG W	20	1		29⁵	101	4	58	4	6
3.41	TEA												T E A				O
3.55								RITCHIE			TEAMS PRESENTED TO HM THE QUEEN						
4.05	BOTHAM	5						. :	1			30					
07			FOSTER	10	. 9† . .	79		3 . x 7 . . 2	5		† Rain (umpires conferred)	31	104		59	2	
12	- . -	6			5(6)	80		. 4½ . 6 . 4 .	10	1	† over WK	32	109		60	6	
17			- . -	11	P 2 . 1	82		. 5 . 4	14			33	110		61		
20	- . -	7			7 6 . 2 4 . . 1	86	7	. .	16			34	115		66		
24			- . -	12	: : : 2 1	91		6 . 1	17		• Low chance to 2nd slip (GOOCH)	35	117		67	7	
28	- . -	8			: P 1	93		. † † . 1 1º .	21		† Botham slipped - sawdust.	36	118			8	
34			- . -	13				7 1 2 . 4 . 4 .	27	3		37	126			16	
38	- . -	9			P 2 . 1	95		. 77 6(6) 9 . 4 2 2	32	4	(NB) NB2	38	136		68	24	7
42			- . -	14	9 . :	97		6 L 3 ½ . . 2 1	36		BOTHAM off. (sub SIDEBOTTOM)	39	140		69	27	
46½	ALLOTT	12						. 5(6) 4 . 5(6) . 2 . . 2	42		3HR	40	144			31	
52			GOOCH	1	: 3 3 : 2 . 4 . 1	102	8	. 4	43	5	50 p'ship: 51 min.	41	153		74	35	
56	- . -	13			3 . 9 75 4 . . 2 1	107	9	. :	44			42	160		81		
5.00			- . -	2	: 4 2	113					Botham back.	43	162		83		
04	- . -	14			2 1	115		6 . . . 4 1 . LB	48		(LB)	44	165		84	36	8
09			- . -	3				6 . . . 1 . . 4	54		M4	45					
11	- . -	15			: 5 ⅓	118		P . : :	57			46	166		85		
16			EDMONDS	6	P 4 . .	120		7 . : : 5	61		Round wkt to RHB.	47	167		86		
20½	- . -	16			: 3 . 2 1	124		. . :	63		/ M5	48	168		87		
25			- . -	7	: . . P 7º .	130					• Dropped sh. leg (GATTING) juggling.	49					
29	EMBUREY	1						: : 5(6) . P8½ 4 . . 1	69	6		50	173			41	
32			- . -	8	8 4 2 1	132		8 . 2/3 1 . 4 .	73	7		51	181		90	46	
36	- . -	2			: : 2 9 P : . . 2 1	138	9	: . .	73	7		52	183	4	92	46	8
5.39	BLSP							†			† umpires conferred. M5 NB 2		B L S P				
6.50	PLAY ABANDONED										26 OVERS LOST 2ND DAY		S T U M P S				
3RD DAY 11.00			FOSTER	15				. . 5(6) 6 L . 2 . .	79			53	185			48	
05	ALLOTT	17			4 . 8/7 . : 2 . . 2 . 1	144					4HR	54	188		95		
10			- . -	16	: 8½ † † P 9 . . 4 . ! :	150	10				• Bisected slips. † Almost played on.	55	193		100		
15	- . -	18			9P .	151		. . P .	84		BORDER's 100: 199'.	56	194		101		
20			- . -	17	9E 4 . . x . .	157	11					57	198		105		
23½	- . -	19			: : : 7 .	162		2/3	85			58	199			49	
28			- . -	18				6 . 3 2/3 †8 . . 4 2 .	91		(W) RITCHIE's 50: 125' 100 p'ship: 125'	59	202			51	9
32½	- . -	20			: : P . 8½† . . 4 .	168	12				† chance to absent. 2nd slip.	60	206		109		
37½			EDMONDS	9				. L 4 . . 3 . . .	97		Round wkt to RHB. M6	61	207				
40	- . -	21			7 . : : 9 1	173		. 9	98			62	207		110		
45½			- . -	10	7 2 4 1	175	13	6 . : : P .	102	7	M6 NB 2	63	212	4	115	51	9

3RD DAY TIME	BOWLERS (EVANS) PAVILION — BOWLER	O.	END	(BIRD) NURSERY — BOWLER	O.	END	SCOREBOARD LEFT SCORING	BALLS	6s/4s	SCOREBOARD RIGHT SCORING	BALLS	6s/4s	NOTES	O.	RUNS	W.	L BAT	R BAT	EXTRAS
							BORDER	175	13	RITCHIE	102	7	M6 NB2	63	212	4	115	51	9
11.49	ALLOTT	22					.:L LB	178		X:P	105		(LB) X Appeal ct wk M7	64	213				10
54				EDMONDS	11		.5(6) 5	181		:7 4	108			65	215		116	52	
57	- · -	23								:8 7 7	114			66	218			55	
12.02				- · -	12		4	182		6:4 4	119			67	220		117	56	
05/07	EMBUREY	3					P 9 7	185		::4	122		2' delay - sightscreen reparation.	68	223		119	57	
10½	Round wkt to LHB			- · -	13		3 6 / 4 1	187	14	??:	126		5HR	69	228		124		
13	- · -	4			·		8	189		::7 8	130			70	230		125	58	
16				- · -	14		5P	190		::7 1 3	135			71	233			61	
19½	- · -	5					6:::				141		M8	72					
22				- · -	15		5t::: 7	195		7b	142		Good stop (bowler)	73	235		126	62	
24½	- · -	6								5P:::	148		M9	74					
26½				- · -	16		::7	198		7:4	151			75	237		127	63	
29	- · -	7					t 3	200		::7 8	155		t over wkt.	76	238			64	
33				- · -	17		::	202		:4 9t	159			77	239			65	
36	- · -	8			·					7:7:	165		M10	78					
38				- · -	18		29/8	205		:4 2	168			79	241		128	66	
42	- · -	9					8 1/2 8 8 / 4 4 1	209	16	8/1 6	170		150 p'ship: 199'	80	251		137	67	
46½				- · -	19		:5 LB	213		7 L 2:	172		(LB)	81	254			69	11
50	- · -	10					:9 4 3	216		:::	175			82	257		140		
53				- · -	20		:18 4	218	17		175	7	M10 NB2	82	261	4	144	69	11
12.55	BLSP												LUNCH						
1.37				EDMONDS	20		8 7t 1E / 2:3	221		6	176		t Gatting (bn leg)	83	266		149		
42	EMBUREY	11					P::: 2 / ::4	227	18				BORDER'S 150: 306'	84	270		153		
44½				- · -	21		1 3 / 1 1	229		½ 6 P / .3: 1	180			85	276		155	73	
49	FOSTER	19					9 9 / 1 1	231		1E 3t2 x / 4.:1	184	8	t over 2nd slip 4 NEW BALL 6HR	86	283		157	78	
53				ALLOTT	24		2 / .1 ...	236		9 1	185		Bo Butcher(2nd) GATTING (badly bruised knee)	87	285		158	79	
59	- · -	20								::: 3 8 1E / .4 2 4	191	10		88	295			89	
2.03½				- · -	25		:::::2LB	242					(2LB) M11	89	297				13
08	- · -	21					1E 4	244	19	P:7 2 / ::1	195		200 p'ship: 243'	90	302		162	90	
12				- · -	26		6 7 7:	249		8 1	196			91	303			91	
17	BOTHAM	10								7: 4: / ©: : 0	204		x Ecu over (NB) (NB) NB4	92	305				15
22				- · -	27		2 8 2 / 1:2:1	254		4 1	205			93	310		166	92	
27	- · -	11					4 1E 2 / .4 1	258	20	L 2 / :1	207			94	316		171	93	
31½				- · -	28		:::	261		:5 1	210			95	317			94	
36	- · -	12								18 L / .W	212	10		95	317	5	171	94	15
37										PHILLIPS		LHB						0	
39	- · -	12								:9 ..	4			96	319			2	
42				- · -	29		5(4) 4 4 9t5t / .4:1	266	21	:	5		t Almost played on.	97	324		176		
46	- · -	13					8E5 t t / :	272	21	5		-	t Round wkt M12 NB4	98	324	5	176	2	15

3RD DAY TIME	BOWLERS (EVANS) PAVILION END BOWLER	O.	(BIRD) NURSERY END BOWLER	O.	BATSMEN SCOREBOARD LEFT SCORING	BALLS	6s 4s	SCOREBOARD RIGHT SCORING	BALLS	6s 4s	AUSTRALIA 1ST INNINGS NOTES	O.	RUNS	W.	'L' BAT	'R' BAT	EXTRAS
					BORDER	272	21	PHILLIPS	5	–	M12 NB4	98	324	5	176	2	15
2·50			ALLOTT	30				3 ∶∶∶∶	11		M13 7HR	99					
54½	BOTHAM	14			↑ ↑ × ∶∶∶	278					†Round wkt (2 balls) M14	100					
3·00			EDMONDS	22	1 ∶∶ 3	279		∶ 6 7/6 1 6 ∶	16	/		101	334		179	9	
05	– · –	15			6/4s 1	280		↑ 2/3 18 18 ∶ 4 · 44	21	1/3	† over slips.	102	347		180	21	
10			– · –	23	P ∶ 3 8† × 3	286					† Diving stop (Gower) M15	103					
12	– · –	16						62 W	22	1/3		103	347	6	180	21	15
13								O'DONNELL							0		
15	– · –	16			∶ ∶ ↑	289		21 ∶ 1	2			104	348		1		
19			EMBUREY	12				∶ ? 7 2 ∶	8			105	350		3		
22	– · –	17			∶ 2 1 ·	292		7/6 6/4 4 2 3	11	1		106	360		181	12	
26			– · –	13				∶ 2 18o ∶ 44 ∶ P ·	17	3	• Dropped slip (Botham)	107	368			20	
30	FOSTER	22			2 1	293		· 6 6 7	22			108	369		182		
34			– · –	14	∶∶ ∶ 7/8	297		∶ 4	24		Round wkt to LHB.	109	370		183		
37	– · –	23			∶∶ P ↑ ∶ 8/9	303	21		24	3	M15 NB4	110	371	6	184	20	15
3·40	TEA														T E A		
4·00			EMBUREY	15	4 1	304		∶ 4 ∶∶ 3	29			111	373		185	21	
03½	BOTHAM	18			4†× ∶	307		L ∶ 2 · 1	32		† Diving stop (Lamb)	112	374			22	
08			– · –	16				4 ∶∶∶	38	4		113	378			26	
11	– · ·	19			× 2 1	309		•4 8† × 5 4 ∶∶	42		• Dropped long leg (Allott) 8HR	114	381		186	28	
15			– · –	17	5/6	310		∶∶∶∶	47			115	382		187		
18	– · –	20			3 5(6)	312		∶ 17 ↑ 6 ∶	51	1/4		116	389		188	34	
22			– · –	18	∶∶ 8/74 4 1	316	22	∶ 2	53			117	394		193		
24½	– · –	21			2/1 E1 3 W	318	22	∶ 1/2	55		50 p'ship: 50 min.	117	398	7	196	35	15
27					LAWSON										0		
29	– · –	21			4F ∶	2						118					
31			– · –	19				∶∶∶ 6/4 4 ∶	61	1/5		119	402			39	
34	– · –	22			† 9 2 1 1	5		†1/64 4 3 4 3 2	64	1/6	† Hit on chest ‡ over wk.	120	413		2	48	
39			EDMONDS	24	9 1	6		∶ 2 ∶ 2 E2 W	69	1/6		121	414	8	3	48	15
41					McDERMOTT										0		
43	– · –	23			4 1	7		1 8E 5 2 ∶ 2 ·	5			122	419		4	4	
47			– · –	25	∶∶ × ∶∶∶∶	13					M16	123					
50	– · –	24			1E	14		4 1†×× 6 1	10		† Hit on back.	124	422		5	6	
53			– · –	26	∶ 7	16		1/2 3 (RO)	11	–		124	425	9	5	9	15
55								HOLLAND							0		
57			– · –	26		16	–	× W	1	–		124	425	10	5	0	15
4·58	AUSTRALIA		ALL OUT								M16 NB4		ALL		OUT		
											752 balls						

3RD DAY TIME	BOWLERS (BIRD) PAVILION END BOWLER	O.	(EVANS) NURSERY END BOWLER	O.	BATSMEN SCOREBOARD LEFT SCORING	BALLS	6s/4s	SCOREBOARD RIGHT SCORING	BALLS	6s/4s	ENGLAND 2ND INNINGS NOTES	END-OF-OVER TOTALS O.	RUNS	W.	L.BAT	R.BAT	EXTRAS
					GOOCH			ROBINSON			(13 OVERS TO BAT)						
5·11	McDERMOTT	1			B -	1		...·↑·.	5		Ⓑ M1	1	1				1
16			LAWSON	1	41 5(6)· 1F 1 2·.·.	6		4 3	6		† Wood misfielded	2	7		3	3	
20½	-·-	2			·P·↑· 5(6) 2	12					†Appeal c WK (legside)	3	9			5	
25			-·-	2	:·. ·8·47 ②·1	12		:	13		NB1	4	12		6		
30	-·-	3			7 7 7 ·241	16	1	4 2·	15			5	21		13	7	
34			-·-	3	8/9 ::·LB	20		4 LB 2·	17		ⓁᴮⓁᴮ	6	26		14	9	3
38	-·-	4		·	5(6) 7 7 †6 1 ·2·:	25		7 1	18			7	30		17	10	
43			-·-	4	·†· :	28		:·7 ·1	21		† hit on arm.	8	31			11	
47	-·-	5	⎫		E9 W	29	1	:·:· 2E 1	24			8⁴	32	1	17	12	3
49			⎬		EMBUREY											0	
51	-·-	5	⎭		8 P 2·	2						9	34		2		
53			HOLLAND	1	⎫			P · P · x ...W	29	-		9⁵	34	2	2	12	3
55					⎬			ALLOTT								0	
57			-·-	1	⎭			·:	1		M2	10					
58	-·-	6			P L Y † 7/8 ·.·.1	8					† bowler warned (pitch damage)	11	35		3		
6·03			-·-	2	::·:·8·PP	14					M3	12					
05½	-·-	7			Y 6 ·1	16	-	L· 5LB	5	-	Ⓛᴮ 1HR	13	37	2	4	0	4
6·10											M3 NB1						
11·00			LAWSON	5	1F 2 ·1	18		·x W	7	-		13⁴	38	3	5	0	4
03								GOWER	LHB							0	
05			-·-	5				:·.	2			14					
07	McDERMOTT	8			7E 7 P½ 2·.·3	22		·↑	4			15	43		10		
12			-·-	6	:·!·:·↑ ·2:	28						16	45		12		
16	-·-	9						2 4.·.·:	10	1		17	49			4	
20			-·-	7	1E†4 EX 44W	31	2				† over slips.	17³	57	4	20	4	4
22					GATTING											0	
24			-·-	7	L4† ·1	2		4 4	11	2	† O'Donnell misfielded	18	62		1	8	
27	-·-	10			P 4 7 7 ·.·.1	6		4 3/1 ·.·1	13			19	64		2	9	
32			-·-	8				8 4 3 2 ·444·1	19	5		20	77			22	
36	-·-	11	⎫					3 E1 ·W	21	5		20²	77	5	2	22	4
37			⎬					LAMB								0	
39	-·-	11	⎭					L·:·LB	4		Ⓛᴮ M4	21	78				5
43			HOLLAND	3	9·PP3 2·:·.·	11		LB	5		Ⓛᴮ	22	81		4		6
46	-·-	12						P E4 6 x 2 ·⑥·.·.	12		Ⓝᴮ NB2	23	82				7
51			-·-	4	4·PP·x ·.·.·.	17					M5	24					
54	-·-	13			P·Y2 ·.·.4	21	1	F4 8 41	14	1		25	91		8	5	
58			-·-	5	·.·6	23		8F 2E EP ·1	18		2HR	26	93		9	6	
12·01	LAWSON	9			·2†·9	28		7 ·1	19		† hit on box.	27	94		10		
07			-·-	6	P·.·P· ·.·.1	34	1		19	1	M6 NB2	28	94	5	10	6	7

79

4TH DAY	BOWLERS (BIRD) PAVILION END		(EVANS) NURSERY END		BATSMEN SCOREBOARD LEFT			SCOREBOARD RIGHT			ENGLAND 2ND INNINGS NOTES	END-OF-OVER TOTALS					
TIME	BOWLER	O.	BOWLER	O.	SCORING	BALLS	6s/4s	SCORING	BALLS	6s/4s		O.	RUNS	W.	'L' BAT	'R' BAT	EXTRAS
					GATTING	34	1	LAMB	19	1	M6 NB2	28	94	5	10	6	7
12.09½	LAWSON	10			· · · ⸱	38		:⁹₁	21			29	95			7	
15			HOLLAND	7				·⁶:····	27		M7	30					
17	— · —	11			LB	39		·:⁷ ·⁸⁴2W	32	1	(LB)	31	98	6	10	9	8
20								BOTHAM								0	
22			— · —	8	P:···:	45					M8	32					
25	— · —	12			P:··:	49		:⁴₁	2			33	99			1	
30			— · —	9				⁷2:·⁴⁴:·P	8	1		34	105			7	
33	— · —	13			¹/2 · ⁹/8	52		⁷₁ :·	11			35	108		12	8	
37			— · —	10	⁴₁ ::	55		PP²E	14			36	110		13	9	
40	· · —	14						·⁷₄·⊙₄³¹	21	2	(NB) NB3	37	116			14	9
45			— · —	11	:::::₁	60		⁸₁	22			38	117			15	
48	— · · —	15						ˣ²²/₁P: ·²⁴···	28	3		39	123			21	
52			— · —	12	::·⁴₁	64		::	30		Gatting 18' on 13.	40	124		14		
55	— · · ·	16			·⁴₃ :⁴₃	68		:⁶₁	32			41	128		17	22	
59			— · —	13	P:··²₃	72	1	9⁵(4)	34	3	3HR	42	132	6	20	23	9
1.02	LUNCH										M8 NB3		LUNCH				
1.40	McDERMOTT	14			⁸P₁ ⁸⁺₁	74		·⁹/5F ⁺²/1⁶₆	38	1/3	† England level.	43	141		22	30	
45			HOLLAND	14	⁹::··:P	80					M9	44					
47	— · —	15			P⁷₁⁸:⁴2:⁴P	85		⁸₁	39			45	144		24	31	
51½			— · —	15				·⁸/9 ·³·	45		M10	46					
54	— · ·	16	·		P⁸₀14⁺⁸··P	91	2	³₁	46		(NB) NB4 50 p'ship: 57 min.	47	151		29	32	10
59½			— · —	16	·₁	92		⁸/9₄:::⁶⁸₁	51	1/5		48	160			41	
2.03	— · —	17						²₂⁴:₄¹PP⁶⁶₁	57	1/6	* Diving chance to extra-cover (HILDITCH)	49	167			48	
07½			— · —	17				P·₄₄⁵³⁵⁸₄	63	1/8	BOTHAM'S 50: 68 min	50	175			56	
11	— · · —	18			⁴LB ↑:	95		⁹F₄:	66	1/9	(LB)	51	181		61		11
15½			— · —	18	::₁	97		²₃:ˣ¹/2₃	70			52	184		64		
19	LAWSON	17			:³₄:²₄₁	102		⁸E₁	71			53	187		31	65	
24			— · —	19	³/4₄:	104	3	³/4₁7²⁶₄⁸	75	1/10		54	196		35	70	
27	— · —	18			↑₁	105		:₁ :⁴₄LB	80	1/11	100 p'ship: 87 min (LB)	55	201			74	12
31½			— · —	20	³₄::	108	4	⁸/9₃	83			56	206		39	75	
34½	— · —	19			:Y₁⁷	111		ˣ³⁵₁ ⁴	86		4HR	57	208		40	76	
39			— · · ·	21	PP³:⁴⁵₁	116		P₁	87		Round wkt.	58	209		41		
42	— · —	20			⁹/6₃	117		³⁺₁:··⁸₁	92		† Botham limping - bruised left foot.	59	213		44	77	
48			— · —	22				PPPP·₁	98		M11	60					
50 52	— · · ·	21			⁴↑₁↑²/3	121		::	100		Physio treatment to Botham.	61	214		45		
57			— · · —	23	³:::::₁	127					MATTHEWS (sub for McDermott) M12	62					
3.00	— · —	22			:⁶₁	129		LB ⁸/7:⁸₂₁	104		(LB)	63	219		46	80	13
05			— · —	24	³⁵₁	130		³6F₄:·:⁶₁	109	1/12		64	225		47	85	
09	O'DONNELL	1			²₁ ²₁	132	4	↑⁷₁:·LB	113	1/12	(LB) M12 NB4 McDermott back.	65	228	6	49	85	14

4TH DAY TIME	BOWLERS (BIRD) PAVILION END BOWLER	O.	(EVANS) NURSERY END BOWLER	O.	BATSMEN SCOREBOARD LEFT SCORING	BALLS	6s 4s	SCOREBOARD RIGHT SCORING	BALLS	6s 4s	ENGLAND 2ND INNINGS NOTES	O.	END-OF-OVER TOTALS RUNS	W.	'L' BAT	'R' BAT	EXTRAS
					GATTING	132	4	BOTHAM	113	1/12	M12 NB4	65	228	6	49	85	14
3·13½			HOLLAND	25	. ³ 1	134		P : ³ W	116	1/12	GATTING'S 50: 192'	65⁵	229	7	50	85	14
15								DOWNTON								0	
17			– · –	25				61 W	1	-		66	229	8	50	0	14
18								EDMONDS								0	
20	O'DONNELL	2			: : : : ⁹1	140						67	230		51		
23			– · –	26	34 P LB :2 ·	144		: ³	2		(LB)	68	233		53		15
26½	– · –	3		·	: : 2 5(6). 8 4 · 1	150	5					69	238		58		
30			– · –	27	5 2 3s :2 1	153		X : P	5			70	241		61		
33	– · –	4			7 1	154		7 1 · :4 :	10			71	242		62		
37			– · –	28	P : : B3 1	158		1 . P	12		† over mkt. 5HR	72	243		63		
39½	– · –	5			4 1	159	5	L : : : P	17	-		73	244	8	64	0	15
3·42	TEA										M12 NB4		T	E	A		
4·01			HOLLAND	29	: : 4 1	162		3 P% : ·	20			74	245		65		
04	McDERMOTT	19			P 7 LB 8F :2 · 4	166	6	P 8 : 1	22		(LB)	75	253		71	1	16
08½			– · –	30	·			3L · · P F	28		† Border hit (rt shin) M13	76					
11	– · –	20			P : · # :·6⁹ 1	172					(4W)	77	258		72		20
16			– · –	31	: : 4 1	175		8 · P : · :	31		Treatment to Border.	78	259		73		
19	LAWSON	23			3 2 · x3↑ :2 · · · ·	181						79	261		75		
23			– · –	32	⌐			: 8 E1 · W	34	-		79³	261	9	75	1	20
24								FOSTER								0	
26			– · –	32	⌐	181	6	: ·11 :·W	3	-	M14	80	261	10	75	0	20
4·27	ENGLAND		ALL OUT								M14 NB4 484 balls		AL	L	OU	T	

4TH DAY TIME	BOWLERS (BIRD) PAVILION END BOWLER	O.	(EVANS) NURSERY END BOWLER	O.	BATSMEN SCOREBOARD LEFT SCORING	BALLS	6s/4s	SCOREBOARD RIGHT SCORING	BALLS	6s/4s	AUSTRALIA 2ND INNINGS NOTES (21 OVERS MIN.)	END-OF-OVER TOTALS O.	RUNS	W.	'L' BAT	'R' BAT	EXTRAS
					HILDITCH			WOOD		LHB							
4·39	BOTHAM	1	}		x . 2↑8 . . W	4	-					0⁴	0	1	0	0	-
41			}		WESSELS		LHB								0		
43	- · -	1	}		8 2 2 ·	2						1	2		2		
45			ALLOTT	1				. L L	6		M1	2					
50	- · -	2			: 8 . 1 x	5		↑ · 8	9			3	4		3	1	
54½			- · -	2	: 6	6		9 · P 4↑8 2 · · 2 1	14		† overthrow (via woods back).	4	9			6	
59	- · -	3	}					· · W	17	-		4³	9	2	3	6	-
5·01			}					RITCHIE							0		
03	- · -	3	}		: 7	7		8↑7 · · 1	2			5	10			1	
06			- · -	3				6 4 · · · x	8		M2	6					
10	- · -	4			: 1 8 · 4 · ↑ · x	13	1					7	14		7		
14			- · -	4	· · P · 4 L ·	18		6 1	9			8	15			2	
18	- · -	5			: · 2½↑P 4 ·	23	2	L8	10		(LB)	9	20		11		1
23			- · -	5				· · 2LB · 8 · x · · W	16	-	(2LB) M3	10	22	3	11	2	3
27								BORDER		LHB					0		
29	- · -	6			P · · · 2/3 · · 4 ·	29	3					11	26		15		
33			- · -	6	: P 1	32		8 · 9 · · 1	3		1HR	12	28		16	1	
37	- · -	7			: : 1 2	35		8 · 9 · 4	6	1		13	33		17	5	
43			- · -	7	3 · · · · ·	41					M4	14					
47½	- · - ·	8						· · 4↑9 · ·	12	2		15	37			9	
52			EDMONDS	1	: P P · · · 3 2	47						16	39		19		
55	- · -	9						· · · x · · 2/1	18			17	40			10	
59½			- · -	2	4 · 1	48		· · · L · 8	23			18	42		20	11	
6·03	EMBUREY	1			· P · · 7 L · · 2 · 1	54						19	44		22		
06			- · -	3	: P L 9 · · 1	58		8 1 · ·	25			20	46		23	12	
09	- · -	2			· · · · · P	64	3		25	2	MS NB -	21	46	3	23	12	3
6·11	STUMPS	-	4TH DAY										S	T	U	M	P S
5TH DAY 11·00			EDMONDS OVER VIKT.	4				· 4LB 5 P x 7	31		(4LB) M6	22	50				7
03	BOTHAM	10			2 2↑4↑ 2 · 1	68		· ·	33		† HIT on shoulder.	23	53		26		
07			- · -	5	: · 2 P · 8 · · 1	74						24	54		27		
10	- · -	11			3 2 · ·	76		6↑ · · 8 4 · · ·	37	3	† Emburey misfielded	25	59		28	16	
14			- · -	6	P · P · P 7 · 1	82					M7	26					
16	- · -	12						↑ 2↑ · 3 · : 4 · · ·	43	4	† Allott misfielded	27	63			20	
20			- · -	7	· x · KP 1	86	3					27⁴	63	4	28	20	7
21					BOON										0		
23			- · -	7	· P 1	2					M8	28					
25	- · -	13			: 8 · 1	4		7 1 · 8 ↑x	47		2HR	29	65		1	21	
29			- · -	8	· · W x	8	-		47	4		29⁴	65	5	1	21	7
31											M8 NB -						

5TH DAY	BOWLERS				BATSMEN						AUSTRALIA 2ND INNINGS					
	(BIRD) PAVILION END		(EVANS) NURSERY END		SCOREBOARD LEFT			SCOREBOARD RIGHT			NOTES	END-OF-OVER TOTALS					
TIME	BOWLER	O.	BOWLER	O.	SCORING	BALLS	6³⁄4s	SCORING	BALLS	6³⁄4s		O.	RUNS	W.	'L' BAT	'R' BAT	EXTRAS
					PHILLIPS	·	LHB	BORDER	47	4	M8 NB -	29⁴	65	5	0	21	7
11.33			EDMONDS	8	P ·	2					M9	30					
34	BOTHAM	14			↑ 2 4 · · ·	5		· · 5(4) 3	50			31	68			24	
38	- ··		- · -	9	6 9 ·	7		3 9/8 · · · ·	54			32	70	1	25		
41½	· ··	15			6 4 4 6 2 4 · 4 · · · 1	13	1				+ all run.	33	75	6			
45½			- · -	10	· P · ·7/8↑ 1	17		· P 7	56		+ via umpire BIRD's foot.	34	77	7	26		
49	EMBUREY	3						6 4 4·P · · 3	62	5	+BORDER 5000 R.	35	84		33		
54			- · -	·11				P 3 · P X 7	68		M10	36					
57	- · -	4			↑9 · ·	18		· · · · 3 4	73	6	+ Round wkt.	37	89	8	37		
12·01			- · -	12	2 3 4LB P 7 2 4 · · 1	23	2	57·	74		(4LB) + high chance to 3m.leg(?) (batting)	38	100	15		11	
05	- · -	5			8/7 8/1½ 1 · X 4 2 4 · · ·	29	4					39	110	25			
09			- · -	13	2 2 3 1	31		8 5(6) P · 1 · ·	78		50 p'ship : 38'	40	116	29	39		
13	- · -	6)			3/2 W	32	4					40	116	6	29	39	11
13		}			O'DONNELL										0		
15	- · -	6)			· · · P P ·	5					M11	41					
18			- · -	14	· · 8 1	7		7 P 8 4 1	82			42	118	1	40		
21	- · -	7			· · · 4¢ · P	13					+ diving ch to S.m-off (GOWER) M12	43					
24			- · -	15	· · X 1E P	18		9 1	83		3HR	44	119		41		
27	- · -	8						· · · · 6 4	89		M13	45					
30			- · -	16	1E · 5(4) 6 · 6 · · 6 · · 2	24	1/-		89	6		46	127	6	9	41	11
12·32	AUSTRALIA	WON BY	4 WICKETS								M13 NB - 276 balls						

83

NURSERY END

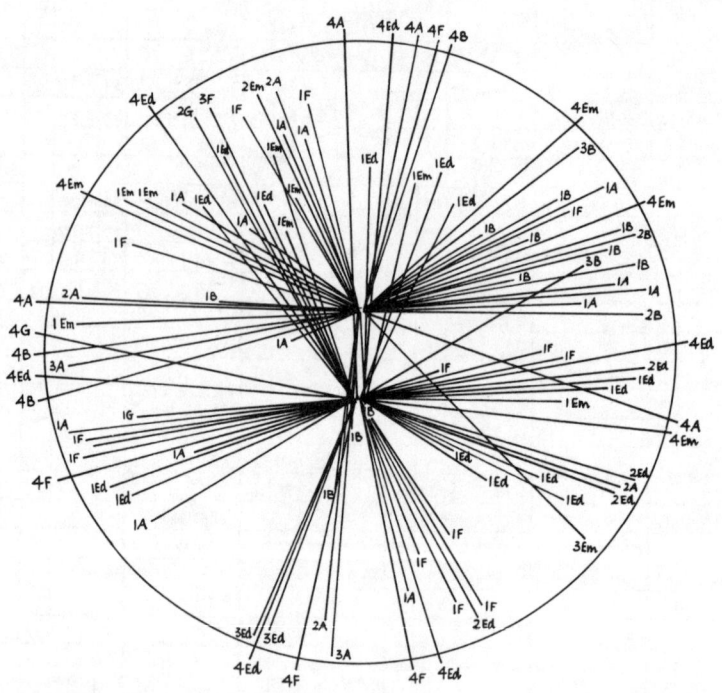

PAVILION END

BOWLER	SYMBOL	R	U	N	S	
		1	2	3	4	6	TOTAL
ALLOTT	A	13	4	2	4	-	43
BOTHAM	B	11	2	2	3	-	33
EDMONDS	Ed	14	4	2	6	-	52
EMBUREY	Em	8	1	1	4	-	29
FOSTER	F	13	-	1	4	-	32
GOOCH	G	1	1	-	1	-	7
TOTALS		60	12	8	22	-	196

A.R. BORDER at Lord's

196   RUNS
318   BALLS
450   MINUTES

(left-handed batsman)

© BILL FRINDALL 1985

THIRD TEST

TRENT BRIDGE

JULY 11, 12, 13, 15, 16

ENGLAND

D.I. Gower (captain), G.A. Gooch, R.T. Robinson, M.W. Gatting,
A.J. Lamb, I.T. Botham, P.R. Downton, A. Sidebottom, J.E. Emburey,
P.H. Edmonds, P.J.W. Allott

AUSTRALIA

A.R. Border (captain), G.M.Wood, A.M.J. Hilditch, K.C. Wessels,
G.M. Ritchie, D.C. Boon, W.B. Phillips, S.P. O'Donnell,
G.F. Lawson, C.J. McDermott, R.G. Holland

May calls for patience in middle order

While the final make-up of England's attack will not be known until shortly before the start of today's third Cornhill Test against Australia at Trent Bridge, their batsmen will also come under scrutiny after the individual lapses that contributed to defeat at Lord's. With a fascinating series poised at 1–1, either side could gain ground with a convincing all-round performance here, and consistency with both bat and ball needs to be the keynote of England's display.

To that end Peter May, chairman of selectors, stressed at last night's pre-match team dinner that he and his colleagues will be looking for a more patient approach, particularly among the England middle order. This hardly comes as a surprise, for the point has often been made in these columns that the way that Gower, Lamb and company bat is based on instinctive strokeplay rather than laying down the foundation for a long innings.

There have, of course, been exceptions – Gower in Pakistan, for instance, and Lamb against the West Indies last year – but overall the tendency of England's middle order to squander wickets needlessly at crucial moments was illustrated at Lord's, apart from Gatting's stoical effort in the second innings which was probably the exception that proved the rule.

England, however, ought by now to have learned from their experiences, first in India last winter and then at Headingley, that one factor for Test match success is the ability to bat for a long time, and perhaps Mr May's words will have served as a timely reminder.

What happens if they do not remains to be seen. The selectors are understandably backing the undoubted quality of the middle order to come good eventually, and are also well aware of the disruptive influence of one-day cricket, but there are candidates waiting in the wings.

As for the bowlers, they are likely to find the hardest surface that groundsman Ron Allsopp has managed to produce this season; for several reasons, not least the weather, Trent Bridge has had only one outright result in first-class cricket so far. By Saturday, or thereabouts, today's pitch, given a continuation of warm, dry weather, should accommodate the batsmen. But initially it is expected there will be something in it for the bowlers, and there should be an encouraging amount of bounce, but probably no great pace.

It may, therefore, be one of those piches on which the side with the faster bowling prevails, which tends to suggest that Australia may make the early running, with Lawson – who has so far promised more than he has achieved – possibly a key figure. If Botham can run in as he did at Lord's, Australia's somewhat variable batting will again be under pressure. But with the unfortunate Foster out of the reckoning, England have to pick two from Allott, Agnew and Sidebottom in support.

When the squad was first named it seemed as though Allott might be omitted, rightly or wrongly. To do so now, however, would mean playing both Agnew and Sidebottom, who have only two Test appearances between them, leaving the side riskily short of experience.

The decision may now be influenced by the pitch's expected lack of pace, which would give Sidebottom his first Test cap and England the insurance of his greater accuracy.

AUSTRALIAN VIEWPOINT
Gilbert's first big test

Dave 'Eddie' Gilbert could have been playing for Essex's Second XI this season, on an Esso scholarship from the Australian Cricket Board. Today, instead, he is expected to make his Test debut for Australia against England at Trent Bridge.

Gilbert and Jeff Thomson came on this England tour when two of the original pace-bowling choices, Rod McCurdy and Terry Alderman, withdrew after signing to play with a 'rebel' Australian team in South Africa later this year. Their replacements, Carl Rackemann and John MacGuire, were unavailable for the same reason.

Gilbert, 24, tall, strongly built and quietly spoken, has taken 68 wickets for an average of 34·57 in 26 first-class matches since his debut for New

South Wales in 1983-84. Those figures include 13 wickets (average 34·84) off 142·2 overs in six matches on this tour.

While Gilbert bowls quickly and accurately enough, doubts have been cast – in Australia, anyway – about whether he does enough with the ball, through the air and off the pitch, to trouble the best batsmen. But he is expected to play today because the Australian tour selectors believe he, rather than all-rounder Simon O'Donnell, will provide more penetrative support for opening bowlers Geoff Lawson and Craig McDermott.

As the most likely all-rounder Australia have found for some years, O'Donnell, 22, would be somewhat unfortunate to be left out of the side. But, at the highest level, he still is more a batsman who bowls than a genuine all-rounder.

STATISTICAL PREVIEW
Target for Robinson

E ngland have won only three of the 14 Trent Bridge Tests against Australia (1905, 1930 and 1977) and have been defeated on four occasions (1921, 1934, 1948 and 1981).

Tim Robinson, who scored a hundred in each innings against Glamorgan in his last match, could become the first Nottinghamshire player to score a century against Australia on his home ground. Surprisingly, in view of the prolific-scoring Nottinghamshire batsmen who have played in Tests there, Reg Simpson is alone in scoring a century for England at Trent Bridge. He achieved this feat twice, against South Africa in 1951 and against Pakistan in 1954.

Ian Botham needs to hit only two more sixes to become the second batsman, after his Somerset predecessor Arthur Wellard, to hit 50 sixes in a first-class season. Wellard reached that target four times between 1933 and 1938, his best performance being the world record of 66 in 1935. The second most prolific hitter of sixes and the holder of the post-war record is John Edrich with 49 in 1965.

Test career batting landmarks beckon Wayne Phillips (927 runs) and Graeme Wood (2,880 runs, including 834 against England).

Gower inspires England with fine hundred

Led by David Gower's unbeaten 107, England's batting flourished on the opening day of the third Cornhill Test at Trent Bridge yesterday, and they were formidably placed at 279 for two when bad light ended play four overs early.

Neither the pitch nor the Australian bowling proved as demanding as might have been expected, and Gower in a chanceless and increasingly selective four-and-a-quarter-hour stay, seized the opportunity to make his first century in 23 innings as England captain.

Nothing extravagant was required from him or his colleagues to maintain a run rate of around four an over for much of the time.

And after Gower and Gooch had put on 116 for the second wicket, Gatting and his captain were very much in control, having added an unbroken 108 at the close.

Now, if the new ball, which will become due early this morning, can be overcome with the mimimum of mishaps, England have an excellent opportunity first to consolidate, then to put the match out of Australia's reach by aiming for a total of 500 or more.

England omitted Agnew, so Sidebottom became the first Yorkshire player to win a cap since Athey four years ago. Australia were unchanged, again opting for only four bowlers.

Although the morning was overcast, Gower chose to bat on winning the toss, perhaps reasoning – correctly, as it turned out – that the pitch's lack of pace would nullify any help it offered the bowlers. In any case, with two spinners, he also had a vested interest in bowling last.

The last vestige of dampness meant that the odd ball would move off the seam or sometimes bounce, though the way Australia bowled early on did much to camouflage this, and England had 50 on the board in only 12 overs.

Mostly this was due to Robinson who, with rather more of the strike, found plenty of bowling that could be tucked off his legs. With two centuries in his last two innings, his timing was perfect and the ball raced to the boundary.

Between times, he illustrated the pitch's mildness by playing a couple of attempted bouncers from Lawson with great comfort and a straight bat off the back foot. He was also quick to drive the half volley, and thus Gooch was able to spend plenty of time in reconnaissance.

All this took place in modest light, and it was immediately after a six-over stoppage that Robinson was caught at slip, driving at a ball from Lawson that held its line. But the pattern had been firmly set, and Australia were beginning to look a bowler short.

This was because of McDermott's tendency to overpitch. He produced a series of full tosses and a chest-high beamer, no doubt accidental, which left Gooch flat on his back after he had overbalanced.

Otherwise, all was very serene, with Gooch operating with increased fluency. He reached his first half-century in a home series against Australia with two fours in one over from O'Donnell, who, at medium pace, had started to look Australia's most suitable bowler for these conditions.

Unfortunately for Australia, when he found the edge or induced a false stroke, the ball barely carried on this pitch and with Gower timing everything from the start, he and Gooch maintained an ideal tempo without recourse to anything risky.

Gower's only problems lay in the occasional undisciplined stroke, but these were isolated moments among many fine and elegant ones. Not surprisingly, in his first innings since being reappointed captain, he looked more relaxed than for some time.

Hereabouts, Australia had another problem when Holland, initially, also overpitched, but he settled down and, although finding nothing in the conditions, again provided the steady stock bowling his side needed with so few attacking options at their disposal.

Gooch, meanwhile, was playing so well, savaging anything that could be driven on the front foot, that it came as a surprise when he eventually fell, well caught by Wessels in the gully when not quite controlling a back-foot force against Lawson.

Gower went on, cutting, pulling and driving in that effortless manner of his when everything is in working order. He reached 100 from 167 balls, and then moved above Tom Graveney to become England's ninth leading run-getter of all time.

Gatting, though clearly setting out his stall for a long stay, also found bowling that could be hooked and cut comfortably, until with the light rapidly worsening, the third wicket pair took the opportunity to avoid a needless upset in final four overs.

AUSTRALIAN VIEWPOINT

Crying need for fifth bowler

The Australian tour selectors' stubborn persistence with only four bowlers contributed to England's domination of the first day's play in the third Test at Trent Bridge yesterday.

Australia got away with a four-pronged attack at Lord's, where they won by four wickets, but it was exposed as manifestly inadequate yesterday on a surprisingly slow, unsympathetic pitch.

There was a crying need for a fifth bowler, preferably Dave Gilbert, who was to make his Test debut until the selectors – Allan Border, Andrew Hilditch, Geoff Lawson and Geoff Dymock – examined the pitch, saw it had been shaved much more closely than they had thought, and decided to retain the all-rounder Simon O'Donnell, and make Gilbert 12th man.

In fairness, the selectors were not to know that Craig McDermott would bowl so badly or that Lawson would make such an indifferent start, though he fought back courageously.

They were aware, however, that O'Donnell's medium-pacers were merely honest rather than penetrative, hence their original intention to play Gilbert ahead of him.

Even without the benefit of hindsight, Gilbert should have played, and if O'Donnell had to be kept in, a batsman – the out-of-form opener Graeme Wood – should have been left out.

Trent Bridge was supposed to provide the quickest pitch of the series, yet it was sluggish to the point of being dormant. While there was bounce in it for the quick bowlers, the ball came off so lazily that the batsmen were rarely inconvenienced.

If the pitch does not deteriorate alarmingly and unexpectedly over the remaining four days, neither side should be bowled out twice. This would then become the sixth drawn match in the past nine Australia-England Tests at Trent Bridge, since and including 1938.

Overnight
England 279 – 2 (D.I. Gower 107 not out, G.A. Gooch 70,
M.W. Gatting 53 not out)

England fail to turn the screw

Though Australia's fortunes changed abruptly for the better in the third Cornhill Test at Trent Bridge yesterday, a lengthy and possibly tortuous path still lies ahead of them when they resume today, 362 behind England with nine wickets standing.

A day which began with David Gower going brilliantly on to 166, his highest score against Australia, veered rapidly away from England from the moment that Gatting was unluckily run out as he backed up after a partnership of 187.

From that point, England's last eight wickets disappeared for 98 runs, four of them at one stage while only three were added, and their total of 456, though substantial enough, fell short of what could have been achieved after such an excellent start.

Moreover, the pitch, which tended to look variable in bounce for bowlers of Australia's pace, appeared extremely mild when England were operating, and spin may need to be their main attacking weapon from an early stage today.

The gates were closed before lunch behind a crowd of some 15,000. By then Gatting and Gower, the latter touching rarefied heights of brilliance, had done most of what was necessary to point England towards a huge total.

Or so it seemed at the time. But if Australia were out of luck early on, they had a generous measure of fortune with the dismissal of Gatting, and afterwards it was, as the saying goes, a different game.

Even before the new ball, taken in the 88th over, it was possible to detect a change in the pitch. Perhaps because the surface was drier and possibly crustier, the ball began to go through at various heights and paces, often much quicker than on the first day.

With 300 soon on the board, and viewed through English eyes, this was an encouraging development and did not stop Gower and Gatting making the next 50 from only 10 overs, helped by a certain amount of shortness and width from the bowling.

This especially suited Gower, who fired off stroke after stroke of marvellous certainty and timing, mostly off the back foot, which took him past 150 for the fifth time in his Test career.

Gatting was by no means inactive, but had again embarked on a largely unselfish supporting role when he was cruelly run out as Gower's fierce drive back down the pitch off Holland was deflected by the bowler into the stumps as Gatting backed up.

As often happens, this was the stroke of luck Australia needed. Seven runs later, O'Donnell produced a ball good enough to have Gower caught behind after a stay of almost six and a half hours. He left to a standing ovation in which the Australians joined, little dreaming, I suppose, at the successes that now lay around the corner, even though England had two new batsmen, in Lamb and Botham, beginning at the same time.

In the event, with Lamb quickly

putting away two full tosses from Holland, and Botham punctuating a careful start with some glorious strokes, the next eight overs produced another 47 runs and Australia seemed in for a testing afternoon session.

Lamb, however, then met a ball from Lawson which hardly bounced to have him lbw, and barely had this surprise been digested when Botham unwisely tried to assault the next, from McDermott, and skied a comfortable catch to cover. So much, for the thoughts (or hopes) of chairman May.

In the same over, Downton departed first ball for the second successive innings, brilliantly caught at square leg by Ritchie as he attempted to put away an undistinguished ball off his legs.

AUSTRALIAN VIEWPOINT

Botham makes mockery of chairman's plea

England yesterday produced the type of disappearing act – losing eight wickets for 98 runs in 26 overs – which has been an Australian habit almost exclusively in recent years.

Mike Gatting, run out in the cruellest possible way, and Allan Lamb, leg before to an unusually low ball from Geoff Lawson, were unlucky – Gatting desperately so.

Ian Botham, however, forfeited yet another chance to build a big innings with a half-push, half-lob, half-drive. Whatever it was, it was an awful shot, which characterised much of the wastefulness that marred the second half of England's innings, besides

Sidebottom, astonishingly in his first Test innings, was then caught hooking at Lawson. The days have clearly gone when Yorkshiremen never played this stroke before August, let alone in a Test match.

Emburey batted well, but quickly ran out of support, and soon Lawson, after taking five wickets in a Test innings for the 10th time, was leading Australia in, no doubt several hours earlier than they had imagined.

Though Hilditch and Wood then began with odd moments of uncertainty, Australia looked likely to end the day much more happily than they began it, until, disappointingly for them, Allott won an lbw decision against Hilditch.

making a mockery of David Gower's stated ambition of reaching a total around 600.

Test teams do not get many better chances to 'kill off' opposing sides than England had at Trent Bridge yesterday, and they threw it away in such careless manner that their chairman of selectors, Peter May, might as well have been talking to the wall on Wednesday, when he called for 'more patience'.

On a tortoise-paced pitch, England's 456 still appears sufficient to rule out the possibility of defeat, but not enough to lessen Australia's chances of drawing the match, provided the wicket does not deteriorate unduly.

Lawson deserves the highest praise for carrying the under-manned Australian attack, and being justly rewarded with his 10th five-wickets-in-an-innings haul in 31 Tests. Lawson, with the ball, and Allan Border, with the bat, are a class above the other 15 members of this Australian touring party, and they will need to keep performing if Australia are to keep the Ashes.

In Australia's innings, Graeme Wood, playing for his place in the team, battled through what must have seemed to him one of the longest innings of his 51-match Test career.

Overnight
England 456 (D.I. Gower 166, M.W. Gatting 74, G.A. Gooch 70;
G.F. Lawson 5 – 103)
Australia 94 – 1 (A.M.J. Hilditch 47)

Defiant Wood puts pressure on England

Graeme Wood's unbeaten 152, the merits of which tended to be overshadowed by later events, kept Australia in contention on the third day of the third Cornhill Test at Trent Bridge, and they ended 90 behind England with five wickets standing.

Wood, in some danger of losing his place after a depressing sequence of low scores in the first two Tests, applied himself with great discipline for almost 8½ hours, facing 369 balls, on a day which gathered momentum and, again, had its fair share of incident.

Much of this was crammed into one over in the final session when Botham, allowing the frustrations of the day to get the better of him, was twice cautioned by umpire Whitehead, for excessive short-pitched bowling and for following through onto the pitch.

At this stage, England had taken the second new ball in an attempt to dislodge Wood and the increasingly impressive Ritchie who, joining forces immediately after the possibility of following on had been avoided, had put on 103 together at the close.

England had started the day without the services of Allott (upset stomach), and Sidebottom managed only four deliveries with the new ball, two of which were pulled to the boundary, when he split his left big toe and had to go off.

Gooch completed the over and continued in the attack. England needed two substitutes, Paul Parker of Sussex and Basharat Hassan of Notts – who had gone to the ground to announce his retirement at the end of the season – and then Botham's problems began.

The day had already proved to be one, for England, where the half chances were not going to hand or sticking when they did, and now Botham, having seen Wood edge him close to Gatting at slip, could not hide his disappointment when Ritchie survived a very close lbw appeal.

From the next ball, Edmonds, running in from third man, held a spectacular tumbling catch off Ritchie's slash high over the slips, only to discover – with a chagrin he shared with the bowler – that it had been a no-ball.

The combination of these episodes, plus a genuine attempt to generate pace and life from a pitch which had none, then led to Botham bowling a series of short-pitched deliveries which brought umpire Whitehead's first warning.

Another warning for running on the pitch followed a few balls later, and Gower was obliged to walk over and try to persuade his distinguished all-rounder not to lose sight of the main objective – to bowl straight and to try to take wickets.

One way and another, England had hardly made the most of the new ball, and umpire Whitehead, standing in only his second Test, had emerged from the whole affair with rather more distinction than Botham, playing in his 76th.

This little farrago tended to disguise

how well England's depleted attack had performed hitherto in restricting Australia to less than three runs an over on such a mild pitch. This was due in no small measure to the efforts of Edmonds and Emburey. Edmonds, operating mainly over the wicket in the hope of pitching in the bowlers' footmarks, produced the day's most telling – and controversial – delivery, which accounted for Border at a time when the Australian captain was taking the spinners on in superb fashion.

He had already struck Emburey for a straight six (only his third scoring stroke) and was clearly determined not to let the Middlesex pair dominate, when Edmonds turned a ball sharply out of the rough and on to a pad to be caught by Botham at slip.

Border may have been unlucky with umpire Whitehead's decision (made, of course, on the evidence of the naked eye and without the benefit of a slow-motion replay) that the ball had hit the inside edge, and his departure, after a stunned moment or two, certainly robbed another large crowd of much rich potential entertainment.

However, Border was, I felt, unwise to allow himself later to be drawn into commenting on the standard of umpiring in the series, even though he was at pains to stress that any mistakes had evened themselves out and his remarks were obviously honest and sincere. I doubt whether there has ever been an error-free Test series, but it is only nowadays that the umpires' efforts seem to be the subject of much continuous and often nauseating debate. Maybe, for a change, the umpires should be asked for their thoughts on the players' mistakes!

Border also revealed how close Australia were to leaving out Wood after scores of only 14, 3, 8, and 6 in the first two Tests. Their reward for putting their faith in character rather than form was the best Test innings any Australian had ever seen Wood play.

His bat was passed early on, by both Botham and Sidebottom. The latter, on his first appearance, overcame an understandably nervous start and obtained, from a full length, what little help there was to be had from this pitch, and Holland, the nightwatchman, became his first victim when he was palpably lbw.

Wessells then dropped anchor and was apparently well set for the lengthy innings needed in support of Wood when Emburey had him caught behind off a ball that turned, and after Border had gone, the off-spinner quickly caught-and-bowled Boon.

Emburey, flinging himself full length, was then within a fraction of holding a one-handed return catch offered by Ritchie before he had scored. Encouraged by that and his later fortune against Botham, Ritchie found his touch and was looking extremely at ease by the close.

AUSTRALIAN VIEWPOINT

Father's call rings right note

G raham Wood strode proudly off the Trent Bridge ground on Saturday night, happy for the first time in five weeks, thinking about his father and knowing he had played the innings of his life in the third Test against England.

Wood's 152 runs in an unfinished 8½-hour vigil represented what he and Allan Border, the Australian captain, later described as the finest of his 97 Test innings. It was his eighth century in 51 Tests and his 20th in 144 first class matches.

Wood was watched by his wife, Angela, and their daughter, Brooke 20 months, and said his first thoughts were for his father, Mal, as he walked off.

'I think he would have been up until 1 o'clock Sunday morning in Perth, watching on television,' said the left-hander. 'He's been the driving force behind me. He's been very supportive. I was pretty pleased for him.

'He rang me on Thursday morning and said he didn't think I was watching the ball. I think he was probably right!'

He added: 'That's the most disciplined innings I've played and the straightest I've played. I don't think I've made runs on a wicket like that against two pretty good spinners.'

Wood's resolve was strengthened by his reputation for not going on to a really big score once he had reached 100. The highest of his previous seven Test centuries was 126 against the West Indies in Guyana in 1978.

'I was very conscious of that, and very conscious of the game's situation,' he said. 'If I'd got out soon after 100 I would have let the team down terribly.

'I was very grateful to be picked for this match. I've had a bad month or so (77 runs in his previous eight innings) and had started asking myself if it was all worth it.'

Wood's saving his Test career and another mature innings from Greg Ritchie, a Peter Burge lookalike, were two of the best things to have happened to the Australians on this tour.

While both captains are talking optimistically about their chances of winning, a draw is the most likely result on such a disappointingly slow wicket.

Overnight
England 456
Australia 366 – 5 (G.M. Wood 152 not out, G.M. Ritchie 65 not out,
A.M.J. Hilditch 47)

Australia go ahead by 83 – then rain

Bad light quickly followed by rain curtailed events in the third Cornhill Test at Trent Bridge yesterday at a point when Australia were trying to capitalise on a first innings lead of 83.

Though survival might not have been a serious problem on a slow, if slightly variable pitch, England had much more to lose than gain when Gooch and Robinson quickly accepted the umpire's invitation to go off after making eight from two overs.

The day was, perhaps inevitably, less compelling than many this series has produced, and Australia were made to work hard to reach 539 all out, their highest total in 54 games against England and their biggest in this country since making 656 at Old Trafford in 1964.

This was built around the stalwart efforts of Wood (172) and Ritchie, whose 146 was his highest Test innings, while Botham, beating the bat with some frequency from a full length, and Edmonds sustained England's attack in daunting circumstances.

England had Allott back after illness, but not Sidebottom, for what was potentially another difficult day for them unless an early breakthrough could be contrived on this mild pitch.

In the event, Wood and Ritchie suggested they could go through the first session together, which would have been their initial objective, and Ritchie began by playing some confident strokes off the spinners who started the day together.

Wood attempted less, which made it something of a surprise when, on the appearance of Botham, he was immediately persuaded to pull his first two deliveries, which were nothing more than very short looseners.

The first stroke dropped not far short of Robinson at mid-wicket and the second was caught by him, ending Wood's stay of just over 10 hours. It was also a blow to Australia if their intention was to bat all day.

The value of Botham's success was immediately emphasised when Phillips began with uncharacteristic hesitancy, and he quickly lost his leg stump to Emburey when he overbalanced attempting to sweep.

Ritchie meanwhile had gone on to an admirable century from 212 balls. He continued to time his strokes well, especially off his legs, though the appearance of O'Donnell gave England another surge of encouragement.

He could make nothing of Botham, who, having made great play of putting two men on the boundary, as if in readiness for a bouncer, went past O'Donnell's bat three times in one over with balls of a very full length.

O'Donnell then produced two highly unconvincing species of hook, getting away with both of them, and an uppish stroke through the covers, all off Botham, while at 14 it looked as though Hassan, the sub, might have caught him off Edmonds from a bat-pad chance.

All this meant that the tempo of the batting suited England more than Australia at this stage, but Ritchie offered the bowlers less hope and still reeled off strokes of quality, occasionally managing to give himself room against the spinners.

He was next to go, however, when Edmonds, again operating over the wicket, probably deceived him through the air as he advanced and clipped his off-stump with a ball that turned out of the rough.

By now, O'Donnell had started to make more satisfactory contact, driving straight and playing profitably off his legs, and with Lawson he saw Australia past their previous highest score at Nottingham, 509 by Bradman's 1948 side.

There were now occasional signs that England's concentration was faltering slightly, notably when Lawson, driving at Allott, was dropped

by Robinson in the covers at 18.

Eventually, Botham removed them both with successive deliveries. O'Donnell, hooking, was caught by Downton somewhere near square leg off a top edge and Lawson was then well picked up by Gooch at slip.

England were spared a potentially awkward 20 overs when the light worsened. Not for the first time Border and his colleagues showed, by standing their ground as the batsmen departed, that they felt the umpires had acted hastily.

But the umpires had already conferred about the deteriorating conditions before Lawson unwisely bowled a bouncer, which may have influenced them. In any case, rain was soon falling in the gathering gloom.

AUSTRALIAN VIEWPOINT

'Fat Cat' laps up cream

G reg 'Fat Cat' Ritchie crowned his confirmation as a Test cricketer with a joyous century against England at Trent Bridge.

His second hundred in his 12th Test was, like Graeme Wood's 172, the finest innings of his career, and ensured that Trent Bridge would host its sixth draw in the past nine Tests between England and Australia.

Ritchie, 25, whose sturdy physique and majestic stroke-play is so reminiscent of the former Queensland Test batsman Peter 'Jumbo' Burge, reached his richly deserved century by leg-glancing John Emburey for two.

As he ran along the pitch, Ritchie,

who owns an indoor cricket centre in Queensland, waved his bat jubilantly, smiling broadly and content in the knowledge that he had been largely responsible for Australia's epic fight-back.

Throughout his six-hour day for 146 runs, Ritchie played with a poise and maturity that suggested he had finally sealed a regular place in the Australian team.

His ability had never been questioned, but doubts had been cast over his concentration and application, for he had often thrown away his wicket.

He owes some of his development on this tour to his captain, Allan Border, and a former Australian captain, Ian Chappell, who have talked him into believing in himself and playing more responsibly.

Ritchie's previous Test century was 106 not out against Pakistan at Faisalabad, in October 1982; and yesterday's handsome innings was his third tour century, following his 100 not out against Sussex and 115 against Leicestershire.

Australia's total of 539 was their highest score in England since the 656 for eight declared in the fourth Test at Old Trafford in 1964, when Bob Simpson – then captain – made his first Test century. He finished on 311.

The other occasion in recent memory on which Australia made more than they did yesterday was 543 for eight in Melbourne (1965-66), when Bob Cowper, a left-hander from Victoria, hit 307.

Overnight
England 456 and 8 – 0
Australia 539 (G.M. Wood 172, G.M. Ritchie 146, A.M.J. Hilditch 47, S.P. O'Donnell 46)

Robinson and Gooch ensure quiet finish

The third Cornhill Test moved unspectacularly to a draw at Trent Bridge yesterday, with England making 196 for the loss of Gooch and Gower from 68 overs and mercifully avoiding early lapses, even though Australia – particularly Lawson – bowled well.

As it happened, the quicker bowlers rather than Holland's leg-spin provided what occasional problems there were, mainly through variations in bounce, but Robinson and Gooch played well, and in doing so removed the possibility of an embarrassing struggle for the later batsmen.

They were helped by a delay of 75 minutes following overnight rain, though, afterwards. Lawson ran in perhaps as convincingly as at any time in the series so far, often generating genuine pace with the new ball on this sluggish pitch.

McDermott broke through in the 28th over, however, defeating an attempted hook by Gooch with his extra bounce. Then Gower, whose memorable first innings (166) earned him the Man of the Match award from Tom Graveney, was caught behind driving at a wide one.

Robinson, however, took the opportunity to spend time in the middle. He remained unbeaten with 77, and needed only two moments of luck, early on, with a leading edge that flew to safety and then when a beamer from McDermott hit a finger but inflicted no serious damage.

Now, with the series level at the halfway stage, the selectors have more breathing space than usual to mull over their options before the fourth Test, which starts at Old Trafford on August 1.

Much has been made of their plans to consider potential fast bowling candidates, such as Lawrence of Gloucestershire and Thomas of Glamorgan, though any changes in this department, if based on this game, would have to be made on evidence that was rather inconclusive.

No one could have legislated for Allott's illness, which kept him out of the attack for a day, or the injury to the newcomer, Sidebottom, who, the selectors stress, was fully fit when he reported for duty.

Nor, especially, could any selector's plans for Trent Bridge have anticipated such a slow pitch on which, overall, Edmonds and Emburey – unsurprisingly – were England's most consistent bowlers, with 121 overs between them for 284 runs, an admirable display of craftsmanship.

Something similar may be required from them if Old Trafford is true to character, but the selectors have several questions to answer about current and past members of the seam-bowling section, even before they decide whether to look elsewhere.

Do they, for instance, want another look at Sidebottom, who was not entirely unsuccessful before his injury? If so, and if Foster is fit, what happens to Agnew? He was omitted here because of the pitch's lack of pace which, if that is to be the yardstick, hardly makes him a starter for Manchester.

If the selectors look outside the camp, they may have noted that Dilley, though in and out of the Kent side, has been bowling by all accounts as fast as ever lately; or remember Cowans's past contribution rather than plump for

AUSTRALIAN VIEWPOINT

More 'bite' needed by bowlers

E ngland will and Australia can be expected to reinforce their bowling in an attempt to produce a result in the fourth Test at Old Trafford from August 1.

The drawn third Test, on an inordinately slow Trent Bridge strip, proved what was known at the start of this Ashes series. England need a new fast bowler to inject more hostility into their attack and to ease the burden on Ian Botham, while Australia require a fifth bowler, preferably another spinner, if Old Trafford lives up to its reputation for being a slow turner.

Both teams are stronger in batting than bowling, and more draws are likely in the remaining three Tests if, as expected, the wickets at Old Trafford,

inexperience at this stage.

The batting, I suspect, will remain unchanged, although it is worth recalling that, after being placed at 358 for two on the second day, it was England who finished up as the only side who might have lost.

Edgbaston and the Oval are as sluggish as that at Trent Bridge.

Allan Border, the Australian captain, said last night: 'The wicket was too good for batting to produce a result.'

David Gower, the England captain, said: 'If the batting plays to its full potential on both sides, we are looking at draws.'

Australia will consider including left-arm orthodox spinner Murray Bennett, or off-spinner Greg Matthews, instead of No. 6 batsman David Boon, at Old Trafford.

They are, however, short of match practice – Bennett five for 278 off 111 overs and Matthews 12 for 356 off 102·2 overs – through not having played in the first three Tests and because matches, between the Tests, were interrupted or ruined by rain.

For all his consistency in the county games, Boon will be hard pressed to hold his Test place after having scored only 56 runs in his first five innings of this series.

Result: Match drawn
England 456 and 196 – 2 (R.T. Robinson 77 not out, G.A. Gooch 48)
Australia 539

ENGLAND 1ST INNINGS v. AUSTRALIA (3RD TEST) at TRENT BRIDGE, NOTTINGHAM on 11, 12, 13, 15, 16 JULY, 1985.   TOSS: ENGLAND

IN	OUT	MINS	No.	BATSMAN	HOW OUT	BOWLER	RUNS	WKT	TOTAL	6s	4s	BALLS	NOTES ON DISMISSAL
11.00	3.16	170	1	G.A.GOOCH	c WESSELS	LAWSON	70	2	171	·	12	132	Reflex gully catch off low, firmly hit out.
11.00	12.31	65	2	R.T.ROBINSON	c BORDER	LAWSON	38	1	55	·	6	54	Edged low to 2nd slip - two-handed juggled catch.
12.33	12.57	381	3	D.I.GOWER *	c PHILLIPS	O'DONNELL	166	4	365	·	17	283	60th (1st for 23 mins) Edged steer at lifting ball.
3.18	12.46	245	4	M.W.GATTING	RUN OUT (HOLLAND)		74	3	358	·	9	162	Backing up - bowler deflected Gower drive into stumps.
12.48	2.13	47	5	A.J.LAMB	LBW	LAWSON	17	5	416	·	3	29	Beaten by ball that kept low.
12.59	2.16	39	6	I.T.BOTHAM	c O'DONNELL	McDERMOTT	38	6	416	·	7	35	Leading edge skier to extra-cover - aiming to mid-wicket.
2.15	2.21	6	7	P.R.DOWNTON†	c RITCHIE	McDERMOTT	0	7	419	·	·	·	1st ball - diving left-handed catch at square-leg.
2.18	2.25	7	8	A.SIDEBOTTOM	c O'DONNELL	LAWSON	2	8	419	·	·	8	Hooked short ball to backward square-leg.
2.23	(3.21)	58	9	J.E.EMBUREY	NOT OUT		16			·	2	26	
2.27	3.00	33	10	P.H.EDMONDS	BOWLED	HOLLAND	12	9	443	·	1	31	Bowled behind legs sweeping at full toss.
3.02	3.21	19	11	P.J.W.ALLOTT	c BORDER	LAWSON	7	10	456	·	1	21	Edged low to 2nd slip.
					EXTRAS	b - lb 12 w 1 nb 3	16			6 0 4 57			782 balls (including 4 no balls)
					TOTAL	(129.4 OVERS, 554 MINUTES)	456 all out						456 all out at 3.21 pm on 2nd day.

* CAPTAIN † WICKET-KEEPER

UMPIRES: D.J.CONSTANT A.G.T.WHITEHEAD

© BILL FRINDALL 1985

BOWLER	O	M	R	W	nb	w
LAWSON	39.4	10	103	5	½	
McDERMOTT	35	3	147	2	-/1	
O'DONNELL	29	4	104	1	-	
HOLLAND	26	3	90	1	-	
			12	-		
	129.4	20	456	10		

2nd new ball taken at 11.29 am 2nd day - ENGLAND 288-2 after 87.1 overs.

HRS	OVERS	RUNS
1	13	52
2	14	51
3	15	63
4	16	41
5	16	58
6	13	23
7	12	52
8	14	62
9	13	45

RUNS	MINS	OVERS	LAST 50 (in mins)
50	54	11.5	54
100	114	25.5	60
150	170	39.1	56
200	232	55.5	62
250	280	69.4	48
300	381	91.5	101
350	427	101.0	46
400	469	111.2	42
450	543	127.1	74

LUNCH: 85-1 (21 OVERS) (26 min (6 overs) lost.) GOOCH 17* (94¹) GOWER 23* (27)

TEA: 182-2 (51 OVERS, 215 MINUTES) GOWER 63* (148¹) GATTING 1* (23¹)

STUMPS: 279-2 (80.4 OVERS) (1st DAY - 9.2 OVERS LOST) 331 MINUTES) GOWER 107* (264¹) GATTING 53* (139)

LUNCH: 369-4 (107 OVERS, 453 MINUTES) LAMB 4* (14¹) BOTHAM 4* (3¹)

ENGLAND reached 416-4 before losing 4 WICKETS for 3 RUNS off 11 BALLS in 12 MINUTES.

14 OVERS 0 BALLS/HOUR
3.52 RUNS/OVER
58 RUNS/100 BALLS

WKT	PARTNERSHIP		RUNS	MINS
1st	Gooch	Robinson	55	65
2nd	Gooch	Gower	116	123
3rd	Gower	Gatting	187	245
4th	Gower	Lamb	7	9
5th	Lamb	Botham	51	36
6th	Botham	Downton	0	1
7th	Downton	Sidebottom	3	3
8th	Sidebottom	Emburey	0	2
9th	Emburey	Edmonds	24	33
10th	Emburey	Allott	13	19

456

AUSTRALIA 1ST INNINGS (IN REPLY TO ENGLAND'S 456 ALL OUT)

IN	OUT	MINS	No.	BATSMAN	HOW OUT	BOWLER	RUNS	WKT	TOTAL	6s	4s	BALLS	NOTES ON DISMISSAL
3.42	12.29	599	1	G.M.WOOD	C' ROBINSON	BOTHAM	172	6	424	-	21	448	8th HS in Test. 3000 Runs. 1000 v Eng. Pulled long-hop to mid-wicket.
3.42	5.52	130	2	A.M.J.HILDITCH	LBW	ALLOTT	47	1	87	·	5	89	Beaten on forward stroke by breakback.
5.54	11.39	57	3	R.G.HOLLAND	LBW	SIDEBOTTOM	10	2	128	·	2	41	Missed pull. HS in Tests. Sidebottom's 1st wkt in inns 12th over.
11.41	1.56	95	4	K.C.WESSELS	C' DOWNTON	EMBUREY	33	3	205	·	3	85	Edged forward push at ball that straightened.
1.58	2.15	17	5	A.R.BORDER*	C' BOTHAM	EMBUREY	23	4	234	1	2	18	Edged via pad to slip.
2.17	3.03	46	6	D.C.BOON	C' AND BOWLED	EDMONDS	15	5	263	·	3	47	Deceived by slower flighted ball - waist-high catch.
3.05	3.02	359	7	G.M.RITCHIE	BOWLED	EDMONDS	146	8	491	·	16	308	2nd HS in Tests. Missed drive at leg-break that clipped off stump.
12.31	12.53	22	8	W.B.PHILLIPS†	BOWLED	EMBUREY	2	7	437	·	·	23	Missed sweep and fell over. 'Arm' ball removed leg stump.
12.55	4.30	156	9	S.P.O'DONNELL	C' DOWNTON	BOTHAM	46	9	539	·	6	117	Skied hook - running catch taken at fine leg.
3.04	4.32	68	10	G.F.LAWSON	C' GOOCH	BOTHAM	18	10	539	·	3	50	Edged to slip - Botham's 2nd wicket in successive balls.
4.31	(4.32)	1	11	C.J.McDERMOTT	NOT OUT		0			·	·		
				EXTRAS		b 6 lb 7 w 2 nb 12	27			1	5		1226 balls (including 18 no balls).

TOTAL 539 all out at 4.32 pm on 4th day. (201·2 OVERS, 783 MINUTES).

LEAD: 83

* CAPTAIN   † WICKET-KEEPER

15 OVERS 2 BALLS/HOUR
2·68 RUNS/OVER
44 RUNS/100 BALLS

WKT	PARTNERSHIP		RUNS	MINS
1st	Wood	Hilditch	87	130
2nd	Wood	Holland	41	57
3rd	Wood	Wessels	77	95
4th	Wood	Border	29	17
5th	Wood	Boon	29	46
6th	Wood	Ritchie	161	244
7th	Ritchie	Phillips	13	22
8th	Ritchie	O'Donnell	54	89
9th	O'Donnell	Lawson	48	66
10th	Lawson	McDermott	0	1
			539	

STUMPS: 94-1 (2nd DAY) (362 BEHIND)
LUNCH: 187-2 (35 OVERS)(150 MINUTES) WOOD 38* (156') HOLLAND 4* (18')
TEA: 289-5 (64 OVERS)(270 MINUTES) WOOD 89* (270') WESSELS 26* (79')
STUMPS: 366-5 (3rd DAY)(90 BEHIND) (100 OVERS)(390 MINUTES) WOOD 125* (390') RITCHIE 21* (36')
LUNCH: 440-7 (131 OVERS)(510 MINUTES) WOOD 152* (510') RITCHIE 65* (165')
TEA: 526-8 (162 OVERS)(632 MINUTES) RITCHIE 113* (277') O'DONNELL 2* (7')
(195 OVERS)(752 MINUTES) O'DONNELL 35* (127') LAWSON 17* (31')

AUSTRALIA'S HIGHEST TOTAL AT TRENT BRIDGE

© BILL FRINDALL 1985

BOWLER	O	M	R	W
BOTHAM	34.2	3	107	3
SIDEBOTTOM	18.4	3	65	1
ALLOTT	18	4	55	1
EDMONDS	66	18	155	2
EMBUREY	55	15	129	3
GOOCH	8.2	2	13	0
GATTING	1	0	2	0
	201·2	45	520	10

HRS	OVERS	RUNS
1	12	42
2	15	36
3	14	38
4	13	48
5	19	62
6	18	39
7	15	43
8	16	36
9	19	39
10	14	41
11	14	38
12	17	30
13	15	47

RUNS	MINS	OVERS	LAST 50 (in mins)
50	66	13.5	66
100	161	37.3	95
150	222	50.3	61
200	283	68.2	61
250	338	84.1	55
300	413	104.4	75
350	487	123.2	74
400	562	147.1	75
450	644	165.2	82
500	726	188.0	82

2ND NEW BALL TAKEN at 4.03 pm 3RD day - AUSTRALIA 289-5 after 100 overs.
3RD NEW BALL TAKEN at 3.30 pm 4th day - AUSTRALIA 512-8 after 193 overs.

ENGLAND 2ND INNINGS (83 RUNS BEHIND ON FIRST INNINGS)

IN	OUT	MINS	No.	BATSMAN	HOW OUT	BOWLER	RUNS	WKT	TOTAL	6s	4s	BALLS	NOTES ON DISMISSAL
4·42	2·57	117	1	G.A.GOOCH	c RITCHIE	McDERMOTT	48	1	79	·	6	91	Late on hook - skied simple catch to mid-wicket.
4·42	5·32	272	2	R.T.ROBINSON	NOT OUT		77			·	4	198	Completed 1000 F·C runs for season. HS v AUS by Notts batsman at Trent Bridge.
2·39	3·20	41	3	D.I.GOWER *	c PHILLIPS	McDERMOTT	17	2	107	·	2	33	Edged wait at width offside ball.
3·22	5·32	110	4	M.W.GATTING	NOT OUT		35			·	5	89	
			5										
			6										
			7										
			8										
			9										
			10										
			11										

EXTRAS b 1 lb 16 w - nb 2 = 19

TOTAL (68 OVERS - 272 MINUTES) 196-2

0 6 17 4 411 balls (including 3 no balls)

15 OVERS 0 BALLS/HOUR
2·88 RUNS/OVER
48 RUNS/100 BALLS

* CAPTAIN † WICKET-KEEPER

BOWLER	O	M	R	W	nb
LAWSON	13	4	32	0	
McDERMOTT	16	2	42	2	
HOLLAND	28	9	69	0	
O'DONNELL	10	2	26	0	
RITCHIE	1	0	10	0	·
			17		
	68	17	196	2	

HRS	OVERS	RUNS
1	13	40
2	15	39
3	14	33
4	17	55

RUNS	MINS	OVERS	LAST 50 (in mins)
50	84	17.2	84
100	152	36.3	68
150	217	53.0	65

BAD LIGHT STOPPED PLAY AT 4.55pm - 17.1 OVERS LOST
STUMPS: 8-0 (2.5 OVERS - 13 MIN) GOOCH 4*, ROBINSON 3*
LUNCH: 40-0 (13 OVERS - 60 MINUTES) GOOCH 25*, ROBINSON 11*
TEA: 112-2 (42 OVERS - 180 MINUTES) ROBINSON 35* (186'), GATTING 4* (18')

MATCH DRAWN
MAN OF THE MATCH: D.I.GOWER
(Adjudicator: T.W.GRAVENEY)

WKT	PARTNERSHIP		RUNS	MINS
1st	Gooch	Robinson	79	117
2nd	Robinson	Gower	28	41
3rd	Robinson	Gatting	89*	110
			196	

© BILL FRINDALL 1985

1ST DAY	BOWLERS (D.J. Constant) PAVILION END		(A.G.T. Whitehead) RADCLIFFE RD END		BATSMEN SCOREBOARD LEFT			SCOREBOARD RIGHT			ENGLAND 1ST INNINGS NOTES	END-OF-OVER TOTALS					
TIME	BOWLER	O.	BOWLER	O.	SCORING	BALLS	6S/4S	SCORING	BALLS	6S/4S		O.	RUNS	W.	'L' BAT	'R' BAT	EXTRAS
					GOOCH			ROBINSON			Heavy cloud - humid						
11.00			LAWSON	1	∶∶∶∶∶	6					M1	1					
05	McDERMOTT	1						x∶∶∶6∶2∶	6			2	2			2	
09	—·—			2	∶∶7∶∶·0·	13					(NB) NB1	3	3				1
14	—·—	2						17 9/74/54/57 4·∶241	12	2	† Umpires discussed light.	4	14			13	
18			—·—	3				∶∶∶∶175	18			5	15			14	
23	—·—	3			∶4∶∶	17	1	67 21	20		Gooch 26' on 0. † Good stop - Ritchie	6	22		4	17	
28			—·—	4				∶3 4↑8/7 ∶·4	26	3		7	26			21	
33	—·—	4			2LB 68 61 8F ∶·4·4	23	3				(2LB) † Ritchie diving stop.	8	36		12		3
37			—·—	5				3/2·3 ↑18↑ 4·4·4	32	6		9	48			33	
42	O'DONNELL	1			7½↑	25		∶∶6P∶	36		† Holland misfielded	10	49		13		
46			—·—	6	∶∶∶∶↑¹	31					M2 † Umpires discussed light.	11					
51	—·—	2			P↑	32		4∶∶∶8	41		50 p'ship: 54 min. † Light discussed.	12	50			34	
55			—·—	7		32	3	∶↑	42	6	† Umpires conferred	12'	50	0	13	34	3
11.56	BAD LIGHT										WELLHAM sub for HILDITCH	B	L		S	P	
12.22			LAWSON	7	↑7 ↑∶	34		∶·0·47 ∶·0·①	47		(NB) NB3 1HR	13	52			35	4
26½	O'DONNELL	3			·6	35		8/7 ∶∶∶7 ∶2∶∶1	52			14	55			38	
30			—·—	8	⌐			E1 _W	54	6		14²	55	1	13	38	4
31			·		⌐			GOWER		LHB						0	
33			—·—	8	⌐			xx27	4		M3	15					
36	—·—	4			x∶8 ∶∶1	38		83 24	7	1		16	62		14	6	
40			—·—	9	9 ∶∶EP8	42		7 ∶34	9	2		17	69		16	11	
44	—·—	5			9 ∶	43		2LB 28/73 ∶·24∶	14	3	(2LB)	18	78		17	17	6
48½			—·—	10	↑∶PP↑∶	49					M4	19					
52½	—·—	6			∶∶77	52		∶8LB ∶2∶	17		(LB)	20	81			19	7
57			—·—	11		52	3	2 5/4↑ ∶22↑∶∶∶	23	3	† Lawson fell.	21	85	1	17	23	7
1.00	LUNCH										M4 NB3	L	U	N	C	H	
1.40	O'DONNELL	7			9 ∶	53		4∶∶∶∶	28		Hilditch back.	22	86		18		
44½			McDERMOTT	5	∶∶4½∶4 ∶∶4	59	4					23	90		22		
48	—·—	8						4∶∶∶x∶4 4	34	4		24	94			27	
52			—·—	6	63 ∶0∶ ∶55 ∶4	66					(NB) NB4	25	95				8
57	—·—	9			4∶8/9 ∶2∶∶	70	5	63 ∶1	36			26	100		26	28	
2.01			—·—	7	↑ 7F6 6 ∶2∶∶	75		LB	37		(LB) 2HR	27	103		28		9
05	—·—	10						∶∶4 18 5∶	43		† Just chest of 2nd slip. M5	28					
08½			—·—	8	7F 6 R6 8 4·21	79	6	G9/8	45		50 p'ship: 56'	29	111		35	29	
13	—·—	11						28 64·4 ∶2∶∶	51			30	113			31	
16½			—·—	9	267 Y6F 7 ∶∶2∶	85						31	115		37		
21	—·—	12			5↑	87		2 3 7E ·421	55	5	† stumps hit - Ro appeal.	32	122			38	
25			—·—	10	4·↑F4F 9 ∶4∶∶	92	7	7 ∶1	56		† Beamer. Gooch fell.	33	128		42	39	
29½	—·—	13			6 5·↑ ∶4∶∶	98	8		56	5	M5 NB4	34	132	1	46	39	9

1st DAY TIME	BOWLERS (D.J. CONSTANT) PAVILION END BOWLER	O.	(A.G.T. WHITEHEAD) RADCLIFFE Rᵈ END BOWLER	O.	BATSMEN SCOREBOARD LEFT SCORING	BALLS	6s/4s	SCOREBOARD RIGHT SCORING	BALLS	6s/4s	NOTES	O.	RUNS	W.	'L' BAT	'R' BAT	EXTRAS
					GOOCH	98	8	GOWER	56	5	M5 NB4	34	132	1	46	39	9
2·34			LAWSON	12				·:··:237	62		M6	35					
38	O'DONNELL	14			:8/9 ↑4↑8 :·4	103	9	2	63		GOOCH'S 50: 156'	36	138		51	40	
43			- · -	13	8/ 7	105		11 33 ·3	67			37	144		53	44	
48	HOLLAND	1			4 4/8 ::·	110		6	68			38	146		54	45	
51			- · -	14	↑↑ 4·8	114		:7	70		(LB)	39	148			46	10
55	- · -	2			6F 5(4) ·F· 8 44 ·:2	120	11				loo p'ship: 98 min	40	158		64		
59			- · -	15	6/7 :· 84	124		↑· 8/9	72		† Umpires discussed light.	41	161		66	47	
3·04	- · -	3			:·6 4	126	12	·: 6 8	76		3HR	42	166		70	48	
07			- · -	16	↑	127		x ·48	81			43	167			49	
11	- · -	4			:·:	130		:·6 3 ·3	84		GOWER'S 50: 119'	44	170			52	
14			- · -	17	4 2 :·W	132	12	:↑	85			44³	171	2	70	53	10
16					GATTING											0	
18			- · -	17	4(6·:	3						45					
20	- · -	5						3 1/4F ··P7 ·4	91	6		46	176			58	
23			- · -	18	:··:↑	7		9/6 44 21	93			47	179			61	
28	- · -	6				8		·P 6 :·7	98			48	180			62	
31			- · -	19				3 8 ··x·	104		M7	49					
35½	- · -	7			44 ·:P↑	14					M8	50					
37½			- · -	20	:↑6	16	-	4··: 3 ·1	108	6		51	182	2	1	63	10
3·41 TEA											M8 NB4				T E A		
4·00	HOLLAND	8			4·: 2 ::·	22					WELLHAM Sub (LAWSON) (2 overs)	52	184		3		
03			McDERMOTT	11	2 4	23	1	::·4 :2 ·1	113			53	189		7	64	
07½	- · -	9			6 3 ·1	25		·6F8 21	117			54	193		8	67	
11			- · -	12	:::·8 3	29		2↑ 2·1	119		† Diving stop (Lawson) on boundary.	55	198		11	69	
15	- · -	10			:4F ·9F :·1	33		7· 2:	121			56	201		12	71	
18			- · -	13	6·:48 :·4	39	2					57	205		16		
22	- · -	11						↑7 3 ·PP 2·:	127		† Round wkt to LHB 4HR	58	207			73	
24			- · -	14	349 ·1	42		8 x 4·:	130	7		59	212		17	77	
28	- · -	12			9/6 ·:8/74 1 :·2	47		6	131			60	216		20	78	
31			- · -	15				776 ··↑ 4	137	8		61	220			82	
35	- · -	13			:·4 :·6	51		:·6	139		50 p'ship: 58'min	62	222		21	83	
37½			- · -	16	:5(6) ·3	53		3/9 3·8/7 1 ·3	143			63	229		24	87	
41½	- · -	14			9 3↑ ·1	55		:2 8 6 ·1	147		† Diving stop (Ritchie)	64	233		26	89	
45			- · -	17	3·:·8 1	59		·F·	149			65	234		27		
49	O'DONNELL	15			7764 2 44·1	65	4					66	242		35		
54			HOLLAND	15	3 ·3	66		6·:4 :·1	154			67	246		38	90	
57	- · -	16			:34 x:·	72					M9	68					
5·00			- · -	16	::	74		:::·8 1	158			69	247			91	
04	- · -	17			↑ ·:4	76	5	:4 32 ·21	162	8	M9 NB4	70	254	2	42	94	10

107

TIME	BOWLER (Pavilion End)	O.	BOWLER (Radcliffe Rd End)	O.	SCORING (Left)	BALLS	6s/4s	SCORING (Right)	BALLS	6s/4s	NOTES	O.	RUNS	W.	L BAT	R BAT	EXTRAS
					GATTING	76	5	GOWER	162	8	M9 NB4	70	254	2	42	94	10
5·08			HOLLAND	17	st::	79		6 6 2/3 .41	165	9	†Removed border's off and middle stump	71	259			99	
13	O'DONNELL	18						†.8.454 .2	171		†Round wkt to LHB WELLHAM sub(HILDITCH)	72	261			101	
18			LAWSON	21	:.4::	85	6				GOWER'S 100: 222'	73	265		46		
23	–·–	19						.P st.33	177		†Stumps hit run bowler M10 5HR	74					
26			–·–	22	7 1	86		.:..	182			75	266		47		
31	–·–	20			:5 x2 .1	91		:	183			76	267		48		
35			–·–	23	:.LB	93		x:11	187		(LB) M11	77	268				11
39	–·–	21			3.:7. 4:::.	99	7				GATTING 50 and 100 p'ship in 123'	78	272		52		
44			–·–	24				85.† 2..1x	193		GOWER 81 on 101	79	274			103	
48½	McDERMOTT	18			728 :.1	103		.6 .1	195			80	276		53	104	
53			–·–	25	:3↑.1	106	7	8.3	196	9		80⁴	279	2	53	107	11
5·56	BAD LIGHT										M11 NB4	BLSP					
6·10	PLAY ABANDONED										9·2 OVERS LOST	STUMPS					
2nd DAY 11·00			LAWSON	25	::	108						81	279	2	53	107	11
02	O'DONNELL	22			P3.3	112		:1† .1	198			82	280			108	
06½			–·–	26	†3† .21	117		LB	199		(LB) †Record E 3rd wkt v A at N'ham	83	283		55		12
11	–·–	23						.:.4	205	10		84	287			112	
15			–·–	27	.:†3	123					M12	85					
20	McDERMOTT	19						6.6.†	211		M13	86					
24½			–·–	28	6s 1	124		:.4.	216		6HR	87	288		56		
29	–·–	20			†...†	130					†NEW BALL M14	88					
33			–·–	29	6.1 4:..	135	8	8.3	217			89	295		60	115	
37	–·–	21						x..L	223		M15	90					
41½			–·–	30	..x .1 7s	141						91	296		61		
46	–·–	22			3s† †	143		:..8 .3	227		†Wood collided with O'Donnell	92	300		62	118	
51			–·–	31				:..† †	233		M16	93					
56	–·–	23			x P4 L 37 .1	148		2 .1	234		†2LB disallowed	94	302		63	119	
12·01			–·–	32	::†8† 4:.	153	9	877 1	235		Repairs to McDermott's boot (1 min)	95	307		67	120	
07	–·–	24			4/8 1	154		6.2/F.16 .2.3	240		†McDermott warned – pitch damage	96	316		68	128	
12			–·–	33				.:4:4† .1	246	11	(W) '150 p'ship: 215'	97	321			132	13
17½	–·–	25			3 8 1	156		:1/42 .41	250	12		98	329		70	138	
22			–·–	34				2 x L 74 .4..43	256	14	7HR	99	340			149	
27	–···	26						33.3† .4.1	262	15	GOWER'S 150: 352'	100	344			153	
32			O'DONNELL	24	9E† 2 .1	158		5 .24 .4	266	16	†Almost bowled	101	351		72	158	
36	–·–	27			6 1	159		P.5(6).4	271	17		102	356		73	162	
41			–·–	25	8 1 :L 1	162		3.7 .1	274			103	358		74	163	
45	HOLLAND	18 7			R0	162	9	3 5	276	17		103²	358	3	74	163	13
46					LAMB	.	–				MATTHEWS sub for LAWSON (1·4 overs)				0		
48	–·–	18						.:.:	280	17	M17 NB4	104	358	3	0	163	13

108

2ND DAY TIME	BOWLERS (CONSTANT) PAVILION END BOWLER	O.	(WHITEHEAD) RADCLIFFE R⁰ END BOWLER	O.	BATSMEN SCOREBOARD LEFT SCORING	BALLS	6⁵/4⁵	SCOREBOARD RIGHT SCORING	BALLS	6⁵/4⁵	ENGLAND 1ST INNINGS NOTES	O.	RUNS	W.	'L' BAT	'R' BAT	EXTRAS
					LAMB	-	-	GOWER	280	17	M17 NB4	104	358	3	0	163	13
12.50			O'DONNELL	26	x : : . . . :	6					M18	105					
54	HOLLAND	19			6 4 : : : :	11	1	²/³⁵	281			106	363		4	164	
56½			– • –	27				2 1E 2 W	283	17		106	365	4	4	166	13
57								BOTHAM							0		
59			• • –	27		11	1	½ 4 : . .	4	1		107	369	4	4	4	13
1.02	LUNCH										M18 NB4		L U	N	C H		
1.40	HOLLAND	20			6F S 47 . 6 4 · 4 : 1	16	3	. 6 1	5		MATTHEWS sub for McDermott (3 overs)	108	379		13	5	
43			O'DONNELL	28	. :	18		6 · 6 3 4 : : 1	9	2		109	384			10	
47/48	– • –	21			: : : : ⁵ᵗ ½ : 4	15	3				Lamb's bat repairs. + stumps hit.	110	388			14	
51			– • –	29	: 6 1	20		: 3 RH9 P 42 : 1	19	4		111	395		14	20	
55	– • –	22			8 1 S6) . 7	24		7 4 41	21	5		112	401		15	25	
58			LAWSON	35	? 1	25		. P X ²/³⁵	26		8HR	113	402			26	
2.05	McDERMOTT	28			7 1	26		: 1 · 2 B/7 2 : 1 4	31	6		114	410		16	33	
09			– • –	36	7 1 : W	29	3	EP 6⁷ 2 . 41	34	7	1 Holland misfielded 50 p'ship: 34 min.	115	416	5	17	38	13
13					DOWNTON									0			
15	– • –	29						4 W	35	7		115	416	6	0	38	13
16								SIDEBOTTOM						0			
18	– • –	29			⁷/⁸ W	1	-	P : 1E 1B 2 .	4		(LB)	116	419	7	0	2	14
21					EMBUREY									0			
23			– • –	37				: . L P ⁶⁸ W	8	-		116	419	8	0	2	14
25								EDMONDS			Matthews sub for Hildich (2.2 overs)			0			
27			– • –	37				L :	2		M19	117					
29	– • –	30			³ †EP . 4 4 : : . . 1	6	1				+ hit on shoulder.	118	423		4		
33			– • –	38	:	7		3 · 1 G 2 : 1	7			119	426		3		
38	– • –	31						· 8 2LB · 3 : . . 2	13		(2LB)	120	430		5	16	
42			– • –	39	3 2 : ³ 2 : 1	11		. :	15			121	433		7		
47	– • –	32			: X X ² 1 · 1	15		: .	17			122	434		8		
51			HOLLAND	23	P ⁸ 1	17		9⁶ · 3 6 2 : . .	21			123	437		9	7	
54½	– • –	33			¹/⁹	18		x : : : 7 : : 1	26			124	439		10	8	
59			– • –	24				: ³ · X X 4 : W	31	1		124	443	9	10	12	16
3.00								ALLOTT						0			
02			– • –	24				·	1			125					
03			– • –	34	3 1 :	20		: X E3⁹/⁶ · 3	5		9HR	126	447		11	3	
06			– • –	25				· 6 2 : : · .	11		M20	127					
10	– • –	35			4⁷ 3 41 : EP	24	2	9/6 3 21	13			128	455		16	6	
15			– • –	26	EP 3 . :	26		2 : 4 . . 1	17			129	456			7	
18	LAWSON	40				26	2	: X E1 · W	21	-		129	456	10	16	7	16
3.21	ALL OUT										M20 NB4		A L	L	O U T		
	TEA										782 balls			T E A			

2ND DAY TIME	BOWLERS (CONSTANT) PAVILION END BOWLER	O.	(WHITEHEAD) RADCLIFFE RD END BOWLER	O.	BATSMEN SCOREBOARD LEFT SCORING	BALLS	6s/4s	SCOREBOARD RIGHT SCORING	BALLS	6s/4s	AUSTRALIA 1ST INNINGS NOTES	END-OF-OVER TOTALS O.	RUNS	W.	L BAT	R BAT	EXTRAS
					WOOD		LHB	HILDITCH									
3·42			BOTHAM	1	x↑ E1 ↑6 ··	6					M1	1					
46½	SIDEBOTTOM	1			· · ·*↑	10		9 8 4 1	2	1	↑Appeal ct wk.	2	5			5	
51			— · —	2	8 1	11		· ↑ 2 · ·9 1 · X	7			3	8		1	7	
55	ALLOTT	1						3 · · · · P 4 · · · ·	13	2		4	12			11	
4·01			SIDEBOTTOM	2	E · 2 1 6·· 1	14		9E · · 2 ⊙4 ·· 2	18	3	NB NB NB 2	5	21		2	17	2
07	BOTHAM	3			2 ↑ 9 · · 1	17		8/6 2 2 ·	21			6	26		3	21	
13			— · —	3	L · 2 ⊙ 1 · 1	22		P ↑9 · 1	23		NB NB 3	7	30		5	22	3
17	— · —	4			· 1 · 8 · 1	26		· ·	25			8	31		6		
22			— · —	4	· 1 · 2 · 4 1 ⊙ ·	33		7 ③	26		NB NB 5	9	36		7	25	4
27	— · —	5			·	34		3 · · · · 7 1	31			10	37			26	
31			— · —	5				X · · · · 1	37		M2	11					
35	— · —	6			7 · 1	36		7/8↑ 4 · 1	41	4	1 HR	12	42		8	30	
40			— · —	6	8 · 6 1 · ⊙ 1	41		· 7 · 1	43		NB NB 6	13	45		9	31	5
44	— · —	7			· ↑8 ↑ · 4 ·	44	1	· 7/8 2 · 2 1	46		↑Round wkt. 50 p/ship: 66 min	14	52		13	34	
49			— · —	7	· · · 3 · ·	49		3 · 1	47			15	53			35	
53	— · —	8			·	50		6 · · 4 · · · 3	52			16	56			38	
57			EDMONDS	1				· P 1 8 P 3 · 4 2 ·	58	5		17	62			44	
5·03	ALLOTT	2			3 L · · · · 1	56					M3	18					
08	·		— · —	2				· · P · · 2 · 1	64		Round wkt to RHB. M4	19					
11	— · —	3			· X 1 1	59		· 7 · 2 ·	67			20	65		14	46	
16			— · —	3	· · · X L P 1	65					M5	21					
19	— · —	4						· · 2 · · · 1	73		M6	22					
23			— · —	4	· · · · 3 8 · 2 1	71						23	68		17		
26	— · —	5			↑ P · 4 · 9 · 4 · 2	77	2				↑ Edmonds Bo att caught (sh. Leg).	24	74		23		
31			— · —	5				8 E P↑ 4 · · · 1	79		↑ nr sh. leg. M7	25					
34	— · —	6			· · · 2 7 · 4 ·	83	3					26	78		27		
38			— · —	6				· · · · 1 1	85		M8 2 HR	27					
41	— · —	7			· · 4 ↑2 1 · 2 · 1	89					↑ Round wkt.	28	81		30		
46			— · —	7	P⊙ P · P 8/6 · 4	95	4					29	85		34		
49	— · —	8	⎰		8 1	96		· 8 · L 1 · W	89	5		29⁵	87	1	35	47	5
5·52			⎱					HOLLAND								0	
54	— · —	8	⎰					Y· 1	1			30					
55			— · —	8	4 1	97		· · · P · P 1	6			31	88		36		
59	— · —	9			E2 3 · 1	99		· · ↑↑ 1	10			32	89		37		
6·03			— · —	9	· L · P · · 1	105					M9	33					
06	EMBUREY	1						4 · 4 P · · 4 1	16	1		34	93			4	
09			— · —	10	P X P P↑ · 8 · · · · · 1	111	4		16	1	↑ Round wkt	35	94	1	38	4	5
6·12	STUMPS										M9 NB 6		S T U M P S				

3RD DAY TIME	BOWLERS (CONSTANT) PAVILION END	O.	(WHITEHEAD) RADCLIFFE END	O.	BATSMEN SCOREBOARD LEFT SCORING	BALLS	6s/4s	SCOREBOARD RIGHT SCORING	BALLS	6s/4s	NOTES	O.	RUNS	W.	'L' BAT	'R' BAT	EXTRAS
					WOOD	111	4	HOLLAND	16	1	M 9 NB 6	35	94	1	38	4	5
11.00	SIDEBOTTOM	8			.•8	113		P × : :	20		GATES CLOSED. PNG PARKER sub	36	95		39		
05			BOTHAM	9	3/1	114		: : : × :	25		for ALLOTT (upset stomach)(3 overs)	37	96		40		
09	– • –	9			: L 3 1/6 L × 9 :	121	6				(NB) NB 7	38	105		48		6
14			– • –	10	17 47 ④ 2 • + :	126	7	: • 4	27		WOOD'S 50: 166 min. (W) NB 8	39	113		54	5	7
20	– • –	10			8 ①	127		8 . 3 . 3 : 1	33		NB 9	40	115		55	6	
24½			– • –	11	1 : . ⊙ : 3	134					(NB) NB 10 3HR	41	116				8
30	– • –	11						× 61 • : 4 : : : :	39	2	• Low chance to 2nd slip (BOTHAM)	42	120			10	
33			– • –	12	× : : . . 8/9 3 4 ④	141	9				NB 11	43	128		63		
38	– • –	12						× L : W	41	2		43³	128	1	63	10	8
39								WESSELS		LHB						0	
41	– • –	12			: . • 248	143		: 7 1	2		(4LB)	44	133		1	12	
45			– • –	13				: : L . × EP7 1	8			45	134		2		
49	– • –	13						P 3 : : : P EP	14		M 10	46					
53			– • –	14	: : 1 : 3 1 : . : 1	149					† Round wkt. M 11	47					
58	– • –	14			P . .	152		: : 961 :	17		† Almost played on.	48	135			3	
12.03			EDMONDS	11	4	153	10	: : 3 7 4 2 2 3	22		† via sh leg's helmet	49	146		67	10	
08	– • –	15						: : P 4 2 P	28		M 12	50					
12			– • –	12	P : 4 : P :	159	11					51	150		71		
14 16	– • –	16			: 1 3 : 20 . 1	164		4 1 :	30		B.HASSAN sub for ALLOTT. (NB) NB12	52	155		74	11	13
22			– • –	13	4 2 : 4 . 4 : 1	169	12	8 1	31			53	161		79	12	
25	– • –	17						: : 2 ⊙ : P P :	38		(NB) NB 13 4HR	54	164		14	14	
30			– • –	14	: : : P .	175					M 13	55					
32	– • –	18			⊙ : : 3	179		2 8 7 • 2 1	41		(NB) NB14	56	168		17	15	
37			– • –	15	: 1 2 : 182	182		7 3 : 2 1	44			57	175		82	21	
41	EMBUREY	2			: : : : :	187		9 1	45		Round wkt	58	176			22	
45			– • –	16				: : L . . 6	51		M 14	59					
47	– • –	3			: : : : :	193					M 15	60					
49½			– • –	17	3 1 : 3	195		: 2 : 7	55		50 p'ship: 71 min	61	180		85	23	
52	– • –	4			3 : : : : 4	201	13					62	184		89		
55			– • –	18	4	202		7† : × 1E 3	60		† Stopped (HASSAN) sh.leg.	63	187			26	
57½	– • –	5					13	P : : : P	66	–	M 16 NB 14	64	187	2	89	26	15
1.00	LUNCH													L U N C H		
1.40			EDMONDS	19	2 4 4 1	204	14	: : : :	70		HASSAN sub (ALLOTT)	65	192		94		
43½	EMBUREY	6			4 9E1 . 4 2 : : :	210	15				WOOD'S (8) : 275'	66	198		100		
47			– • –	20				: 2 . 8	76		M 17	67					
50	– • –	7			2 : P : : :	216					M 18	68					
52			– • –	21	:	217		× 3 9 × 9 4 2 . 1	81	1		69	205		33		
55	– • –	8				217	15	: 2 : 81 . . W	85	1	M 18 NB 14	69⁴	205	3	100	33	15
56																	

111

3RD DAY TIME	BOWLERS (CONSTANT) PAVILION END BOWLER	O.	(WHITEHEAD) RADCLIFFE RD END BOWLER	O.	BATSMEN SCOREBOARD LEFT SCORING	BALLS	6s/4s	SCOREBOARD RIGHT SCORING	BALLS	6s/4s	AUSTRALIA 1ST INNINGS NOTES	O.	RUNS	W.	'L' BAT	'R' BAT	EXTRAS
					WOOD	217	15	BORDER	-	LHB	M18 NB14	69⁴	205	3	100	0	15
1·58	EMBUREY	8						··	2		M19	70					
2·00			EDMONDS	22	8 · ·3 P 1	222		6	3			71	207		101		1
03	- · -	9						9E ·44)9E 8 8 2 · 64 · 1	9	1/1		72	220			14	
07			- · -	23	3 · 1	223		2 x 3 23/9 2 · · 2 1	14		5HR	73	226		102	19	
10	- · -	10			· P 4 · 1	226		· 67 ·4	17	1/2		74	231		103	23	
14			- · -	24	94 2 1	228		EP W	18	1/2		74³	234	4	106	23	15
15½								BOON								0	
17½			- · -	24.				···	3			75					
19	- · -	11			8 · 1	232		· 8	5			76	236		107	1	
22			- · -	25				·· ···	11		· Between slips M20	77					
26	- · -	12			· 8 · 1	234		6 6 Pf ·	15		† Appeal at sh leg (2nd)	78	237		108		
28½			- · -	26	· P ··· 1	240					M21	79					
31	- · -	13			· 1	241		···· 63	20			80	238			2	
34			- · -	27				··· 7 ·4 · 1	26	1		81	242			6	
37	- · -	14			4 · P 3 · · 3	245		··	28			82	245		111		
39½			- · -	28	3 · ·· 9E 1	250		·	29			83	246		112		
42½ 45½	DRINKS - · -	15			· 8 ··· 9 · 2	256						84	248		114		
48			- · -	29				4 · P P P ·	35	2		85	252			10	
51	- · -	16			·4 · 1	258		····	39			86	253		115		
54			- · -	30	··· · 8/9	263		·	40			87	254		116		
57	- · -	17			···· 3 4·	269	16				WOOD 3000 in TESTS	88	258		120		
59			- · -	31	··	271		·· 2/9 4 1	44	3		89	263			15	
3·02	- · -	18						6· 5 W	47	3		89³	263	5	120	15	15
03								RITCHIE								0	
05	- · -	18						5· · ·	3		· Low c+b chance M22	90					
08			- · -	32	½P · · P 2 ··· 1	277					6HR	91	265		122		
11	- · -	19						· 3 6† · · 7 · 2 · · 1	9		† Emburey dropped ball	92	268			3	
15			- · -	33	5 · · 3 1	281		·7 3 2	11			93	271			6	
18	- · -	20			·· x	283		4 · 4 8 · 4 · 1	15	1		94	276			11	
21			- · -	34				7 1E P 2 P 4 · · · · · · ·	21		M23	95					
24	- · -	21			·· 75 · 1	286		· · 8	24			96	278		123	12	
27			- · -	35				P P P 7 2 7 · · · · ·	30	2		97	282			16	
30	- · -	22			75 · 1	287		··· P P 8 · 1	35			98	284		124	17	
33			- · -	36	·· 6 P 290	290		9E 9E 2 · 1	38			99	287			20	
37	- · -	23			3 · 1	291	16	··· 5 8 4 · 1	43	2		100	289	5	125	21	15
3·40	TEA										M23 NB14			T	E	A	
4·02			BOTHAM	15	1E1 x † 1 · · · 1	295		· ½	45		· Dropped Gatting (1st slip). † 1 NEW BALL	101	291		126	22	
06	SIDEBOTTOM	19						7 3 · 6 4 · · 4	49	4	· Sidebottom foot	101⁴	299			30	
14	GOOCH	1			·	295	16	·· · 1	51	4	† Jarvis · PARKER sub. M23 NB14	102	299	5	126	30	15

3RD DAY TIME	BOWLERS (CONSTANT) PAVILION END BOWLER	O.	(WHITEHEAD) RADCLIFFE RD END BOWLER	O.	BATSMEN SCOREBOARD LEFT SCORING	BALLS	6s/4s	SCOREBOARD RIGHT SCORING	BALLS	6s/4s	AUSTRALIA 1ST INNINGS NOTES	END-OF-OVER TOTALS O.	RUNS	W.	L BAT	R BAT	EXTRAS
					WOOD	295	16	RITCHIE	51	4	M 23 NB 14	102	299	5	126	30	15
4.15			BOTHAM	16	.9...4	301					M 24	103					
19	GOOCH	2						4 P 4t P	57		† Diving stop (HASSEN) M25	104					
23	- . -		- . -	17	:: 1t	304		4t7 8 3 4 2 1	60	5	† wood's H.S in Tests ‡ Round wkt.	105	307		127	37	
28	- . -	3						7 P .. 2	66		7 HR	106	308			38	
31			- . -	18	tt9	305		2 L 9/8 3 .	71		† Round wkt.	107	310		128	39	
35	- . -	4			V2 P	307		: 4 : 75 . : 1	75		50 p'ship: 74 min (NB) NB 16	108	312		129	40	
40			- . -	19	⊙4.:.t	313	17	4tH ⊙	77		• Rolling catch-dure on run (EDMONDS).	109	318		133	41	16
46	- . -	5						:: 4 5(4) 2 :.	83		† BOTHAM hurt + led - pitch damage.	110	320			43	
51			- . -	20	7 1	314		3 . : 7 t18 : ⊙ : . :	89		† Intimidation. (NB) (LB) NB 17	111	323		134		18
56	- . -	6						L 4 5 6 . 9 1	95			112	324			44	
5.00			EMBUREY	24	t:	315		P : : : 6	100		† Round wkt to LHB.	113	325			45	
05	- . -	7						: : : 6	106		M 26	114					
08			- . -	25	: : : . 4 8 56) . 4	321	18					115	329		138		
11	- . -	8						: 7 3 . 7 7 . 4	112	6		116	333			49	
14			- . -	26	. : : : .	327					M 27	117					
17	EDMONDS	37			:	328		: 6 . 8 : : 1	117		Round wkt to RHB RITCHIE'S 50: 112'	118	334			50	
21½			- . -	27	: 6 : 2	330		: : 3 9 : 4 1	121	7		119	341		140	55	
25	- . -	38			L :	332		4 : : 8 : 1	125			120	342			56	
28			- . -	28	: x 6P) :	337		8 1	126			121	343			57	
31	- . -	39			5	338		t: : . 7 1	131		8 HR	122	344			58	
34			- . -	29	P . : 3B	341		8 ::	134		(3B)	123	348			59	21
38	- . -	40			: 5(4) P : 4 2 : .	347	19					124	354		146		
41			- . -	30	: : .	350		: P 9 : 3	137			125	357			62	
44	- . -	41			: L . : P	354		: 7	139			126	358			63	
47			- . -	31				: P . P	145		M 28	127					
50	GOOCH	9			: 8/9 : 1 : 1	358		L 8 : 1	147			128	361		148	64	
54			EDMONDS	42	: 4 . x : P	364	20				WOOD's 150: 503: 100 n'ship: 147 min.	129	365		152		
56½	EMBUREY	32			: : : 5	368		16 8 . 1	149			130	366			65	
59½			- . -	43		368	20	7 Pt . . L:	155	7	† Round wkt. M 29 NB 17	131	366	5	152	65	21
6.02	STUMPS										HASSAN sub (SIDEBOTTOM)		S T U M P S				
4TH DAY 11.00	EMBUREY	33			: x . . 5 .	374					Round wkt to LHB M 30	132					
03			EDMONDS	44	:	375		4 4/5 6 . 8 : 4 . : 1	160	8	Round wkt to RHB.	133	371			70	
07	- . -	34						: : : : : . P	166		M 31	134					
10			- . -	45	: P 3 P	381					M 32	135					
12	- . -	35						6 . 7 . : :	172		M 33	136					
15			- . -	46	: : : . 3	386		3 4	173	9		137	376		153	74	
18	- . -	36			3 . P . P 4	392	21					138	380		157		
21			- . -	47				7 6t P . : : 2	179		† Mishit - no mid-on	139	382			76	
24	- . -	37			. : : : . 8	398	21		179	9	M 34 NB 17	140	382	5	157	76	21

4th DAY TIME	BOWLERS (CONSTANT) PAVILION END BOWLER	O.	(WHITEHEAD) RADCLIFFE END BOWLER	O.	BATSMEN SCOREBOARD LEFT SCORING	BALLS	6/4	SCOREBOARD RIGHT SCORING	BALLS	6/4	AUSTRALIA 1st INNINGS NOTES	O.	RUNS	W.	'L' BAT	'R' BAT	EXTRAS
					WOOD	398	21	RITCHIE	179	9	M34 NB17	140	382	5	157	76	21
11·27			EDMONDS	48	:::	401		::3	182		9 HR	141	383			77	
30	EMBUREY	38			1 .8	404		9 3 :7/8 1	185			142	389		159	81	
34			– · –	49	53 P·3	410					M35	143					
36	– · –	39			:	411		:5 6/7 6 8 ·4·1	190	10		144	394			86	
40			– · –	50	::P·	416		8/7	191			145	395			87	
43	ALLOTT	10			7 1	417		:5 L3 ·1	196		Heavy cloud–cool.	146	397		160	88	
48			– · –	51	3 35 :1	419		P IE 47 ··1	200			147	399		161	89	
51	– · –	11			15 9 :22::	424		LB	201		(LB)	148	404		165		22
56			– · –	52	::3t 1	427		:5/6 1	204		† WOOD 1000 + ENG.	149	406		166	90	
12·00	– · –	12			656 ·x5	433					M36	150					
04½			– · –	53	P8/7	435		4 1 75P 4:1	208	11		151	412		167	95	
08	– · –	13			IE 8 :2 1	438		:47 ·4	211	12	150 p'ship: 224'	152	419		170	99	
13			EMBUREY	40	x:··LB	443		9 2	212		Round wkt to LHB. (LB) RITCHIE'S 2nd·233'	153	422			101	23
19	– · –	14			1/2 1	444		::P6·	217			154	423		171		
24			– · –	41	4s :1	446		:P··	221		10 HR	155	424		172		
28	BOTHAM	21			7 7 ·W	448	21					155	424	6	172	101	23
29					PHILLIPS		LHB								0		
31	– · –	21			8 1	1		:↑·8/7 4	224	13		156	429		1	105	
36			– · –	42	:2 1 P6P	7					M37	157					
39	– · –	22			4 ·475	12		2 1	225			158	430			106	
43			– · –	43	2 ·:	16		4+6 4 1	227	14	† HS in Tests.	159	435			111	
48	– · –	23			4 :1/3 7/8 ·1	21		7 1	228			160	437		2	112	
52			– · –	44	:x ·W	23	–					160	437	7	2	112	23
53					O'DONNELL										0		
55			– · –	44	:P·	4					M38	161					
57	– · –	24			x+x x 37/6 :·2	9	–	8 1	229	14	† Dropped ball.	162	440	7	2	113	23
1·02 LUNCH											M38 NB17			L U N C H			
1·41			EMBUREY	45				P ::::	235		M39	163					
44	BOTHAM	25			:↑:·8:+4	15	1				(W)	164	445		6		24
48½			– · –	46	7:7	18		7·6 2:1	238			165	448			116	
52	– · –	26						129 IE 4↑ :224:	244	15		166	456			124	
56			– · –	47	B+	19		::::7	249		(B) † LEAD	167	458			125	25
59	– · –	27			4 17 :2	21		:466	253			168	461		8	126	
2·05			EDMONDS	54	P::·	25		P4	255		11 HR	169	462			127	
07½	– · –	28			:	26		4··4/7 3	260			170	465			130	
12			– · –	55				6·3 ·23	266		M40	171					
15	– · –	29			3 x↑7·8/7 4	32	2					172	469		12		
20			– · –	56	:PP:	37		6 1	267			173	470			131	
22	– · –	30			5	38	2	3↑L x9 1	272	15	M40 NB17	174	471	7	12	132	25

114

4TH DAY TIME	BOWLERS (CONSTANT) PAVILION END BOWLER	O.	(WHITEHEAD) RADCLIFFE Rᴰ END BOWLER	O.	BATSMEN SCOREBOARD LEFT SCORING	BALLS	6ˢ/4ˢ	SCOREBOARD RIGHT SCORING	BALLS	6ˢ/4ˢ	NOTES	AUSTRALIA 1ˢᵀ INNINGS END-OF-OVER TOTALS O.	RUNS	W.	'L' BAT	'R' BAT	EXTRAS
					O'DONNELL	38	2	RITCHIE	272	15	M 40 NB 17	174	471	7	12	132	25
2.27			EDMONDS	57	.7.:.ᴵ³⁄₄:	278	16					175	475			136	
30	EMBUREY	48			:·ᴾ 6 ᴾ:·ᴼ	44						176	476		13		
33½	- · -			58	7ᴾ:::·ᴾ	50		·			M 41	177					
36	- · -	49			·6ᴺ·4 .·.·	54		ᵛ¹⁄₃·· 8	280				178	481		14	140	
40			- · -	59	:ᴾ⁴ᴾ:	58		:·6	282		·Dropped S. point (SUB - HASSAN)	179	482			141	
43	- · -	50						:·:·ˣ·⁷⁄₈:	288		M 42	180					
45			- · -	60	⁴:·	59		:·9 6 7·	293			181	483		15		
48½	- · -	51		·	⁴⁄₈· 8·	61		ᴾᵀ·:·:·⁷⁄₈	297		† rebounded into face	182	486		17	142	
52½			- · -	61	:·⁵⁴::·ᴾ:	67					M 43	183					
56	GATTING	1			⁴ 8ᵀ·::·3:				303		† 80 p'ship : 84 min	184	488			144	
59			- · -	62	:⁴4	69		·:·³⁄₄ᴾ·ˣᴵ·ᵂ	308	16	NB 18	185	491	8	18	146	25
3·02								LAWSON								0	
04	EMBUREY	52			:::·⁴	73		::	2		12 HR	186	492		19		
09			- · -	63	⁸·	74		:·:·:·ᵀ·:	7		† Round wkt.	187	493		20		
12	- · -	53			:·2·²·⁴⁸:	80	3					188	501		28		
15			- · -	64				:·ᵛ¹⁄₄·ᴾᴾ·	13	1		189	505			4	
17½	- · -	54			::·7⁸	84		::·	15			190	506		29		
21			- · -	65	⁸·:·⁸	86		:·:ᴾ⁸·	19		Ⓑ	191	508			5	26
25	- · -	55						:²⁄₄ᴾ·:·	25	2		192	512			9	
27		·	- · -	66	⁸:·::·:	92					M 44	193					
30	BOTHAM	31			†·:·³·⁷⁸·¹⁷⁸	31					† NEW BALL † Trod on ball - changed	194	513			10	
36			ALLOTT	15	⁷²⁴·⁵⁶·⁴	94	4	:·⁴⁴·:·⁸ ⁴·3	35	3	† GOWER misfielded & damaged hand.	195	526	8	35	17	26
3·41	TEA										M 44 NB 18	T	E	A			
4·01	BOTHAM	32			⁴·↑:·²⁄₃	99	5	²↑·	36			196	531		39	18	
06			ALLOTT	16				³·3⁄₄↑·:·	42		· Dropped cover (ROBINSON) M 45	197					
11	- · -	33			ˣ²⁴⁷⁄₃	102		ˣ²↑·:	45			198	532		40		
15			- · -	17	:·ᴾ·³7·	108	6					199	536		44		
20	- · -	34			:²·↑	110		ˣ·ˣᴮ	49		Ⓑ	200	538		45		27
25	- · -	18			:·7·:ᴾ·⁹:	116					13 HR	201	539		46		
30	- · -	35			↑⁹ᵂ	117	6				(crossed)	201¹	539	9	46	18	27
					McDERMOTT										0		
31	- · -	35			- ·	- ·		Eᴵ ᵂ	50	3		201²	539	10	0	18	27
4·32	ALL OUT										M 45 NB 18 1226 balls	ALL	OUT				

4TH DAY TIME	BOWLERS (WHITEHEAD) PAVILION END BOWLER	O.	(CONSTANT) RADCLIFFE RD END BOWLER	O.	BATSMEN SCOREBOARD LEFT SCORING	BALLS 6s/4s	SCOREBOARD RIGHT SCORING	BALLS 6s/4s	ENGLAND 2ND INNINGS NOTES	END-OF-OVER TOTALS O.	RUNS	W.	L BAT	R BAT	EXTRAS
					GOOCH		ROBINSON		(20 OVERS LEFT)						
4.42			LAWSON	1		3		3	† just short of 2nd slip	1	5		2	3	
47	McDERMOTT	1				6	:LB	6	(LB)	2	8		4		1
52			— · —	2	EP 4	11 ·		6	—	2⁵	8	-	4	3	1
4·55	BAD LIGHT								M· NB·		B	L	S	P	
6·25	PLAY ABANDONED								RAIN at 5·10pm		S	T	U	M	P S
5TH DAY 12·16			LAWSON	2		12			START DELAYED M1 -18 OVERS LOST	3					
17	McDERMOTT	2				17	4/1	7		4	10		5	4	
21½			→ -	3	2· 9	20		10	(NB) NB 1	5	13		8		
27	— · · —	3			†©: 9	23	2 5 † 3½ 2·:!	14	† false run-followed through-kept ball	6	18		9	7	2
32			— · —	4			·:··· 6	20	M2	7					
36½	— · —	4			Bt 67 ·3	26	:2E	23	† Phillips hit on leg by ball! (B)	8	23		12	8	3
41			— · · —	5	↑↑ · · X	32			M3	9					
45½	HOLLAND	1			:P S 8	36	8	25	Round wkt	10	25		13	9	
48			— · · —	6	©·:·4	43 1			(NB) NB 2	11	30		17		4
55	— · · —	2			S· 3/4 ·4	47 2	2/1	27		12	35		21	10	
58			— · · —	7	†8 ·4·:··	51 3	L8/4	29	—	1HR	13	40	-	25	11	4
1·03	LUNCH								M3 N2		L	U	N	C H	
1·40½	HOLLAND	3					3 2 6· 2	35	Round wkt	14	42			13	
43½			LAWSON	8	6 2 7 ↑ :·:·	57				15	44		27		
48	— · —	4					7 67 22····	41		16	48			17	
52			— · —	9	3·:↑↑ 3½	63			† Appeal at 2nd slip	17	49		28		
56	— · · —	5			6 5 ·PP ·4·	69 4			50 p'ship: 84'	18	53		32		
59½			— · —	10			:·†PLP	47	M4	19					
2·04	— · —	6			3· 8 :4·1	73 5	7 8 ↑:1	49		20	59		37	18	
07			— · —	11	↑·:·LB	77	P 2 ·!·	51	(LB)	21	61			19	5
11½	— · · —	7			6/1	78	7··· ·2···	56		22	64		38	21	
14			— · —	12	8 8 2 1	80	†8/†·x	60	† Good stop (O'Donnell)	23	67		41		
19	— · —	8			·P ·PSP	86			M5	24					
21½			— · —	13	4/4	87 6	7··4 ·2·!	65		25	74		45	24	
26	McDERMOTT	5			:	88	:LB	70	(LB) M6	26	75				6
31			HOLLAND	9			3···7	76	M7 Round wkt.	27					
34	— · —	6			6 9 t7 2 1 W	91 6	P 4 ·!1	79	2HR	28	79	1	48	25	
37					GOWER	LHB							0		
39			— · —	10	6·::	3	·:·7	82		29	80			26	
42	— · —	7			·:·3	5	X·P 3† ··3	86	1000 F-C RUNS FOR SEASON ARREARS CLEARED	30	83			29	
47			— · —	11			5:·7/8 P7 ·2·!	92		31	85			31	
50	— · —	8			·: X P	11			WELLHAM Sub (WOOD) M8	32					
55			— · —	12			::··2·	98		33	87			33	
58 3·00	— · —	9			6···1 2	15 -	::	100 -	Repairs to Phillips' hand. M8 NB2	34	88	1	1	33	6

5TH DAY TIME	BOWLERS (WHITEHEAD) PAVILION END BOWLER	O.	(CONSTANT) RADCLIFFE RD END BOWLER	O.	BATSMEN SCOREBOARD LEFT SCORING	BALLS	6s/4s	SCOREBOARD RIGHT SCORING	BALLS	6s/4s	ENGLAND 2ND INNINGS NOTES	END-OF-OVER TOTALS O.	RUNS	W.	L BAT	R BAT	EXTRAS
					GOWER	15	-	ROBINSON	100	-	M8 NB2	34	88	1	1	33	6
3.04			HOLLAND	13		16			105			35	89		2		
07½	McDERMOTT	10			LB	21			106		(LB)	36	94		5	34	7
12			- · -	14		27	2					37	105		16		
15	- · -	11			W	33	2	LB	107	·	(LB) NB3	38	107	2	17	34	8
20					GATTING										0		
22			- · -	15					113		· Just short of slip M9	39					
25	- · -	12				6						40	108		1		
29			- · -	16		12					M10 3HR	41					
33	- · -	13				13	-		118	-	† Robinson injured hand - treatment	42	112	2	4	35	8
3.40	TEA										SHEILA BALL M10 NB3		TEA				
4.00			HOLLAND	17		16			121		WELLHAM sub (LAWSON) -4 overs	43	113		5		
03	McDERMOTT	14				20	1		123			44	118		10		
08			- · -	18		23			126	1		45	123		11	39	
10	- · -	15				26			129		(4LB)	46	128		12		12
15			- · -	19		32					M11	47					
17	- · -	16				37	2		130		(4LB)	48	137		16	40	16
22			- · -	20		40			133			49	140			43	
25	O'DONNELL	1							139			50	142			45	
29			- · -	21		45			140		† over wkt	51	143		17		
32	- · -	2				51					· c&b chance (high to right) M12	52					
36			- · -	22					146	2	ROBINSON's 50: 216	53	152			54	
38½	- · -	3				55			148			54	155			57	
42			- · -	23		59	3		150		50 p'ship: 62 min.	55	160		21	58	
45	- · -	4							156	3		56	164			62	
49			- · -	24		65					† Appeal at slip (hook) M13	57					
51	- · -	5							162			58	167			65	
56			- · -	25					168		† Diving stop (RITCHIE) M14 4HR	59					
59	- · -	6				69			170		(2LB) (LB)	60	172		22	66	19
5.03			- · -	26		75					M15	61					
05	- · -	7				77			174			62	175		23	68	
10			- · -	27					180			63	177			70	
12½	- · -	8				83					M16	64					
17			- · -	28					186		M17	65					
20	- · -	9				84			191			66	180		26		
25			RITCHIE	1		89	5		192		off breaks - 1st bowl of Test cricket.	67	190		35	71	
28½	- · -	10				89	5		198	4	Ritchie misfielded.	68	196	2	35	77	19
5.32	MATCH	DRAWN									M17 NB3 411 balls		STUMPS				

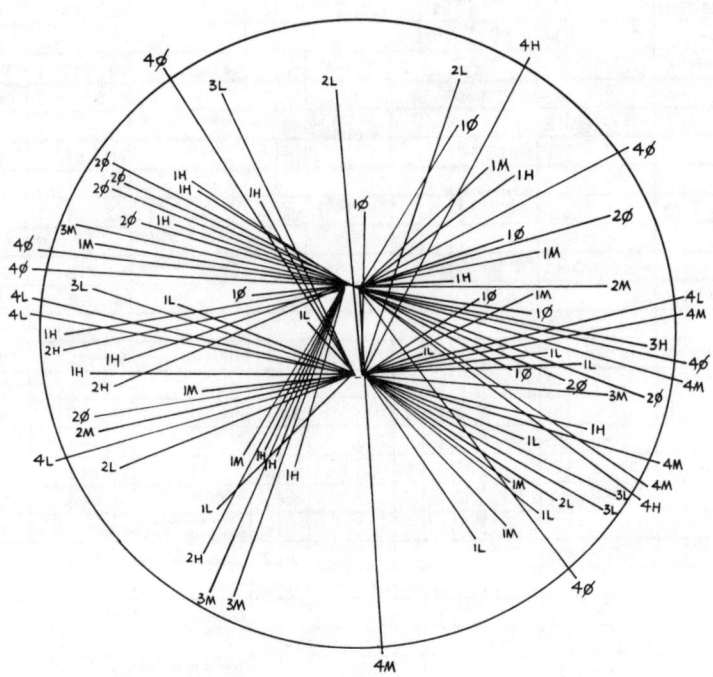

RADCLIFFE ROAD END

PAVILION END

BOWLER	SYMBOL	R U N S					
		1	2	3	4	6	TOTAL
HOLLAND	H	13	3	1	2	-	30
LAWSON	L	9	4	4	4	-	45
McDERMOTT	M	8	2	4	5	-	44
O'DONNELL	Ø	7	8	-	6	-	47
TOTALS		37	17	9	17	-	166

D.I. GOWER at Trent Bridge

166 RUNS
283 BALLS
381 MINUTES
(left-handed batsman)
© BILL FRINDALL 1985

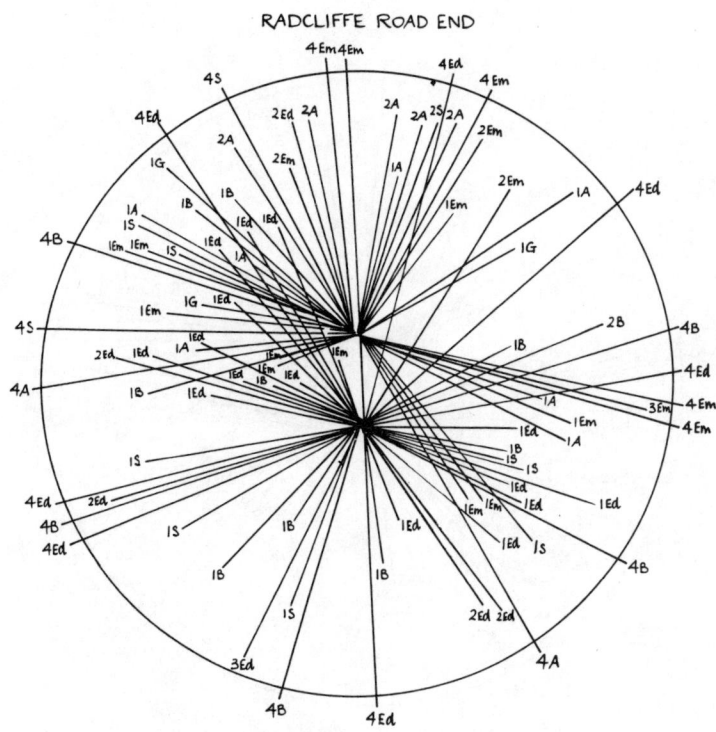

RADCLIFFE ROAD END

PAVILION END

BOWLER	SYMBOL	RUNS				
		1	2	3	4	6	TOTAL
ALLOTT	A	7	5	-	2	-	25
BOTHAM	B	9	1	-	5	-	31
EDMONDS	Ed	15	5	1	7	-	56
EMBUREY	Em	10	3	1	5	-	39
GOOCH	G	3	-	-	-	-	3
SIDEBOTTOM	S	8	1	-	2	-	18
TOTALS		52	15	2	21	-	172

G.M. WOOD at Trent Bridge

172   RUNS
448   BALLS
599   MINUTES

(left-handed batsman)

© BILL FRINDALL 1985

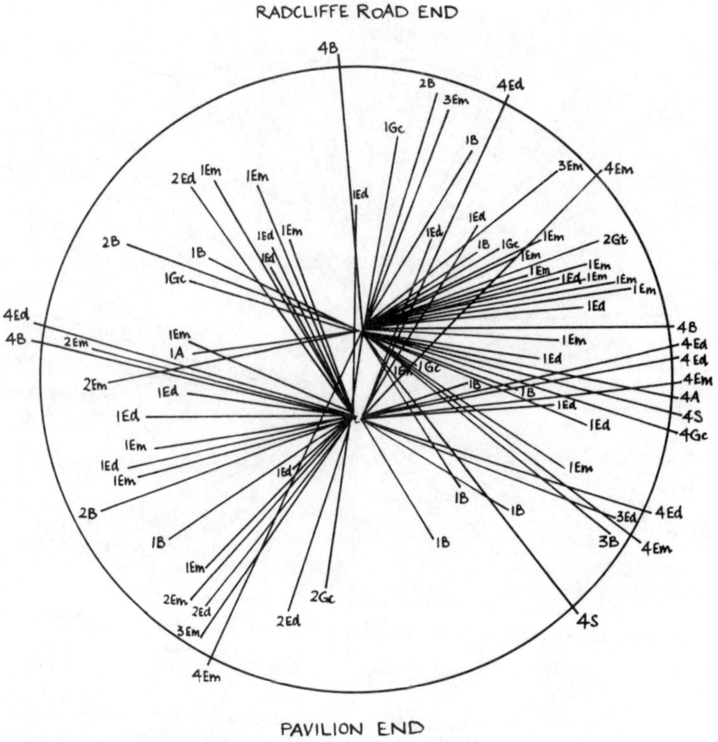

RADCLIFFE ROAD END

PAVILION END

BOWLING	SYMBOL	R U N S				
		1	2	3	4	6	TOTAL
ALLOTT	A	1	·	·	1	·	5
BOTHAM	B	9	3	1	3	·	30
EDMONDS	Ed	14	3	1	5	·	43
EMBUREY	Em	17	3	3	4	·	48
GATTING	Gt	·	1	·	·	·	2
GOOCH	Gc	4	1	·	1	·	10
SIDEBOTTOM	S	·	·	·	2	·	8
TOTALS		45	11	5	16	·	146

G.M. RITCHIE at Trent Bridge

146   RUNS
308   BALLS
359   MINUTES

© BILL FRINDALL 1985

FOURTH TEST

OLD TRAFFORD

AUGUST 1, 2, 3, 5, 6

ENGLAND
D.I. Gower (captain), G.A. Gooch, R.T. Robinson, M.W. Gatting,
A.J. Lamb, I.T. Botham, P.R. Downton, J.E. Emburey,
P.H. Edmonds, P.J.W. Allott, J.P. Agnew

AUSTRALIA
A.R. Border (captain), K.C. Wessels, A.M.J. Hilditch, D.C. Boon,
G.M. Ritchie, W.B. Phillips, G.R.J. Matthews, S.P. O'Donnell,
G.F. Lawson, C.J. McDermott, R.G. Holland

Tricky pitch could help England

While history offers England some slight hope, today's fourth Cornhill Test match against Australia at Old Trafford is otherwise shrouded in considerable doubt, with both sides unsure of the final make-up of their teams.

England's 12 all reported fit yesterday, but as ever the balance of the attack remains open until the last moment. Australia have sundry individual ailments, though none seems likely to prove serious.

Not least, there is the weather. It has not spared this corner of England, and the result is a square which is unsatisfactorily damp (although the pitch is said to be firm enough, though moist), and the nets were unsurprisingly unfit for use yesterday.

So Australia were denied the hard workout they needed after yet another period of limited activity, and, like England, who managed only brief fielding practice, they are not quite sure what to make of the pitch. It is brown in appearance, not dissimilar (to the distant eye and with the aid of a vivid imagination) to a strip of baked mud in Faisalabad or Lahore, but its moisture and the likelihood of continuing cloud-cover means either captain could have misgivings about batting first.

All this might tempt England to omit a spinner, though I sincerely hope not. If it is England's lot to be bowling this morning, Emburey and Edmonds could be effective and, in any case, most Old Trafford pitches this season have turned at some stage, even during three-day games.

In the end, it might come down to the England selectors simply choosing their five best bowlers, which you might think is what they should always do. This would mean omitting one of Allott, Agnew and Ellison. The case for each bowler is pretty strong: Allott is on familiar territory, and Ellison would be expected to move the ball around in these conditions. Agnew, having just taken nine wickets in an innings, is now bowling as fast and as straight as at any time in his career.

Australia are in a similar quandary. Originally, they expected to require two spinners, but now they are less sure, partly because the balance of their side, with usually only four bowlers, is different. In any case, they have no-one of the quality of the English pair.

Whoever plays, awkward batting conditions would be a help for England, whose main priority, with the series level and only two Tests after this, must be to bowl out Australia twice. Curiously, when the series began, batting looked like being Australia's main worry, but so far it has not worked out quite like that.

This suggests that England again will have to perform with high efficiency to maintain their run of success here. They have won seven times against Australia's four, the last three in succession, and in 1981 with the aid of Botham's memorable 118 from 102 deliveries.

Perhaps in anticipation of something similar, would-be spectators have already paid some £250,000 in advance ticket sales, which represents an increase of more than £100,000 on the West Indies Test last year.

STATISTICAL PREVIEW

Two records in danger

If Ian Botham can take seven wickets in this match he will overhaul the record aggregate for any bowler in Tests against Australia – 128 by Bob Willis in 35 tests (8 more than Botham). Recent speculation that Botham gains most of his wickets from the lower batting order is unfounded. The first five batsmen have provided 165 of his 329 Test wickets, and the last five only 137.

Botham needs three more sixes to overtake Arthur Wellard's 50-year-old world record for the most in a season. His 64 sixes account for 30% of his aggregate of 1,270 runs and have been struck at the phenomenal rate of 2·9 per innings.

When he scores his 34th run, David Gower will become the ninth England batsman to score 5,000 runs in Tests. Allan Border requires 45 runs to become the first left-handed Australian captain to score 1,000 first-class runs on a tour of England since Joe Darling in 1905. Bill Lawry fell 94 short in 1968.

Australia's recent malaise of dropped slip catches appears to have been cured. Both sides have had ten chances in that area and, whilst Botham (3), Gooch and Gatting have missed half of theirs, Australia have failed to snap up only one.

Spinners and Botham take the honours

Australia were dismissed for 257 after being put in on the first day of the fourth Cornhill Test at Old Trafford yesterday, which was a reflection of their own variable batting and the persistence of England's bowlers in conditions that offered only minimal assistance.

The pitch, though damp, turned out to be nothing more than a slow one, requiring a degree of patience by both sides, and unsurprisingly perhaps it was Australia who struggled to come to terms with it.

Nevertheless, they had reached 97 for one before the accuracy of Emburey and Edmonds, who took three for six in 13 deliveries, induced frustration which led to the middle order being swept away.

Boon's 61, his highest Test score, saw them through that stage, but four wickets by Botham restored England's control until O'Donnell capitalised on his good fortune – and England's later shortcomings – to make 45 from 78 balls.

After, presumably, much deliberation, England omitted Ellison. Thus even before a ball was bowled, their seam attack achieved a rare distinction, for all three members, Botham, Agnew and Allott, were born in Cheshire.

Alas, not even this little local knowledge was initially of much use to them as they strove in turn to wrest some life from a slow, grassless pitch after Gower had, unsurprisingly, opted to bowl first.

Though the day was overcast, it was also cool, and there was negligible movement through the air and, until Allott was eventually given the downwind Stretford end, not much off the seam.

Wessels, opening in place of the injured Wood, and Hilditch were therefore not unduly troubled. Indeed, until the introduction of spin they touched four runs an over, with Wessels missing little that allowed him room to cut or force.

When Emburey appeared after not much more than an hour, Wessels was caught at slip by Botham as he drove, possibly slightly off-balance, at a flighted delivery, while Allott, yielding only 14 runs in nine overs, went past Hilditch's bat more than once.

Hilditch otherwise looked capable of playing the lengthy innings his side needed, until he fell to Gower's juggling catch at silly point as he pushed forward to a ball from Edmonds that drifted in to hit pad, then bat.

Boon, meanwhile, had made a tentative start, which was hardly a surprise in view of his hitherto modest series. But two straight-driven fours off Agnew were a reminder of the power of his strokes at other levels.

Border also began with a resounding stroke off Agnew, but then Edmonds' continuing accuracy induced a rare rush of blood from the Australian captain, who went down the pitch, heaved across the line and was neatly stumped.

If that was one bonus, another

followed in the same over, Ritchie, perhaps beaten through the air, went forward and then back, eventually giving Edmonds a simple return catch as he tried to adjust to a ball that straightened.

Boon went past an admirable half-century and with Phillips restored order, but it was still England's afternoon. And soon after tea, Botham, finding more movement than earlier, produced a highly penetrative spell. He had Phillips caught behind cutting and then removed Boon, after a stay of some three and a quarter hours, with the aid of Lamb's brilliant low catch in

the gully off a firm hit, before bowling Matthews, who played no stroke.

Lawson quickly followed, and when McDermott was palpably lbw to Emburey, England looked like finishing the job very quickly, especially as O'Donnell needed a generous amount of luck against Botham.

Eventually he started to make contact and with Holland added 33 for the last wicket before Edmonds was recalled and with his first ball bowled O'Donnell, which merely emphasised England's lack of imagination during this phase.

AUSTRALIAN VIEWPOINT

Border's stroke of shame

Australia would not be completely disillusioned with their first-innings score of 257 at Old Trafford yesterday, even if it should have been much more after a convincing opening partnership of 71.

Graeme Wood's enforced withdrawal with a broken nose and 11-stitch gash in his left eyebrow and forehead was a serious setback, and the early dismissals of Allan Border and Greg Ritchie compounded Australia's problems.

For a change, batting was somewhat easier on the first morning of a Test when the new ball came onto the bat reasonably enough, and England's quick bowlers did not use the conditions as well as expected.

When David Gower won the toss, he had no other choice than to bowl first

because of the doubts – even fears – both teams had about the damp, under-prepared pitch, which was exposed as a tired, crusty pudding, unfit for a five-day match.

On such a sluggish surface, John Emburey and Phil Edmonds revealed their class in cracking the Australian innings wide open, and the incomparable Ian Botham sunk it with an inspired second spell, which was a big improvement on his disappointing opening.

Edmonds could not have reckoned on the help he received from Border, who looked to be trying to emulate Botham's batting belligerence with a wild dismissal shot that Edmonds later described as 'a pure slog'.

It is difficult to be too critical of Border for he has played aggressively and successfully throughout this tour. Yet it still was an awful-looking shot – one that seemed totally unnecessary at that stage (118 for two) and unworthy of an Australian captain, particularly as it was only the 18th ball he had faced.

David Boon, fighting for his Test career, had to overcome what must have been almost intolerable personal pressure to top score with a determined, often handsome 61 – only his second half-century in 11 Test innings. Earlier this week, Border had said of Boon: 'I want to stick with him because I really do think he can become a good player. He's a good, compact little competitor. One good score and he'll be away as a Test player.'

Overnight
Australia 257 (D.C. Boon 61, A.M.J. Hilditch 49, S.P. O'Donnell 45;
Edmonds 4 – 40, Botham 4 – 79)

England lay solid base for big lead

England, tempering their batting carefully to meet the demands of Old Trafford's sluggish pitch, emerged only 24 runs behind with seven wickets in hand on the second day of the Fourth Cornhill Test yesterday.

Not too often in recent years have England batted all day for fewer than three runs an over, but their rediscovered application served them well against accurate Australian bowling and left a position from which it should be possible to aim for a substantial lead.

Even the loss, in quick succession, of Gooch and Gower, whose partnership of 121 was the focal point of the day, proved only a temporary blemish, and Gatting and Lamb went through the final session most responsibly, adding 85 from the last 31 overs.

England were helped by two fielding lapses, though neither ultimately cost Australia as much as they probably feared. If McDermott, with all three wickets, was Australia's most successful bowler, O'Donnell was probably their unluckiest.

Ten overs, or 40 minutes, were lost to the weather. Had it been an hour, play could have gone on till 7 p.m., and there seems no reason why this regulation should not be amended to cover delays of up to an hour, which would have given yesterday's capacity crowd a full ration of cricket.

Remarkably, play started on time, even though overnight rain had penetrated the modest covers on the square, while the light perked up appreciably after a grey dawn.

England's start was much more colourful, Gooch quickly producing a ringing square cut for four off Lawson, and 21 came from the first three overs, while the bowlers sought their rhythm.

In Lawson's case, it was not immediately located. He had problems with his delivery stride, not surprising perhaps with the pitch retaining its dampness, but there was an early bonus for Australia when Robinson was well caught at slip by Border off McDermott.

Robinson had looked more tentative than usual outside his off stump, and this dismissal owed something to the bat being further away from body than desirable, while Gooch then saw a leading edge off McDermott lob just over the bowler's head.

All this suggested much care was still required, especially by players who need the ball coming on to the bat, and immediately after a stoppage for rain, Gower, when four, was missed at slip by Boon off McDermott.

After that, Gower played very straight and was highly selective outside off stump, and though Gooch found he could not always time everything, they did much to suggest that England could hope to bat for at least two days, which must have been their objective.

So a period of mostly solid entrenchment followed, with the pair content to await lapses in line and length, and Gooch also playing so straight that once umpire Bird bore the brunt of a firm stroke off Holland which struck an ankle.

Gower, when 34, reached 5,000 runs in Test cricket – it is his 74th game – and all remained well, though when O'Donnell appeared he was miserably out of luck against both batsmen.

Both got away with an inside edge in the same over, but the most important lapse came when Gooch, at 59, escaped. Boon, diving to his left, at first slip, touched but could not hold a fast-travelling chance.

Curiously Phillips, the wicket-keeper, did not move, otherwise it would probably have been his chance. Poor O'Donnell then saw Gooch edge him for four through the slips, before Gower twice drove him for more elegant boundaries.

It had been a good, old-fashioned afternoon's Test cricket, watched indeed by a large, old-fashioned crowd behind whom the gates had long since been closed, as Australia yielded only 86 runs from 30 overs.

With the sun also managing to shine intermittently, it seemed almost too good to last. And soon after tea, McDermott, now operating with the wind at his back, broke through much as Botham had the previous day.

The second-wicket partnership had lasted 43 overs when Gooch, 26 short of his first century against Australia, was lbw after a stay of some 3½ hours.

In McDermott's next over, Gower, middling a hook, seemed to have cleared Hilditch on the square leg boundary, but the fielder took a remarkable catch tumbling backwards which earned him the congratulations of the entire Australian side.

England now had two new batsmen, Gatting and Lamb, beginning at the same time, which is never ideal, but both seemed to have observed what the pitch demanded and another spell of earnest consolidation followed.

AUSTRALIAN VIEWPOINT

Boon not immune from catching 'disease'

David Boon dropped two catches at Old Trafford yesterday, just when the Australians were preening themselves for having found a reliable slip fieldsman. Fielding there for Australia is akin to sailing through the Bermuda Triangle – you can disappear without trace.

At the very least you contract a seemingly incurable disease, which makes your hands so slippery that you rarely are able to catch a cricket ball, no matter how hard you try.

Boon was considered the most dependable of all the greasy-fingered occupants of the Australian slips cordon over the past three series. Yet he missed two straightforward chances yesterday. He dropped David Gower at four (28 for one) off Craig McDermott, and Graham Gooch at 59 (118 for one) off Simon O'Donnell.

Boon's dropping of Gower was especially costly, as the England captain and his powerful opening batsman Gooch went on to share a second-wicket partnership of 121 in

Gower on his way to 166 at Trent Bridge, his first hundred as England captain.

Left: Graeme Wood on his way to a fine 172. Unfortunately for Australia, this was his only innings of note, and in his other eight knocks in the series he scored a total of 88.

Left, below: Ian Botham holds the ball aloft and appeals for a catch off Phil Edmonds. Allan Border, who felt he had not made contact with the bat, was given out, to raise England's hopes of a win.

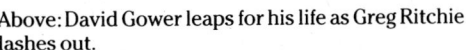

Above: David Gower leaps for his life as Greg Ritchie lashes out.

Left: Ritchie is delighted with his hundred. He went on to make a handsome 146 as Australia continued their fight-back.

Overleaf: Simon O'Donnell hooks Ian Botham during his bright knock of 46. Australia compiled 539, their highest Test total in England for over 20 years, ensuring that England could not win. England survived the last day for the loss of only two wickets and the match was drawn.

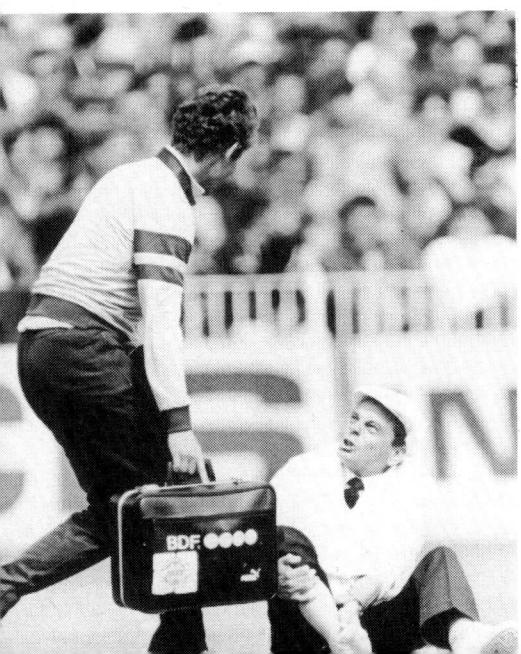

Above: Ian Botham is jubilant as he has David Boon brilliantly caught by Allan Lamb (out of picture). Boon was top scorer with 61 as Australia, put in to bat, slumped to 257 all out on the first day at Old Trafford.

Left: Umpire Dickie Bird appeals for first aid after being struck on the ankle by a straight drive from Graham Gooch.

Left: Australia's young
bowling hero Craig
McDermott (8–141) traps
Gooch lbw.

Right: Mike Gatting on his way
to an impeccable 160, his first
Test hundred in England, as
England compile a formidable
482–9 declared.

Left: Allan Border
characteristically sweeps
Emburey past Ian Botham
during his magnificent
match-saving hundred.

Right: Paul Downton in
contrite pose after 'dropping'
Allan Border off Botham in
the first over of the last day
with the Australian captain
still on his overnight score of
49. He went on to an unbeaten
146, and Downton took some
stick for missing what would
have been hailed as a
breathtaking catch had he
held it.

Border walks back to the pavilion as yet again the rain comes down on the last day at Old Trafford, flanked by Gower and Botham protecting his bleached locks. Half the day's play was lost through rain as England's bowlers toiled without success in their efforts to remove Border permanently.

just over three hours, until the hard-working McDermott removed both of them within seven balls immediately after tea.

Last year the Australians' continual fielding blunders ruined whatever slim chance they had of competing on equal terms with the West Indies in the Caribbean and in Australia.

They were credited with dropping no fewer than 53 catches in the five home Tests against the West Indies and in the World Series Cup and World Championship of Cricket tournaments.

In this English 'summer' they have missed more than 30, though no-one is quite sure of the exact count because it does get rather monotonous keeping score and, in fairness, Boon, at least, had provided a glimmer of hope that sanity had returned.

It is all the more galling because if there was one thing Australian teams could do, it was field. Some of the old-timers, and not so old-timers, say the Australians should do away with their baseball gloves when they practice.

That might be a start. If you have any other ideas, write to Allan Border.

Overnight
Australia 257
England 233 – 3 (G.A. Gooch 74, D.I. Gower 47, M.W. Gatting 45 not out)

England plan to charge, then declare

M ike Gatting's impeccable innings of 160 sustained England throughout most of the 52 overs permitted by the weather in the fourth Cornhill Test at Old Trafford on Saturday, leaving them 191 ahead with four wickets standing.

Though it was only Gatting's third Test hundred, his first in this country and his first against Australia, it was accomplished in a manner which suggested he had been reeling them off for years rather than, for so long, struggling to become established at this level.

Of its many qualities, concentration was probably the key factor. This kept him going with remarkably few errors for almost six hours, and also enabled him to take in his stride first Lamb's unfortunate run out and then a would-be Botham mini blitz which was out of context with everything that had gone before.

Before play began at 2 p.m., another large and remarkably patient crowd must have watched the hard-working groundstaff struggling after overnight rain with sheets of tarpaulin, and tried to equate these primitive, inadequate covering methods with the large amounts of money taken at the box office these days.

But the cricket itself was compelling enough, especially when Gatting and Lamb were both going so well together in a fourth-wicket partnership that added 156, though I suspect both would be quietly surprised and grateful when Border opted to take the new ball as soon as it became available.

The old one had not bounced overmuch on this slow pitch and it had frequently been hammered into the ground by mistimed strokes from two such strong back-foot players. The new one came on to the bat much quicker and, with the bowling initially short, its first five overs produced 38 runs and England were on their way.

It was also surprising that McDermott, having bowled so effectively with what might be laughingly described as the breeze at his back the previous evening, found himself labouring into a near gale, while Lawson – whose bowling still lacks something – had the more favourable end.

Still, Gatting and Lamb played so well that Australia's attack, fast or slow, might have been taken apart had they remained together. Both timed the ball well and played with the straightness demanded by the pitch's low bounce, and it was clear something special would be needed to separate them.

It came when Gatting called his partner for a single for a firm push to cover, and Matthews, with probably only one stump to aim at, ran out Lamb with a direct hit. The margin was so clear-cut that Lamb did not bother to glance at umpire Shepherd.

Matthews' out-cricket, like that of many of his colleagues, gave Australia some compensation on a difficult day. His bowling may seem bland, but his fielding is positively Bland-like.

There might have been a time when Gatting would have brooded over that episode and perhaps got himself out soon afterwards, but not now. Nor did he change his selective approach when Botham appeared and predictably tried to prove that a batsman of his strength could play strokes on this pitch, even without any time spent in reconnaissance.

With Gatting playing so well, Botham was under no obligation to go after the bowling from the start, but he did so, with mixed results. It was hardly a surprise when, fed a short ball by McDermott, he was well caught off a hook in the bowler's leg-trap which, for Botham, was some distance from the one which Laker employed here in 1956.

After that, Downton – who had been dismissed first ball in his two previous innings – sensibly pushed the ones, while Gatting reached three figures (for the first time this season, too) from 179 deliveries. The stroke, a square drive off the back foot off O'Donnell, was one Gatting might have nominated in advance if he had been given the option.

An inside edge off O'Donnell which could not have missed leg stump by much was, hereabouts, a rare blemish. Otherwise, Gatting made 64 of the 91 added with Downton with crisp strokes all round the wicket – and, let it be said, no suggestion of padding up!

By now assorted selections of 1985 meteorological delights were threatening the ground. Remarkably, they passed it by, though the light was bad enough for a less prosperously placed side to have accepted the umpires' offer before Gatting provided McDermott with his fifth wicket and departed to the sort of ovation he must have wondered would ever come his way on an English Test ground.

Before the day's most convincing downpour ended play, Emburey produced two uncomplicated blows for four and the half-frozen sun-starved Australians were left wondering whether the weather would now be their ally.

The crowd finished drenched but no doubt delighted, but I wonder if the obscene, football-style chanting of a section of them gave offence to the ground authorities, the police and those sitting nearby who were forced to endure it – and if not why not?

AUSTRALIAN VIEWPOINT

Murky Manchester may aid Australia

Whatever happens in the fourth Test today – and Manchester's murky, wet weather suggests it will not be much – England are starting to appeal as a slightly more stable side than Australia.

Allan Border's team are giving the impression of clinging to the Ashes by their fingernails, and it will be something of a minor miracle if they can hang on, given the on-and-off field problems that have confronted them.

Few Australian teams have had to endure so much consistently depressing weather as this one. It has affected players' opportunities, performances and attitudes in matches against the counties and has helped create abnormally slow Test wickets, even by English standards.

Geoff Lawson and Craig McDermott, rated Australia's trump cards, have suffered the most yet they still have performed splendidly to take 16 and 21 wickets respectively in the Tests.

Lawson has not been anywhere near one hundred per cent fit or healthy all tour and McDermott also has had fitness and illness worries. Moreover, it is a serious setback for Australia that Bob Holland's legspin bowling and his confidence are being affected by the ultra slow wickets.

Border, who seemingly could do no wrong with the bat, must agonise for two more days before learning whether his reckless swish of last Thursday has weakened his chances of keeping the Ashes.

On Saturday night, he was optimistic that Australia could bat for five sessions to save the match, because the wicket was playing faster as it dried and he thought it would be at its best for batting on the fourth and fifth days. Border conceded, though, that 'a day of rain wouldn't go astray.'

David Gower, England's captain, said: 'I would be very disappointed not to win, given two clear days. But we have to wait for the weather to sort itself out.'

As the rain persisted last night, it appeared to be sorting itself out in Australia's favour.

A draw at Old Trafford and another at Edgbaston, where everyone keeps saying the wicket is weighted too heavily in favour of batsmen to produce a result, would leave England exceedingly anxious about their prospects of having to win at the Oval to recapture that famous little urn.

Overnight
Australia 257
England 448 – 6 (M.W. Gatting 160, G.A Gooch 74, A.J. Lamb 67, D.I. Gower 47)

Border leads battle to foil England

Allan Border placed himself staunchly between England and victory in the fourth Cornhill Test at Old Trafford yesterday with a dogged display of self-denial that left Australia entering the last day 33 runs behind, with six wickets standing

For three hours, Border batted with admirable judgement against the spin of Edmonds and Emburey, which eluded some of his colleagues, after Australia had embarked on the task of saving the match with a deficit of 225.

Though the ball turned only intermittently, the two spinners bowled with accuracy, guile and variation enough to induce error, and Australia were reduced to 138 for four before Border and Ritchie saw them through an increasingly tense final session.

All this, on a day when the rain again miraculously avoided the ground, came after McDermott had emerged with 8-141, the 10th Australian to achieve the feat in a Test innings and the third youngest bowler, after Valentine and Venkat, to do so.

The ground had recovered improbably well from another overnight soaking, and play began on time. With the day also fair, at least by present standards, England batted on, though not quite according to plan.

They were disrupted by McDermott who, bowling with exemplary straightness from the downwind end, hit the stumps three times in 17 deliveries to remove Downton,

Edmonds and Allott, the first two with extremely good balls.

In nine overs England added 34, mainly thanks to Emburey, at which point Gower declared, which denied McDermott the opportunity of becoming only the second Australian (after Arthur Mailey) to take nine wickets in an innings.

Still, it took his tally for the series to 24, and at the age of only 20 McDermott has now taken 34 in his first six Tests. And this in an alleged summer when he has had neither the sun on his back nor glimpsed any pitch with pace or bounce.

Matthews then appeared as Hilditch's opening partner, which may have been more in deference to Wessels' preferring to bat at No. 3 than to any deep-laid tactical ploy, though it did give Australia the desirable left- and right-hand combination.

They got through until lunch together, though Hilditch caused a stir by sweeping Emburey for six off the last ball of the morning, which was straight enough to have embarrassed if he had not made contact.

If that was somewhat unexpected from a side trying to save the game, so was Matthews' decision to go down the pitch to Edmonds in the first over of the afternoon, the bowler holding on to a firmly struck return catch.

Hilditch, meanwhile, had all kinds of problems during one particularly good over from Edmonds, who had turned the occasional ball quite sharply and off whom Wessels, when 10, was almost caught off bat and pad.

Despite this, it was some time before

Gower used his spinners in harness. Before that happened, anyway, Emburey returned to bowl Hilditch who, in some disarray, played across the arm ball.

By now Wessels was playing well. A long innings has eluded him in this series, but the hour of need had now arrived and, with great selectivity, he and Border dug in against the spinners.

Border, though showing neat footwork agair st the spinners, otherwise showed no sign of repeating his first innings indiscretion, and there developed an absorbing struggle during which Edmonds received a warning from umpire Bird for following through on the operational part of the pitch.

The spinners tried every variation, though it seemed that, on this pitch, the slower they bowled the more effective they might be. The next breakthrough came on the stroke of tea.

This time, Wessels – aiming to on-drive a ball from Emburey that was drifting in invitingly – gave the bowler a low return catch when the spin bit sufficiently to find something akin to a leading edge.

Boon, whose limited Test experience could hardly have prepared him for a situation like this, was next to go. He, too, was lured down the pitch and, beaten through the air, perhaps, by Emburey, was bowled by a ball that turned just enough.

Border went on, using his pads as often as possible, stifling what spin there was on other occasions and scoring no fewer than 34 of his 49 runs in singles. It was a tremendous effort.

What little luck he needed came when the odd ball squirted to safety through the close cordon of fielders off bat and pad, and Ritchie stayed carefully with him; though, in the last over, he survived an appeal for a close catch off Edmonds.

AUSTRALIAN VIEWPOINT

Captain content to take his time

A llan Border and Greg Ritchie batted with all the considerable skill and care they could muster at Old Trafford late yesterday to revive Australia's hopes of holding England to a draw in the fourth Test.

Border, who passed 1,000 runs for the tour when he reached 37, looked intent on atoning for the rush-of-blood swipe that caused his downfall in the first innings.

That 34 of his 49 runs were gathered in singles (plus two twos, one three and two fours) was indicative of the grim 186-ball, three-hour struggle he had with nagging spinners John Emburey and Phil Edmonds.

For Australia to save the match Border may well need to better his marathon 123 not out in a second innings total of 402 at Old Trafford in 1981, when England won by 103 runs.

Greg Matthews believed he could serve Australia best by opening the batting in the second innings, which allowed Kepler Wessels to revert to No. 3 and David Boon to No. 5. Border agreed and rearranged his batting order yesterday.

Matthews' efforts in this Test – seven and 17, 0-21 off nine overs and a brilliant piece of fielding to run out Allan Lamb – support the suspicion that he is just short of Test class, while remaining a capable, energetic competitor at first-class level.

Craig McDermott's 8-141, including yesterday's burst of 3-8 in 14 balls, was further proof of the way he and, to a lesser extent, Geoff Lawson have carried Australia's attack in this series.

He has had to shoulder almost an unfair burden for a 20-year-old in his first full series, and an Ashes contest at that. Yet he is the leading wicket-taker in the series, with 24 at 26·58 apiece. He is averaging a wicket every seven overs.

This is only McDermott's 28th first class match, including his sixth Test, since his debut for Queensland in 1983-84. He now has 91 wickets at 29·8.

Overnight
Australia 257 and 192 – 4 (K.C. Wessels 50, A.R. Border 49 not out,
A.M.J. Hilditch 40)
England 482 – 9 dec (McDermott 8 – 141)

Weather helps gritty Border foil England

Australia saved the fourth Cornhill Test at Old Trafford yesterday thanks to a formidable combination of Allan Border's sustained diligence and a lengthy intervention from the weather, which restricted the day's operations to 50 overs.

That was patently not enough for England's bowlers on such a mild pitch, and Australia lost only one more wicket in finishing at 340 for five, Border taking out his bat after an admirable display of concentration lasting almost six hours.

Yet he had not added to his overnight 49 when he was missed by Downton off an awkward chance, and all concerned may well go to their graves wondering how much this episode might have changed the course of history.

Ironically, it occurred during an isolated over bowled by Botham purely to allow the spinners to change ends after heavy rain (the forecast had promised a 'mainly dry' day, incidentally) had eased the pressure on Australia by delaying the start for 90 minutes.

From the first ball, Border obtained an inside edge to which Downton, obliged to change direction abruptly, managed to get a glove as he dived down the leg side. Alas, the ball did not stick.

Though it was the type of chance that could have eluded any wicketkeeper, Downton may now find he has to live with it, as he did after missing a rather more straightforward one in 1981 which, it could be argued, changed the course of that series.

On such slender threads are series often won and lost. Afterwards, Border offered no other detectable chance, and indeed played so well that it is tempting, if perhaps slightly unpatriotic, to suggest that he might have saved his side even with a full day's play.

Without his stabilising influence, Emburey and Edmonds might have prevailed, even though the pitch was possibly even slower than hitherto and it was clear that nothing was going to happen quickly enough to dislodge batsmen intent only on survival.

The one wicket to fall owed something to a sudden surge of aggression by Ritchie, who went down the pitch to Emburey and, beaten through the air, was bowled off an inside edge.

By then, the spinners had the encouragement of a new ball, but although Emburey got a couple to bounce, this gave England only illusory hope, and the highly disciplined Phillips kept his captain company for the final 44 overs in which 127 were added.

Though some 40 overs remained when the arrears were cleared, another shower in mid-afternoon intervened and gave the spinners a dampish ball to use and soon Border was celebrating his seventh century of the tour.

Surprisingly, though his innings might not have saved just the Test but also the Ashes, it did not earn him the Man of the Match award from Ray

Illingworth, who gave it instead to McDermott, for his eight-wicket achievement, no doubt taking into consideration it was done on a pitch offering negligible help.

Now the series moves on, at 1-1, to Edgbaston next week. Contrary to some expressed theories, pitches there this season have not always been entirely unhelpful to bowlers, and there must be some chance of one that could produce an outright result, especially in the current climate.

To help achieve that, England will need to look again at their modest fast-bowling resources. Agnew, unsurprisingly, was unsuccessful here, so perhaps Foster or Cowans will come into consideration. But surely there will be no more talk of leaving out a spin bowler after the efforts – again – of Edmonds and Emburey.

AUSTRALIAN VIEWPOINT

Ah, rain, lovely rain

David Gower said last night that England were the better team and had had 'a powerful moral victory' over Australia at Old Trafford.

To my mind, his was the usual frustrated lament from a captain who had been unable to force a win after his team had controlled most of the first four days of a five-day match.

For the jubilant Australians, a draw was almost as good as a win, given all the circumstances that led to their denying England a 2-1 lead in the series.

It was somewhat ironic that the miserable weather the Australians had cursed all tour finally befriended them when they needed it most.

With some assistance from above – ah, rain, lovely rain – Allan Border completed another monumental mission of courage that earned him his 14th century in 70 Tests and his 32nd in 156 first-class matches, including his seventh in 11 matches on this tour.

When told of Gower's 'moral victory' comment, Border said: 'England have to take the points from the game, but they must be very disappointed. This was the one to win.

'It's all very well to have a moral victory, but we're pretty happy. Fighting it out for an honourable draw gives a real spurt for Edgbaston next week.'

Border praised England's spinners John Emburey and Phil Edmonds for producing 'as fine a spell off spin bowling as I've faced'. But the fact remained that, for all the rain, and nearly half the last day's play lost, England still bowled 50 overs and took only one wicket while Australia scored 148 runs.

It might have been a moral victory for England, but guess who was celebrating last night?

Result: Match drawn
Australia 257 and 340 – 5 (A.R. Border 146 not out, K.C. Wessels 50,
A.M.J. Hilditch 40; J.E. Emburey 4 – 99)
England 482 – 9 dec

AUSTRALIA 1ST INNINGS v. ENGLAND (4TH TEST) at OLD TRAFFORD, MANCHESTER on 1,2,3,5,6 AUGUST, 1985. TOSS: ENGLAND

IN	OUT	MINS	No.	BATSMAN	HOW OUT	BOWLER	RUNS	WKT	TOTAL	6s	4s	BALLS	NOTES ON DISMISSAL
11-00	12-23	83	1	K.C.WESSELS	C' BOTHAM	EMBUREY	34	1	71	-	3	60	Edged drive to slip.
11-00	1-50	131	2	A.M.J.HILDITCH	C' GOWER	EDMONDS	49	2	97	-	4	93	Silly point - juggled catch. Ball rebounded from pad - hit bat.
12-25	4-36	191	3	D.C.BOON	C' LAMB	BOTHAM	61	6	198	-	6	146	HS in Tests. Cut hard to deep gully - sharp catch.
1-52	2-29	37	4	A.R.BORDER*	ST DOWNTON	EDMONDS	8	3	118	-	1	18	Down wicket - pulled across line. First stumping of rubber.
2-31	2-33	2	5	G.M.RITCHIE	C' AND BOWLED	EDMONDS	4	4	122	-	1	3	Mistimed short ball that held up - simple catch.
2-35	4-21	85	6	W.B.PHILLIPS†	C' DOWNTON	BOTHAM	36	5	193	-	4	71	Top-edged cut.
4-23	5-00	37	7	G.R.J.MATTHEWS	BOWLED	BOTHAM	4	7	211	-	.	25	Played no stroke to breakback that removed off stump.
4-38	6-14	96	8	S.P.O'DONNELL	BOWLED	EDMONDS	45	10	257	1	3	78	Beaten by 'arm' ball.
5-02	5-20	18	9	G.F.LAWSON	C' DOWNTON	BOTHAM	4	8	223	-	.	17	Edged push at away seamer.
5-22	5-23	1	10	C.J.McDERMOTT	LBW	EMBUREY	0	9	224	-	.	1	Padded up to 'arm' ball - first ball.
5-25	(6-14)	49	11	R.G.HOLLAND	NOT OUT		5			-	.	27	
				EXTRAS	b - lb 3 w 1 nb 3		7			1	22	539 balls (including 4 no balls)	
				TOTAL	(89.1 OVERS - 374 MINUTES)		**257**						ALL OUT AT 6.14 pm (90th over of 1st day)

* CAPTAIN   † WICKET-KEEPER

UMPIRES: H.D.BIRD, D.R.SHEPHERD

© BILL FRINDALL 1985

14 OVERS 2 BALLS/HOUR
2·88 RUNS/OVER
48 RUNS/100 BALLS

BOWLER	O	M	R	W
BOTHAM	23	4	79	4
AGNEW	14	0	65	0
ALLOTT	13	1	29	0
EMBUREY	24	7	41	2
EDMONDS	15.1	4	40	4
			3	
	89.1	16	257	10

W	HRS	OVERS	RUNS
4½	1	12	51
0 -⅓	2	14	34
-	3	15	40
-	4	17	43
-	5	14	43
	6	14	35

RUNS	MINS	OVERS	LAST 50 (in mins)
50	56	11.4	56
100	138	30.4	82
150	210	50.0	72
200	280	66.3	70
250	366	87.4	86

LUNCH: 85-1 (27 OVERS)(122 MIN) HILDITCH 43* (156b) BOON 6* (19b)

TEA: 168-4 (58 OVERS)(241 MIN) BOON 51* (156b) PHILLIPS 18* (65b)

WKT	PARTNERSHIP		RUNS	MINS
1st	Wessels	Hilditch	71	83
2nd	Hilditch	Boon	26	46
3rd	Boon	Border	21	37
4th	Boon	Ritchie	4	2
5th	Boon	Phillips	71	85
6th	Boon	Matthews	5	13
7th	Matthews	O'Donnell	13	22
8th	O'Donnell	Lawson	12	18
9th	O'Donnell	McDermott	1	1
10th	O'Donnell	Holland	33	49
			257	

2ND NEW BALL taken at 5.59 pm on 1st day - AUSTRALIA 246-9 after 86 overs.

138

ENGLAND 1ST INNINGS — IN REPLY TO AUSTRALIA'S 257 ALL OUT

IN	OUT	MINS	No.	BATSMAN	HOW OUT	BOWLER	RUNS	WKT	TOTAL	6s	4s	BALLS	NOTES ON DISMISSAL
11:00	4:06	209	1	G.A.GOOCH	LBW	McDERMOTT	74	2	142	·	9	144	Late on fast breakback - played back.
11:00	11:18	18	2	R.T.ROBINSON	C BORDER	McDERMOTT	10	1	21	·	2	12	Edged steer at widish ball waist-high to 2nd slip.
11:21	4:15	197	3	D.I.GOWER *	C HILDITCH	McDERMOTT	47	3	148	·	5	140	(5000 runs when 34) Hooked to long-leg boundary - tumbling catch.
4:08	6:05	357	4	M.W.GATTING	C PHILLIPS	McDERMOTT	160	6	450	·	21	266	(1st in 40 Test innings in England. Edged cover drive - 'walked'.
4:17	3:13	194	5	A.J.LAMB	RUN OUT (MATTHEWS)		67	4	304	·	8	135	Direct throw from cover-point - Gatting's stroke.
3:15	3:49	34	6	I.T.BOTHAM	C O'DONNELL	McDERMOTT	20	5	339	·	3	25	Hooked bouncer to deep backward square-leg (running catch).
3:51	11:01	134	7	P.R.DOWNTON †	BOWLED	McDERMOTT	23	7	448	·	1	82	Break back - second ball of fourth day.
6:07	11:46	62	8	J.E.EMBUREY	NOT OUT		31		-	·	3	37	
11:03	11:08	5	9	P.H.EDMONDS	BOWLED	McDERMOTT	1	8	450	·	·	7	Yorked leg stump - late inswinger.
11:10	11:28	18	10	P.J.W.ALLOTT	BOWLED	McDERMOTT	7	9	470	·	1	11	Middle stump out - attempting slog over long-on.
11:30	11:46	16	11	J.P.AGNEW	NOT OUT		2			·	·	8	
				EXTRAS	b 7 lb 16 w - nb 17		40			0	5³		867 balls (including 21 no balls)

TOTAL (141 OVERS - 631 MINUTES) **482-9 DECLARED** at 11:46am on 4th day

(LEAD: 225)

13 OVERS 2 BALLS/HOUR
3.42 RUNS/OVER
56 RUNS/100 BALLS

* CAPTAIN † WICKET-KEEPER

WKT	PARTNERSHIP		RUNS	MINS
1st	Gooch	Robinson	21	18
2nd	Gooch	Gower	121	188
3rd	Gower	Gatting	6	7
4th	Gatting	Lamb	156	194
5th	Gatting	Botham	35	34
6th	Gatting	Downton	91	115
7th	Downton	Emburey	18	17
8th	Emburey	Edmonds	2	5
9th	Emburey	Allott	20	18
10th	Emburey	Agnew	12*	16
			482.	

RSP 11:33 to 12:14 1ST DAY (24-1)   10 OVERS LOST (41')

LUNCH: 55-1 (15 OVERS, 31 MINUTES) GOOCH 18* (81 min) GOWER 15* (60 min)

TEA: 141-1 (45 OVERS, 203 MINUTES) GOOCH 73* (203 min) GOWER 46* (182 min)

STUMPS: 233-3 (2ND DAY) (80 OVERS, 341 MIN.) GATTING 45* (130 min) LAMB 38* (121 min)

TEA: 354-5 (107 OVERS, 472 MIN.) GATTING 103* (261 min) DOWNTON 7* (20 min)

STUMPS: 448-6 (3RD DAY) (132.4 OVERS, 585 MIN.) (LEAD: 191) DOWNTON 23* (135') EMBUREY 12* (16')

ENGLAND added 34 RUNS in 46 MINUTES off 8.2 OVERS for the loss of 3 WICKETS on the fourth morning (McDERMOTT 3-14 in 4.2 OVERS)

BOWLER	O	M	R	W	nb
LAWSON	37	7	114	0	9
McDERMOTT	36	3	141	8	7
HOLLAND	38	7	101	0	-
O'DONNELL	21	6	82	0	1
MATTHEWS	9	2	21	0	-
	141	25	482	9	23 / 25

HRS	OVERS	RUNS
1	11	37
2	13	39
3	15	42
4	15	51
5	16	39
6	15	42
7	11	54
8	13	61
9	13	45
10	13	40

RUNS	MINS	OVERS	LAST 50 (in mins)
50	73	13.2	73
100	146	29.5	73
150	223	49.1	77
200	283	66.0	60
250	359	84.5	76
300	410	94.3	51
350	466	105.4	56
400	521	118.3	55
450	590	133.5	69

© BILL FRINDALL 1985

2nd NEW BALL taken at 2:30pm on 3rd day. - ENGLAND 256-3 after 87 overs.

AUSTRALIA 2ND INNINGS — 225 RUNS BEHIND ON FIRST INNINGS

IN	OUT	MINS	No.	BATSMAN	HOW OUT	BOWLER	RUNS	WKT	TOTAL	6s	4s	BALLS	NOTES ON DISMISSAL
11·57	2·34	118	1	A.M.J.HILDITCH	BOWLED	EMBUREY	40	2	85		3	88	Played back to straight ball (bowled through bat-pad gap).
11·57	1·41	65	2	G.R.J.MATTHEWS	Cᵗ AND BOWLED	EDMONDS	17	.	38	.	.	42	Held fierce chest-high drive – second post-lunch ball.
1·43	3·38	115	3	K.C.WESSELS	Cᵗ AND BOWLED	EMBUREY	50	3	126	.	8	112	Low return catch – beaten in flight.
2·36	(5·32)	346	4	A.R.BORDER*	NOT OUT		146		334	.	13	334	(1000 F-C RUNS) WHEN 57
4·00	4·28	28	5	D.C.BOON	BOWLED	EMBUREY	7	4	138	.	1	36	Down wicket – drove outside off-break.
4·30	2·13	127	6	G.M.RITCHIE	BOWLED	EMBUREY	31	5	213	1	3	102	Played on – inside edge rolled into stumps.
2·15	(5·32)	125	7	W.B.PHILLIPS†	NOT OUT		39			.	6	130	
			8										
			9										
			10										
			11										

EXTRAS: b 1 lb 6 w – nb 3 → 10

TOTAL (140 OVERS – 466 MINUTES) **340-5**

2ᵇ 36 844 balls (including 4 no balls)

* CAPTAIN † WICKET-KEEPER

© BILL FRINDALL 1985

BOWLER	O	M	R	W	nb		HRS	OVERS	RUNS
BOTHAM	15	3	50	0	-		1	14	31
ALLOTT	6	2	40	0	-		2	14	54
EDMONDS	54	12	122	1	.		3	21	36
EMBUREY	51	17	99	4	1		4	19	38
AGNEW	9	2	34	0	2		5	20	31
GATTING	4	0	14	0	-		6	18	29
LAMB	1	0	10	0	-		7	20	69
	140	36	340	5					

RUNS	MINS	OVERS	LAST 50 (in mins)
50	82	19·2	82
100	152	38·5	70
150	231	65·1	79
200	315	93·2	84
250	390	117·5	75
300	430	130·0	40

2ND NEW BALL taken at 1·51 pm on 5ᵗʰ day – AUSTRALIA 200-4 after 94 overs.

18 OVERS 0 BALLS/HOUR
2·43 RUNS/OVER
40 RUNS/100 BALLS

WKT	PARTNERSHIP		RUNS	MINS
1ST	Hilditch	Matthews	38	65
2ND	Hilditch	Wessels	47	51
3RD	Wessels	Border	41	62
4TH	Border	Boon	12	28
5TH	Border	Ritchie	75	127
6TH	Border	Phillips	127*	125
7TH				
8TH				
9TH				
10TH				
			340	

LUNCH: 38-0 (15 OVERS) (64 MIN.)
TEA: 126-3 (49·5 OVERS) (182 MINUTES) HILDITCH 20* MATTHEWS 17* BORDER 15* (62 min)
STUMPS: 192-4 (90 OVERS) (304 MIN) (33 BEHIND) (4ᵗʰ DAY) BORDER 49* (184') RITCHIE 22* (92')
RAIN DELAYED START UNTIL 12·30pm (10 MINUTES) PLAY RSP at 12·40 – 3 OVERS (22 OVERS LOST)
LUNCH: 194-4 (93 OVERS) (314 MIN) BORDER 50* (194') RITCHIE 23* (102')
RESTART at 1·48 pm – RSP (TEA TAKEN) at 3·10pm. (18·3 OVERS) BORDER 93* (274') PHILLIPS 6* (53')
TEA: 253-5 (394 MINUTES)

MATCH DRAWN
MAN OF THE MATCH: C.J. McDERMOTT
(Adjudicator: R. ILLINGWORTH)

FOURTH TEST
SHEET 1

1ST DAY TIME	BOWLERS (D.R. SHEPHERD) STRETFORD END BOWLER	O.	(H.D. BIRD) WARWICK RD END BOWLER	O.	BATSMEN SCOREBOARD LEFT SCORING	BALLS	6s/4s	SCOREBOARD RIGHT SCORING	BALLS	6s/4s	AUSTRALIA 1ST INNINGS NOTES	END-OF-OVER TOTALS O.	RUNS	W.	'L' BAT	'R' BAT	EXTRAS
					WESSELS			LHB HILDITCH									
11·00	BOTHAM	1			4/7 1 3P 4+4 ·.	6	2				(W)	1	9		8		1
07			AGNEW	1	:	7		7/8 2 · · 2 2 · · · 3	5			2	14			5	
12	– · –	2			4 3	8		3 · 1 · · 7 1	10			3	19		11	7	
16			– · –	2	L · 28 · x ·O· 2·	14		3 3	11		(NB) NB1	4	25		13	10	2
20½	– · –	3			·			8 2 · x : : : :	17			5	27			12	
25			– · –	3	: · · · P 9 1	20	·					6	28		14		
28½	– · –	4			6(6) · 1	23		: 1 2 4 1	20	1		7	34		15	17	
33			– · –	4	: · x 23/4 23	28		1/2 1	21			8	40		20	18	
37½	– · –	5			: P · 4 · 2 ·	34						9	42		22		
43			ALLOTT	1	· P	35		· L · · 7	26		sawdust – 1 min delay	10	43			19	
49½	– · –	6			8	36		PL · 9 4/9 : · 4 1	31	2		11	49		23	24	
54			– · –	2	P: · · 2 :	41		4/9	32		50 p'ship : 56 min. 1HR	12	51		24	25	
58	– · –	7			· 4 1	42		: : · 3 7 4 1	37	3	Round wkt to LHB	13	57		25	30	
12·04			EMBUREY	1	7 4 4 4 3 24 : : ·	48	3				† Gatting hit (leg). # didn't other U.B.	14	63		31		
08	ALLOTT	3			4 P L 4 · · · 3	52		1/2E 1	39			15	67		34	31	
13½			– · –	2	: : : · : ·	58					M1	16					
16½	– · –	4			:	59		x · P x 8 : · · 1	44			17	68			32	
22			– · –	3	E1 W	60	3	8 8 2 1	46			17/3	71	1	34	35	2
23					BOON										0		
25			– · –	3	: P :	3						18					
27	– · –	5						6/7 2 · x · · 2 · · · 1	52			19	73			37	
32			– · –	4	7 1 : :	6		: P 2 1	55			20	75		1	38	
35	– · –	6			: 8 : · 1	8		: 8t · 7/3 : · · 1	59		† Edmonds misfielded	21	76			39	
39½			– · –	5	9 1 : · 9	9		· · · P 3	64			22	78		2	40	
42½	– · –	7			5(6) 1	10		: : : · 8	69			23	79		3		
47			– · –	6	P 8 · · 7 : 1	14		6 P 1 ·	71			24	82		5	41	
50	– · –	8			7 · x 6 : · · 1	19		7 : 1	72			25	84		6	42	
55			EDMONDS	1	: :	21		: · · at 1	76		Round wkt 2HR † to absent S. point.	26	85			43	
58	– · –	9			:	21	–	: 8 · 8 : : : · 1	82	3	M2	27	85	1	6	43	2
1·02	LUNCH												L U N C H				
1·41			EDMONDS	2	LL : P 2 P 4·	27	1					28	89		10		
44	AGNEW	5						1 6 Lx 2 · 24 · · 0 · ·	89	4	(NB) NB2	29	96			49	3
49			– · –	3	4 1	28		x : : 3 W	93	4		29/5	97	2	11	49	3
50½								BORDER		LHB						0	
52½			– · –	3				: 1	1		over wkt.	30					
54	– · –	6			x FSt · 5(4) · · · 3	32		7 3 : 1	3		† Hit bowler's stump.	31	100		14		
59			– · –	4	PP · · PP : · ·	38					M3	32					
2·01½	– · –	7			1 P · x : · ·	43		· 9 O1	5		(NB) NB 3	33	102			1	4
06			– · –	5	8/9 : · : 8	47	1	7 : 1	7	–	* Almost played on. M3 NB3	34	104	2	15	2	4

TIME	BOWLER (Stretford End)	O.	BOWLER (Warwick Rd End)	O.	SCORING (Scoreboard Left)	BALLS	6s/4s	SCORING (Scoreboard Right)	BALLS	6s/4s	NOTES	O.	RUNS	W.	L BAT	R BAT	EXTRAS
					BOON	47	1	BORDER	7	-	M3 NB 3	34	104	2	15	2	4
2·10	AGNEW	8			:4:4¹	52	2	:	8			35	109		20		
14½			EDMONDS	6	::4²:P	58					M 4	36					
17	-·-	9						4...:⁴	14	1		37	113			6	
21			-·-	7	:::3::	64					M 5	38					
24	-·-	10			:4:6/3	68		7/1 2/1	16			39	118		23	8	
28			-·-	8	⎫			7.X W	18	1		39²	118	3	23	8	4
29					⎪			RITCHIE								0	
31			-·-	8	⎪			4.W	3	1		39⁵	122	4	23	4	4
33					⎬			PHILLIPS		LHB						0	
35			-·-	8	⎭			:	1			40	123			1	
37	EMBUREY	7			::6	71		3.8 :	4		Round wkt to LHB. 3HR	41	125		24	2	
41			-·-	9	P¹³:4:::	77	3				† EDMONDS warned - pitch damage.	42	129		28		
44½	-·-	8						:4...X	10			43					
47			-·-	10	:7:PPP	83					M 7	44					
50	-·-	9						:5::::	16		M 8	45					
52			-·-	11	P¹/₈L:5 :2 :1	88		::	17			46	132		31		
56	-·-	10			7/8 1	89		2·3⁵::::	22			47	133		32		
59			-·-	12	:LP:7 :	94		2 1	23			48	135		33	3	
3·03	-·-	11			::⁸	96		:4 2·4 43	27	1		49	142			10	
06			-·-	13	P⁷¹⁸:4¹	100	4	:¹³	29			50	150		38	13	
10	ALLOTT	10			::³⁴¹⁶:4¹	104	5	::	31			51	155		43		
16			EMBUREY	12	:::⁸	109		.	32			52	156		44		
19	-·-	11			² :::	113		:⁴⁸	34			53	158		45	14	
23			-·-	13	7 :	114		:::²·³1	39			54	160		46	15	
26	-·-	12			P:5(6):4¹:::	120	6				Boon's 50: 145 min	55	164		50		
31			-·-	14				7::¹:.	45		M 9	56					
33	-·-	13			4 6 1	122		8::·9 1	49			57	168		51	18	
38			-·-	15		122	6	:P:..:6	55	1	M 10 NB 3 4HR	58	168	4	51	18	4
3·40	TEA													T E A		
4·01	BOTHAM	8			::² 1	125		:4·4²/₃	58	2	50 P'ship: 70 min.	59	173		52	22	
06			EDMONDS	14	²3 6::	129		:³ 3	60			60	179		55	25	
10	-·-	9						L:2¹/₃7 7 :4·:	66	3		61	183	·		29	
15			-·-	15	.²³:2: ::	134		7 1	67			62	187		58	30	
19	-·-	10	⎫					7·4 61 2·4W	71	4		62²	193	5	58	36	4
21			⎬					MATTHEWS		LHB						0	
23	-·-	10	⎭					P::	2			63					
26			EMBUREY	16	PP:9:2::	140						64	195		60		
29	-·-	11						4..·2::	8			65	197			2	
33			-·-	17	.³4P6:1	145	6	.	9	-	M 10 NB 3	66	198	5	61	2	4

1ST DAY TIME	BOWLERS (SHEPHERD) STRETFORD END BOWLER	O.	(BIRD) WARWICK RD END BOWLER	O.	BATSMEN SCOREBOARD LEFT SCORING	BALLS	6/4	SCOREBOARD RIGHT SCORING	BALLS	6/4	NOTES	O.	RUNS	W.	'L' BAT	'R' BAT	EXTRAS
					BOON	145	6	MATTHEWS	9	-	M10 NB 3	66	198	5	61	2	4
4·36	BOTHAM	12			²W	146	6					66	198	6	61	2	4
					O'DONNELL										O		
38	- · -	12			E¹ x .4 : :	5	1					67	202		4		
42			EMBUREY	18				6· 1 P : ·2LB .2 : : ·	15		· Bo chance (ALLOTT). (2LB)	68	206			4	6
46	- · -	13			: : : x ·³/4	11	2					69	210		8		
50			- · -	19				3† ² · L P · : · :	21		† Diving Stop (EDMONDS). M11	70					
53	- · -	14			4 · 7 : · 1	14		: · :	24			71	211		9		
57			- · -	20	7 : : : P ·	20					M12 5HR	72					
5·00	- · -	15						x̂ W	25	-		72	211	7	9	4	6
								LAWSON								O	
02	- · -	15						x x : · x	5		M13	73					
05			- · -	21	8 : 1	22		P : ·³ P ·	9			74	214		10	2	
09	- · -	16			: 7 8 : x 2 2 : ·	28						75	218		14		
13½			- · -	22				: : : : ³ P 2 ·	15			76	220			4	
16	- · -	17			4 2 : · 1	32		6 E¹ · W	17	-		77	223	8	17	4	6
20								McDERMOTT								O	
22			- · -	23	: 4 1	34		L W	1	-		77³	224	9	18	O	6
23								HOLLAND								O	
25			- · -	23				: P ¹†	3		† Run refused.	78					
27	- · -	18			x 6† x LB · : :	38		· : x ·	5		† Run refused. (LB) M14	79	225				7
31			- · -	24	: 8 1	40		P : : :	9			80	226		19		
34	- · -	19			2† 4 L 7 · · 1	46					† Run refused. M15	81					
38			AGNEW	11	: ²† ¹/0 6†³ · : · 3	51		9 2 1 : 1	11		† Run refused. NB 4 · Botham overthrows.	82	232		23	2	
43	- · -	20			4† : : ·²³/2Ⓛ 2 2 1	57					† Run refused.	83	237		28		
46			- · -	12	: 2† ²/6 7 : · : 1	61		P† ² :	13		† Runs refused.	84	240		31		
51	- · -	21			: P · ¹²³4 · · · 4 ·	67	3				† Run refused	85	244		35		
55			- · -	13				: : : ½ P ·	19		6HR	86	246			4	
59	- · -	22			† 8† 7† : : ·⁵/4Ⓛ	72		· ·	20		† NEW BALL † Runs refused	87	247		36		
6·03			- · -	14	6 · ¹⁶/⁶† : 2 6 ·	77	1/3	4 : 1	21			88	257		45	5	
08	- · -	23						⁵ · P · : : : ·	27		M 16	89					
13			EDMONDS	16	x̂ W	78	1/3		27	-		89³	257	10	45	5	7
6·14	AUSTRALIA	ALL	OUT								M 16 NB 4	ALL	OUT				
											539 balls						

FOURTH TEST
SHEET 4

2ND DAY TIME	BOWLERS (SHEPHERD) STRETFORD END BOWLER	O.	BOWLERS (BIRD) WARWICK Rd END BOWLER	O.	BATSMEN SCOREBOARD LEFT SCORING	BALLS	6s/4s	BATSMEN SCOREBOARD RIGHT SCORING	BALLS	6s/4s	ENGLAND 1ST INNINGS NOTES	O.	RUNS	W.	L BAT	R BAT	EXTRAS
					GOOCH			ROBINSON									
11·00	LAWSON	1			⊙··1	4		··1	3		NB 1	1	3		1	1	1
06			McDERMOTT	1	·1	5		·44·1	8	2		2	13		2	10	
11½	·-·	2			··22·4	11	1					3	21		10		
17			·-·	2				··W	12	2		3	21	1	10	10	1
18½								GOWER		LHB	M1					0	
21			·-·	2				·1	2		Pitch damage McDermott warned	4					
23	·-·	3			x·3/4 ·x	15		·1	4			5	23		11	1	
28			·-·	3	set·P·	19	1	L·7	6	-	in air behind bowler. Umpires consulted – drizzle	6	24	1	11	2	1
32	·-·	4															
11·33 RAIN											(10 OVERS LOST)		R	S	P		
12·14	LAWSON	4			·⊙··2··	13					NB 2	7	27			4	2
19			McDERMOTT	4	·1	21		2·⊙·	18		Dropped BOON (1st40) NB 3	8	31		12	6	3
25	·-·	5			····⊙1	28					NB 4	9	33		13		4
30½			·-·	5	··7·8	33			19			10	34		14		
35	·-·	6			4·7	37		⊙·1	22		NB 5 1HR	11	37		15	7	5
41			·-·	6	·14	40		9⊙·⊙	27		NB 7	12	40		16	8	6
46½	·-·	7			2·1	41		···⊙4	33	1	NB 8	13	46		17	12	7
52			·-·	7	9·1 ⊙·7	44		42·1	37	2	NB 9	14	55		18	19	8
57	·-·	8				44	1	···89	43	2	Almost played on M2 NB9	15	55	1	18	19	8
1·02 LUNCH													L	U	N	C	H
1·40			McDERMOTT	8	·P LB	47		1 ·4·	46		LB	16	58		19	20	9
44½	LAWSON	9			·2··	53						17	60		21		
50			·-·	9				3·····3	52			18	63			23	
54	·-·	10						····P·	58		M3	19					
58½			·-·	10		54		·2···	63			20	66		22	25	
2·03	·-·	11			4·LB	57		··3	66		M4 LB	21	67				10
07			·-·	11	77 V/2 ·1	60	2	···	69		50 p'ship: 89 min.	22	72		27		
12	·-·	12			·1·7	65		1st	70		Just short of gully	23	75		29	26	
17			HOLLAND	1	4·8f	68		···	73		2HR	24	76		30		
20	·-·	13			·2⊕20·0	77	3				NB NB 12	25	87		39		12
27			·-·	2	···1	83					M5	26					
30	O'DONNELL	1						·4···	79	3		27	91			30	
34			·-·	3	4·1	85		·P··	83			28	92		40		
37	·-·	2			·1	88	4	··8/9	86		Almost played on	29	98		45	31	
42			·-·	4	··st	91		·6·1	89		Bird hit on leg (saved 3 runs)	30	100		46	32	
46	·-·	3			st·614·	97					hit stumps M6	31					
50			·-·	5				··644	95			32	101			33	
53	·-·	4						75·4	101		5000 RUNS	33	102		34		
57/59			·-·	6		97	4	····2·	107	3	Treatment to BIRD M6 NB 12	34	104	1	46	36	12

144

2ND DAY TIME	BOWLERS (SHEPHERD) STRETFORD END BOWLER	O.	(BIRD) WARWICK RD END BOWLER	O.	BATSMEN SCOREBOARD LEFT SCORING	BALLS	6s/4s	SCOREBOARD RIGHT SCORING	BALLS	6s/4s	ENGLAND 1ST INNINGS NOTES	O.	RUNS	W.	'L' BAT	'R' BAT	EXTRAS
					GOOCH	97	4	GOWER	107	3	M6 NB 12	34	104	1	46	36	12
3.01	O'DONNELL	5			.347.4	103					M7 Gooch's 50: 163	35					
05			HOLLAND	7	:4².⁵ᵗ.	107	5	:8 1	109		† Removed middle stump.	36	109		50	37	
09	— • —	6						3...³.	115		M8	37					
13			— " —	8	⁵⁽⁶⁾ 4.²²¹	113	6				•	38	118		59		
17	— • —	7			ᴺᴮ4.5⁵ᵗ	119					• Dropped slip (Boon) M9 3HR	39					
21			— • —	9				664:.:	121		M10	40					
23	— • —	8			ᴱ¹4.⁵⁽⁴⁾4.:.	125	8				100 p'ship : 164 min.	41	126		67		
28			— • —	10	⁴ᴾ•⁴4.::	130	9	⁵⁽⁶⁾	122		† Round wkt.	42	131		71	38	
31	— • —	9						3.:4.³4	128	5		43	139			46	
35½			— • —	11	⁶ᴾ7 :·¹	133		ᴸ.::	131			44	140		72		
38	— • —	10			ᴸ:.:³.	138	9	:	132	5		45	141	1	73	46	12
3.42	TEA										M 10 NB 12				T E A		
4.00			HOLLAND	12	::⁶ᶠ¹	141		ᴾ:.⁶	135		Round wkt.	46	142		74		
04	McDERMOTT	12			ᴾ.ᴸ.W	144	9					46³	142	2	74	46	12
06					GATTING										0		
08	— • —	12			ᴾ³ᴾ :.¹	3					M11	47					
10			— • —	13	:::⁵⁽⁴⁾4:	8	1	ᴸ¹	136			48	147		4	47	
13	— • —	13						⁵:·⁺⁸⁹:⊙·W	140	5	ⓃⒷ NB 13	48³	148	3	4	47	13
15								LAMB								0	
17	— • —	13			..	10		⁸¹ 1	1			49	149			1	
19½			— • —	14	:³¹	12		⁸¹ ::ᴾ	5			50	153		7	2	
24	— • —	14			⁸⁄⁸⁸⁸ 4 2 1	15	2	:::.	8			51	160		14		
28			— • —	15	⁵⁴³.³.³⁹ ::·¹	21						52	161		15		
30½	— • —	15			³⁵ 4 3.:.	26		²ᴱ¹	9			53	163		16	3	
35			— • —	16				::³⁄²ᴾ7ᴱ⁴⁄¹ 4.·.²	15	1	4HR	54	169			9	
38	— • —	16			⁶⁸¹ ᶠ:.:	30		⁷.⁷⁸ 2.⊙¹	18		NB 14	55	173		17	12	
42½			— • —	17				.ˣᵗ::.¹	24		† st asst umpt. M12	56					
47	— • —	17			ᴸ4ᴾ.⁺⁷⁄²⁷⁄⁸ 4.¹	36	3					57	178		22		
51	— • —	18			⁸¹	37		ᴾ²74ᴾ :².:	29			58	181		23	14	
54½	— • —	18			:.⁴³⁵.¹ :	42		4. :³⁰	30			59	183		24	15	
59½			— • —	19				.44.ᴱ⁸²	36		M13	60					
5.02	MATTHEWS	1			³.::.³.	48					M14	61					
05			— • —	20	.ˣ⁶1	51		:³.¹ :	39			62	185		25	16	
08½	— • —	2			:⁹.:³⁵¹ 2 ¹	57						63	188		28		
11			— • —	21	4³4.⁴⁴⁵: 4.¹	63	4				† Diving stop (Wessels)	64	192		32		
14½	— • —	3			⁵⁸ᶠ.⁴¹1	66		:⁴ᶠ.³ ᴮ	42		Ⓑ† Diving (Border)	65	197		33	19	14
17½			— • —	22	ᴾ.²4.¹	69	5	:4³.¹	45		50 p'ship : 61 min.	66	202		37	20	
21	LAWSON	14						:::².⁷.¹	51			67	205			23	
25			MATTHEWS	4	.ᴾ⁶1	72	5	ᴮ. .ᴾ	54	1	Ⓑ M14 NB 14	68	207	3	38	23	15

145

2ND DAY TIME	BOWLER (SHEPHERD) STRETFORD END	O.	BOWLER (BIRD) WARWICK Rd END	O.	SCOREBOARD LEFT SCORING	BALLS	6s/4s	SCOREBOARD RIGHT SCORING	BALLS	6s/4s	NOTES	O.	RUNS	W.	L BAT	R BAT	EXTRAS
					GATTING	72	5	LAMB	54	1	M14 NB14	68	207	3	38	23	15
5.29	LAWSON	15			3... ..	78					M15	69					
34			MATTHEWS	5	:::P	82		:8 /1	56		5 HR	70	208			24	
38	-.-	16			:8 :.	86		1 8 /1	58		Delay - reflection from TV camera	71	211		39	26	
43			-.-	6	?	87		4::: 8/7	63			72	212			27	
46	-.-	17			::	88		8/7 .. 9 .4:	68	2		73	217			32	
51			-.-	7	3 4 5 . 8	74					(B) M16	74	218				16
54	-.-.	18			:::: x	80					M17	75					
59½			HOLLAND	23	P8 /1	90		. :: 2B	84		(2B)	76	221		40		18
6.02½	-.-	19			7 /1	91		. :: 4 3	89			77	223		41	33	
07			-.-	24	6F P 7 4P .4:	96	6	6S /1	90			78	228		45	34	
10	-.-	20						7/9† ... LB	96		† Round wkt. (LB) M18	79	229				19
15½			-.-	25		96	6	4 P P P† ::	102	3	† Over wkt.	80	233	3	45	38	19
6.18	STUMPS										M18 NB14		STUMPS				
3RD DAY 11.00	START DELAYED										Heavy overnight rain - showers throughout morning. 35 OVERS LOST						
1.00	LUNCH																
2.00	MATTHEWS	8			.::::4 3	102	7					81	237		49		
03			HOLLAND	26				: 6†7f .4: 52 3	108	4		82	241			42	
06	-.-	9			6 3S /1	104		7 2 :.4 7	112	5	GATTING'S 50: 137' 100 p'ship: 129'	83	248		50	48	
09			-.-	27	6::: 8	109		:	113			84	249		51		
12/15	LAWSON	21			.4 3/2 . 9	114		x	114		Ball changed 6HR	85	250		52		
20			McDERMOTT	19	P: 2LB 4 7	119		↑	115		(2LB)	86	253		53		21
25	-.-	22			3 3 7 2 . 1	122		:.: :	118			87	256		56		
30			-.-	20	†7 3/43/2 3 4 1 0	127	8	7 8½ /1	120		† NEW BALL LAMB's 50: 154 min (NB) NB 15	88	267		64	50	22
35	-.-	23			2 .1 2.0	130		78† 2.. /1	124		† Return, hit Gatting on wrist (Holland)	89	273		67	53	
42			-.-	21	4 Y 4 3 3† 2 . 1	136					† NB 16	90	276		70		
47	-.-	24			3 3/2 . L 6 .4 . 4	142	10				† Misfield (Matthews)	91	284		78		
52			-.-	22				2 6/5 †: .4: 4	130	7	† Missed hook (chest)	92	294			63	
57	-.-	25			E†: . L .7S .O1	148		4	131		† lbw front of 1st slip	93	296		79		23
3.03			O'DONNELL	11	7 x†: . LB	154					† Appeal ct wk. (NB) M19	94	297				24
07	-.-	26			66 2 /1	156		17 . LB .4:	135	8	150 p'ship: 189 min (LB)	95	304		81	67	25
13			-.-	12	3 /1	157		RO	135	8		95	304	4	81	67	25
13								BOTHAM									0
15	-.-	12						7 . x: .	5		M20 7HR	96					
19	McDERMOTT	23			1 8 . F. :: 2 . 1	163						97	306		83		
24			-.-	13	:	164		P . P 6 2 /1	10			98	307			1	
28	-.-	24			8 3 .4.	166	11	P P x 7 ::	14			99	312		87	2	
33			-.-	14	P 9	168		P 6 7 4† .44:	18	2	† Good stop (Marsh)	100	322		88	11	
37	-.-	25			8/7 † 3 3 6 6 4...	174	12					101	326		92		
42			-.-	15	EP4 .4:	177	13	3 7† :. 3	21	2	† Diving stop (Border) M20 NB17	102	333	4	96	14	25

	BOWLERS				BATSMEN					ENGLAND 1ST INNINGS	END-OF-OVER TOTALS					
3RD DAY	(SHEPHERD) STRETFORD END		(BIRD) WARWICK RD END		SCOREBOARD LEFT			SCOREBOARD RIGHT			NOTES						
TIME	BOWLER	O.	BOWLER	O.	SCORING	BALLS	6s/4s	SCORING	BALLS	6s/4s		O.	RUNS	W.	'L' BAT	'R' BAT	EXTRAS
					GATTING	177	13	BOTHAM	21	2	M20 NB17	102	333	4	96	14	25
3.46	McDERMOTT	26						6 8 64) 8⁴ 24 W	25	3		102	339	5	96	20	25
49								DOWNTON								0	
51	— · —	26						7 :	2			103					
52½			O'DONNELL	16	: 3 4 . . : 2 P	183	14				GATTING'S 100: 244'	104	343		100		
57	— · —	27			: 4	185		6 8/78/79 4⁴	6	1		105	348			5	
4.03			— · —	17	9 5⁴ 2 .	187		. . : ○ 8	11		† Almost bowled NB 18 NB	106	352		102	6	26
07	— · —	28			: : . : 6P 2	192	14	E2	12	1		107	354	5	103	7	26
4.11	TEA		·								M20 NB 18				TEA		
4.30			O'DONNELL	18	8 2 7/6 . : 2 4 2 4 . .	198	16					108	365		114		
35	LAWSON	27			7/3 3 3 3 : :	204					M21 8HR	109					
40			— · —	19	3 2 4 2 4 2 - .	208	17	LB :	14		LB	110	373		121		27
45	— · —	28			6 3 2 . 4 P 6	213	18	.	15			111	379		126	8	
50			HOLLAND	28				: 2B P - . P	21		2B M22	112	381				29
53	— · —	29			7 : 2	217		. 9	23			113	384		128	9	
58			— · —	29	9 : : : 4 :	223					M23	114					
5.02	— · —	30			: 24	226		X : 7	26			115	385			10	
07			— · —	30	: : :	229		6 : LB	29		LB M24	116	386				30
10	— · —	31			LB 230	230		E2 : . 9	34		LB	117	388			11	31
15			— · —	31	: 3 3⁴ 4 1	236	20				† Diving stop (Boon) 50 p's hip: 66 min.	118	397		137		
18	— · —	32			: : 6 3	239		4 L :	37			119	400		140		
23			— · —	32	6 . 64) 1	242		8 :	40		Round wkt	120	403		142	12	
28	— · —	33			6 7 : 1 2 0 1	246		: : 4	43		NB NB 19	121	408		145	13	32
33			— · —	33	8	247		: : 8 : P⁴	48		† Appeal cr sh leg. 9HR	122	410		146	14	
37	— · —	34			†4 5/6 P 8 4 : 1	251	21	3 :	50		† umpires conferred : batsmen offered light	123	415		151		
42			— · —	34	: 4	253		: : 4 ⁴/3	54		GATTING'S 150: 329 min	124	416		152		
44	— · —	35			2LB 1 . 1	255		: 6 ⁴ ⁴9	58		2LB	125	420		153	15	34
48 52	DRINKS		— · —	35				: P . 8 8/9 2 :	64			126	422			17	
55	McDERMOTT	29			6 4 : 4 : 2 : 2 .	261						127	424		155		
6.00			— · —	36	1 5 6 2 1	263		: 8 : 25 : 1	68			128	428		158	18	
04	— · —	30			2 T 5 E1 2 · W	266	21				† Diving stop (Matthews)	128	430	6	160	18	34
05½					EMBUREY											0	
07	— · —	30			7 : 1	3						129					
10			— · —	37				: : P . . : 2 .	74			130	432			20	
12	— · —	31			: : P 67 : 4 · 0	10	1				NB NB 20	131	437		4		35
17			— · —	38	9 : 3	12		L6 8 · 1 . 7/6	78			132	442		7	22	
21	— · —	32			3 2t 4 1	14	2	: 9 1	80	1	† heavy rain.	132	448	6	12	23	35
6.23	STUMPS										M24 NB 20		RSP	-	STUMPS		

FOURTH TEST
SHEET 8

4TH DAY TIME	BOWLER (SHEPHERD) STRETFORD END	O.	BOWLER (BIRD) WARWICK RD END	O.	SCOREBOARD LEFT SCORING	BALLS	6s/4s	SCOREBOARD RIGHT SCORING	BALLS	6s/4s	NOTES	O.	RUNS	W.	'L' BAT	'R' BAT	EXTRAS
					EMBUREY	14	2	DOWNTON	80	1	M 24 NB 20	132	448	6	12	23	35
11·00	McDERMOTT	32						ᵡW	82	1		133	448	7	12	23	35
01								EDMONDS								0	
03			O'DONNELL	20	9 · · · ᵡ · · ·	16		P · · 3 ᵞ/8	4			134	450		13	1	
07	— · —	33						· 3 ᵞ/4 · · · W	7	–		134	450	8	13	1	35
08								ALLOTT								0	
10	– · · –	33						ᵡ ᵞ P · · ·	3		M 25 10 HR	135				0	
13			— · · —	21	ᵞ/3 4/5 6 ᵞ · · 4 3	20	3	ᵡ 4/5 · ·	5		† 200 LEAD	136	458		20	1	
17	– · · –	34			2 · 2 2 · 1	23		4 · 7 6 4 · 1	8	1		137	466		23	6	
23			LAWSON	36	8/9 1 · · ᵡ 2 · · 2	27		5 6/1 · 1	10		† Rebounded off bowler's hand to m-on.	138	470		26	7	
28	– · · –	35						ᵡ W	11	1		138	470	9	26	7	35
								AGNEW								0	
30	– · · –	35			· · 2	28		P ᵞ · 0 · 1 ᵡ · 5	5		NB † Run refused NB 21	139	473		27	1	36
36			— · —	37	2 5 6 LB 1	32		1 P ·	7		LB † increase.	140	476		28	2	37
40	– · · –	36			8/8 2LB 7 ᵞ · 2 · 1 ·	37	3	LB · ·	8	–	2LB LB	141	482	9	31	2	40
11·46	DECLARATION										M 25 NB 21		DECLARED				
											867 balls						

148

4TH DAY	BOWLERS (BIRD) STRETFORD END	O.	(SHEPHERD) WARWICK Rd END	O.	BATSMEN SCOREBOARD LEFT SCORING	BALLS	6s/4s	SCOREBOARD RIGHT SCORING	BALLS	6s/4s	AUSTRALIA 2ND INNINGS NOTES	END-OF-OVER TOTALS O.	RUNS	W.	L BAT	R BAT	EXTRAS
TIME	BOWLER	O.	BOWLER	O.	MATTHEWS			LHB HILDITCH									
11.57	BOTHAM	1			LB	1		· ³ ⁹ · ³/₁	5		(LB)	1	3			2	1
12.01			ALLOTT	1				P ² · · · ₁	11		M 1	2					
06	— · —	2			8 · P P	7					Rabant to Botham's M 2 left hand.	3					
11			— · —	2	· · ᴸ	10		3 · ² · · ₁	14		Sawdust.	4	4			3	
17	— · —	3			¹/₂ · ·	14		³ ⁷/₃	16			5	9		2	6	
21			— · —	3				· · · · · ² ᴸ	22		M 3	6					
25	— · —	4			8 ¹/₂ · · ⁷⁵ · ₁	18		⁶/₇₂ 2 ₁	24			7	14		4	9	
30			— · —	4	· · ₁ ⁷	21		ˣ · ·	27			8	15	5			
34	— · —	5			· ᴱᴾ⁵/₄ 1 · P · 2 4	27	1					9	21	11			
38			— · —	5	· · ·	30		7 7 ⁸ · ₁	30			10	22			10	
42	— · —	6			· · 3 ·²/₃ · 4	35	2	ᵢ	31			11	27	15	11		1
47			EDMONDS	1				1ᶠ 1ᵉ 7 · · ₂ · · ₁	37		Round wkt.	12	29			13	
51	— · —	7			· ⁴/₁	37		⁷³ · ˣ ² · ₁	41			13	31	16	14		
55			— · —	2				² · · P · ₁	47		M 4 1 HR	14					
58	EMBURY	1			· P ⁸ · · ₁	40	2	⁷ · ⁷ · · 6	50	/.	Round wkt to LHB.	15	38	—	17	20	1
1.01	LUNCH										M 4 NB - over wkt to LHB.	LUNCH					
1.40			EDMONDS	3	)₋W ⁵	42	2					15²	38	1	17	20	1
41					WESSELS			LHB							0		
43			— · —	3	· P · ·	4					M 5	16					
46	AGNEW	1						· ² · ²² · · 2 ·	56			17	40			22	
50		·	— · —	4	· P P ⁸ · · ₁	8		· · ˣ	58			18	41	1			
53	— · · —	2			· · · 4 ⁷ P⁴ · ₁	14	1					19	46	6			
58½			— · —	5	³/₄ ³ · ᴮ 4 · · ₁	19	2	P	59		* dropped close point (GOWER) (B)	20	51	10			2
2.02	— · · —	3			4 · ²/₃ · P⁴⁶ · 2 ·⊙₁	25		· ₁	60		(NB) NB 1	21	55	13			3
06½			— · —	6	⁸ ₁	26		P L · 3(4) · · 4	65	/₁		22	60		14	26	
10	— · · —	4			ₓ† · · · ⁴³ ₁	31		·	66		† Appeal ct wkt.	23	61	15			
14			— · —	7	³/₃ · ³/₃	34		6² · 8	69			24	65	18	27		
17	— · · —	5			4 · ³ · · ₁	37	3 4	9⁰ · · ⁷ · ⊙₁	73	1/₂	* Low leg side chance to wkt. (NB) NB 2	25	75	22	32	4	
23			— · —	8	· ₁	38		2 ²/₃ 2 · ·¹/₃ 4 · · ₁	78	1/₃		26	80			37	
26	— · —	6						· · 3 2 · · ·	84		M 6	27					
30			EMBURY	2	⁸ ⁸ ₁ ₁	40		² · ᴱᴾ⁹ ˣ 3 · · W	88	1/₃	2HR	28	85	2	24	40	4
34								BORDER		LHB						0	
36	— · · —	7			· · · · · ᴮ	46					M 7	29					
41			— · —	3	⁸ ₁	47		⁵(4) · · · ⁷ · 2 ₁	5			30	89	25	3		
43	EDMONDS	9			· · · · · ³/₁ 4 ·	53					M 8	31					
46			— · ·	4	³ ³ 4 ₁	55	4	·· · ⁸ · ₁	9			32	95	30	4		
49	— · · —	10			· · · ⁷ · · · ₁	61					M 9	33					
51			— · —	5				· · · · · · ₁	15		M 10	34					
54	— · · —	11			· P · P ³ 4 ₁	67	4		15	-	M 11 NB 2	35	95	2	30	4	4

149

4TH DAY TIME	BOWLERS (BIRD) STRETFORD END BOWLER	O.	(SHEPHERD) WARWICK RD END BOWLER	O.	BATSMEN SCOREBOARD LEFT SCORING	BALLS	6s 4s	SCOREBOARD RIGHT SCORING	BALLS	6s 4s	NOTES	O.	END-OF-OVER TOTALS RUNS	W.	'L' BAT	'R' BAT	EXTRAS
					WESSELS	67	4	BORDER	15	–	M 11 NB 2	35	95	2	30	4	4
2.57			EMBUREY	6	:⁵ᴾ²/³	72		⁶:	16			36	96			5	
59	EDMONDS	12			:⁴ᴾ⁴	75		:⁶/⁵ .	19			37	98		31	6	
3.03			- · -	7	ᴾ×:ᴾ.ᴾ.	81					M 12	38					
06	- · -	13			ᴾ.⁹²/²:44	85	6	⁵⁽⁴⁾⁷ᵇᶠ.	21		Over wkt	39	107		39	7	
09			- · -	8	:2:88	88		::⁹/⁸	24			40	110		41	8	
12	- · -	14						⁴³ᴸᴾ⁷⁶:2...	30			41	112			10	
15			- · -	9	:::ᴸ:³/²	94					M 13	42					
18	- · -	15						³/⁴.4ᴾ:ᴾ	36		M 14	43					
20			- · -	10	:1⁷/⁸⁸	98		×⁴	38			44	114		42	11	
22½	- · -	16			⁴/³:17	101		:.ᴸ⁵⁽⁶⁾	41		† Round wkt	45	115			12	
25			- · -	11	†:.	102		⁷:ᴾ.4	46		† over wkt	46	116			13	
29	- · -	17						ᴾ:::⁶⁸	52			47	117			14	
31½			- · -	12				:::⁴::⁵	58		M 15	48					
33½	- · -	18			:ᴾ.†×⁴³:4	108	7				† Round wkt 3 HR	49	121		46		
37			- · -	13	†ᴾ⁸/¹×⁵:4:W	112	8	⁷ᵇ	59		† Round † over WESSELS 50:115'.	49⁵	126	3	50	15	4
3.38	TEA				BOON						M 15 NB 2		TEA	0			
4.00			- · -	13	::	1						50					
01	EDMONDS	19			⁶⁵⁽⁶⁾ᴾ:4:	4	1	.::⁵⁽⁴⁾	62		Round wkt to Boon	51	131		4	16	
05			- · -	14	.:⁵	6		ᴾᴾᴾ⁴:	66		Round wkt to Border	52	132			17	
08	- · -	20			:::⁸1	9		⁸ᴾ:⁸1	69			53	134		5	18	
11			- · -	15	:::ᴾ:	15					M 16	54					
13	- · -	21			::1	17		:::⁵⁽⁶⁾1	73			55	135			19	
15			- · -	16	:†.:⁷:1	21		⁶:ᴾ1	75		† Round wkt	56	137		6	20	
18	- · -	22			ᴸ:2:5.:	27					M 17	57					
21			- · -	17				:5×†.6² ::	81		† Almost bowled - turned sharply. M 18	58					
24	- · -	23			4:::⁷⁵	32		:	82			59	138		7		
27			- · -	18	):::W	36	1					59⁴	138	4	7	20	4
28					RITCHIE									0			
30			- · -	18	⁶ᴾ:.	2					M 19	60					
32	- · -	24						ᴾ::5ᴾ⁶1	88			61	139			21	
35			- · -	19	⁷:1	3		ᴾᴾᴸ⁸ᴸᴮ1	93		ⓁⒷ	62	142	1	22	5	
38	- · -	25			:ᴾ:1	6		:ᴾ⁴1	96		Edmonds warned (pitch damage)	63	143		23		
41½			- · -	20	:⁷1	8		:ᴾᵛ:⁸1	100			64	144		24		
45	- · -	26			ᴾ²⁶.4:1	11	1	:::⁴1	103			65	149		5	25	
48			- · -	21				⁷ᶠ:××ᴾ.ᴾ4:::ᴼ	110	1	ⓃⒷ NB 3	66	154			29	6
52	- · -	27			:4.⁵⁽⁶⁾1	15		ᴾ⁵⁽⁶⁾1	112			67	156		6	30	
55			- · -	22	†:3.⁹⁸:2.1	19		†.⁶:1	114		† over wkt † Round · w. sh extra (Gower) →	68	159		8	31	
58	- · -	28			⁶:2:1	24		ᴸᴮ	115		ⓁⒷ M 20 4 HR	69	160				7
5.01			- · -	23	⁵/2	25	1	:::⁵.4	120	1	M 20 NB 3	70	163	4	10	32	7

4TH DAY	BOWLERS (BIRD) STRETFORD END		(SHEPHERD) WARWICK RD END		BATSMEN SCOREBOARD LEFT			SCOREBOARD RIGHT			AUSTRALIA 2ND INNINGS NOTES	END-OF-OVER TOTALS					
TIME	BOWLER	O.	BOWLER	O.	SCORING	BALLS	6s 4s	SCORING	BALLS	6s 4s		O.	RUNS	W.	'L' BAT	'R' BAT	EXTRAS
					RITCHIE	25	1	BORDER	120	1	M20 NB3	70	163	4	10	32	7
5.04	EDMONDS	29			::	27		::: 8	124			71	164			33	
07			EMBUREY	24				:9: :76 6	130		• chance to	72	165			34	
10	− · −	30						: : :43 136			† BORDER 1000 F-c RUNS ON TOUR.	73	168			37	
13			− · −	25	. : :	30		:: 4 1	139			74	169			38	
16	− · −	31						P 5 4 : 4 145				75	170			39	
19			GATTING	1				. : 7 : 5 8 151		2		76	174			43	
22	EMBUREY	26			x 8	32		5/6 : : : P 155				77	175		11		
25			EDMONDS	32	: 5(4) P P 9 6 38		1					78	181		17		
30	− · −	27						: : : : : P 161			M21	79					
32			− · −	33	: 4 6F 5(4) 2 1 42			5 P 163			† misfielded.	80	184		20		
35	− · −	28			: : : 7 : 48						M 22	81					
37			− · −	34	: : : 51			P P 4 166				82	185			44	
40	− · −	29						. : 12 8 . 4 172			• Hard ch - L/point (BONER) M23	83					
43			− · −	35	8. 5 : : : 57						• Near s-point (GOWER) M24	84					
46	− · −	30			: 6 : 8 62			7 1 173				85	186			45	
48½			− · −	36	L P 6 :7 6 67			8P 3 174			† over wkt	86	187			46	
51	− · −	31						: : : 4 180			50 p'ship : 83 min.	87	188			47	
54			− · −	37	7 8(4) 69			: L : 1 184			5 HR	88	190		21	48	
58	− · −	32			9 : : : : 75						M25	89					
59½			− · −	38	P : : 7 1 79		1	: 8 186		2		90	192	4	22	49	7
6.02 STUMPS											M25 NB3	STUMPS					
5TH DAY 11.00											22 OVERS LOST						
12.30	BOTHAM	8			7 6	80		. . . . : 8(4 191			• Dropped wk - low inside edge to his rt.	91	193		23		
34			EMBUREY	33	: : : P 7 : 86						Round wkt M26	92					
37	EDMONDS	39			P : 87		1/1	: : : 6 : 7 1 196		2	BORDER'S 50 : 193'	93	194	4	23	50	7
12·40 RAIN											M 26 NB 3	RSP					
12·50 LUNCH											2 OVERS LOST	LUNCH					
1·30 RAIN											2 OVERS LOST	RSP					
1·40			EMBUREY	34		87	1/1		196	2	M26 NB3	93	194	4	23	50	7
1·41 RAIN											2 OVERS LOST						
1·48			EMBUREY	34				2LB 3/2 7 8 : • P . 4 : : : . 202		3	(2LB)	94	200			54	9
51	BOTHAM	9			† . . P . 6 93						NEW BALL M27	95					
55			AGNEW	8	: 94			. : : 8 8/7 2 1 207				96	203			57	
2·00	− · −	10			: ! 96			. . : 1/2 211				97	204			58	
04			− · −	9	: 3 4 3 44 100		1/3	7 8 : 1 213				98	213		31	59	
08	− · −	11						: : : ! 1 219			M 28	99					
12			EMBUREY	35	P 8x : W 102		1/3					99³	213	5	31	59	9
13					PHILLIPS		LHB								0		
15			− · −	35	: : : x x 4		-		219	3	M29 NB3	100	213	5	0	59	9

5TH DAY TIME	BOWLERS (BIRD) STRETFORD END BOWLER	O.	(SHEPHERD) WARWICK RD END BOWLER	O.	BATSMEN SCOREBOARD LEFT SCORING	BALLS	6s/4s	SCOREBOARD RIGHT SCORING	BALLS	6s/4s	AUSTRALIA 2ND INNINGS NOTES	O.	RUNS	W.	'L' BAT	'R' BAT	EXTRAS
					PHILLIPS	4	-	BORDER	219	3	M29 NB3	100	213	5	0	59	9
2·16	BOTHAM	12						4 2 2/31 7 · · 2 1 · · 2	225			101	217			63	
20			EMBUREY	36	P 52 · · · P	10					Round wkt M30	102					
23	EDMONDS	40			· x · 4 ·	15		1	226			103	218			64	
26			- · -	37	4 · · 15	19		· 8 · 1	228		+ over no	104	219			65	
28	- · ·	41						P 4 5 · x 6	234		M31	105					
30½			- · -	38	52 · P L · ·	25					M32 6HR	106					
33	- · ·	42			· · 4	28		· · 2/9	237			107	220			66	
35			- · -	39				9 P · 7F · 4 · 1	243	4		108	224			70	
38	- · ·	43			· · · · · P	34					M33	109					
40			- · -	40	· · 3 1	37		· · · 9†	246		† SCORES LEVEL	110	225			71	
42½	- · ·	44			· · · 3 1	41		1 4 2 1	248			111	228			74	
45			- · -	41				· · · · 9 · 1	254		M34	112					
47½	- · ·	45			· · · 1 · P 1	47					† Round M35	113					
50			- · -	42				6 3 · · · 3 4 2	260	5		114	234			80	
53	- · ·	46			· · · 2/7 1	51		· · 8 1	262		PHILLIPS on 0 for 29'.	115	236		1	81	
55			- · -	43	· · · 3 1	55		8/7 · 3 1	264			116	239		2	83	
58½	- · ·	47						· · 8/7 4 2 1 · 4 2 4	270	7		117	249			93	
3·02			· - · ·	44	· · 6 · · 3 4	61	1					118	253		6		
05	ALLOTT	6				61	1	· · · †	273	7	† Light discussed	118	253	5	6	93	9
3·08	BAD LIGHT										M 35 NB 3		B	L	S	P	
3·10	RAIN - TEA										13 OVERS LOST		T	E	A		
4·20	ALLOTT	6			· 1	62		4 2 · 1	275			119	254			94	
23			EMBUREY	45	· 1/4 2 · 4 1	65	2	16 · · 4 1	278		† Round wkr.	120	261		11	96	
27	EDMONDS	48			· · 1	67		· 4 3 67 · · 3	282		50 p'ship : 61 min.	121	264			99	
29½			- · -	46	· 3 1	69		2 L 3 L8 2 · 4 ·	286	8	BORDER's 100: 283' L8	122	271			105	10
33	- · -	49			· 4 · · 2/3 · · 4	74	3	3 1	287			123	276		15	106	
36			- · -	47	· 1 · · 1	77		· 7 6 2 1	290		† Round wkr.	124	279			109	
38½	- · -	50						· · 8/7 4 1L · 4 · 4	296	10		125	287			117	
42			- · -	48	8 1	78		4 2 4 36 1	301		7 HR	126	288		16		
45	- · -	51			· 6 3 · · 1	83		9/7 1	302			127	290		17	118	
48			- · -	49	3 · · · 9 1	88		6 1	303			128	292		18	119	
50½	BOTHAM	13			3F P 2 x · 4F · 4 · · 1	94	4				Round wkt - 0B	129	296		22		
54			EDMONDS	52	3 4 · 1	96		8 · P 3 8/9 1 · · 2	307			130	300		23	122	
57	EMBUREY	50			· · 4 · · 3 1	102					M 36	131					
59			- · -	53	· · · 1	105		· 4 3 1	310			132	301			123	
5·02½	- · -	51			· · · 1	108		4 · 5(4) 1	313		20 OVERS 1	133	302			124	
05			- · -	54	· · 1 · 6 1	112		5/6 · 8 1	315		2	134	305		24	126	
08	BOTHAM	14			P 7 1	114		9 · 2 6 4 · · 1	319	11	3 Round wkr - 0B	135	310			131	
12			GATTING	2	3 4 † 1	117	4	4 3 1L 1	322	11	4 M36 NB 3	136	311	5	24	132	10

5TH DAY TIME	BOWLERS (BIRD) STRETFORD END BOWLER	O.	(SHEPHERD) WARWICK Rd END BOWLER	O.	BATSMEN SCOREBOARD LEFT SCORING	BALLS	6s/4s	SCOREBOARD RIGHT SCORING	BALLS	6s/4s	AUSTRALIA 2ND INNINGS NOTES	END-OF-OVER TOTALS O.	RUNS	W.	'L' BAT	'R' BAT	EXTRAS
					PHILLIPS	117	4	BORDER	322	11	4 M36 NB3	136	311	5	24	132	10
5·16	BOTHAM	15			9 6 / 4 1	119	5	†9 ·†3 6 / 4 · ¹ .	326	12	† OVER WKT. 100†1109¹ ξ ROUND WKT	137	321		29	137	
20			GATTING	3	· : 1 4 / 4 1 :	124	6	8 / 1	327		6	138	327		34	138	
24	LAMB	1			:(2)1 96	127		4 8 3 / 2 4 1 .	331	13	7 NB4 † Nearly bowled	139					
29			— · —	4	4 / 1 6 ·1	130	6	4 8 / · 1 ·.	334	13	8 Round WKT - OB	140	340	5	39	146	10
5·32	MATCH DRAWN										M36 NB4 844 balls	STUMPS					

WARWICK ROAD END

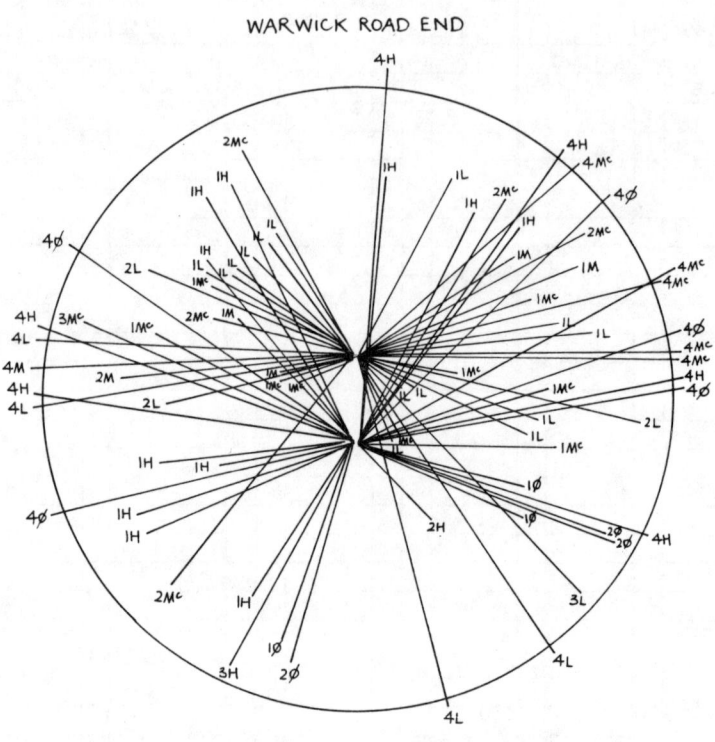

STRETFORD END

BOWLER	SYMBOL	R U N S				
		1	2	3	4	6	TOTAL
HOLLAND	H	11	1	1	6	-	40
LAWSON	L	14	3	1	4	-	39
McDERMOTT	Mc	9	5	1	5	-	42
MATTHEWS	M	4	1	-	1	-	10
O'DONNELL	Ø	3	3	-	5	-	29
TOTALS		41	13	3	21	-	160

M.W. GATTING at Old Trafford

160 RUNS
266 BALLS
357 MINUTES

© BILL FRINDALL 1985

154

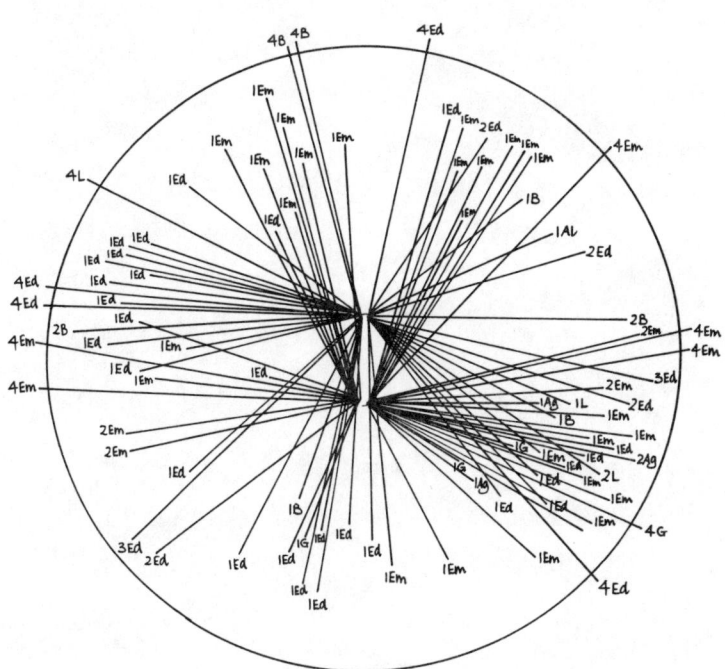

WARWICK ROAD END

STRETFORD END

BOWLER	SYMBOL	R U N S				
		1	2	3	4	6	TOTAL
AGNEW	Ag	2	1	-	-	-	4
ALLOTT	Al	1	-	-	-	-	1
BOTHAM	B	3	2	-	2	-	15
EDMONDS	Ed	28	4	2	4	-	58
EMBUREY	Em	26	4	-	5	-	54
GATTING	G	3	-	-	1	-	7
LAMB	L	1	1	-	1	-	7
TOTALS		64	12	2	13	-	146

A.R. BORDER at Old Trafford

146 RUNS (not out)
334 BALLS
346 MINUTES

(left-handed batsman)

© BILL FRINDALL 1985

FIFTH TEST

EDGBASTON

AUGUST 15, 16, 17, 19, 20

ENGLAND

D.I. Gower (captain), G.A. Gooch, R.T. Robinson, M.W. Gatting,
A.J. Lamb, I.T. Botham, P.R. Downton, J.E. Emburey, R.M. Ellison,
P.H. Edmonds, L.B. Taylor

AUSTRALIA

A.R. Border (captain), G.M. Wood, A.M.J. Hilditch, K.C. Wessels,
G.M. Ritchie, W.B. Phillips, S.P. O'Donnell, G.F. Lawson,
C.J. McDermott, J.R. Thomson, R.G. Holland

Botham begins fifth Test under cloud

I an Botham is to appear before the Test and County Cricket Board's disciplinary committee accused of dissent during the third Test, it was announced yesterday as he and his England colleagues reported to Edgbaston for today's fifth Cornhill match against Australia. While the timing of this announcement seems a little unusual, it hardly comes as a surprise after the episode at Trent Bridge in which Botham let his frustration get the better of him on the third day.

Botham's cup of woe overflowed during an eventful interlude with the new ball which reached its height when, after three times being narrowly denied a wicket, he was given two warnings in one over by umpire Alan Whitehead. The first was for following through on the pitch, the second for excessive use of short-pitched bowling, and at the end of the over Botham could be seen, not least in close-up on television, giving vent to his feelings.

David Gower, England's captain, said afterwards that he had seen nothing untoward in the incident. It is true that down the years bowlers have been known to utter the odd expletive or two, often to themselves, but nowadays the attitude and behaviour of cricketers frequently give cause for concern.

It now seems clear that umpire Whitehead, who was standing in only his second Test, felt that Botham's behaviour was excessive. He also reported two Australians, Allan Border, the captain, and Geoff Lawson, who apparently later offered their apologies for incidents in which they were involved. Botham, however, is understood to have declined to sign a letter of apology to the umpire.

If the disciplinary committee ultimately agree with the umpire's reports, it is important that their decision gives him the strongest possible backing and serves as an encouragement to other officials to step in and take firm action when necessary.

As the case is now *sub judice*, nothing more needs to be said at the moment, except that it seems unusual that the Test and County Cricket

Board have apparently asked Peter May, chairman of selectors, to supply written evidence. He had left the ground at the time of the incident and first heard of it while listening to the BBC's Test Match Special. Though he has since discussed it with the parties involved, such evidence would surely be deemed inadmissible in a court of law.

Botham has twice appeared before the disciplinary committee, to answer charges arising out of remarks he made about Australian umpires and then about Pakistan after his early return home from England's visit there last year. He was fined on both occasions.

If Botham can translate his apparent disenchantment at the Board's decision into aggressive bowling, he might provide England with some much-needed penetration. Whoever England omit from their 12 today, they will be very light on Test match experience in the seam-bowling department.

The likelihood of a slow, slightly damp pitch suggests that Agnew may be the unlucky one, which would give Taylor, his Leicestershire team-mate, his first appearance and Ellison his first of the series and sixth in all.

Ellison reported fit yesterday as the monsoons continued, denying England net practice after the Australians had managed to get in two and a half hours earlier in the day. But the rains may leave conditions in which Ellison, Taylor and Botham could be effective.

History provides England's greatest encouragement. No Test has been drawn here since 1973 and the last seven have ended in four days or less, with India beaten in a matter of two and a half days in 1974 and Pakistan in only 20 hours in 1978.

No batsman scored 50 when England triumphed over Australia here in 1981, and although today's pitch is on the part of the square which tends to produce better batting surfaces, there must be a chance that it may be similarly low and slightly variable in bounce. Unfortunately, Edgbaston's famous massive cover – the Brumbrella – is not functioning well enough to be risked. And although Warwickshire have acquired extra covers from elsewhere, this match is more at the mercy of the weather than it might have been.

AUSTRALIAN VIEWPOINT

Border plays his five-bowler trick

A ustralia will take five bowlers into the fifth Test, seeking a win that would snuff out England's chances of regaining the Ashes Greg Chappell's team took at home in 1982-83. There is no more talk of a draw on Edgbaston's supposedly plumb pitch, which according to head groundsman Bob Franklin yesterday has 'quite a bit of moisture in it' and will favour seam bowlers.

A round of golf with Ian and Greg Chappell, the former Australian captains, at Moor Park on Sunday evening reinforced Allan Border's belief that Australia must adopt a positive stance and attack England with more bowling strength. Hence, there is the desire to recall Jeff Thomson, who is striving to overcome a burst blood vessel in his left foot. If Thomson cannot prove his fitness this morning, the fast-medium Dave Gilbert, 24, seems certain to make his Test debut in place of batsman David Boon.

The other change to the Australian XI will be the reinclusion of left-hand opening batsman Graeme Wood for off-spinning all-rounder Greg Matthews. Wood has recovered from a broken nose and a gashed forehead.

Thomson has had a remarkably injury-free career – barring the dislocated shoulder he suffered in a collision with Allan Turner in Adelaide in 1976. It would be a cruel stroke of misfortune if, on the eve of his 35th birthday, a foot injury denied him the chance to play in his 51st Test and to take his 200th wicket and his 100th in 21 Tests against England. He has 199 and 99 respectively.

Thomson has fond memories of Edgbaston, because he played an important part in Australia's only victory in six Tests there – by an innings and 85 runs in 1975. He made his highest Test score (49) and took five wickets in England's second innings of 173 after Dennis Lillee and Max Walker had taken five wickets each in the first innings of 101 on a wet wicket.

Border believes the Australian batsmen have been placed under too much strain through England having scored more than 400 in three of the four Tests. England managed only 290 and 261 when beaten at Lord's. He also feels, quite rightly, that the balance of his side will not be affected by bringing in a fifth bowler and promoting batsman-wicketkeeper Wayne Phillips to No. 6 and promising all-rounder Simon O'Donnell to No. 7.

STATISTICAL PREVIEW

Result expected

The last seven Edgbaston Tests have produced results before the fifth day, including England's only defeats in 22 matches there (by Australia in 1975, West Indies 1984). Only two complete days of Test cricket have been lost in Birmingham – fewer than at any other current English ground. No complete day of Test cricket has been lost in England since 28 June 1982, when Old Trafford lost its 26th day in 54 matches.

Gatting needs 77 runs to become the fourth England batsman after Compton (1948), Barrington (1964) and John Edrich (1968) to score 500 runs in a home series against Australia. Border, whose first-class tour average (79·21) exceeds that of this season's leading domestic batsman (Viv Richards – 78·25), is 46 runs short of scoring 500 runs in a series in England for the second time (533 in 1981). Sir Donald Bradman (1930, 1934 and 1948) is the only Australian to have achieved this feat more than once. Wood (975), Gooch (890) and Gatting (856) are all within reach of their thousandth run in Anglo-Australian Tests.

England pay for missed chances

England, frustrated by the weather and two crucial lapses in the field, were left to reflect upon what might have been in the fifth Cornhill Test at Edgbaston yesterday, when Australia made 181 for two from the 64 overs possible. David Gower, who had been named at the start of the day as England's captain in the West Indies next winter, saw his decision to bowl first undermined when Wessels and Border both escaped chances in the formative stages of their innings.

Thus encouraged, they added an unbroken 89 together, with Wessels' ability to accumulate carefully coming into its own on another slow pitch, though he also survived two difficult late chances before ending with 76 not out.

Gower's appointment, in his 19th Test as captain, is partly a reflection of the selectors' satisfaction with his progress in a series where he has not been helped by the current shortage of high-class fast bowling in English cricket.

England omitted Agnew, Australia opted for Thomson as their fifth bowler, and Gower chose to field first, the first English captain ever to do so in two successive Tests against Australia.

This obviously had much to do with the dampish pitch and yet another overcast day, but it was an acceptable attacking gesture anyway at this stage of the series, especially against opponents again playing only five specialist batsmen.

In the event, the pitch proved unsurprisingly slow and low in pace and bounce, which tended to defeat Botham's early attempts to dislodge Wood and Hilditch, both instinctive hookers, by inviting the stroke and putting two men out for it.

In these conditions, both batsmen could control the stroke, contributing to Australia's encouragingly brisk start, which ought to have been denied them with the ball coming only reluctantly onto the bat.

Taylor found what little movement there was from a fuller length, though not always managing to make the batsmen play, and it was when Botham pitched the ball up that he had Wood caught, left-handed, by the diving Edmonds at short square leg.

Ellison, replacing Taylor after four overs, found negligible movement through the air, but produced the accuracy needed. And when Taylor reappeared, having switched ends, Wessels, then 13, was missed by Botham in the slips. The chance was not easy, though Botham has been known to hold his share of them, Wessels slashing a short ball to him at head height. Botham got both hands to the chance before spilling it as he lurched backwards.

Hilditch, meanwhile, had managed to time anything over-pitched well, but when Edmonds appeared he was caught behind down the leg side in his second over, getting what must have been the faintest of touches to a ball that drifted across him, so that Downton appeared to be the last to appeal.

Downton could have followed that with an even more important piece of work when, on the stroke of lunch, Border strayed down the pitch against Edmonds, but turned round to see the ball on the ground, not in the wicket-keeper's gloves, and thus escaped a stumping chance.

Rain wiped out the entire afternoon session and beyond, bringing the extra hour into use. On resumption, Border, who was below his best for some time, and Wessels were made to work much harder for their runs.

From time to time, the ball still moved off the seam, suggesting this may remain one of those pitches where batsmen never feel entirely at home, and there was some slight help for the spinners, especially Edmonds when operating into the rough.

Border, when 13, survived a close appeal for lbw, and hereabouts another bonus for England was Taylor's last spell, in which he troubled both batsmen with his accuracy, occasional movement and neat variations of pace.

Driving remained not quite straightforward, and when Wessels twice ventured the stroke, in the 70s, he survived a difficult chance to the diving Robinson, off Ellison, then a hard, low caught-and-bowled which just carried to Taylor.

AUSTRALIAN VIEWPOINT

Omens good for Wessels

Keppler Wessels has made a habit of scoring one big hundred a series, and he is threatening to do it again in Australia's first innings of the fifth Test at Edgbaston.

He needed more than his fair share of luck to reach 76 yesterday, because he was dropped at 13, 72 and 73 – an unusually generous offering for a batsman who invariably makes his opponents pay a high price for giving him a life.

Wessels made the highest of his four Test centuries, 179, in Adelaide in 1983-84, after Pakistan's Azeem Hafeez had missed a catch at fine leg off Sarfraz Nawaz when he was only seven.

For all Ian Botham's all-round genius, one wonders about the wisdom of his waiting in slips with his hands resting on his knees, as he was doing again yesterday when he missed Wessels off the luckless Les Taylor, when Australia were 68 for one.

Allan Border, now only 15 runs short of 500 for the series, could consider himself fortunate that the umpire David Shepherd did not give him out leg before to Phil Edmonds when 13, at 117 for two.

The ball often deviated or spun appreciably on yet another slow wicket, and batting was nowhere near as easy as it might have appeared from a distance, even if the bowling seemed gentle fodder compared with the cannon-balls fired by the West Indians.

Overnight
Australia 181 – 2 (K.C. Wessels 76 not out, A.R. Border 43 not out)

Australia are 335–8 despite Ellison's 5–77

Richard Ellison's admirable, controlled swing bowling which brought him five wickets for 77 in his first match of the series, was not enough to sustain England in the fifth Cornhill Test at Edgbaston yesterday, and Australia emerged from another rain-affected day at 335 for eight.

Ellison, exploiting more helpful conditions in the morning sessions, moved the ball disconcertingly late, and, by taking four wickets for 12, including those of Border and Wessels in successive overs, reduced Australia to 218 for seven.

At that point England seemed capable of compensating for their lapses of Thursday. But on a day in which only 49 overs proved possible, events went increasingly awry for them after a lengthy stoppage.

They found the second new ball less accommodating and it cost 85 runs from its first 20 overs, while Lawson, who had almost been forced to retire hurt after being struck on the elbow by Botham, restored Australia's fortunes with an unbeaten 53 from 83 balls.

Australia's hopes of developing their strong position were thwarted when they discovered the ball moving around much more than hitherto, both through the air and off the seam. This may have been the result of a combination of lower cloud, a milder day and the pitch unsurprisingly retaining its moisture.

Whatever the logistics, Ellison hugely relished the conditions. In successive overs he removed Border and Wessels, giving England back much of what they had lost the previous day, and continued to swing the ball late from a full length.

In this sense he now seems a better equipped bowler than when he first appeared last year, with limited experience, and by finding a line around off stump he made the batsmen play more often than not.

Before he broke through, Botham had two close lbw calls rejected, but in the sixth over of the day England obtained the wicket they wanted when Border, perhaps deceived by a change of pace, played a shade too early off his legs and Edmonds swooped to hold the catch.

Two overs later, Wessels met a good ball from Ellison which, angled across him, also moved off the seam to end a stay of almost four hours with a straightforward catch to Downton, and England, remarkably, found themselves with two new batsmen to attack.

Even in these conditions, Botham started to lapse into shortness, but before this could become another costly folly he was replaced by Taylor, who began to pass the bat at encouraging intervals, and neither Ritchie nor Phillips showed many signs of permanence.

Ritchie, playing tentatively forward in front of his pad, then edged Ellison's outswinger to Botham at second slip, giving the bowler three wickets for 10 runs in 25 deliveries, and one run later O'Donnell was caught behind off Taylor. This was from an excellent delivery, pitching around off stump and leaving the batsman, and it was hardly surprising that when the first rain arrived (a mainly dry day had been forecast) it was Australia who showed signs of wanting to make an excuse and leave.

Play continued in drizzle after the umpires had twice conferred, and the irritation at this may have had something to do with the eventual departure of Phillips, who had dealt firmly with the odd long hop and half volley. He made great play of borrowing a cloth from umpire Constant to dry his bat handle. The next ball from Ellison was, for once, invitingly short and wide and Phillips drove it hard off the back foot but straight to Robinson at cover.

There was then time only for Lawson to take a painful blow on the elbow from a short-pitched ball by Botham before the weather miserably closed in,

much as it had the previous day, and the afternoon session was again washed away.

By then England had logically taken the new ball, but it was 5.15 p.m. before they had a chance to exploit its possibilities fully. In the event it did less than its predecessor, though that was partially due to Botham again dropping short and yielding 30 runs in six overs.

When he pitched it up, he could not hold a return catch offered by McDermott, who was now attacking anything resembling a full length. The young fast bowler then became Ellison's fifth victim, with the aid of Gower's splendid tumbling catch at extra cover, but the extra 60 minutes were to prove anything but the happy hour for England, as Lawson and Thomson took their ninth-wicket partnership to an unbeaten 59 at the close.

AUSTRALIAN VIEWPOINT

Three Modern Millers

What a revival! Who dared suggest Australian cricket was bereft of all-rounders?

Fast bowlers Geoff Lawson, Craig McDermott and Jeff Thomson resembled Keith Millers of the 1980s as they helped themselves to 117 match-saving, and maybe Ashes-saving, runs for the eighth and ninth wickets.

Lawson always has looked a technically correct lower-order batsman, yet his invaluable, unbeaten 53 was only his third half century in 52 Test innings.

McDermott, an outstanding all-rounder in junior ranks, made his 35 stylishly enough to indicate he has much more to offer Australia as a run-getter.

Thomson celebrated his 35th birthday with some old-fashioned slogging on the same ground where he had sprinted to his highest Test score (49) 10 years ago.

> **Overnight**
> **Australia 335 – 8 (K.C. Wessels 83, G.F. Lawson 53 not out, A.R. Border 45; R.M. Ellison 5 – 77)**

Robinson and Gower offer victory hope

David Gower and Tim Robinson gave England another glimpse of the promised land in the fifth Cornhill Test at Edgbaston on Saturday with two innings of the highest class. Their partnership left Australia's attack looking as devastated and down-at-heel as any of recent memory from that country.

Each made his second century of the series, Gower ending with an unbeaten 169 made from 238 balls and Robinson with 140 not out, from 279 balls.

Throughout a rare sunny afternoon, they threatened to rewrite the record books, and by scoring at a remarkable four runs an over during a stand that added an unbroken 317 for the second wicket, they compensated time lost to the weather and opened up the game for their side.

A memorable day for a capacity crowd began improbably enough when Gower ran out Lawson from the very first ball. Thomson called for a risky single for a push into the covers and, after some hesitation, Lawson was beaten by the captain's underarm throw.

From the fifth ball, Ellison, who had called up an extra gully, had Holland caught there without scoring, giving him figures of 6-77 for a display of bowling that emphasised his development in the 12 months since his Test debut.

After that, England might have scripted the scenario themselves.

Gooch, who had collected a pair by courtesy of Thomson on his debut here in 1975, became his 200th Test victim, though not before he had had time to expose the shoddiness of much of the Australian bowling. He drove two very wide half volleys from Lawson to the cover boundary before being caught behind off a Thomson outswinger, but Gower and Robinson maintained the destruction, reeling off one brilliant stroke after another so that by lunch England had made 103 from only 22 overs.

Robinson, troubled early on by the occasional good delivery from Lawson, later located a rich diet of leg-stump half volleys which he dealt with expertly, and with Gower punching the bowling away off the back foot the pair made their first 50 from only seven overs.

During the interval Border clearly re-thought his tactics, and, with Lawson and O'Donnell bowling very straight and just short of a length to defensive fields, Gower and Robinson spent a more restricted hour, though importantly they did not allow themselves to become frustrated.

Eventually the supply of loose balls started to flow again. The result was batting that was disciplined, clinical and selective, and more than a passing reminder of the way England had played in Madras last winter which, incidentally, set up the platform for victory in not dissimilar circumstances.

The pair passed 100 together in 27 overs before Robinson reached three figures from 193 balls with a resounding hook for four off Thomson. Gower soon followed him, though he experienced his most anxious moments in the nineties. At 93, only the faintest of inside edges probably saved him from becoming an lbw victim to Thomson, while Holland was unlucky with two balls that spun sharply out of the rough, providing a bat-pad chance that eluded Border, and a near lbw.

If that was close enough for Holland to look extremely disappointed, at least the umpires here have consistently given the batsmen the benefit of the doubt, as Australia should be the first to testify.

Later, as the pair maintained their tempo, the ball was in the air a lot but regularly avoided the field. If that was one indication of the way the rub of the green was going, it also had much to do with batting that was Gower-Robinson and bowling that was Heath Robinson.

By bowling their overs slowly, Australia also condemned themselves to a long (two hours twenty minutes) and increasingly testing final session during which Robinson and Gower amassed 158 from only 38 overs and ruthlessly went past one milestone after another.

Gower by now was doing much as he pleased, lifting Holland for six and four in one over which took England past the 300 mark in only 73 overs, and the 300 partnership soon followed. It was only the seventh of its kind for England in Test cricket.

AUSTRALIAN VIEWPOINT

Facts of life by Border

Australia's poorly directed bowling in unfavourable conditions has again placed unfair pressure on their batsmen to save the fifth Test and, quite possibly, the Ashes.

In a grim replay of the drawn fourth Test, Allan Border, the captain, is resigned to his team's having to bat for at least the last four sessions (about 130 overs) to save the match and keep the series tied at 1–1.

'Another day of rain wouldn't go astray,' said Border yesterday, mocking the words he had used after the third day of the fourth Test.

'It's going to be very, very hard to do what we did last time twice in a row; but we'll just show them that it can be done.

I think we can do it. It's going to take another monumental effort. Someone will have to get a big, slow hundred.

'We're under pressure again with our batting, and the bowling has been the cause of it.'

To the surprise of no one, Border said he had been 'very disappointed' with the Australian bowling on Saturday: 'It's not a question of the blokes not giving their best,' he said. 'They just made it too easy for England to score – it was just like one-day cricket.

'Tim Robinson's and David Gower's ability to get balls away for fours was uncanny. It might have been just one of those days. I hadn't experienced one like it. Now we're having to try to save the match after batting for the first two-and-a-bit days. That's ridiculous.'

Border said he was disappointed

with the umpires' 'inconsistent' interpretations of the rain and poor light when Australia were batting before lunch on Friday.

For the first time this tour, Border declined to give his usual Press conference on Saturday night. Instead, he stayed in the dressing room with his players, speaking to the bowlers individually and conducting a team meeting. 'I just told the blokes the facts of life and what's expected of them,' he said. 'I thought I was the best bowler and that's ridiculous, too.'

Overnight
Australia 335
(K.C. Wessels 83, G.F. Lawson 53, A.R. Border 45; R.M. Ellison 6 – 77)
England 355 – 1 (D.I. Gower 169 not out, R.T. Robinson 140 not out)

Ellison burst puts Australia on the rack

R ichard Ellison brought an increasingly remarkable day to an almost unbelievable climax in the fifth Cornhill Test at Edgbaston yesterday by taking four wickets for one run in 15 deliveries to reduce Australia to 37 for five – still 223 behind. They included the prized scalps of Wessels and Border – the two men most likely to play long, disciplined innings – and left Australia facing a daunting struggle today to save the game and avoid going 2-1 down in the series. Ellison has so far taken 10 for 79 in the match.

England had gone on to declare at 595 for five, with Gower achieving the highest score of his career, 215, and Gatting scoring his second successive century.

The final demoralising session accurately reflected how Australia's morale had sagged after being comprehensively outplayed for the best part of two days.

Though the ball did nothing extravagant, Botham made the breakthrough by persuading Hilditch to hook, after again baiting the trap on the boundary. Then Ellison improbably followed his first innings spell of four for 12 by removing Wessels, Holland, Wood and Border while only four runs were scored.

Wessels, dropped by Emburey from a straightforward slip catch off Taylor before scoring, was caught behind driving at a widish ball from Ellison, who with his next delivery had Holland, the nightwatchman, palpably lbw.

In Ellison's next over, Wood, perhaps undone by a little extra bounce as he aimed through midwicket, was caught off a leading edge, and Border once again found himself cast in the role of the most wanted Australian since Ned Kelly.

But Ellison bowled him with a ball that may have swung just enough to defeat his defensive stroke, brushing a pad en route. It left Australia needing some rare heroics from their remaining batsmen and England hoping the weather for once will relent and allow them to finish what they so memorably started.

After rain had delayed the start for 55 minutes, Robinson and Gower found themselves confronted with bowling similar to Saturday's especially from McDermott, who, with Lawson, was kept going for the first two hours.

This was not so much a well-deserved penance, but probably had more to do with the time they took to bowl an over as Australia went on the defensive. But early on Lawson's accuracy was rewarded with Robinson's wicket.

He played on, trying to force a ball that came back, after the epic partnership had reached 331, which had been bettered for England's second wicket against Australia only by the 382 made by Hutton and Leyland at the Oval in 1938.

Two successive fours through the covers off McDermott, who hereabouts conceded 24 from three overs, launched Gower fluently. Otherwise he and Gatting wisely avoided anything extravagant as they completed the addition of 48 runs from the 13 overs possible before lunch.

More rain delayed the resumption, after which Gower, though perhaps not touching the heights of the earlier part of his innings, went past 200 with a typical stroke through the covers, which took him to the highest score of his career. It also overtook Compton's aggregate of 562 in 1948, the previous best by an English batsman in a home series against Australia.

This coincided with some mediocre out-cricket during which Gower, at 208 and 214, was dropped by Ritchie off a full toss and Thomson off a long hop, deliveries which offered a clue to the name of the bowler (McDermott).

Gatting's care in becoming established now started to repay him, and he began to time some good-looking strokes before Gower eventually departed, to a standing ovation, when he cut Lawson into Border's hands after a stay of 451 minutes.

Gatting followed this with more punishing strokes, including one ferocious blow back over McDermott's head, and with Lamb gradually finding his timing, the afternoon session yielded 142 runs, even though Australia had managed only 25 overs.

This scorching tempo well suited England's requirements, and the fourth-wicket partnership had produced 109 in only 20 overs, despite deep defensive fields, when Lamb mistimed a stroke off his legs and was caught at midwicket.

Enter Botham with the scoreboard reading 572 for four – shades of Arthur Wood and his comment: 'I'm just the man for a crisis.' Even by Botham's standards, his start was explosive, in a situation where he had scope to express himself as he wished.

So ... he drove his first ball from McDermott stunningly for six into the pavilion. Two balls later he lifted him for another, off a perfectly decent good-length delivery, and followed this with an onside four – 16 in a matter of four minutes.

McDermott then produced a full toss – not an unintelligent ball in the circumstances – which Botham could only lift from high on the bat to deep midwicket, where Thomson held a well-judged catch. But the gesture to the crowd which followed it was not so well judged.

Still, this, plus Lawson's inability to bowl an over in less than seven minutes, seemed a reflection of Australia's increasingly fraught start.

How fraught, England were to discover, probably more than they dared hope, when they declared the moment Gatting completed a high-class century from only 125 balls.

Another collapse so Gower takes honours

D avid Gower, England's captain, already can claim a moral victory for his team in the fifth Test, and he will not get an argument from an Australian, as he did after the drawn fourth Test.

Richard Ellison's astonishing 15-ball demolition of Australia's second innings at Edgbaston late yesterday has given England an iron grip on the Ashes and seemingly ruined 16 weeks of hard work by the Australians.

Only rain, which is forecast for late today, but probably will not arrive soon enough, can save Australia, as it helped to do at Old Trafford.

Ellison's destructive swing and seam bowling has given him the exceptional analysis of 10–79 off 36·5 overs in this abnormally one-sided match.

Australia have not enjoyed much luck, particularly with the awful weather throughout the tour and again at Edgbaston. But England's overwhelming dominance with bat and ball over the past five days has confirmed the suspicion that they are the stronger, more resilient side.

Australian batting collapses are nothing new. The galling thing about yesterday's rout was that it started when Andrew Hilditch, the vice-captain, was out, hooking carelessly for the third time in the series as he fell into Ian Botham's obvious, much-maligned two-men-on-the-boundary trap.

Overnight
Australia 335 and 37 – 5 (R.M. Ellison 4 – 2)
England 595 – 5 dec (D.I. Gower 215, R.T. Robinson 148,
M.W. Gatting 100 not out, A.J. Lamb 46)

Rain relents and England go 2–1 ahead

England overcame their twin adversaries, Australia and the weather, in memorable style at Edgbaston yesterday to win the fifth Cornhill Test by an innings and 118 runs with 11·5 overs of a taut and ultimately controversial day remaining. They now lead by 2–1 with one Test left.

Their luck changed abruptly after rain had prevented a start until mid-afternoon, for not only did the clouds roll away but they revealed a silver lining in the shape of a freak dismissal which changed the course of the final session.

This involved the departure of Phillips, caught by Gower when his powerful cut rebounded off Lamb's instep at silly point and was given out only after the umpires had conferred.

From that point, Australia lost their last five wickets for 29 runs in 48 minutes, first to the spin of Edmonds and Emburey and finally to Botham, and were dismissed for 142. Ellison, with 10–106 in the game, took the Man of the Match award.

So Australia contrived to lose a Test in which they had been placed at 189 for two on the first day. The match had gone remarkably England's way from the moment that Gower ran out Lawson from the first ball on Saturday and followed that with his majestic double century.

Gower had also masterminded affairs with much aplomb but, unfortunately, Allan Border chose what should have been the high point in the England captain's career to make a churlish comment about the umpires for the decision he reckoned cost his side the match.

While admitting that Australia scarcely deserved to emerge unbeaten, Border said: 'There was no way in the world that the umpires could tell that the batsman was out. He should have been given the benefit of the doubt.'

How Border could presume to have had a better view of the episode, even with the aid of television, than the square-leg umpire is a mystery.

The spinners introduced much needed subtlety plus a cluster of close fielders, and Phillips had made 59 from 89 balls in that uncomplicated way of his when he clipped a short one from Edmonds fiercely off the back foot. Lamb and Gower took evasive action, but Gower reacted quickly enough to sense that the ball was looping towards him, from, it transpired later, Lamb's left instep.

It was some moment for umpire Shepherd, in only his second Test. With his view obscured by Gower, he took the obvious move and consulted his colleague at square leg. Umpire Constant, who, incidentally, had regularly moved from square leg to point and back to ensure an unobstructed view, promptly upheld the appeal.

After Old Trafford, where sundry close catches had never quite gone to hand, this, after 28 overs, was a choice piece of luck – one which may eventually decide the destiny of the

Ashes. And a neat piece of bowling by Emburey brought the next success. Finding some drift, he turned an off-break just enough to obtain a bat-pad catch off Ritchie – who departed instantly without waiting for the decision – and the last hour arrived with three wickets required.

In the first over, Lawson went to Gower's juggling catch after a jabbed defensive stroke at Edmonds, and for a while the ball squirted agonisingly here and there off the spinners.

Gower then pulled out another plum by recalling Botham, who in successive overs prised out O'Donnell and McDermott, thus becoming the most successful English bowler against Australia, with 130 wickets, as the epic victory was completed.

All this, almost equally unbelievably, took place in bright sunshine.

AUSTRALIAN VIEWPOINT

No wheels left on the bowling wagon

Luck and umpiring decisions aside, Australia's inadequate bowling against England's more stable batting line-up on slow, low pitches is the decisive difference between the teams in this Ashes series.

Justice prevailed at Edgbaston yesterday when England, by taking five wickets for 29 off 15·3 overs, clinched their second win of the series after rain had given Australia an undeserved chance of scrambling a draw.

The wheels have fallen off the Australian bowling wagon over the past three and a half weeks, in which time the tourists have taken 21 wickets for 1,732 runs – a wicket every 82 runs.

Northants made 258 for three, England scored 482 for nine declared in the fourth Test, Middlesex ran up 397 for four declared and England sprinted to 595 for five in the fifth Test.

Geoff Lawson, who was to be Australia's bowling ace, has been weakened all tour by sundry injuries and illnesses, including asthma.

Lawson and Craig McDermott, 20, have shared 44 wickets in the first five Tests, yet neither is, nor can be, satisfied with his performances, even allowing for the sluggish pitches.

Lawson has figures of 2–281 off 87 overs since his five-wicket haul in England's only innings of the third Test.

McDermott's persistent leg-side attack in the fifth Test, in the face of regular punishment, defied explanation, even if he can be in part excused by some because of his age and inexperience.

Lawson and McDermott have lacked support, with Bob Holland, the leg-spinner, having taken just 1–355 off 115 overs since his match-winning 5–68 in the second Test, and Simon O'Donnell is simply not doing enough to trouble Test-class batsmen.

Result: England beat Australia by an innings and 118 runs
Australia 335 and 142 (W.B. Phillips 59; R.M. Ellison 4–27)
England 595–5 dec

AUSTRALIA 1ST INNINGS v ENGLAND (5TH TEST) at EDGBASTON, BIRMINGHAM on 15,16,17,19,20 AUGUST 1985. TOSS: ENGLAND

IN	OUT	MINS	No.	BATSMAN	HOW OUT	BOWLER	RUNS	WKT	TOTAL	6s	4s	BALLS	NOTES ON DISMISSAL
11-00	11-53	53	1	G.M. WOOD	C't EDMONDS	BOTHAM	19	1	44	·	3	45	Edged via thigh pad to short-leg - left-handed diving catch.
11-00	12-52	112	2	A.M.J. HILDITCH	C't DOWNTON	EDMONDS	39	2	92	·	5	71	1000 runs in 16th Test. Legside catch - edged 'arm' ball.
11-55	11-32	228	3	K.C. WESSELS	C't DOWNTON	ELLISON	83	4	191	·	8	204	Edged outswinger.
12-54	11-22	159	4	A.R. BORDER*	C't EDMONDS	ELLISON	45	3	189	·	5	111	Turned inswinger low to backward short leg.
11-24	12-02	38	5	G.M. RITCHIE	C't BOTHAM	ELLISON	8	5	207	·	1	22	Edged outswinger to 2nd slip.
11-34	12-30	56	6	W.B. PHILLIPS†	C't ROBINSON	ELLISON	15	7	218	·	3	42	Cut long hop low and hard to cover-point.
12-04	12-13	9	7	S.P. O'DONNELL	C't DOWNTON	TAYLOR	1	6	208	·	·	3	Edged inswinger that cut away on pitching.
12-15	11-00	140	8	G.F. LAWSON	RUN OUT (GOWER)		53	9	335	·	7	93	First ball of 3rd day. Direct hit from cover - Thomson's call.
12-32	6-07	69	9	C.J. McDERMOTT	C't GOWER	ELLISON	35	8	276	·	4	51	Skied offdrive - superb two-handed running, diving catch.
6-09	11-03	55	10	J.R. THOMSON	NOT OUT		28				1 2	43	
11-01	11-03	2	11	R.G. HOLLAND	C't EDMONDS	ELLISON	0	10	335	·	·	4	Shin-high catch at backward point. Mistimed drive.

EXTRAS: b - lb 4 w 1 nb 4   1 6 38 4

TOTAL **335** ALL OUT at 11-03 am on 3rd day.
(113.5 OVERS - 469 MINUTES)   6.89 balls (including 6 no balls)

14 OVERS 3 BALLS/HOUR
2.94 RUNS/OVER
49 RUNS/100 BALLS

* CAPTAIN † WICKET-KEEPER
UMPIRES: D.J. CONSTANT, D.R. SHEPHERD
© BILL FRINDALL 1985

BOWLER	O	M	R	W
BOTHAM	27	1	108	1
TAYLOR	26	5	78	1
ELLISON	31.5	9	77	6
EDMONDS	20	4	47	1
EMBUREY	9	2	21	0
			4	1
	113.5	21	335	10

HRS	OVERS	RUNS	
½	1	13	44
½	2	14	50
1½	3	18	42
-	4	16	38
1½	5	14	24
	6	11	27
	7	15	51

RUNS	MINS	OVERS	LAST 50 (in mins)
50	65	15.0	65
100	131	31.1	66
150	206	52.2	75
200	304	75.5	98
250	378	91.0	74
300	431	103.4	53

LUNCH: 96-2 (28 OVERS)(122 MIN.)
RAIN PREVENTED RESTART UNTIL 4-55pm - 175 MIN (43 OVERS LOST)
STUMPS: 181-2 (1st DAY) 64 OVERS (251 MIN.) NETT LOSS: 26 OVERS   WESSELS 76*(96) BORDER 43*(137)
RSP at 12-51pm
LUNCH: 230-7 (87 OVERS)(362 MIN.)   LAWSON 6*(84) McDERMOTT 5*(19)
TEA: 248-7 (89.5 OVERS)(373 MIN.) (35 OVERS in 11 MIN)   LAWSON 11*(47) McDERMOTT 18*(30)
STUMPS: 335-8 (2nd DAY)(113 OVERS)(466 MIN.) NETT LOSS: 41 OVERS   LAWSON 53*(140) THOMSON 28*(52)
WESSELS 33*(67) BORDER 2*(8)

3RD MORNING - AUSTRALIA LOST TWO WICKETS IN 3 MINUTES OFF 5 BALLS WITHOUT ADDITION
AUSTRALIA'S 8TH AND 9TH WICKET PARTNERSHIPS WERE RECORDS FOR THIS SERIES AT EDGBASTON.

WKT	PARTNERSHIP		RUNS	MINS
1st	Wood	Hilditch	44	53
2nd	Hilditch	Wessels	48	57
3rd	Wessels	Border	97	159
4th	Wessels	Ritchie	2	8
5th	Ritchie	Phillips	16	24
6th	Phillips	O'Donnell	1	9
7th	Phillips	Lawson	10	15
8th	Lawson	McDermott	58	69
9th	Lawson	Thomson	59	52
10th	Thomson	Holland	0	2

335

2ND NEW BALL taken at 12-42 pm on 2nd day - AUSTRALIA 229-7 after 86-2 overs.

ENGLAND 1st INNINGS

IN REPLY TO AUSTRALIA'S 335 ALL OUT

IN	OUT	MINS	No.	BATSMAN	HOW OUT	BOWLER	RUNS	WKT	TOTAL	6s	4s	BALLS	NOTES ON DISMISSAL
11·13	12·01	48	1	G.A.GOOCH	c't PHILLIPS	THOMSON	19	1	38	·	4	29	Edged out-swinger. Thomson's 200th wkt (51 Tests) & 100th v ENG (21 Tests).
11·13	12·10	393	2	R.T.ROBINSON	BOWLED	LAWSON	148	2	369	·	18	293	3rd Test. Breakback - Edged backfoot force into leg stump.
12·03	3·08	452	3	D.I.GOWER *	c't BORDER	LAWSON	215	3	463	1	25	314	(11th Tests. Ms. Mistimed drive - gentle catch to cover-point.
12·12	(5·14)	214	4	M.W.GATTING	NOT OUT		100			·	13	127	(4th in Tests - 2nd in successive innings.
3·10	4·55	86	5	A.J.LAMB	c't WOOD	McDERMOTT	46	4	572		5	62	Clipped half-volley to mid-wicket.
4·57	5·08	11	6	I.T.BOTHAM	c't THOMSON	McDERMOTT	18	5	592	2	1	7	Skied full toss to deep mid-wicket - falling catch.
5·11	(5·14)	3	7	P.R.DOWNTON †	NOT OUT		0			·	·	0	
			8	J.E.EMBUREY									
			9	R.M.ELLISON	did not bat								
			10	P.H.EDMONDS									
			11	L.B.TAYLOR									
				EXTRAS	b 7 lb 20 w - nb 22		49						

3 6s   66 4s   852 balls (including 28 no balls)

TOTAL (134 OVERS - 609 MINUTES)   595-5 DECLARED at 5·14 pm on 4th day.

ENGLAND'S HIGHEST TOTAL v. AUSTRALIA AT EDGBASTON

* CAPTAIN   † WICKET-KEEPER

BOWLER	O	M	R	W	nb
LAWSON	37	1	135	2	11
McDERMOTT	31	2	155	2	2
THOMSON	19	1	101	1	9
HOLLAND	25	4	95	0	-
O'DONNELL	16	3	69	0	-
BORDER	6	1	13	0	-
			27		
	134	12	595	5	

2ND NEW BALL taken at 6·21 pm on 3rd day - ENGLAND 342-1 after 85 overs.

© BILL FRINDALL 1985

HRS	OVERS	RUNS
11	11	43
2 2	13	63
3	13	38
4	15	58
5	14	53
6	16	86
7	12	46
8	13	50
9	12	58
10	13	93

RUNS	MINS	OVERS	LAST 50 (in mins)
50	63	12·3	63
100	102	20·4	39
150	179	37·3	77
200	232	49·5	53
250	298	65·4	66
300	326	72·5	28
350	375	86·1	49
400	443	99·2	68
450	494	109·4	51
500	540	119·3	46
550	571	126·2	31

13 OVERS 1 BALLS/HOUR
4·44 RUNS/OVER
72 RUNS/100 BALLS

WKT	PARTNERSHIP		RUNS	MINS
1st	Gooch	Robinson	38	48
2nd	Robinson	Gower	351	343
3rd	Gower	Gatting	94	107
4th	Gatting	Lamb	109	86
5th	Gatting	Botham	20	11
6th	Gatting	Downton	3*	3
			595	

LUNCH: 103-1 (22 OVERS) ROBINSON 42* (107) GOWER 36* (57)
  (107 MIN)

TEA: 197-1 (49 OVERS) ROBINSON 77* (228) GOWER 80* (118)
  (138 BEHIND) (228 MIN)

STUMPS: 355-1 (87 OVERS) ROBINSON 140* (378) GOWER 169* (322)
  (3RD DAY) (20 AHEAD) (378 MIN)

4TH DAY'S START DELAYED BY 55 MINUTES - RAIN.

LUNCH: 403-2 (100 OVERS) GOWER 197* (397) GATTING 8* (52)
  (LEAD: 68) (447 MIN)

TEA: 545-3 (125 OVERS) GATTING 81* (170) LAMB 35* (61)
  (LEAD: 210) (565 MIN)

331 - ENGLAND'S SECOND-HIGHEST PARTNERSHIP FOR ANY WICKET AGAINST AUSTRALIA.

AUSTRALIA 2ND INNINGS (260 RUNS BEHIND ON FIRST INNINGS)

IN	OUT	MINS	No.	BATSMAN	HOW OUT	BOWLER	RUNS	WKT	TOTAL	6s	4s	BALLS	NOTES ON DISMISSAL
5.25	5.37	12	1	A.M.J.HILDITCH	c ELLISON	BOTHAM	10	1	10	·	1	14	Hooked short ball to deep backward square-leg.
5.25	6.46	81	2	G.M.WOOD	c ROBINSON	ELLISON	10	4	35	·	1	51	Skied onside hit - leading edge to short cover.
5.39	6.32	53	3	K.C.WESSELS	c DOWNTON	ELLISON	10	2	32	·	1	36	Edged loose drive at slower ball - low catch to his left.
6.34	6.35	1	4	R.G.HOLLAND	LBW	ELLISON	0	3	32	·	·	1	First ball - pushed across line of straight ball. 'PAIR'.
6.37	6.54	17	5	A.R.BORDER*	BOWLED	ELLISON	2	5	36	·	·	17	Breakback - clipped pad top. ELLISON (to mess in Match) 4 in 15b.
6.48	4.54	126	6	G.M.RITCHIE	c LAMB	EMBUREY	20	7	117	·	·	103	Edged off-break via pad to silly point - walked.
6.56	4.40	104	7	W.B.PHILLIPS†	c GOWER	EDMONDS	59	6	113	·	11	90	50 off 78 balls. Cut via silly point's instep to silly mid-off.
4.42	5.23	41	8	S.P.O'DONNELL	BOWLED	BOTHAM	11	9	137	·	1	39	Drove over yorker. BOTHAM's 120th wkt v AUS (ENGLAND record)
4.56	5.02	6	9	G.F.LAWSON	c GOWER	EDMONDS	3	8	120	·	·	8	Edged push to silly point - held rebound off chest.
5.04	5.28	24	10	C.J.McDERMOTT	c EDMONDS	BOTHAM	8	10	142	·	1	22	Low catch - falling to left at forward short leg.
5.25	5.28	3	11	J.R.THOMSON	NOT OUT		4			·	1	5	
				EXTRAS	b1 lb 3	w - nb 1	5						

TOTAL (64.1 OVERS - 242 MINUTES) **142** ALL OUT at 5.28 pm on 5th day. 386 balls (including 1 no-ball).

* CAPTAIN † WICKET-KEEPER

BOWLER	O	M	R	W
BOTHAM	14.1	2	52	3
TAYLOR	13	4	27	0
ELLISON	9	3	27	4
EDMONDS	15	9	13	2
EMBUREY	13	5	19	1
			4	
	64.1	23	142	10

© BILL FRINDALL 1985

HRS	OVERS	RUNS
1	14	32
2	13	26
3	17	41
4	19	38

RUNS	MINS	OVERS	LAST 50 (in mins)
50	106	23.5	106
100	180	44.3	74

15 OVERS 5 BALLS/HOUR
2.21 RUNS/OVER
37 RUNS/100 BALLS

WKT	PARTNERSHIP		RUNS	MINS
1st	Hilditch	Wood	10	12
2nd	Wood	Wessels	22	53
3rd	Wood	Holland	0	1
4th	Wood	Border	3	9
5th	Border	Ritchie	1	6
6th	Ritchie	Phillips	77	104
7th	Ritchie	O'Donnell	4	12
8th	O'Donnell	Lawson	3	6
9th	O'Donnell	McDermott	17	19
10th	McDermott	Thomson	5	3
			142	

STUMPS: 37-5 (4th DAY) (223 BEHIND)
(21 OVERS RITCHIE 0*(0)
95 MINUTES) PHILLIPS 1*(4)

5TH DAY: START DELAYED UNTIL 2.30pm. 2 balls - 1 min. MAL.
TEA: 80-5 (37 OVERS RITCHIE 12*(71 min.)
154 MINUTES) PHILLIPS 31*(63 min)

ENGLAND WON BY AN INNINGS
AND 118 RUNS (WITH 11.5 OVERS TO SPARE)

MAN OF THE MATCH: R.M.ELLISON (10-104)
(Adjudicator: F.S.TRUEMAN)

1ST DAY TIME	BOWLERS PAVILION END (D.J. CONSTANT) BOWLER	O.	CITY END (D.R. SHEPHERD) BOWLER	O.	BATSMEN SCOREBOARD LEFT SCORING	BALLS	6s 4s	SCOREBOARD RIGHT SCORING	BALLS	6s 4s	NOTES	END-OF-OVER TOTALS O.	RUNS	W.	L. BAT	R. BAT	EXTRAS
					HILDITCH			WOOD		LHB	overcast – cool strong SW wind.						
11.00	BOTHAM	1			x.2.4.†	3	1	...9	3		No 3rd man. sawdust (2 min)	1	5		4	1	
06			TAYLOR	1				... 21.	9		† Good stop (LAMB) M1	2					
09	– · –	2			L.8/7. 7.211.	7		.1.7/8	11	•	• In air – short of deep sq. leg (LAMB).	3	9		7	2	
13			– · –	2	..2.1	10		76.1	14			4	11		8	3	
17	– · –	3			+9/8	11		⊙.4.3.2.7.3.24	20	2	NB † Hit on helmet NB1 ↑ Round wkt.	5	23		9	13	1
22			– · –	3	9. LB 1	13		3.9. 3.4.6 41	24	3	LB	6	30		10	18	2
26	– · –	4			..:.4.P.: 4 1	19	2				HILDITCH 1000 RUNS in 16 TESTS.	7	34		14		
31			– · –	4				.P. 78. ⊙.:	31		NB NB2	8	35				3
35	– · –	5			:.8 1	21		.... :	35		BOTHAM warned (pitch damage)	9	36		15		
39			ELLISON	1	7: 4.:..	27	3					10	40		19		
43	– · –	6			:2.30	30		..1.7/8	38			11	43		21	19	
47			– " –	2				:.:.P.	44		M2	12					
51	– · –	7 ⎤			L.7/8 1	32		8P7/8 W	45	3		12.8	44	1	22	19	3
53		⎬						WESSELS		LHB						0	
55	– · –	7 ⎦						:.:.:	3		1 HR	13					
58			– · –	3	L.:....	38					M3	14					
12.01	– · –	8			.4	39	4	:.:. 6/8.1/2. 2.7.3	8		† ball examined.	15	53		26	5	
06			– · –	4	:.2.:.	44		8/9	9			16	56		28	6	
10½	TAYLOR	5						3/2.: P 1/2.:.P 4	15	1		17	62			12	
15			– · –	5	:.:.2 1	47		P.P. ...	18			18	63		29		
19	– · –	6			:.2.3. 22:...	53						19	67		33		
23			– · –	6	.::::	58		8.1	19			20	68			13	
27	– · –	7			..	60		: 7.8.1. 7	23		• Dropped 2nd slip (BOTHAM)	21	69			14	
31			– · –	7				8.7.:.:.4.7 1	29		Ball examined.	22	70			15	
35	– · –	8			.:1 1	62		:.4.8 4.3	33	2		23	78		34	22	
40			EDMONDS	1	:.2/3 1	66		7/8.7 4.1	35	3	Round wkt to RHB.	24	84		35	27	
46	– · –	9						.:.4.:: 1	41	4		25	88			31	
50			– · –	2	5/6.2.: .29 4.:::W	71	5					25.5	92	2	39	31	3
52					BORDER		LHB								0		
54			– · –	2	.6P 1							26					
55	– · –	10			:.:.7 1	4		2.1 ::	44		2 HR	27	94		1	32	
59			– · –	3	P.9. 64† 1	8	–	8.1	46	4	• 3rd chance (v. difficult)	28	96	2	2	33	3
1.02	LUNCH										M3 NB2			LUNCH			
1.15	RAIN																
3.40	TEA	•									43 overs lost			TEA			
4.55	EMBUREY	1			.:	9		:.:.:.8 1	51		Round wkt.	29	97			34	
57			EDMONDS	4				:.PT.:.:	57		NB disallowed. M4	30					
5.00	– · –	2			:.1 P.	13		:.8.1	59			31	99		3	35	
03			– · –	5	6 1	14	–	3.3 :.4.P.:	64	4	M4 NB2	32	103	2	4	38	3

1ST DAY TIME	BOWLERS (CONSTANT) PAVILION END BOWLER	O.	(SHEPHERD) CITY END BOWLER	O.	BATSMEN SCOREBOARD LEFT SCORING	BALLS	6s 4s	SCOREBOARD RIGHT SCORING	BALLS	6s 4s	AUSTRALIA 1ST INNINGS NOTES	O.	RUNS	W.	'L' BAT	'R' BAT	EXTRAS
					BORDER	14	–	WESSELS	64	4	M4 NB2	32	103	2	4	38	3
5·06	EMBUREY	3			. P . . . ³/₂ 4	20	1					33	107		8		
09			EDMONDS	6	: :	21		6 ³/₄ . . ³/₃	69			34	110			41	
12	– . –	4						P . ·Ọ· .	76		NB NB3	35	111				4
15			– . –	7	9E . P 9 2 . . 1	25		1+6	78		† Round wkt.	36	114		11		
19	BOTHAM	9			P . . ²/₃ † 2 . . 2	31						37	116		13		
23			– . –	8	L . 6 . . .	34		. . ³/₇	81		over wkt.	38	117			42	
26	– . –	10						L	87		M5	39					
30			– . –	9	³ L . EP 1	38		P 7/8	89			40	119		14	43	
33	– . –	11			X 8/9	41		. X 2 . 1	92			41	121		15	44	
37			– . –	10	P . . P 8 4 . 1	46		³ 1	93			42	123		16	45	
40	– . .	12			2 1	47		8/9 . . ²/3 3 4	98	5	WESSELS 50: 116.	43	129		17	50	
44			– . –	11	9 P . . 1 . .	51		. 2 . 1	100			44	131		18	51	
47	– . –	13						. . . 3 4 2 4 . 1	106	6	3HR	45	136			56	
52			– . –	12	³ 1	52		. . . . 9E 1	111			46	138		19	57	
55	TAYLOR	11			6 ³ . ² P 1	58					M6	47					
59			– . –	13	9E 1 7 P . 1 (4)			. . 1	118	7	NB4 Sop'ship: 73 min. † Diving stop (Taylor)	48	143			62	
6·03	– . –	12			X † EP . 8	63		7 1	119		† Round wkt.	49	144			63	
06½			– . –	14				† 1	125		† Appeal ct sh leg (Ealting). M7	50					
10	– . .	13			2 . S . 1 . .	67		P 7 1	127			51	146		20	64	
13½			– . –	15	3/2 1 4 3/2 1	71		1 2 1	129		† s.m. off's shadow on pitch – moved to mw	52	149		21	66	
17	– . –	14			P 4 F X . 1	75		. 2 . 1	131			53	150			67	
22½			EMBUREY	5				 1	137		Round wkt. M8	54					
25	– . –	15			6/2 4 3/4 X 5 (4) . 4 . 1	82	3				NB5	55	158		29		
30			– . –	6				. 7 . 1	143		• Difficult st. chance M9	56					
33	– . –	16			³/₄ † P 6 P PL 4 1	88	4				over wkt. † Lamb 'torpedoed'.	57	162		33		
37			– . –	7				. 2 . 1 4 . . 1	149	8	over wk°	58	166			71	
40	– . –	17			³ ³ 2 1 . . 3	92		8/7 75 1	151			59	172		37	73	
44			ELLISON	8				S 9³ 1	157		• Cover – Robinson diving low to left.	60	173			74	
48½	– . –	18						P 7 P 5° . . . 1	163		• Hard, low c Ð b. 4HR	61	174			75	
53			– . –	9	3 8/7 4 7/6 1	97		9 1	164		† Diving stop (Edmonds)	62	175			76	
56	EDMONDS	16						P . . . . ²/₃ 1	170		M10	63					
59½			– . –	10	6 L . 8 . 4 . . 2 . .	103	5		170	8		64	181	2	43	76	
7·04	STUMPS										M10 NB5		STUMPS				

178

2ND DAY TIME	BOWLERS (CONSTANT) PAVILION END BOWLER	O.	(SHEPHERD) CITY END BOWLER	O.	BATSMEN SCOREBOARD LEFT SCORING	BALLS	6s/4s	SCOREBOARD RIGHT SCORING	BALLS	6s/4s	AUSTRALIA 1ST INNINGS NOTES	END-OF-OVER TOTALS O.	RUNS	W.	L BAT	R BAT	EXTRAS
					BORDER	103	5	WESSELS	170	8	overcast - cool. M10 NB5	64	181	2	43	76	4
11.00	BOTHAM	14						. . . : ² . 176				65	182			77	
03			ELLISON	11				: ⁸ 182			M11	66					
07	— · · —	15			¹ · · ↑ · · 105			: ↑ : ↑ 186				67	184		44	78	
11			— · · —	12				. . . . ⁴ 192			M12	68					
15	— · · —	16			· ⁵ : ⁷⁸ 109			. . . ³ 194				69	188		45	81	
19½			— · · —	13	· W 111		5	: . ↑ 197			↑ in air - no gully.	69	189	3	45	82	4
22					RITCHIE											0	
24			— · · —	13	· . 1							70					
25	— · · —	17			· ⁴ . 4			⁵ ⁴ ⁵/⁹ 200				71	190			83	
29			— · · —	14				4 ⁸ . . W 204		8	Ⓦ	71	191	4	0	83	5
32								PHILLIPS LHB								0	
34			— · · —	14				· · 2				72					
35½	— · · —	18			⁴ · : ² ⁷/⁸ 10		1				M13	73	197		6		
40			— · · —	15				⁸↑ · · · 4 8			↑ just short of cover	74					
44½	TAYLOR	19			· · ⊙ · ⁴ · ˣ 17						NB NB6 5HR	75	198				6
50			— · · —	16				ᵖ ³/⁴ · ¹⁸⁸⁷ · 43 14		1	AGNEW sub (Botham boot repairs - 2 overs)	76	205			7	
54	— · —	20						⁶ · · · ⁵ 20			M14	77					
59			— · · —	17	: · ² · ⁸¹ W 22		1				↑ 1 overthrow (cover)	77	207	5	8	7	6
12.02					O'DONNELL						Agnew sub (Edmonds)					0	
04			— · · —	17				· · 1				78					
05	— · · —	21						: ˣ · ⁸ 26			M15	79	·				
09½			— · · —	18	⁸¹ 2			· ³ : ᴾ ᴾ 31				80	208		1		
13	— · · —	22			⁸¹ W 3		–					80	208	6	1	7	6
13½					LAWSON						Edmonds back.					0	
15	— · · —	22			: ˣ ⁸¹ 3			² ² 4 · 33		2		81	213		1	11	
19			— · · —	19	² : . ˣ . 9						M16	82					
23	— · · —	23						· · ³ : ᴾ . 39		3		83	217			15	
27			— · · —	20	: ² 11			⁵ · ³/² W 42		3		83	218	7	2	15	6
30					McDERMOTT			: 1			umpires discussed drizzle.					0	
32			— · · —	20								84					
33	— · · —	24			⁶ : ⁴ ↑ 14			· · ⁷ 4				85	221		4	1	
37			— · · —	21	ˣ 2LB ³ : ² · · 20						(2LB) 6HR	86	225			6	8
41	BOTHAM	19			ᴾ ↑↑ ˣ 23		–	⁴ ᴱᴾᴵ LB · · 7		1	↑ NEW BALL (LB) ↑ Elbow hit - treatment - 4 min.	87	230	7	6	5	9
50			— · · —	22													
12·51	RAIN										M16 NB6			R	S	P	
12·51	LUNCH													L U N C H			
1·30			ELLISON	22				ˣ · ˣ ˣ ²/³²¹³ · · 2 · 13		1		88	232	7	6	7	9
1·33	RAIN										M16 NB6			R	S	P	
											6 overs lost						

2ND DAY	BOWLERS (CONSTANT) PAVILION END		(SHEPHERD) CITY END		BATSMEN SCOREBOARD LEFT			SCOREBOARD RIGHT			AUSTRALIA 1ST INNINGS NOTES	END-OF-OVER TOTALS				
TIME	BOWLER	O.	BOWLER	O.	SCORING	BALLS	6s/4s	SCORING	BALLS	6s/4s		O.	RUNS	W.	L BAT	R BAT	EXTRAS
					LAWSON 23	-		McDERMOTT 13	1		M16 NB6	88	232	7	6	7	9
1·58	BOTHAM	20			7 3¾ 3 1	25		¼/3 2 ⁵⁄₄↑ 1 42	17	2	† Bruising stop (cover) –Robinson.	89	243		10	14	
2·02			ELLISON	23	1↑ 1	26	-	4 7 ⁵⁄₆ 4 : 2 : 2 :	21	2		89⁵	248	7	11	18	9
2·06	BAD LIGHT										M16 NB 6		B L S P				
2·15	RAIN												R A I N				
3·40	TEA										41 overs lost		T E A				
5·15			ELLISON	23				7	22			90	248	7	11	18	9
15½	BOTHAM	21			: ↑ x 3 : ³ : : : 4	32	1					91	252		15		
20			– · –	24	: : 7	35		·ˣ 95† :	25		† H3 6 Tests.	92	253			19	
22½	– · –	22						5 ˣ · · ⁷⁄₈ ⁶⁄₄ : · · : 2	31			93	255			21	
27			– · –	25	P · P 4 4/3↑	41					† Helmet fell off. M17	94					
31	– · –	23			↑/3 3	42		ˣ 9 ˣ↑⁵⁄ : · 1 :	36		† Almost bowled. • Dropped c + b.	95	259		18	22	
35			– · –	26	6 3	43		6 8 ˣ 7 42 · · 2	41	3	50 p'ship : 53 min.	96	270		21	30	
39½	– · –	24			3 1	44		⁴⁄₈ 6 · · 4 · ·	46	4		97	275		22	34	
43			– · –	27	ˣ ˣ : : † :	50					M18	98					
48	EDMONDS	17			: P : † :	55	1	3 1	47	4	Round wkt.	99	276	7	22	35	9
5·51	BLSP										M18 NB6		B L S P				
6·05			ELLISON	28				· 4 3 4 · W	51	4		99⁴	276	8	22	35	9
07								THOMSON			Crossed					0	
09			– · –	28	: :	57					M19	100					
11	TAYLOR	25						: : : : ˣ	6		M20 7HR	101					
15			– · –	29	: ⁴⁄₁ ⁶⁄₄ :	62	2	2† 1	7		† First bounce to third man.	102	282		27	1	
19	– · –	26						4 · 4/5 6 8 6 7 : · 2 · 24	13	1		103	290			9	
24			– · –	30	5 ⁵⁄₄ 4 8 · ˣ 4 4 : 1	68	4				• v. hard c + b (LH).	104	300		37		
27	BOTHAM	25			: 8 : 4 : 2 : 1	72		7 V2 · 1	15			105	305		40	11	
32			– · –	31	7 : 1	74		⁵⁽⁴⁾ · 4 1/2 6 · 1 : 1	19	1/1		106	314		41	19	
36	– · –	26						ˣ ↑ ˣ · 4 6 · : : : 1	25			107	315			20	
41			EDMONDS	18				· 7 · 4 7 : : : 24	31	1/2		108	321			26	
44	– · –	27			3 ˣ 3 · † 4 : : · 1	80	5					109	325		45		
48			– · –	19				P P · · 6 ·	37		M21	110					
52	EMBUREY	8			↑1 9 4 4 · · · :	86	7				50 p'ship : 44 min. LAWSON'S 50 : 132'	111	333		53		
55			– · –	20	: :	88		: ⁵ P † 1	41			112	334			·27	
59	– · –	9			: : : : : ·	93	7	7 1	42	1/2		113	335	8	53	28	9
7·01	STUMPS										M21 NB6		S T U M P S				
3RD DAY 11·00			ELLISON	32	²⁰	93	7	³⁵	43			113¹	335	9	53	28	9
					HOLLAND						(Crossed)				0		
01			– · –	32	: 6 : ⁶⁷ W	4	-		43	1/2		113⁵	335	10	0	28	9
11·03	AUSTRALIA ALL OUT										M21 NB6		A L L O U T				
											689 balls						

180

3RD DAY TIME	BOWLERS (CONSTANT) PAVILION END BOWLER	O.	(SHEPHERD) CITY END BOWLER	O.	BATSMEN SCOREBOARD LEFT SCORING	BALLS	6s 4s	SCOREBOARD RIGHT SCORING	BALLS	6s 4s	ENGLAND 1ST INNINGS NOTES	END-OF-OVER TOTALS O.	RUNS	W.	'L' BAT	'R' BAT	EXTRAS
					ROBINSON			GOOCH									
11.13			LAWSON	1	⊙ᵇᵖ...!ˣ	7					(NB) NB 1	1	1				1
18	McDERMOTT	1			7:::.⁸⁄₄₂⁷⁸	6	1				•	2	7	6			
23	- • -		- • -	2				7 .²¹ 2.4•	13	1		3	13		6		
28	- • -	2			!⊙:..ᴸᴾ:	13					† Appeal ct wk (legde) (NB) NB2	4	14				2
33			- • -	3				P ³²⁄₃...⁷ 4④...	20	3	NB 3	5	22		14		
38	- • -	3			:.⁶ᵖ ⁸ᴾ:.²⁴⁸	19	2					6	26	10			
42			- • -	4	⊙:.::	25		7¹	21		(NB) NB 4	7	28		15	3	
48	- • -	4		•	.¹ ᴾ:ˢ	29		ᴸᴮ ᴸᴮ	23		(LB) (LB)	8	31	11		5	
52¼			- • -	5	:⊙: ..ᵗᵗ	34		7 ᴸᴮ 4•	25	4	† hit on shoulder (NB) NB5	9	37		19	7	
59	THOMSON	1						..⊙W	29	4	(NB) NB6	9⁸	38	1	11	19	8
12.01								GOWER		ᴸᴴᴮ					0		
03	- • -	1						..²⁄₄	3	1		10	42		4		
05			- • -	6	ˣ:.³:ᴾᵗ³	40					1 HR	11	43	12			
09½	- • -	2			¹...⁶₃	45		.:	4			12	46	15			
15			- • -	7	⁴⁄₃ᵗ⁷⁶ ⁹⁵⁺ ₂¹:ᴸ 4:	49	3	7 ᴸᴮ 2:	6		† Lofted - mistimed	13	56	22	6	9	
20	- • -	3						⁵⁄₆². ⁶ ¹ˢᵗ ³ 2.4:	13	3	† Undredged cut. NB7	14	66		16		
25			McDERMOTT	5	ᴾᴱ¹ ⁷¹:	53		4 ⁷ˢ :1	15		† Good stop (Thomson) NB 8	15	68	23	17		
29	- • -	4		•	::.⁴⁄₂⁴⁴ ⊙₂₄	58	4	.⁹ᴱ	17		(NB) # Nr c.t b NB 8	16	76	29	18	10	
34			- • -	6	ᴱ¹ ⁶ᴾ.⁸⁄₇ᴾ⁶³ :(4)4.2:	65	6	⊙	18		NB 10	17	87	39	19		
41	- • -	5						₃.⁴²⁷ᵗ. ⊙	25		50 p'ship: 38 min. NB 11	18	88				11
46			HOLLAND	1	7¹ :	67		::.⁷⁄₆	29		Round wkt to LHB.	19	90	40	20		
49	- • -	6			ᵗ₃ :7	70		.³⁄₄) 7	32			20	93	41	22		
53			- • -	2	:.⁶₁	72		⁶ ⁵ ᴾ⁶ 4..3	36	4		21	100		29		
57	- • -	7			³:.⊙..⁹	78	6	7¹	37	4	(NB) NB 12	22	103	1	42	30	12
1.00	LUNCH										NB 12 M-	L U N C H					
1.40			O'DONNELL	1	⁶ ⁶ᵗ¹ :	81		4 .³₁	40		† Holland misfielded	23	105	43	31		
44½	LAWSON	8			¹⁷₁	83		³ ⁴⁹₃	44		2 HR	24	106		32		
49½			- • -	2	⁸ ᵇᴾ⁷ 2.4	86	7	ᴱ¹ .¹₁	47			25	113	49	33		
54	- • -	9						.::.⊙⁶₁	54		(NB) NB 13	26	114				13
59			- • -	3	::.⁸₄ᴾ:	92	8				ROBINSON'S 50: 128'	27	118	53			
2.03	- • -	10						:³⁴₁⊙:.ᵗ:¹	61		(NB) NB 14	28	119				14
08			- • -	4	.⁴.ᵗᵗ² 4	98					† Good stop (Ritchie) M 1	29					
13	- • -	11			::	100		.⁴ .⁹ᴱ₁	65			30	120		34		
18			- • -	5				7.⁶.::	71		M2	31					
22	- • -	12			⁵ : ² :.¹	103		...²	74			32	121	54			
27			- • -	6	⁶₁	105		ˣ.⁷.4:	78	5		33	126	55	38		
31	- • -	13			7₁	106		.::.⁴	83			34	127	56			
36			- • -	7	⁸⁹⁄₈ : ³ ⁵⁴ 2²:.:	112						35	131	60			
40	- • -	14			↑	113	8	:.²ᵗ⁴⁸⁹ .⁴₁	88	6	† Good stop (Wessels) M 2 NB 14	36	136	1	60	43	14

3RD DAY TIME	BOWLERS (CONSTANT) PAVILION END BOWLER	O.	(SHEPHERD) CITY END BOWLER	O.	BATSMEN SCOREBOARD LEFT SCORING	BALLS	6s/4s	SCOREBOARD RIGHT SCORING	BALLS	6s/4s	ENGLAND 1ST INNINGS NOTES	END-OF-OVER TOTALS O.	RUNS	W.	L.BAT	R.BAT	EXTRAS
					ROBINSON	113	8	GOWER	88	6	M2 NB14	36	136	1	60	43	14
2.45			O'DONNELL	8	7	114		4·21	93	7	100 p'ship: 123 min. GOWER: 125' 3HR	37	144		61	50	
49	LAWSON	15			41	120	9		94		(NB) NB 15	38	151		66	51	15
54½			THOMSON	8		121		·4LB	100		(NB) (LB) NB 16	39	153				17
59½	McDERMOTT	7				106		4·P·4	106		M 3	40					
3.04½			- · -	9		123		4·43	111	9	(NB) NB 17	41	166		67	62	18
09	- · -	8						4·2·	117	10		42	172			68	
14			- · -	10		130			123	11	(NB) NB 18	43	173			74	19
18	- · -	9						·24	123	11		44	179			74	
23			HOLLAND	3		135		6	124			45	182		69	75	
27	- · -	10			41	138	10	·4LB	127		(LB) 150 p'ship: 169'	46	189		75		20
31½			- · -	4		144					M4	47					
34½	- · -	11				146		41	131	12	(B)	48	195			80	21
39			- · -	5		152	10		131	12		49	197	1	77	80	21
3.41	TEA										M 4 NB 18				T	E	A
4.00	LAWSON	16						·2·⊙	138		(NB) NB 19	50	200			82	22
05			HOLLAND	6		158					M5	51					
07	- · -	17				160		·1	142		4HR	52	202		78	83	
12			- · -	7		166						53	203		79		
15	- · -	18				173					† Ball changed. (NB) NB 20	54	204				23
21			- · -	8		176		·7	145			55	208		82	84	
25	- · -	19			·43	183	11				(NB) NB 21	56	216		89		24
30			- · -	9		186		2·2	148			57	221		90	88	
32½	- · -	20			·3	190		·3	150			58	227		93	91	
38			- · -	10		191		2·	155		(LB)	59	233		96	93	25
43	THOMSON	11			4	197	12				† Hit stumps (bowled). ROBINSON'S 100': 273'	60	237		100		
47			- · -	11		201		·3	157		† Bat/pad: S.A.(Border) 200 p'ship: 227 min.	61	240			96	
50	- · -	12						4·st·1	163		† Hit stumps. M 6	62					
54			- · -	12		207					M 7	63					
56	- · -	13			41	210	13	·1	167		† Good stop (Hilditch). (NB) NB 22	64	247		105	97	26
5.00 02	DRINKS			- · -	13		215			168		5HR	65	248		106		
05	- · -	14			·1·⊙	220		41	170	13	GOWER'S 100': 247' 2nd 50 in 122' (WESSELS) (NB) NB 23	66	255		107	102	27
09½			- · -	14		222		24	174	14		67	262			109	
13	- · -	15				223		4·4	179	15		68	268		108	114	
19			- · -	15		228	14		180			69	276		115	115	
23	McDERMOTT	12				232		·4	186	16		70	281			120	
27½			- · -	16		232		·6	188			71	282			121	
31	- · -	13			41	236	15	3·1	190		250 p'ship: 271 min.	72	292		121	125	
35			- · -	17		237		64	195	17		73	304		122	136	
39	BORDER	1				238	15	4·1	200	18	* st appeal. M 7 NB 23	74	310	1	123	141	27

3RD DAY TIME	BOWLERS (CONSTANT) PAVILION END BOWLER	O.	(SHEPHERD) CITY END BOWLER	O.	BATSMEN SCOREBOARD LEFT SCORING	BALLS	6s/4s	SCOREBOARD RIGHT SCORING	BALLS	6s/4s	ENGLAND 1ST INNINGS NOTES	O.	RUNS	W.	'L' BAT	'R' BAT	EXTRAS
					ROBINSON	238	15	GOWER	200	1/18	M7 NB 23	74	310	1	123	141	27
5.43			O'DONNELL	9	:1: ×33 :	244	16					75	314		127		
47	BORDER	2			6/7 :1	245		3:.3:.6	205		Round wkt to LHB	76	316		128	142	
50			- · -	10	6/7 3 :2	247		:.2.8 :4:1	209	1/19		77	325		132	147	
55	- · -	3			7F:1 676 2 :	253						78	327		134		
58			- · -	11	45 ::	255		:.2.2 :.41	213	1/20	Round wkt to LHB	79	332			152	
6.02	- · -	4			3:.:.:	259		7 8/7	215		Gower changed bat	80	333			153	
05			HOLLAND	18	::.6	262		3:.7 4:	218	1/21	300 p'ship: 306'	81	339		135	158	
09	- · -	5			6/7:.7 ::	267		7	219		6HR	82	341		136	159	
12			- · -	19	62 :	269		7:.9 75	223			83	342			160	
15	- · -	6						3:.5.56	229		M 8	84					
18			- · -	20	66 P :.3	275					M 9	85					
21	LAWSON	21			:4..	279	17	13 9 :1	231		† NEW BALL	86	347		140	161	
25			THOMSON	16		279	17	2.:.4:.	238	1/22	NB 24	87	355	1	140	169	27
6.29	STUMPS										M9 NB 24		STUMPS				
4TH DAY 11.00	START DELAYED RAIN										13 OVERS LOST						
11.55	LAWSON	22			:.0:.0:..	287					NB NB NB 26	88	357				29
12.01			McDERMOTT	14	:4 3 5/6 2	290	18	8 ×1 2.1	241			89	366		146	172	
06	- · -	23			1/3 6× 2 W	293	18	2 1	242		NB 27	89	369	2	148	173	29
10					GATTING										0		
12	- · -	23			:.x.	3						90					
15			- · -	15				2:..2 3E :41	248	1/23		91	376			180	
20	- · -	24			:1	4		::.:1	253			92	377			181	
24			- · -	16				x 3/4 2 :44 ::.	259	1/25	† Round wkt to LHB	93	385			189	
30	- · -	25			8 :4.:	9		9	260		7HR	94	387		1	190	
35			- · -	17	×66.2 ::..	14		6/6	261			95	388			191	
40	- · -	26			3:.LB 4	17	1	2 7 :1	264		LB	96	394		5	192	30
44½			- · -	18	6:.8 :2::.	23						97	396		7		
49	- · -	27			:..3	26		:.LB	267		LB M10	98	397				31
54½			- · -	19				3:.4.9 :.2	273			99	399			194	
59	- · -	28			:1 :.7	30	1	88 21	275	1/25		100	403	2	8	197	31
1.04	LUNCH										M10 NB 27		LUNCH				
2.13			McDERMOTT	20	:8.2 :4:2	34	2	V/2 :.1	277		8 overs lost Round wkt to LHB	101	410		14	198	
17½	LAWSON	29			::.3 :1	38		LB 2 :.	279		LB So p'ship: 66'	102	413		15	199	32
22			- · -	21	4 8	39		:.0:..×1 :.3	285		NB 4LB NB 28	103	421			202	37
27	- · -	30						4 5 1 7 3 :.22:1	291		GOWER'S 200 (410') HS in TESTS. Rec ag AUS.	104	426			207	
32½			- · -	22	8/7 9 41	41	3	2 3 :1 :.73-	295		* DROPPED COVER (RITCHIE)	105	432		20	208	
37	- · -	31			3 7:.3 :1	45		3 :. × :1	297			106	435		22	209	
42	- · -			23	3 3 8 :.	49		Y 7 :1	299		8 HR	107	437		23	210	
46	- · -	32			7 :1	50	3	x:.3 48 P :.1	304	1/25	4LB M10 NB 28	108	443	2	24	211	41

4TH DAY TIME	BOWLERS (CONSTANT) PAVILION END BOWLER	O.	(SHEPHERD) CITY END BOWLER	O.	BATSMEN SCOREBOARD LEFT SCORING	BALLS	6s/4s	SCOREBOARD RIGHT SCORING	BALLS	6s/4s	ENGLAND 1ST INNINGS NOTES	O.	RUNS	W.	'L' BAT	'R' BAT	EXTRAS
					GATTING	50	3	GOWER	304	1/25	M10 NB 28	108	443	2	24	211	41
2·52			McDERMOTT	24	3 G 1	52		3 7 8 4 .. 2 1	308		*Dropped 44 h 24 leg (THOMSON)	109	447		25	214	
57	LAWSON	33			4·4	55	5	:: 2	311			110	456		33	215	
3·02			– ··	25	4 .14 37 .. 1	59	6	LB 4	313		LB LB	111	463		38		43
08	– ··	34						W 2/3	314	1/25		111	463	3	38	215	43
								LAMB								0	
10	– ··	34			:: 67	61		† : 2 1	3		†bat handle	112	464			1	
15			O'DONNELL	12	6 : 1	63		7 3 . LB	7		LB M11	113	465				44
19	– ··	35			: 1	64		:4 :: 4	12	1		114	470			6	
23			– ··	13	LB 1 7	66		1/2 3 1/2	16		LB	115	475		39	9	45
27	– ··	36			1	67		3 81 1 LB 244.	21	3	LB	116	488		40	20	46
32			– ··	14	:: 3	70		: 2 . 1	24			117	490		41	21	
36	THOMSON	17			8P6 . 1	73		: 4 8	27			118	492		42	22	
40			– ··	15	L X . 1	75		6 . 2 . 1	31		9HR	119	495			25	
45	– ··	18			7/6 1 56) 4 2 1	78	7	TBY . 4	34	4	50 p'ship: 42 min	120	507		49	30	
50			– ··	16	1 56)3 2.4 . 4	83	9	8/9	35		GATTING'S 50: 149	121	519		60	31	
54½	– ··	19			. 2 . 4 .	88	10	9	36			122	526		66	32	
4·00			HOLLAND	21	P LB 1 3	92		9 4t 1	38		LB †McDonnell misfielded	123	532		69	34	47
04	McDERMOTT	26			5(4) 2 2t x 23 4 . 1 . 1	98	11				† 1 short (run 2)	124	538		75		
09			– ··	22	3E F4+/3 1 41	101	12	P EP4 . : 1	41	4	+50 in series	125	545	3	81	35	47
4·11	TEA										M11 NB 28				T E A		
4·30	McDERMOTT	27			4 1	102		7P 7 7 P1/5 1	46			126	547		82	36	
35			HOLLAND	23	2Bt 1 7 P 2 . 1	106		4 9 1	48		†Ross hit sound/pec (28)	127	552		83	38	49
38	– ··	28			: 1 x 3 1	110		8 . 1	50			128	556		86	39	
43			– ··	24	4t 3 4 1 1	113		7 2 7 1	53		†wood misfielded	129	560		88	41	
46	– ··	29						5 . 7 . 7 1	59		M12	130					
50			– ··	25	3/4 8/9 P : 6 4 . : 2	118	13	8/9 1	60		100 p'ship: 82 min	131	568		95	42	
54½	– ··	30						7/6 7 4 W	62	5		131³	572	4	95	46	49
55								BOTHAM								0	
57	– ··	30						5(6)6/7 56/9 6 . 64	4	2/1	10 HR	132	588			16	
5·01			LAWSON	37	3 3t 8/7 . : 1	122		3 6 1	6		†Phillips hit on wrist	133	592		97	18	
08	– ··	31						7F W	7	2/1	Treatment to Phillips (crossed)	133³	592	5	97	18	49
								DOWNTON								0	
11	– ··	31			: 7 7 . 6 2 . 1	127	13	–	–		GATTING's 100: 214	134	595	5	100	0	49
5·14	DECLARATION										M12 NB 28 832 balls		DEC	LARED			

4TH DAY	BOWLERS				BATSMEN						AUSTRALIA 2ND INNINGS					
	(SHEPHERD) PAVILION END		(CONSTANT) CITY END		SCOREBOARD LEFT			SCOREBOARD RIGHT			NOTES	END-OF-OVER TOTALS					
TIME	BOWLER	O.	BOWLER	O.	SCORING	BALLS	6⁵/4⁴	SCORING	BALLS	6³/4³		O.	RUNS	W.	'L' BAT	'R' BAT	EXTRAS
					HILDITCH			WOOD		LHB							
5.25	BOTHAM	1			: 74 ↑7 22 ↑1	5		.	1			1	5		5		
29½			TAYLOR	1	.6 7 ½ 1	9		:.	3			2	6		6		
34	- · -	2			.x .1E 8↑ 4W	14	1	.				2⁵	10	1	10	O	-
37					WESSELS											0	
39	- · -	2			:	1						3					
40			- · -	2	⊙ ..	4		...↑5	7		(NB) NB1	4	12		1	1	
44½	- · -	3						↑. ↑ .43 : 4 ...	13	1	† Round wkt.	5	16		5		
49			- · -	3	:. ↑1E•	8		::	15		* Dropped 1st slip (EMBUREY)	6	17		1		
52	- · -	4			:. 7 1	11		:↑ ↑.	18			7	18		2		
56½			- · -	4	:.2↑ 1	15		:8 1	20			8	20		3	6	
6.00	- · -	5						.2↑ ...:	26			9	22		8		
05			- · -	5	:.96 43	18	1	.. L7 1	29			10	30	10	9		
08	- · -	6			.x 232	23		8↑ 1	30			11	31		10		
13			ELLISON	1				.. ...:	36		M1	12					
18	- · -	7			.P· LB	27		.↑	38		(LB) M2	13	32				2
22			- · -	2	:.....	33					M3 1HR	14					
26	TAYLOR	6						444 P3L 1	44		M4	15					
31½			- · -	3	P·E1 W	36	1					15³	32	2	10	10	2
32					HOLLAND											0	
34			- · -	3	W	1	-					15⁴	32	3	0	10	2
35					BORDER											0	
37			- · -	3	.:	2					M5	16					
38½	- · -	7			4↑ 1	3		LB L L5 :. .	49		(LB) † BORDER 500 runs in series.	17	34		1		3
43			- · -	4	L. 9 .↑ 1	7		: 87 W	51	1		18	35	4	2	10	3
46								RITCHIE								0	
48	EDMONDS	1			34. . P5	13					M6	19					
51			- · -	5	. .: W	17	-	LB .	1		(LB)		36	5	2	0	4
54					PHILLIPS		LHB									0	
56			- · -	5	4↑ 1	1						20	37		1		
57	- · -	2			:......	7	-		1	-	M7	21	37	5	1	0	4
7.00	STUMPS										M7 NB1	STUMPS					
5TH DAY 11.00	RAIN																
12.30	LUNCH											LUNCH					
1.10	RAIN										42 overs lost						
2.30			ELLISON	6		7	-	.:	3	-		21²	37	5	1	0	4
2.31	BAD LIGHT & RAIN										3 overs lost	B L S P - RAIN					
2.43			- · -	6	4.4 4.	9	1	.75 .1	5			22	42		5	1	
46	TAYLOR	8						5.....	11		M8	23					
50			- · -	7	.37 .4.1 4/1 3 .4.	15	3		11	-	† Good stop (Edmonds) M8 NB1	24	50	5	13	1	4

5TH DAY TIME	BOWLERS (SHEPHERD) PAVILION END BOWLER	O.	(CONSTANT) CITY END BOWLER	O.	BATSMEN SCOREBOARD LEFT SCORING	BALLS	6s/4s	SCOREBOARD RIGHT SCORING	BALLS	6s/4s	NOTES	AUSTRALIA 2ND INNINGS END-OF-OVER TOTALS O.	RUNS	W.	'L' BAT	'R' BAT	EXTRAS
					PHILLIPS	15	3	RITCHIE	11	-	M8 NB1	24	50	5	13	1	4
2·54½	TAYLOR	9						·····⁵	17		M9	25					
58			ELLISON	8	:²/9 6½: ·7/4	21	5					26	58		21		
3·02	– · –	10						:: ·³P:	23		M10 2HR	27					
06			– · –	9	4³·7⁴::::	27	6					28	62		25		
10	– · –	11						:²⁴·⁷ᴸ²·³	29			29	67			6	
15			EDMONDS	3	:	28		³:::³³	34		Round wkt.	30	70			9	
18½	– · –	12			:·ᴸ·	31		P7 6/3	37			31	73			12	
23			– · –	4	²⁹⁶·	33		ᴮ :::³	41		Ⓑ sunlight.	32	75		26		5
25½	– · –	13			ˣ6·:³4:	39	7					33	79		30		
30			– · –	5				:⁵†P³/³⁷⁴/	47		† over wkt. † Round wkt. M11	34					
33	EMBUREY	1			†:::³·P:	45					† Round wkt M12	35					
35½			– · –	6				:::·⁵†··	53		over wkt. † Round wkt M13	36					
38½	– · –	2			P³/²⁸·1	48	7					37	80	5	31	12	5
3·41	TEA							4·:P	56	-	over wkt-¾ R½B.						
											M13 NB1				T E A		
4·00			EDMONDS	7	7:·³:·ᴸ:	54					over wkt.	38	82		33		
02	BOTHAM	8			·:⁺³·⁴⁷/	59	8	7	57		† ⁵-1 field. 50 p'ship: 70 min.	39	87		37	13	
07			– · –	8				: ⁷¹⁵ ⁶†⁶2/2·1·	63		Round wkt. † warning -pitch damage	40	91			17	
10½	– · –	9			ˣ1⁸/⁹ˣ44·:·	65	10					41	99		45		
15			– · –	9				P³/44·†·P·	69		† over wkt. ‡ 2nd warning M14	42					
17½	– · –	10			†·²:·†⁷/	71					† Round wkt. M15	43					
21			EMBUREY	3				:⁷ᴮ ᴾP:P	75		M16 3HR	44					
24	– ·²·	11			²/1:⁸/7 ⁶⁄₂⁴/2	77					∘ Low to point's left (Robinson).	45	103		49		
28			– · –	4				7⁵ᴸ⁷·:	81		M17	46					
31	– · –	12			⁸3ˣ·³⁴2·:4/1	83	11					47	110		56		
35			– · –	5	:⁶/⁷3	85		::::	85		PHILLIPS 50: 94' Round wkt to LHB	48	113		59		
38	EDMONDS	10			ˣP:·³W	90	11					48⁵	113	6	59	17	5
40					O'DONNELL										0		
42	– ·∘·	10			ᴱ¹/⁺·1	1					∘ Hand chance-slip (Botham) M18	49					
43½			– · –	6	·⁷	3		:::·⁸/⁷	89			50	114			18	
46	– · –	11						:·⁴2:6·:2·	95			51	116			20	
49			– · –	7	:·⁷P·:	9					M19	52					
50½	– · –	12						:::·⁴···	101		M20	53					
53			– · –	8	:·⁹1	11		:⁶ᴮW	103	-		53⁴	117	7	1	20	5
54								LAWSON							0		
56			– · –	8				P:·	2			54					
57	– · –	13			·P::::	17					M21	55					
59			– · –	9	·6†4:	21		:⁸/⁹3	4		† Getting hit on leg.	56	120			3	
5·01	– · –	14				21	-	:::W	8	-	20 OVERS M21 NB1	56⁴	120	8	1	3	5
02																	

5TH DAY TIME	BOWLERS (SHEPHERD) PAVILION END BOWLER	O.	(CONSTANT) CITY BOWLER	END O.	BATSMEN SCOREBOARD LEFT SCORING	BALLS	6s/4s	SCOREBOARD RIGHT SCORING	BALLS	6s/4s	AUSTRALIA 2ND INNINGS NOTES OVERS LEFT	END-OF-OVER TOTALS O.	RUNS	W.	'L' BAT	'R' BAT	EXTRAS
					O'DONNELL	21	-	McDERMOTT		-	19.2 M 21 NB1	56⁴	120	8	1	0	5
5.04	EDMONDS	14						7 ∴	2		19 M22	57					
05			EMBUREY	10	4/5 2 : P : 2 2 3	27					18	58	124		5		
08	— · —	15			: 6P .	30		+ 6 : : 1	5		+ over wkt. 17	59	125			1	
10½			— · —	11	::	32		9E P : 3 : 1	9		16	60	126			2	
14	BOTHAM	13			5 . : 7	35		X 6 1 82 : 4 1	12	1	15	61	131			7	
19			— · —	12				4 E9 : : P	18		14 M23	62					
21	— · —	14 ⎫			3 ½ 7X 2 · 4 W	39	1					62⁴	137	9	11	7	5
23		⎬		·	THOMSON											0	
25	— · —	14 ⎭			. : P	2					13 4HR	63					
26			— · —	13	P : 7 · 4	5	1	:: 7 1	21		12	64	142		4	8	
28	— · —	15				5	1	7 W	22	1	11.5 M23 NB1	64⁴	142	10	4	8	5
5.28	AUSTRALIA ALL OUT										386 balls		ALL		OUT		
	ENGLAND WON BY AN INNINGS AND 118 RUNS																

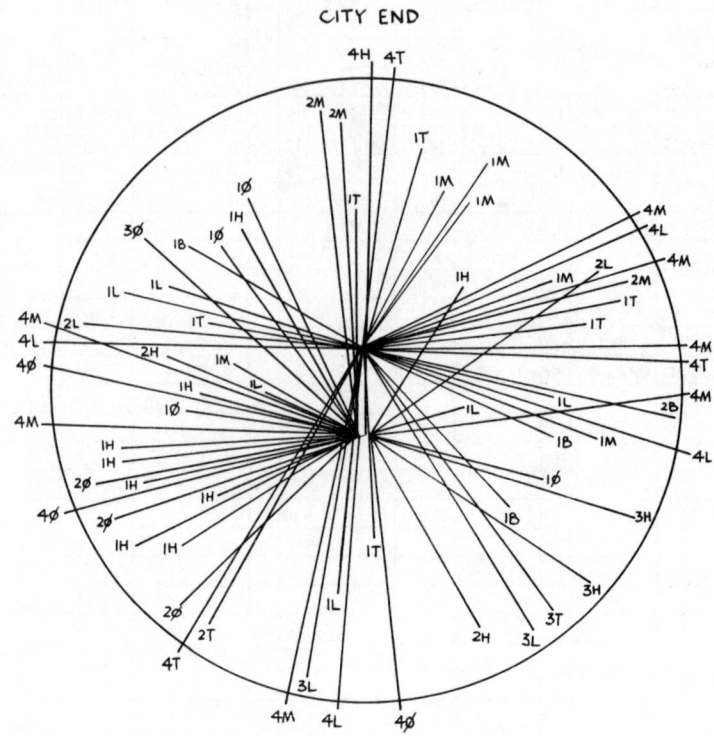

CITY END

PAVILION END

BOWLER	SYMBOL	R U N S					
		1	2	3	4	6	TOTAL
BORDER	B	3	1	-	-	-	5
HOLLAND	H	9	2	2	1	-	23
LAWSON	L	6	2	2	4	-	32
McDERMOTT	M	6	3	-	7	-	40
O'DONNELL	Ø	4	3	1	3	-	25
THOMSON	T	6	1	1	3	-	23
TOTALS		34	12	6	18	-	148

R.T. ROBINSON at Edgbaston

148 RUNS
293 BALLS
393 MINUTES

© BILL FRINDALL 1985

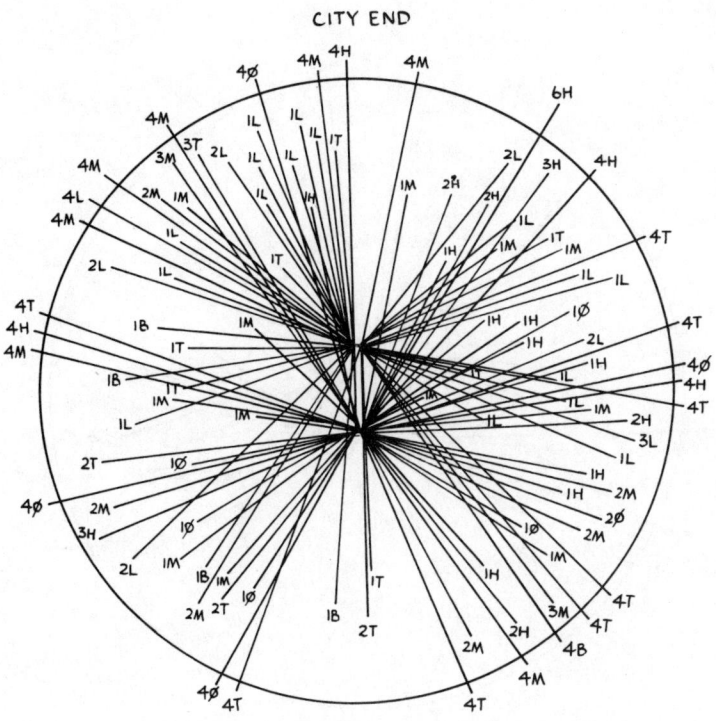

CITY END

PAVILION END

BOWLER	SYMBOL	RUNS					TOTAL
		1	2	3	4	6	
BORDER	B	4	-	-	1	-	8
HOLLAND	H	9	4	2	4	1	45
LAWSON	L	16	5	1	1	-	33
McDERMOTT	M	12	6	2	7	-	58
O'DONNELL	Ø	5	1	-	4	-	23
THOMSON	T	7	3	1	8	-	48
TOTALS		53	19	6	25	1	215

D. I. GOWER at Edgbaston

215 RUNS
314 BALLS
452 MINUTES
(left-handed batsman)

© BILL FRINDALL 1985

189

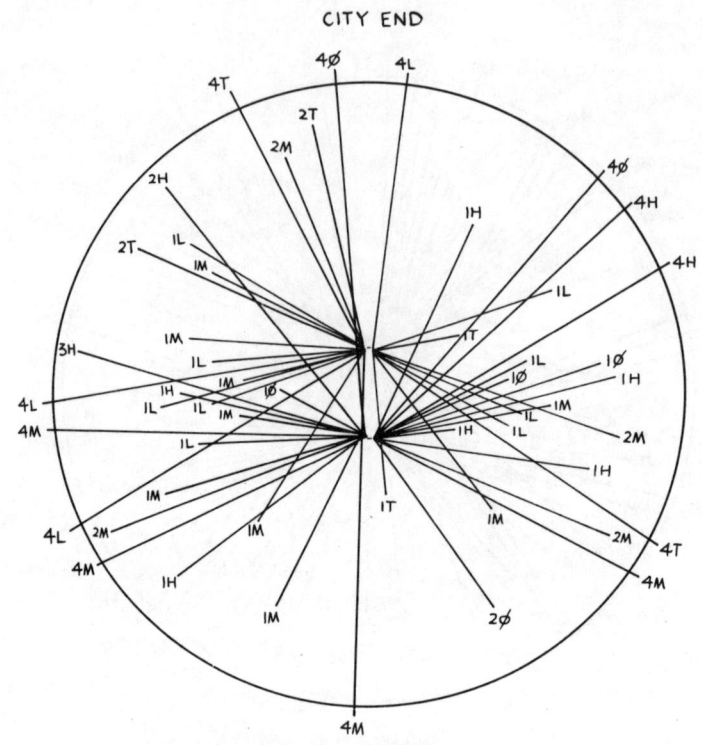

CITY END

PAVILION END

BOWLER	SYMBOL	R U N S				
		1	2	3	6	TOTAL
HOLLAND	H	6	1	1	2	-	19
LAWSON	L	9	-	-	3	-	21
McDERMOTT	M	9	4	-	4	-	33
O'DONNELL	Ø	3	1	-	2	-	13
THOMSON	T	2	2	-	2	-	14
TOTALS		29	8	1	13	-	100

M.W. GATTING at Edgbaston

100 RUNS (not out)
127 BALLS
214 MINUTES

© BILL FRINDALL 1985

SIXTH TEST

THE OVAL

AUGUST 29, 30, 31, September 2

ENGLAND

D.I. Gower (captain), G.A.Gooch, R.T. Robinson, M.W. Gatting,
A.J. Lamb, I.T. Botham, P.R. Downton, J.E. Emburey,
R.M. Ellison, P.H. Edmonds, L.B. Taylor

AUSTRALIA

A.R. Border (captain), G.M. Wood, A.M.J. Hilditch, K.C. Wessels,
D.M. Wellham, G.M. Ritchie, W.B. Phillips, G.F. Lawson,
M.J. Bennett, C.J. McDermott, D.R. Gilbert

Botham injury only England worry

T he doubt over Ian Botham's fitness is the only cloud, literal or metaphorical, on England's horizon as they prepare to complete their grip on the Ashes in the final Cornhill Test at the Oval today. Botham will not know until after a net this morning whether he will appear in his 79th Test, though I doubt whether he will let an injured knee prevent him from competing in a game for which all tickets for the first four days have been sold.

That being so, I imagine England will name the side that triumphed by an innings at Edgbaston, knowing a draw will suffice but perhaps suspecting that they are equipped to overcome Australia again. Without Botham, of course, Bill Athey would play and much more use, perhaps, would be made of Graham Gooch's bowling on a ground where, as was seen last year, the ball can swing.

The choice of Athey as a late standby for Botham may, at first glance, seem unusual, but it mainly reflects the fact that there is no ready-made replacement. Athey has a Test average of only 2·83 from six innings, mainly due to his being catapulted into the series in the Caribbean five years ago from Australian grade cricket with little or no acclimatisation. He is nevertheless a player of class and one in prime form. I imagine that Peter May, chairman of selectors, sees something of his youthful self in the way that the tall, upright Yorkshireman, now playing for Gloucestershire, bats, and there, in a sense, is the key to England's approach here.

They need to maintain the disciplined, selective attitude which was an important factor in the way they scored 595 for five at Edgbaston, and they may well be blessed with the pitch and the weather to do so. If they are lucky with the toss, they should be able to set out their stall to bat for two days or more, which would effectively put Australia out of contention and give England's bowlers time to do their job.

The pitch is a tribute to the way groundsman Harry Brind has overcome the monsoons of August, producing a strip so firm and dry. Bob Holland, Australia's leg-spinner, almost shed a tear of frustration when he saw it yesterday and then learned that, after all the surfaces he has been con-demned to operate on, he was not to have the chance to bowl on this one.

England's 10-wicket bowling hero Richard Ellison in action at Edgbaston.

Below: Ellison, behind Border, is jubilant as he captures the Australian captain's wicket, caught by Edmonds for 45.

Left: Ian Botham has Geoff Lawson in trouble again. But despite this injury, the Australian fast bowler made 53 to help his side to an innings of 335 that extended into the third day – after they were put in to bat.

Right: Umpires Constant and Shepherd consult about the conditions as rain and bad light make England's task difficult at Edgbaston.

Left: Tim Robinson sweeps during his historic second-wicket partnership of 331 with David Gower. After England had taken the last two Australian wickets without addition on the Saturday morning and lost Gooch at 38, the pair took England's score to 355 without further loss by the end of the day. Robinson went on to amass 148 and Gower a scintillating 215.

Right: Mike Gatting continued the good work, and Gower declared at 595–5 as soon as the Middlesex captain reached his hundred.

The controversial incident that finally put England on the road to victory on the last day of the rain-hit Edgbaston Test. Edmonds, the bowler (right) appeals, together with Botham and Gower, who clasps the ball having caught a rebound from Allan Lamb's boot. Wayne Phillips, Australia's last hope, is given out and the Australians collapse to defeat.

Above: Another record-breaking second-wicket stand for England. Gooch and Gower take a breather during their partnership of 351 in the last Test, at the Oval, having virtually guaranteed that the Ashes were on their way back to England.

Left: McDermott, having bowled Robinson for three, despairs as England pile up 376–3 on the first day.

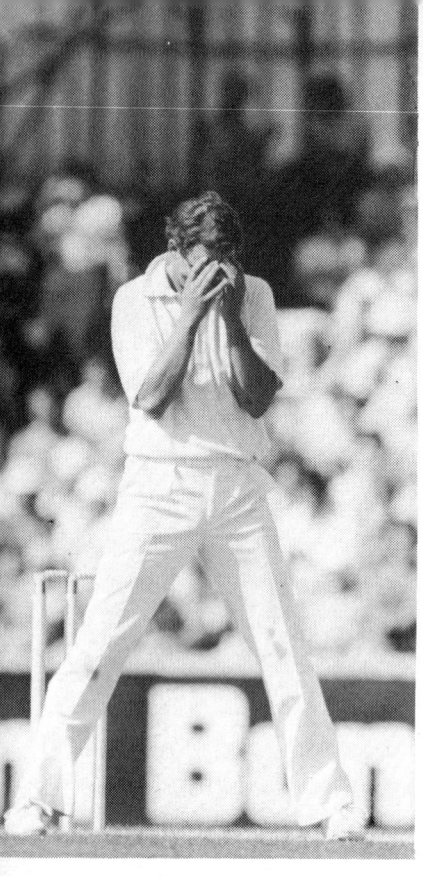

Murray Bennett (above), brought in for the last Test to bolster the Australian attack, is perhaps wishing that he'd been left out as Gooch (above right) and Gower (right) pile on the agony.

Opposite page: Ian Botham (left) leaps high as he has Wayne Phillips caught behind by Downton during Australia's second-innings collapse.

Ellison (left) hugs keeper Downton after again capturing the highly prized wicket of Allan Border. As they and David Gower watch the Australian captain walk off after a brave 58 – no other Australian scored more than 11 – they know that nothing can now stop a second consecutive innings victory for England.

It's 'drinks on David Gower' as the England team celebrate regaining the Ashes.

By the standards of those seen earlier in this entertaining series, it should have a degree of bounce, and I suppose therein lies a hazard for England's batsmen until they have had time to adjust against McDermott, Lawson and company. If they do, the full-house crowds should have ample evidence of the way England's batsmen have scored at a remarkable 59 runs for 100 balls in this series, the fastest ever against Australia, though I doubt whether the Australians will bowl as accommodatingly as they did at Birmingham.

It was at the Oval that Len Hutton's side regained the Ashes in 1953, with Edrich and Compton together at the end, and England have had more success against the old enemy here than at any other home ground.

AUSTRALIAN VIEWPOINT

Thomson & Holland go in Australian gamble

A ustralia have taken a necessary gamble by including three players who have yet to play in the series in their 12 for the sixth and final Test at the Oval, starting today, which they need to win to retain the Ashes. All from New South Wales, the three are Dave Gilbert, 24, fast-medium, Murray Bennett, 28, slow left arm, and Dirk Wellham, 26, a batsman.

Jeff Thomson, the fast bowler, and Bob Holland, the leg-spinner, are dropped. Wellham, 12th man in the fifth Test, will be preferred to Simon O'Donnell, an all-rounder, but Australia may select O'Donnell, medium pace, as their fourth bowler at the expense of Bennett.

The pitch is likely to be quicker, providing more bounce, than any in the series, but yesterday's forecast by Harry Brind, the Oval's ground controller, that his pitch will take turn from about the fourth day should convince the selectors to prefer Bennett to O'Donnell. O'Donnell's bowling has not been sufficiently tight or penetrative in five Tests, as shown by his figures of 6–487 (average 81·16) from 145·4 overs.

Before hearing of the Australian 12, Mr Brind said he would 'certainly play the leg-spinner (Holland).' While the Oval would have suited him more than other venues, including Lord's, where he took five second innings wickets, the selectors believe he has lost his attacking edge. They also feel his style of bowling has become too familiar to the English batsmen, particularly David Gower and Mike Gatting.

Gilbert, tall, strong and tireless, and with 29 first class matches behind him, including nine this tour, will make his Test debut as the third paceman in support of Geoff Lawson and Craig McDermott. They should not be disappointed by a firm, dry strip which looks much more like an Australian wicket than the five 'sponges' previously served up.

The inclusion of Wellham for his fifth Test has a parallel here four years ago, when he made his Test debut in the sixth Test at the Oval and scored 24 and 103.

Allan Border, the Australian captain, says his players are 'back in the groove' after their seven-wicket victory over disappointing Kent on Tuesday.

STATISTICAL PREVIEW

6–4 on a draw

In 28 Tests at Kennington Oval, Australia have suffered 12 defeats and gained only five victories. Six of the ten post-war Ashes Tests there have been drawn.

Bill Athey, whose three previous caps were gained as a Yorkshire player, could become Gloucestershire's 25th England representative. He would also be their first since David Allen made the last of his 39 appearances – against West Indies at Old Trafford in 1966. In the intervening period England have played 187 of their 616 official Tests.

David Gower, whose aggregate of 575 is a record for England in a home Ashes series, needs another 82 to become the ninth English batsman to score 2,000 runs against Australia.

Gower & Gooch run riot in stand of 351

England put the final Cornhill Test, and with it the Ashes, out of Australia's reach, barring miracles, at the Oval yesterday, when centuries by Graham Gooch and David Gower enabled them to exploit perfect batting conditions and amass 376 for three from 90 overs.

Gooch hit an unbeaten 179, the highest Test score of his career, and figured in a second-wicket partnership of 351 with Gower, whose 157 was his third century of the series.

Though Gower needed some luck early on, Gooch batted with clinical certainty and growing fluency in making his first century in 40 innings against Australia.

Their partnership has been exceeded only five times in English Test history, and was the second highest for any wicket against Australia.

Not for the first time, Australia found the Oval a graveyard for their bowlers, and having performed indifferently early on when the new ball bounced, they were ultimately dealt with in devastating and memorable fashion.

Gooch and Gower scored at four an over, while England touched a remarkable rate of 78 runs per 100 balls.

Under a cloudless sky, it added up to high-class entertainment for a capacity crowd of around 16,000, as Australia's out-cricket stood up well and Lawson and McDermott, of their bowlers, performed valiantly in increasingly discouraging circumstances.

Botham was declared fit, so England were unchanged, with Athey 12th man. Also unchanged was the quality of much of the Australian bowling, which played its part in enabling England to make 100 from 25 overs before lunch after Gower had won the toss.

True, the rub of the green went resolutely against them, but they were guilty of failing to make the most of a pitch that, as promised, had a refreshing amount of pace and bounce.

Perhaps the sight of this, as ever, tended to encourage a certain degree of shortness, and when Robinson went in the eighth over he was perhaps startled to receive a ball of full length, a swinging yorker in fact, from McDermott which bowled him.

While Gooch paced himself carefully from the start, Gower needed some luck from time to time, starting when, at two, McDermott got one to bounce off a remote part of the bat only to see the ball lob safely over the slips.

He followed this with a top-edged hook against Gilbert and at 31 edged Lawson perilously close to Hilditch at third slip, all of which suggested that for once, on this pitch, even Gower did not have time to spare.

More sketchy strokes followed. Gower obtained four over the slips when he chased a wide ball from Lawson, escaped with an inside edge from the next delivery, then got himself into a tangle against a McDermott bouncer which mercifully avoided both bat and body.

Between times, however, both he and Gooch found plenty of bowling that could be forced or driven, and Gooch, scoring mainly in the arc between mid-on and mid-off, or picking off anything loose, had started to build his innings in exemplary fashion.

His bat was not often passed. Indeed, he had played and missed only once – and that at a widish ball at this stage – and it was clear that even a niggardly over rate and an outfield slowed by the rains of August would not spare Australia.

When the left-arm Bennett appeared, he unsurprisingly found nothing in the pitch (would Holland's leg spin have extracted more?), and was soon bowling a very defensive line some way outside the off-stump.

Even so, Gower was able to fetch him over the top a time or two, and the partnership moved past 100 in only 23 overs, helped by three fours by Gooch off one over from the otherwise accurate Lawson.

Afterwards, the pair went on remorselessly, offering negligible hope to the bowlers. Bennett by now had started to lapse into shortness and paid the price, and when Border appeared, Gower swept him for his 12th four to reach three figures from, remarkably, only 123 balls.

Gooch soon followed, taking 71 deliveries more, which was testimony to the way he had seemed determined to make the most of pitch and bowling from the start. By now he was batting formidably well, cutting and driving and timing the ball so sweetly that even a defensive push would beat the field.

Australia were permitted one or two last glimmers of salvation, when McDermott troubled both batsmen in one unlucky over and the persevering Lawson proved that it was possible to pass Gooch's bat, before the assault was inevitably stepped up.

Then the strokes began to flow. Bennett was driven from yards down the pitch, the faster bowlers were pulled, cut and driven, and despite much athletic out-cricket, the partnership passed 300 in 67 overs.

Gower, at 137, survived a hard chance off Lawson before he was eventually caught in the gully cutting at McDermott, while the departure of Gatting, caught at slip off Bennett, gave Australia a late, somewhat unexpected bonus.

Tourists' hopes in ashes

Australia's Ashes campaign sunk in an overwhelming torrent of runs from England's best batsmen, Graham Gooch and David Gower, at the Oval yesterday.

Having already effectively elbowed Australia out of the sixth Test, England will formally reclaim cricket's oldest and most prized 'trophy' on Tuesday night.

On the hottest day of the series, in front of an increasingly noisy, capacity crowd, the Australian bowlers laboured and sweated through 90 overs, acting as mere tools to service the classy Gooch-Gower machine on the fastest, bounciest pitch of the series.

The batsmen could play their shots with absolute certainty, knowing the ball would not deviate or bounce dubiously, as it had done occasionally on slow, low pitches in the previous five Tests.

The Australian attack again was embarrassingly impotent, exposed as deficient in quality and quantity, especially against two excellent performers enjoying such favourable batting conditions.

The ball flowed onto the bat so comfortably that the easiest long-term prediction about the result was a high-scoring draw. Yet England have scored so quickly again that they still will have time to press for victory.

Statistics reveal the Australian bowlers' inadequacies in England's last four innings – 196 for two in the second innings of the third Test, 482 for nine declared in the fourth Test, 595 for five declared in the fifth Test and yesterday's 376 for three.

This makes a total of 1,649 for 19 at an average of 86·79 per wicket.

Gower's majestic 157 lifted his aggregate in nine innings in this series to 732 – an average of 81·33.

Only Wally Hammond (905 in nine innings, in Australia in 1928–29) and Herbert Sutcliffe (734 in nine innings, in Australia in 1924–25) have made more runs for England in an Ashes series.

Sir Donald Bradman is the only Australian to have scored more than 700 in an Ashes series, and he did it three times – 974, in England in 1930; 810, in Australia in 1936–37; and 758, in England in 1934.

The second new ball already is five overs overdue, and the Australians can be expected to take it immediately play resumes today, while Gower contemplates an unbeatable England total in excess of 600.

Overnight
England 376 – 3 (G.A. Gooch 179 not out, D.I. Gower 157)

Australia in deep trouble at 145–6

England, bowling with more efficiency than they latterly batted, reduced Australia to 145 for six with a telling mixture of seam and spin in the final Cornhill Test at the Oval yesterday, leaving them still requiring 120 to avoid the follow-on.

Curiously, 13 wickets fell in the day on the pitch where batsmen had lorded it on Thursday, starting when Gooch went four short of his maiden Test double century. Although England reached 464, they had lost their last nine wickets for 93 runs.

But if their batsmen failed to turn the screw, their bowlers soon began to work their way through some unprepossessing, if at times unlucky, Australian batting, even though the ball again did nothing extravagant.

The exception was Edmonds's use of the rough outside the left-handers' off-stump, which enabled him to take the important wicket of Border, who just played on after being deceived through the air, and then remove Phillips, cutting at a ball which spun into him.

Before play began, Gower was talking in terms of a total of 600 or more. When Gooch took 11 off the day's first over from Lawson, this looked only a modest ambition, especially with the outfield clearly much faster after its morning out.

But the ball was new, the bowlers were fresh and their line better, and they enjoyed the luck that had eluded them the previous day. The result was, for England, anticlimax, and for Australia the unexpected capture of seven wickets for 61 runs.

It all started, as these things often do, with a miscalculation by Gooch, who went back rather than forward to his 310th ball, one of full length, and chipped a return catch which McDermott held well, low and left-handed.

In the next over, Emburey could not control an attempted cut against Lawson and was caught at point. This left Lamb and Botham starting together against a newish ball, which is not always the best of omens.

So it proved this time. Lamb never looked at ease and was still far from settled when Lawson produced an excellent bouncer which caught him in at least two minds and, losing his balance, he was caught off what could be kindly described as an attempted hook.

Botham made no attempt to play himself in, which even great players have been known to do. It is a pity he does not always appear to value his wicket as much as the opposition do.

Overall it was a rum Botham display, considering England's needs, and it unsurprisingly ended when he was caught behind aiming a lavish drive at a very wide ball from Lawson, leaving Downton and Ellison to do what they could by more straightforward means.

This did not amount to much. Ellison became Gilbert's first Test victim, meeting a ball that bounced; McDermott forced his inswinger through a large 'gate' left by Downton, and Edmonds was lbw to Lawson after a few vigorous blows, though not before Phillips had dropped him – a comfortable chance – off the same bowler.

It left an odd-looking England scorecard, with the next highest contribution after the centuries from Gooch and Gower the extras column (50). Still, it had finished as an odd-looking batting display.

There was, however, little wrong, eventually, with the England bowling. If Botham was unlucky to have Wood dropped by Emburey at slip early on, the opposite might have applied when he won an lbw decision against him soon afterwards.

Hilditch, remarkably, again managed to fall for Botham's ploy of feeding his instinctive hook and Emburey prised out Wessels for the sixth time in 10 innings with an excellent delivery which drifted in and straightened to clip his off-stump.

By now Ellison had embarked on an admirably accurate spell in which he found the full length ball would swing, and he had Wellham caught behind before Edmonds got to work.

AUSTRALIAN VIEWPOINT

Fatal flaw of Hilditch

A nother disputed umpiring decision, this time involving Graeme Wood, and another suicidal hook by Andrew Hilditch ruined Australia's hopes of capitalising on the remarkable, brave fight-back by their bowlers at the Oval yesterday.

Umpire Ken Palmer gave Wood out leg before in Ian Botham's fourth over, but television replays showed the ball had hit the left-handed opener on the top flap of his right pad and almost certainly would have bounced over the stumps.

In Botham's seventh over, Hilditch surrendered his wicket by hooking straight to Graham Gooch at deep fine leg – the third time in the series, and the second in a row, he had been caught on the leg boundary hooking.

That the Australian vice-captain, who is sufficiently intelligent to have gained a law degree, could be lured into such an obvious trap again was maddeningly inexcusable and almost justification for him to be denied any future executive position within the team.

Hilditch walked off slowly, head bowed and rightly feeling guilty. He could have stretched out on the ground and cried, and apologised a thousand times and he would not have received a morsel of sympathy from any Australian spectator or TV viewer.

> **Overnight**
> **England 464 (G.A. Gooch 196, D.I. Gower 157; G.F. Lawson 4 – 101,**
> **G.J. McDermott 4 – 108)**
> **Australia 145 – 6**

England turn the screw on Australia

England maintained their domination of the sixth Cornhill Test so utterly at the Oval on Saturday that, even though only 59 overs were permitted by the weather, Australia still lost another eight wickets and were pushed to the brink of their third defeat of the series.

Not since 1977, when they were beaten by an innings at Leeds, had an Australian side faced the ignominy of following on in an Ashes match, and after Gower had answered the question that had been exercising everyone, they finished needing 161 to make England bat again with six wickets standing.

But two of them belong to the redoubtable Border and the maturing Ritchie, who had played so well for some 3¼ hours in completing an unbeaten 64 in the remnants of Australia's first innings, that there was surely a good case for his remaining padded up and reappearing at a much earlier stage when they batted again.

That might have enabled Australia to avoid exposing all their increasingly vulnerable early batsmen, notably Hilditch, who, after starting the series with 119 and 80 at Leeds, has finished it looking like a man who is having a nightmare that he is batting against Botham – and has woken up to find that he is.

It is pure hypothesis now, of course, as is the great debate about whether Gower's best move tactically would have been to bat again, a topic which not only apparently divided the England dressing room but also sundry former Test captains present, such as Hutton, Illingworth, Denness, Lewis and Lloyd (who, by the way, would not have enforced the follow-on).

There was merit in both arguments, and Gower admitted later that he had been pondering for some time what course to take. The scorecard proves him correct, but, without hindsight, he would have weighed the fact that his bowlers were still fresh, the day was cool and, most important of all, the opposition were psychologically at their nadir.

The other school of thought worried that Australia might make enough runs to put England at risk in the fourth innings. But what if, after batting again, England had been reduced to, say, 70 for five by Lawson and McDermott?

It was not entirely improbable after England's somewhat mixed performance on Friday, which tended to reinforce the view, suggested beforehand, that the liveliness of this pitch would require batsmen on both sides to adjust after all the slow and low ones that have featured in the series.

So much for theories. The happy facts show that, even on a restricted Saturday, the full-house crowd received excellent value, and the delay perhaps spared the Test and County Cricket Board the knotty problem of what to do about some £140,000 worth of tickets sold for Monday if the game had not gone that far.

Such has been the interest generated by this series, not least

England's success, that it is without precedent, certainly in post-war years, for the fourth day of a Test to be sold out in advance. Certain contingency plans were discussed, but no decision was reached and the Board are open to constructive suggestions in case the situation arises again.

From the start the day was agreeably tense, and when Botham plucked a spectacular right-handed slip catch from above his head to give the deserving Taylor Lawson's wicket, Australia were 192 for eight – still 73 from the follow-on figure.

The next ball bounced enough for McDermott to offer a chance from a mixture of bat and thigh, which was all but caught by Edmonds; after that McDermott and Ritchie made 43 from nine overs in a way that suggested the follow-on controversy might not even arise.

McDermott struck the ball cleanly – and often some distance – in making 25 from 23 deliveries, and perhaps because of this Ritchie made no discernible attempt to take command and resist the numerous long singles he was offered.

The target had been whittled down to thirty when Robinson's accurate return ran out McDermott when he started hesitantly for a single to cover; Gilbert then played on to a ball from Botham that bounced and followed him, and Australia were not only batting again but plagued by rain, which might also have come into Gower's reckoning.

They were obliged to make three starts, the last after a 2½-hour hold-up which gave England's attack respite, if they needed it, having required only 32 overs to complete the first part of their task.

In the sunlit evening, Botham bowled with considerable hostility and speed, so much so that Downton found himself having to move several yards further back than earlier in the match.

Wood, perhaps half-looking for a shorter ball, played on to him, and Wessels had a torrid time of it for a batsman who had been expected to provide much dogged resistance to the England bowlers.

Wessels has lately looked as if his mind is elsewhere, and he eventually reached for a very wide one which Downton caught superbly at full length in front of first slip, to whom it would probably not have carried.

Between these events, Hilditch, now off balance physically, skewered a catch to cover off Taylor, and then Ellison, having fed Wellham a series of outswingers, completed England's day by having him very lbw with one that merely held its line.

Experienced men let Border down

T he English critics were correct after all. Through no fault of Allan Border's, history will deem his team one of the weakest of the 27 to have fought for the Ashes in England.

Border, an an apprentice captain and master batsman, is among only four of the 17 Australians who have enhanced their reputations on this tour. The others are Craig McDermott, Greg Ritchie and Wayne Phillips.

McDermott, at the age of 20, in his first full Test series, has taken 30 wickets to justify his ranking as the most exciting young fast bowler in the world, even if he bowled badly in the fifth Test.

Ritchie has made 422 runs in 10 completed innings, usually in a disciplined, often regal, manner that has confirmed his development as a mature Test-class player who finally has gained a permanent place in the Australian side.

Phillips has been a most valuable all-rounder – a free-hitting, authoritative strokemaker and an adequate, if ungainly and originally reluctant, wicketkeeper, until he dropped two catches, one easy, one hard, in England's first innings at the Oval on Friday.

Border has not received sufficient regular support from his most senior players – fast bowlers Geoff Lawson and Jeff Thomson and batsmen Graeme Wood, Andrew Hilditch and Kepler Wessels.

Most of Lawson's 22 wickets, at a costly 37·72 apiece, have not been taken early enough in England's innings. Injuries and illnesses – including asthma – slow pitches and the class and depth of England's batting have combined to reduce his effectiveness, although his desire and effort cannot be queried.

Thomson played only two Tests, the first and fifth, and, sadly, provided only rare glimpses of the Thommo of old.

Wood simply has not been consistent enough, with 260 runs (average 28·88). Apart from his heroic 172 in the third Test, he has failed eight times – 14, 3, 8, 6, 19, 10, 22 and 6.

Wessels, from whom at least one big century was expected, has reached 50 only three times in scoring 368 (ave 33·45) – 36, 64, 11, 28, 33, 34, 50, 83, 10, 12 and 7.

Overnight
England 464
Australia 241 (G.M. Ritchie 64 not out) and 62 – 4

Glory for Gower as the Ashes are won

E ngland completed victory over Australia with rather more ease than could have been expected in the sixth Cornhill Test at the Oval yesterday, capturing their last six wickets for 58 runs to triumph by an innings and 94 and win an absorbing series 3–1.

From the third day at Edgbaston, England have proved unstoppable with bat and ball, and before lunch David Gower had joined the ranks of England captains who have stood on the Oval balcony celebrating the return of the Ashes – in his case with a replica of the famous urn.

For him, the moment was particularly sweet, coming as it did some 12 months after the annihilation by the West Indies, or, if you like, following suggestions from some quarters this summer that he should resign because of his chequered form.

Since those unhappy days, however, he has completed 732 runs in the series and become only the second England captain, after D.R. Jardine, to win both a series in India and regain the Ashes ... and that in less than a year.

He was unsurprisingly named man-of-the-series by Tony Lewis, and Gooch collected the Man-of-the-Match award for his 196, after Ellison, with four wickets in eight overs, Botham and Taylor had completed the *coup de grace*.

For Australia, the cool, overcast morning, which helped Ellison particularly to move the ball about, was an all-too-familiar reminder of the gloomy weather that has haunted them, and us, more or less since they arrived.

The crowd, some perhaps recalling Bailey and Watson in 1953, might have half wondered if Border and Ritchie, another left- and right-hand combination, might also achieve something remarkable, but, in more daunting circumstances, it was not to be.

Once Ritchie had gone, getting the faintest of touches to Ellison's outswinger, the ball regularly found the edge, the catches stuck, with a particularly good one by Botham, and Taylor had the pleasure of completing victory with a return one off Bennett.

England thus took a series that somehow survived miserable weather, was often played to capacity crowds (which should ensure an excellent share-out for the counties), and which at the outset both sides probably felt would be much closer.

Yesterday's victory was England's 86th against the Australians. Of 257 encounters, England have lost 96 matches and drawn 75.

203

Border: 'We are too soft'

Australia's cricketers must toughen their mental approach on overseas tours, their captain Allan Border admitted yesterday.

'We need fellows who are prepared to really slog it out for a full tour,' he said at the Oval after England had won the sixth Test and the Ashes with a day and two full sessions to spare.

Australia have an appalling record in Tests abroad since their short tour of New Zealand early in 1977, winning only six, losing 22 and drawing 17.

Border said: 'I wish I knew why. I think some players' minds wander in the latter part of a long, hard trip. When things are not going as planned, they think about going home.

'Maybe it's an area we've got to work harder at – a tougher mental approach to being on tour. The pitch at the Oval gave us our best chance of the series to win.

'I would have thought everyone would have been on a high, but our performances have gone straight downhill at a rapid rate over the past couple of weeks.

'We always seem to start a tour well and finish like this. Nearly every tour I've been on has been exactly the same,' added Border.

Australia's performances in the last two Tests – they lost the fifth at Edgbaston by an innings and 118 runs – suggested that the critics 'might have been right' when they suggested his team was one of the weakest to have come to England.

'We have had a fairly inexperienced side. Our 1981 side here was a great deal more experienced. Put Dennis Lillee into our side now and we would have a fair side.'

Border said it was 'difficult to answer' whether the inclusion of experienced batsmen and former Test captains Kim Hughes and Graham Yallop would have boosted the Australians.

But he conceded that England's 3–1 margin in the series was 'justifiable – the result of superior batting in the last three Tests.'

Result: England beat Australia by an innings and 94 runs
England 464
Australia 241 and 129 (A.R. Border 58; R.M. Ellison 5 – 46)

SIXTH TEST
ENGLAND 1ST INNGS

ENGLAND 1ST INNINGS v AUSTRALIA (6TH TEST) at KENNINGTON OVAL, LONDON on 29,30,31 AUGUST, 2 SEPTEMBER 1985. Toss: ENGLAND

IN	OUT	MINS	No.	BATSMAN	HOW OUT	BOWLER	RUNS	WKT	TOTAL	6s	4s	BALLS	NOTES ON DISMISSAL
11.01	11.18	424	1	G.A.GOOCH	c And Bowled	McDERMOTT	196	4	403	—	27	310	(5th (1st Aus) HS in Test). Drove full toss - low catch following through
11.01	11.36	35	2	R.T.ROBINSON	BOWLED	McDERMOTT	3	1	20	·	·	21	Yorked off stump by fast late in-swinger.
11.38	6.14	357	3	D.I.GOWER *	c Bennett	McDERMOTT	157	2	371	·	20	215	2000 R v Aust. Fierce gully catch held at second attempt. (12th)
6.16	6.41	25	4	M.W.GATTING	c Border	BENNETT	4	3	376	·	·	27	Edged low to slip who dived forward. leg break.
6.43	11.25	27	5	J.E.EMBUREY	c Wellham	LAWSON	9	5	405	·	1	17	Night-watchman. Cut short ball chest high to cover.
11.20	11.49	29	6	A.J.LAMB	c McDermott	LAWSON	1	6	418	·	·	15	Top-edged hook at bouncer to deep fine-leg.
11.27	12.00	33	7	I.T.BOTHAM	c Phillips	LAWSON	12	7	425	·	2	23	Edged firm-footed drive at widish ball.
11.51	1.45	74	8	P.R.DOWNTON †	BOWLED	McDERMOTT	16	8	452	·	1	46	Late in-swinger removed middle stump - through gate.
12.03	12.47	44	9	R.M.ELLISON	c Phillips	GILBERT	3	9	447	·	·	32	Faint edge - defensive back stroke.
12.48	2.02	34	10	P.H.EDMONDS	LBW	LAWSON	12	10	464	·	2	26	Hit across full length ball.
1.47(2.02)		15	11	L.B.TAYLOR	NOT OUT		1		-			10	First Test innings

EXTRAS: b 13 lb 11 w - nb 26 — 50 — 742 balls (including 32 no balls)

TOTAL: (118.2 OVERS - 547 MINUTES) — 464 all out at 2.02 pm on 2nd day

6s total: 0   4s total: 53

* CAPTAIN † WICKET-KEEPER

UMPIRES: H.D.BIRD, K.E.PALMER
© BILL FRINDALL 1985

12 OVERS 5 BALLS/HOUR
3.92 RUNS/OVER
63 RUNS/100 BALLS

BOWLER	O	M	R	W	nb
LAWSON	29.2	6	101	4	9
McDERMOTT	31	2	108	4	7
GILBERT	21	2	96	1	10
BENNETT	32	8	111	1	-
BORDER	2	0	8	0	-
WESSELS	3	0	16	0	-
			24		
TOTAL	118.2	18	464	10	

HRS	OVERS	RUNS
1	11	38
2	14	62
3	14	54
4	15	66
5	13	68
6	12	61
7	14	52
8	10	31
9	14	26

2ND NEW BALL taken at 11.02 am on 2nd day
- ENGLAND 380-3 after 90-3 overs.

RUNS	MINS	OVERS	LAST 50 (in mins)
50	72	14.0	72
100	120	25.0	48
150	174	38.0	54
200	222	49.0	48
250	266	59.3	44
300	313	69.5	47
350	361	79.2	48
400	420	92.5	59
450	521	112.1	101

LUNCH: 100-1 (25 OVERS) GOOCH 35*(26) / (120 MIN.) GOWER 44*(83)

TEA: 220-1 (54 OVERS) GOOCH 94*(24th)(246) / (240 MIN.) GOWER 100*(203)

STUMPS (1ST DAY): 376-3 (90 OVERS) GOOCH 179*(405) / (405 MIN.) EMBUREY 0*(2¹)

LUNCH: 452-8 (114 OVERS) DOWNTON 16*(49) / (525 MIN.) EDMONDS 1*(12¹)

ENGLAND LOST THEIR LAST 9 WICKETS FOR 93 RUNS - INCLUDING 7 FOR 88 ON SECOND DAY. McDERMOTT 30 WICKETS IN RUBBER. LAWSON ACHIEVED A SPELL OF 3 FOR 3.

351 - ENGLAND'S SECOND - HIGHEST PARTNERSHIP FOR ANY WICKET AGAINST AUSTRALIA.

WKT	PARTNERSHIP		RUNS	MINS
1st	Gooch	Robinson	20	35
2nd	Gooch	Gower	351	337
3rd	Gooch	Gatting	5	25
4th	Gooch	Emburey	27	20
5th	Emburey	Lamb	2	5
6th	Lamb	Botham	13	22
7th	Botham	Downton	7	9
8th	Downton	Ellison	22	44
9th	Downton	Edmonds	5	17
10th	Edmonds	Taylor	12	15
			464	

AUSTRALIA 1ST INNINGS

IN REPLY TO ENGLAND'S 464 ALL OUT

IN	OUT	MINS	No.	BATSMAN	HOW OUT	BOWLER	RUNS	WKT	TOTAL	6s	4s	BALLS	NOTES ON DISMISSAL
2·14	2·45	31	1	G.M.WOOD	LBW	BOTHAM	22	1	35	·	3	26	Beaten by inswinger - hit on shoulder previous ball.
2·14	3·14	60	2	A.M.J.HILDITCH	C' GOOCH	BOTHAM	17	2	52	·	1	32	Hooked bouncer to long-leg.
2·47	4·02	55	3	K.C.WESSELS	BOWLED	EMBUREY	12	3	56	·	·	51	Missed cut at arm-ball.
3·16	5·21	105	4	A.R.BORDER*	BOWLED	EDMONDS	38	5	109	·	4	67	Played back - off break deflected into wicket by inside edge.
4·04	4·57	53	5	D.M.WELLHAM	C' DOWNTON	ELLISON	13	4	101	·	2	41	Edged outswinger.
5·01	(1·46)	195	6	G.M.RITCHIE	NOT OUT		64			5	155		
5·23	6·01	38	7	W.B.PHILLIPS†	BOWLED	EDMONDS	18	6	144	·	2	29	Missed square-cut - off-break turned sharply.
6·03	11·43	50	8	M.J.BENNETT	C' ROBINSON	ELLISON	12	7	171	·	1	46	Head high catch at cover-point - drove at outswinger.
11·45	12·14	29	9	G.F.LAWSON	C' BOTHAM	TAYLOR	14	8	192	·	1	26	Edged drive to 2nd slip - right-handed high leaping catch.
12·16	12·51	35	10	C.J.McDERMOTT	RUN OUT (ROBINSON/EMBUREY)		25	9	235	1	2	23	Hesitated over single to cover who returned to bowler.
12·53	1·46	13	11	D.R.GILBERT	BOWLED	BOTHAM	1	10	241	·	·	21	Fended short-pitched ball into wicket. First Test innings.
				EXTRAS	b - lb 5 w 2 nb -		5			1s 2s 4s			
				TOTAL	(84 OVERS - 342 MINUTES)		241			all out at 1.46pm on 3rd day.			

*CAPTAIN †WICKET-KEEPER

14 OVERS 4 BALLS/HOUR
2·87 RUNS/OVER
48 RUNS/100 BALLS

BOWLER	O	M	R	W	w/n		HRS	OVERS	RUNS
BOTHAM	20	3	64	3	2/-		1	13	52
TAYLOR	13	1	39	1			2	15	31
ELLISON	18	5	35	2			3	14	33
EMBUREY	19	7	48	1			4	16	42
EDMONDS	14	2	52	2			5	16	42
			3	1					
	84	18	241	10					

© BILL FRINDALL 1985

RUNS	MINS	OVERS	LAST 50 (in mins)
50	58	12·3	58
100	140	32·3	82
150	229	55·4	89
200	300	73·5	71

TEA: 56-2 (19 OVERS / 87 MINUTES) WESSELS 12* (54') BORDER 1* (25')

STUMPS: 145-6 (52 OVERS / 216 MIN.) (2ND DAY) 319 BEHIND RITCHIE 20* (69') BENNETT 0* (7')

LUNCH: 237-9 (82 OVERS / 336 MIN.) 227 BEHIND RITCHIE 60* (189') GILBERT 1* (7')

AUSTRALIA invited to follow-on
(223 RUNS BEHIND)
(FIRST INSTANCE AGAINST ENGLAND SINCE LEEDS 1977)

WKT	PARTNERSHIP		RUNS	MINS
1st	Wood	Hilditch	35	31
2nd	Hilditch	Wessels	17	27
3rd	Wessels	Border	4	26
4th	Border	Wellham	45	53
5th	Border	Ritchie	8	20
6th	Ritchie	Phillips	35	38
7th	Ritchie	Bennett	27	50
8th	Ritchie	Lawson	21	29
9th	Ritchie	McDermott	43	35
10th	Ritchie	Gilbert	6	13
			241	

AUSTRALIA 2ND INNINGS   FOLLOWING-ON 223 RUNS BEHIND

IN	OUT	MINS	No.	BATSMAN	HOW OUT	BOWLER	RUNS	WKT	TOTAL	6s	4s	BALLS	NOTES ON DISMISSAL
1-59	5-31	37	1	A.M.J.HILDITCH	C'GOWER	TAYLOR	9	2	16	.	.	27	Chipped gentle catch to cover.
1-59	5-21	27	2	G.M.WOOD	BOWLED	BOTHAM	6	1	13	.	1	18	Played on - crooked defensive jab at short ball.
5-23	5-57	34	3	K.C.WESSELS	C'DOWNTON	BOTHAM	7	3	37	.	.	21	Edged drive at widish ball - fine catch - diving in front of slip.
5-33	12-08	157	4	A.R.BORDER*	C'BOTHAM	ELLISON	58	7	114	.	7	92	Edged to 2nd slip - driving at ball that bounced generously.
5-59	6-19	20	5	D.M.WELLHAM	LBW	ELLISON	5	4	51	.	.	17	Beaten by late inswing.
6-21	11-18	59	6	G.M.RITCHIE	C'DOWNTON	ELLISON	6	5	71	.	.	42	Edged drive at widish outswinger.
11-20	11-49	29	7	W.B.PHILLIPS†	C'DOWNTON	BOTHAM	10	6	96	.	1	24	Top-edged square-cut.
11-52	12-35	43	8	M.J.BENNETT	C AND BOWLED	TAYLOR	11	10	129	.	1	29	Slower ball - simple return catch.
12-10	12-26	16	9	G.F.LAWSON	C'DOWNTON	ELLISON	7	8	127	.	1	10	Edged drive at outswinger.
12-28	12-30	2	10	C.J.McDERMOTT	C'BOTHAM	ELLISON	2	9	129	.	.	4	Edged drive at outswinger - high catch at 2nd slip.
12-33	(2-35)	2	11	D.R.GILBERT	NOT OUT		0			.	.	-	Did not face a ball.

EXTRAS b 4 lb - w - nb 4 = 8

TOTAL (46.3 OVERS - 223 MINUTES) **129** ALL OUT at 12:35 pm on 4th day

284 balls (including 5 no balls)

* CAPTAIN   † WICKET-KEEPER

12 OVERS 3   BALLS/HOUR
2-77   RUNS/OVER
45   RUNS/100 BALLS

WKT	PARTNERSHIP		RUNS	MINS
1st	Hilditch	Wood	13	27
2nd	Hilditch	Wessels	3	8
3rd	Wessels	Border	21	24
4th	Border	Wellham	14	20
5th	Border	Ritchie	20	59
6th	Border	Phillips	25	29
7th	Border	Bennett	18	16
8th	Bennett	Lawson	13	16
9th	Bennett	McDermott	2	2
10th	Bennett	Gilbert	0	3
			129	

	RUNS	MINS	OVERS	LAST 50 (in mins)
	50	80	16-2	80
	100	183	39-0	103

BOWLER	O	M	R	W	NB	HRS	OVERS	RUNS
BOTHAM	17	3	44	3	1	1	12	33
TAYLOR	11-3	1	34	2	3	2	13	26
ELLISON	17	3	46	5	3	3	13	37
EMBUREY	1	0	1	0	-			
					4			
	46-3	7	129	10				

© BILL FRINDALL 1985

RSP 2·14 to 2·24 pm and 2·29 to 5·15 pm (56 MIN. LOST)

TEA: 12-0 (4·4 OVERS, 20 MIN.) HILDITCH 7*, WOOD 5*
(3RD DAY) 161 BEHIND

STUMPS: 62-4 (27 OVERS) BORDER 26 (89)
(28 MIN.) RITCHIE 6 (41)
NETT 96 MIN (29 OVERS) LOST

ENGLAND WON BY AN INNINGS & 94 RUNS with a day and 70·3 overs to spare.

ENGLAND WON RUBBER 3-1 AND REGAINED ASHES LOST IN JANUARY 1983

PLAYER OF THE MATCH: G.A.GOOCH
PLAYER OF THE SERIES: D.I.GOWER
(Adjudicator: A.R.LEWIS)

129

1ST DAY	BOWLERS (H.D. BIRD) PAVILION END	O.	(K.E. PALMER) VAUXHALL END	O.	BATSMEN SCOREBOARD LEFT	BALLS	6s/4s	SCOREBOARD RIGHT	BALLS	6s/4s	ENGLAND 1ST INNINGS NOTES	O.	RUNS	W.	'L' BAT	'R' BAT	EXTRAS
TIME	BOWLER		BOWLER		SCORING			SCORING				END-OF-OVER TOTALS					
					ROBINSON			GOOCH									
11.01			LAWSON	1				¹/² · ·¹4B · ·	6		(4B) M1	1	4				4
06	McDERMOTT	1			⁷/8 1	1		⁷/6 x · ·¹⁶ 2 · ·	11			2	7		1	2	
11	— · —			2	∴ ˣ³·³⁵·1	7						3	8		2		
15½	— · —	2			↑⁴4B · ·P46 ·⊙·	14					(4B) (NB) NB1	4	13				9
21			— · —	3				6↑·⁷· · · · ·⊙· · ·	18		(NB) NB2	5	14				10
27	— · —	3			LB · 72↑ ·	19		⁷3	19		(LB)	6	18			5	11
31			— · —	4	⁷1	20		³ ³⁷· ·1 · · ·	24			7	20		3	6	
36	— · —	4			ˣˣ W	21	—					7'	20	1	3	6	11
					GOWER		LHB								0		
38	— · —	4			·⊙·↑²³·2	6					(NB) NB3	8	23		2		12
43½			GILBERT	1				6·6·¹/²6 · · · ·4	30	1		9	28			11	
48	— · —	5			³8↑ ·6²	8		· Y·(18) · ·	35		(NB) •Behind slips. NB4	10	30		3		13
53			— · —	2	²3 · · · ·⁵4	13	1	⁹	36		1 HR	11	38		10	12	
58	— · —	6						· ⁵(6)L 6↑·8 4 · ·⊙·1	43	2	(NB) NB5	12	44			17	14
12·03½			— · —	3				6 ³ 4 · ·	49		M2	13					
08	LAWSON	5			· ²/³3	15		· · ⁵⊙·⁷	54		(NB) NB6	14	48		13		15
13			— · —	4	(4)·²:·↑·	22	2				NB7	15	54		19		
18	— · —	6			·↑↑	25		6 ·⁹6P	57			16	55			18	
22½			— · —	5	↑²3·2·	29		⁵·⁹1	59			17	58		21	19	
27	— · —	7						⊙·3⁴⁶⁵⁶⁴²↑ 4²· ·	66	3	(NB) NB8	18	65			25	16
32½			— · —	6	¹/²⁵(6)· 4↑↑8·6 22⊙·4·2	36	3				(NB) 50 p'shp: 56' NB9	19	76		31		17
38	— · —	8			4↑4¹/²·2 ·	41	4	LB	67		(LB) •HILDITCH(4½½)	20	81		35		18
43			BENNETT	1				4·26·4	73		Round wkt. M3	21					
46½	McDERMOTT	7			⁶/³9↑↑ 4·1	43	5	6↑8 4 46 ·4·1	77	4	↑ Nr played on.	22	91		40	30	
51½			— · —	2				· · · · ·4	83		M4	23					
54	— · —	8			↑²4²↑·³ ·4 · ·	49	6					24	95		44		
59			— · —	3				⁹6⁵⁹⁸/²2· · ·2·1	89	4	2HR	25	100	1	44	35	18
1·01	LUNCH										M4 NB9				L U N C H		
1·40½	McDERMOTT	9						F7·³ ³↑·2·	95			26	102			37	
45			BENNETT	4	∴ · ·⁶	55					Over wkt. M5	27					
48½	— · —	10			·⊙	57		6↑B · ⁹/⁵ · · ·4	100	5	(B) NB10	28	108		45	41	19
54			— · —	5	6· · ·⁶⁶ 4 · · · ·	63	7					29	112		49		
57	— · —	11						· 1 · ⁵ ² · 4·2 · ·	106	6		30	118			47	
2·01			— · —	6	⁶ˢ1 · · · ·	68		⁸	107		100 p'shp: 105 min GOWER'S 50: 105 min	31	120		50	48	
05	GILBERT	7			⁹1	69		6⁷P·ˣP↑ · · ·⊙·	114		(NB) NB11	32	121		51	56	20
09½			— · —	7	⁹1	70		· ·⁶⁶ ³⁹(6) · ·44	119	8	Round. wkt. GOOCH'S 50: 151'	33	130		51	56	
13	— · —	8			⁹⁶1	70		·⁵(6)8/7↑↑ ·42· ·	125	9	NB12	34	137		52	62	
18			— · —	8	6· ·⁶44	76	8					35	141		56		
21½	— · —	9				76	8	↑³ ³ · · ·⁶ ⊙· · · · · ·	132	9	(NB) NB13 M5	36	142	1	56	62	21

1ST DAY TIME	BOWLERS (BIRD) PAVILION END BOWLER	O.	(PALMER) VAUXHALL END BOWLER	O.	BATSMEN SCOREBOARD LEFT SCORING	BALLS	6s/4s	SCOREBOARD RIGHT SCORING	BALLS	6s/4s	ENGLAND 1ST INNINGS NOTES	O.	RUNS	W.	'L' BAT	'R' BAT	EXTRAS
					GOWER	76	8	GOOCH	132	9	M5 NB13	36	142	1	56	62	21
2·26			BENNETT	9	: 6	78		: : : :	136			37	143		57		
29½	GILBERT	10			3 3/2 4 · 1 · 4 · 4 · O · : 3	85	9				NB NB14	38	151		64		22
34½			— · —	10	6 · 6 1	87		8 : · : 5	140		3 HR	39	154		66	63	
38	— · —	11			9/2 1	89		EP 6 8 LB · · 2 ·	144		LB	40	158		67	65	23
41½ DRINKS 45			— · —	11				4 : · 3 : · : 4	150	10		41	162			69	
48½	LAWSON	9			1 x 8/7 3 4 · : 1	94		8/9 1	151			42	164		68	70	
53			— · —	12				: : : 3 · 8/2 1	157			43	166			72	
56	— · —	10			4 3 3 · 1 · 1 9 · 4 · : 1	100	10				150 p'ship : 161 min	44	171				
3·01			— · —	13	7 6/7 7s 4/5 · 2 1 2 ·	105		1 9	158		over. † Round.	45	177		78	73	
05	— · —	11						6 : 7 1 4 8 4 4 · 2	164	12	† all run.	46	187			83	
10			— · —	14	6 6 7 1 1 · 3 · :	109		7 1 · 6 1	166		† GOWER 2000 « A.	47	193		82	85	
14	— · —	12						6 6/ 3 3 · 3 : · 3	172		M6	48					
18½			— · —	15	3 3 · 7 2/3 1 4 ·	112	11	8 1 6 · 1 1	175		† over.	49	203		90	87	
23	*	13						: 3 · : 4/9 · 2 1	181			50	206			90	
28			BORDER	1	: 7P 1	114		: 8 4 · : 1	185		Round wkt to RMB.	51	208		91	91	
31	BENNETT	16			7 : 5 · 9 1 · 2 1	120						52	211		94		
34½			— · —	2	9 6 9 · 6 2 · 4 · :	126	12				GOWER'S 100 : 199'	53	217		100		
37½	— · —	17			: 1	127	12	: 6 · 9 9 · 2 1	190	12	200 p'ship : 203' 4 HR	54	220	1	100	94	23
3·40	TEA										M6 NB14			T E A			
4·00			GILBERT	12	: · 6 † : ·	130		· 6 6 · · 3	193		† short of mid-on	55	223			97	
04	McDERMOTT	12			: 1 † 1	132		6F 6 5 LB 4 · · ·	197	13	GOOCH'S 100 : 245' LB	56	228			101	24
08½			— · —	13	O · 3 · 7 1 · 4 1	137	13	6 6/7 · 3	199		NB NB15	57	236		104	104	25
13½	— · —	13						P 3 · : P 4 x 4 ·	205	14	† Ro appeal (BORDER)	58	240			108	
18			— · —	14	4O · 4 3 3 · 1 1	143	14	O 7/ · 1	207		NB NB NB17	59	247		109		27
23	— · —	14			3 9/6 2 · 2 1	146		6 : :	210			60	250		112		
28½			WESSELS	1	: : : 3 · 3 · 2 ·	152						61	252		114		
31½	— · —	15						: 3 · : 7 48 2 1	216			62	255			111	
36			— · —	2	: : · 4 3 1	156		6 8	218			63	258		116	112	
39½	— · —	16			: 4 17 1	158	15	: : · 1/2 3	222			64	265		120	115	
44			— · —	3	7 : · 3 6 8 · 4 4	163	17	1 3	223		250 p'ship : 250'	65	276		128	118	
47½	LAWSON	14						: : : O · 2 : 1	230		NB NB18	66	277				28
54			BENNETT	18	8/6 1	164		: 4 3 7/8 7 4 · 2 4	235	16	over wkt. 5 HR	67	288		129	128	
58	— · —	15			1/2 1 48 4 1	166	18	7 x · : 1	239		† PIGEONS ON PITCH.	68	293		134		
5·03 06 DRINKS			— · —	19	6 : · 5/6 1	170		: 5/4 1	241			69	295		135	129	
09½	— · —	16			x 1	171		4 9 7/8 1 4 4 6 4 · ·	246	17	† Good stop (WESSELS)	70	300			134	
15			— · —	20	x · 6 : 1	174		7/9 7 1 4	249	18	† Good stop (BORDER)	71	306		136	139	
19	— · —	17			2 3/ 1 · 1	176		: : 6P 27	253		† misfield (VELLHAM) « Dropped catch (WESSELS)	72	309		138	140	
24			— · —	21	6 6 3 3 : 2	182					M7	73					
26½	— · —	18			2 1 4 2 2 · 1	185	18	: LB · · 1	256	18	† Gilbert misfielded M7 NB18 LB	74	313	1	141	140	29

1st DAY TIME	BOWLERS (BIRD) PAVILION END BOWLER	O.	(PALMER) VAUXHALL END BOWLER	O.	BATSMEN SCOREBOARD LEFT SCORING	BALLS	6s/4s	SCOREBOARD RIGHT SCORING	BALLS	6s/4s	ENGLAND 1st INNINGS NOTES	O.	RUNS	W.	'L' BAT	'R' BAT	EXTRAS
					GOWER	185	18	GOOCH	256	18	M7 NB 18	74	313	1	141	140	29
5·32			BENNETT	22	6 6 8 1	188		2 5 3 8 2 4 1	259	19	300 p'ship: 298'	75	321		142	147	
36	LAWSON	19						·↑6 ·· ∅④NB	04	20	†Round wkt. NB NB NB NB21	76	328			151	32
43½			GILBERT	15	3 ·· 4 ³⁹ 01	194		5	269		GOOCH 150 in 343' NB NB22	77	330		143		33
49	—·—	20			7 ·· 2↑3 ·· 4	200	19				†Good ship (Bennett) GOWER's 150: 323'	78	334		147		
54			—·—	16	3 4	201	20	15 5 2 4 4 4② ·2·3	275	21	Gooch's HS in Tests 6HR	79	349		151	162	
6·00	BENNETT	23			8	202		P 4 7⁸ 3↑8 ·41 44	280	24	Round wkt. to RHB †Maxfield (wood)	80	363		152	175	
05			McDERMOTT	17	6 L 5⁴⁰ 788 ·· 2 · 1	207		2	281			81	368		155	177	
09	—·—	24			·· ··· 8 · 1	213						82	369		156		
12			—·—	18	7/3 2 W	215	20	8 1	282		350 p'ship: 336'	82³	371	2	157	178	33
14					GATTING										0		
16			—·—	18	7 · ↑8	3						83	372		1		
19	—·—	25			·· 3 · 5⁶ ·	9					M 8	84					
22			—·—	19				7 5↑↑ · 4 3	288		†Edged on to helmet. M 9	85					
26½	—·—	26			4 ·· ··· 9 1	15						86	373		2		
29½			—·—	20	x 7 · ↑8	19		G 4/3 ·	290			87	374		3		
34	—·—	27			4 ·· P · ·	25					M 10	88					
37			—·—	21	↑8	26		·· 7 6 8⁷ 1	295			89	376		4	179	
41	—·—	28			1E W	27	—					89¹	376	3	4	179	33
					EMBUREY										0		
43	—·—	28			P ·· · ·	5			295	24	M 11 NB 23	90	376	3	0	179	33
6·45	STUMPS												S T U M P S				
2ND DAY 11·00			LAWSON	21				·4·4·3	301	26	† NEW BALL	91	387			190	
05	McDERMOTT	22			8 2 1 ·4	7	1	7 6 · ↑8	305			92	392		4	191	
10			—·—	22	∅ x x ·⁴4	13		8/7 75 4 1	307	27	NB NB 25 7HR	93	401		7	196	34
16	—·—	23			∅1	14		· ∅ W	310	27	NB NB 27	93²	403	4	8	196	35
18								LAMB							0		
20	—·—	23			2 3 2	16		4 8 ·	2		LB	94	405		9		36
24			—·—	23	W	17	1					94¹	405	5	9	0	36
25					BOTHAM										0		
27			—··—	23	·· ·· 3 x 1	5					M 12	95					
31	—·—	24			7 1	6		··· 8 P · 1	7			96	407		1	1	
35			—·—	24	8 3 ··	9		↑P ∅ · ·	11		†Appeal at gully NB NB 28	97	409		2		37
41	—·—	25			· 8 5⁶ ·↑4 4 4	16	2				NB † Just wide of gully (BORDER) NB 29	98	418		10		38
46½			—·—	26				·L· ↑8	15	—		98¹	418	6	10	1	38
49								DOWNTON							0		
51			—·—	25				·· 1 · 2	2		M 13	99					
52½	—·—	26			· 3 ↑4 8↑ 2 ·	22					4B	100	424		12		42
57½			—·—	26	W	23	2	P · 7 1	5	—		100⁴	425	7	12	1	42
12·00	DRINKS										M13 NB 29						

2ND DAY TIME	BOWLERS (BIRD) PAVILION END BOWLER	O.	(PALMER) VAUXHALL END BOWLER	O.	BATSMEN SCOREBOARD LEFT SCORING	BALLS	6s/4s	SCOREBOARD RIGHT SCORING	BALLS	6s/4s	ENGLAND 1ST INNINGS NOTES	O.	RUNS	W.	'L' BAT	'R' BAT	EXTRAS
					ELLISON	.	LHB	DOWNTON	5	–	M13 NB29	100	425	7	0	1	42
12.03			LAWSON	26	:·.3	2						101					
05	McDERMOTT	27			::	4		4:·.7 2·:1·	9			102	428			4	
10	– · –		– · –	27				↑4LB ...↑	15		(4LB) M14 8HR	103	432				46
15	– · –	28			⊙::↑:↑x3↑	11					(NB) NB 30	104	433				47
20			GILBERT	17	.	12		4:·7:·s(b) 2·:1·	20			105	436			7	
24½	– · –	29						:..:4↑:8↑·	26	1		106	440			11	
29			– · –	18	x4::.½	17		↑	27		ELLISON 29' on O. O'Donnell sub (McDermott)	107	441	1			
34	BENNETT	29			.:3:::::	23					every wkt M15	108					
37			– · –	19				:..::⊙s(b) ·:2:	34		(NB) NB 31	109	444			13	48
41½	– · –	30			:P½2:P:	29						110	446			3	
44½			– · –	20	P:s1 :..W	32	–	LB .:	35		(LB)	110	447	8		3	13	49
47					EDMONDS									0			
48¾			– · –	20	·L·	2					M16	111					
50	– · –	31			P 8	4		4 : P::.	39		Round wkt	112	449			1	14	
53½			– · –	21	:↑⊙.::3	11					(NB) NB 32	113	450				50
58	– · –	32				11	–	::·3:::: 2	45	1		114	452	8	1	16	50
1.00	LUNCH										M 16 NB 32		LUNCH				
1.40			LAWSON	28	x8Lo·:↑:P 2	17					· Dropped wk M17	115					
45	McDERMOTT	30						x W	46	1		115'	452	9	1	16	50
								TAYLOR						0			
47	– · –	30						6P4↑8 :.·::	5		M18	116					
51			– · –	29	x8/74L2↑ :·2·:·4:	23	1				9HR	117	458			7	
56	– · –	31			6	24		.96· ↑:xt:	10		· Dropped wk (legside) ↑ Appeal ct wkt.	118	460			8	1	
2.00½			– · –	30	4 W	26	2	:·:	10	–		118²	464	10	12	1	50
2.02	ALL OUT										M18 NB 32		ALL OUT				
											742 balls						

2ND DAY TIME	BOWLERS (BIRD) PAVILION END BOWLER	O.	BOWLERS (PALMER) VAUXHALL END BOWLER	O.	SCOREBOARD LEFT SCORING	BALLS	6/4	SCOREBOARD RIGHT SCORING	BALLS	6/4	NOTES	O.	RUNS	W.	L BAT	R BAT	EXTRAS
					HILDITCH			WOOD		LHB	52 OVERS DUE						
2.14			BOTHAM	1				x 1 2 1°6.9 4·2·4·4	6	2	(W)	1	11			10	1
20	TAYLOR	1			2 :·7/9 2 7 ·2· 1	5		:·4 ·3	8		NB 1	2	19		5	13	
26	— · —		— · —	2	P 6 6P·8 ·2·1	9		4 1 6J	10		Treatment to Botham left foot.	3	23		8	14	
30	— · —	2			2 1	11		: LB	14		(LB)	4	25		9		2
34½			— · —	3	:	12		2·4 ·:4/9	19	3	· Dropped Wk.	5	32			21	
39	— · —	3			L · LB	15		·1 LB	22		(LB) (LB)	6	35			22	4
43			— · —	4	ꟼ			:··9L ·W	26	3	† Hit on arm.	6	35	1	9	22	4
45					Y			WESSELS		LHB						0	
47			— · —	4				3·9 ·1	2		M 1	7					
49	— · —	4			1/8 8† ·1	18		4 P 3 2·1	5		† Pitch damage – warning.	8	39		10	3	
54			— · —	5	4 2 4/9 : · 4	21	1	4 3 3 ·1·1	8			9	44		14	4	
58	— · —	5						1/8 ·P7 :·:8 1	14		† Appeal ct Wk.	10	45			5	
3.02			— · —	6	↑1/9	23		x 3 ·1 x4 ·1	18			11	47		15	6	
06½	— · · —	6			6 ·:··6·	29					M 2	12					
10			— ꟼ —	7	†2 :4/9 ·2·W	32	1	4 2·4	21		1 HR	13	52	2	17	9	4
14					BORDER		LHB									0	
16	— · —	7			6·:	2		:··:7	25			14	53			10	
21½			ELLISON	1				Y 6 · P·:	31		M 3	15					
26	— · —	8			2 4/6 ·7 :	5		3 ·1	34			16	55		1	11	
30½			— · —	2				·· x ·:1	40		Athey sub (Botham)	17	56			12	
34	EMBUREY	1						2 2 P·	46		Round wkt to LHB. M 4	18					
38			— · —	3	·· :1P · 1	11	–		46	–	M 5 NB 1	19	56	2	1	12	4
3.41	TEA													T E A		
4.01	EMBUREY	2						· 1/3 x · x ··:·W	51	–	· Dive by s. mid off. (Gower)	19⁵	56	3	1	12	4
02½								WELLHAM								0	
04½	— · —	2						·:1	1		M 6	20					
06			ELLISON	4	:·2·4 ·1	16		9 ·1	2			21	58		2	1	
10	— · —	3						·P ·5/7·:	8		M 7	22					
13			— · —	5	4 1 7 ··:·:·1	22	1					23	63		7		
16½	— · · —	4			·:··P 9	28					M 8	24					
20			— · · —	6				·3 ··· x	14		M 9	25					
23½	— · · —	5			3/2 3 2 5/6 ·7 4·42· 1	34	3					26	74		18		
26½			— · —	7	†1 7 ·41	38	4	·7 ·1	16			27	80		·23	2	
30½	— · —	6						P:·:·7 ·3	22		2 HR	28	83			5	
34			— · —	8				·:··x	28		M 10	29					
37	— · · —	7			· 8·:8 ·2·3	44						30	88		28		
40½			— · —	9	3 : ·4 ··1	49		·2	29			31	89		29		
44	— · —	8			5 5/6)	51		·:4/6 7 ·4	33	1		32	94		30	9	
47½			— · —	10	2 2·:·:·1	57	4		33	1	M 10 NB 1	33	96	3	32	9	4

2ND DAY TIME	BOWLERS (BIRD) PAVILION END BOWLER	O.	(PALMER) VAUXHALL END BOWLER	O.	BATSMEN SCOREBOARD LEFT SCORING	BALLS	6s/4s	SCOREBOARD RIGHT SCORING	BALLS	6s/4s	AUSTRALIA 1ST INNINGS NOTES	O.	RUNS	W.	'L' BAT	'R' BAT	EXTRAS
					BORDER	57	4	WELLHAM	33	1	M 10 NB 1	33	96	3	32	9	4
4·52	EDMONDS	1						5 6 4 P 4 · · 4 · ·	39	2	Round wkt	34	100			13	
56			ELLISON	11	8/5 1	58		6 1 · W	41	2		34³	101	4	33	13	4
57 DRINKS								RITCHIE								0	
5·01½			— · —	11				: : .	3			35					
04	— · —	2			4 1	59		4 : : 4 ³ 1	8			36	103		34	1	
08			— · —	12	· 1/3	61		: 7⁴ · · 3 1	12		† Diving stop (Edmonds)	37	105		35	2	
12	— · —	3			6(6)6/4 2 1	63		3 3 6 6 1	16			38	109		38	3	
15½			— · —	13				† : P † 4 6 1	22		M 11	39					
19½	— · —	4			: : : W	67	4					39⁴	109	5	38	3	4
2φ					PHILLIPS		LHB								0		
23	— · —	4			: 6 1	2					M 12	40					
25			BOTHAM	8	3 6 7/3 P 6 1 4 · 1	6	1	† : 8/7 1	24		† Almost bowled on	41	115		5	4	
30	— · —	5			6 P : : : 7 1	12					3 HR	42	116		6		
33½			— · —	9	6P †7 3	14		· 1/3 · 4 · 3 1	28		Ⓦ	43	120		9		5
38	— · —	6			1	15		4 5(6) · 3 ⁸ · 4 · 4 1	33	2		44	130		10	13	
41½			— · —	10				P † 3 · 1/2 7 1	39	3		45	136			19	
46	— · —	7			3 4 · : · 3 1	21	2					46	140		14		
48			— · —	11				: : x 6 † 1	45		M 13	47					
52½	— · —	8			761 1	22		: : 2 ¾ 1	50			48	141		15		
56			EMBUREY	9	: 1 8	24		6 : 4 † 1	54		† Missed stumping	49	142		16		
59	— · —	9			6P : : 2 x W	29	2					49⁵	144	6	18	19	5
6·01					BENNETT		RHB								0		
03	— · —	9			P 1	1						50					
04½			— · —	10	: : P 4 1	5		7 8 : : 1	56			51	145			20	
08	— · —	10			: 1	5	—	4 · · : 1	62	3	M 14 NB 1	52	145	6	0	20	5
6·10 STUMPS														S T U M P S		
3RD DAY 11·00			BOTHAM	12	: · 2/9 1	8		· · : 2 1	65			53	146		1		
04½	EMBUREY	11			: P · · 6 1	14					M 15	54					
06½			— · —	13	? · : 1	18		3 †6† 1	67		† Just behind mid-on	55	147			21	
11	— · —	12			7 1	19		7 : : 3 96 3 2 1	72			56	153		2	26	
14			— · —	14	† : · · · : 1	25					M 16	57					
18	— · —	13			8 4	26	1	: : : 5 8 1	77		4 HR	58	158		6	27	
20½			— · —	15	: 65 1	28		x : 1 † : 1	81			59	160		7	28	
25	— · —	14			3 6† 8 2 1	30		5 · 2 : 1	85		† 1 overthrow (LAMB)	60	165		10	30	
28½			— · —	16	7 1 † ·	32		· † · 5(6) 1	89		Round wkt — (BALLS 1,2→6)	61	167		11	31	
32½	— · —	15			: : : P† P : 1	37		8 1	90		† LB disallowed.	62	168			32	
35½			ELLISON	14	· · · : 1	40		: : 4 1	93			63	169			33	
39½	— · —	16			6 P P † 64 4	44		: 8 1	95		† Appeal ct Gower — S. mid-off	64	171		12	34	
42½			— · —	15	3 3/2 W	46	1		95	3	M 16 Out @ 43½. NB 1	64²	171	7	12	34	5

3RD DAY TIME	BOWLERS (BIRD) PAVILION END BOWLER	O.	(PALMER) VAUXHALL END BOWLER	O.	BATSMEN SCOREBOARD LEFT SCORING	BALLS	6s/4s	SCOREBOARD RIGHT SCORING	BALLS	6s/4s	AUSTRALIA 1ST INNINGS NOTES	O.	RUNS	W.	'L' BAT	'R' BAT	EXTRAS
					LAWSON	.	.	RITCHIE	95	3	M16 NB1	64²	171	7	0	34	5
11.45½			ELLISON	15	∶∶∶4̇	4	1					65	175		4		
47½	EMBUREY	17						6 4 7 ∶∶∶	101		M17	66					
50			– · –	16	7·5	5		3 3 · 4 ·	106			67	176		5		
54½	TAYLOR	9			· 2 x · 6/7 x	11						68	180		9		
59			– · –	17				1 4 ∶ EP 3 4	112			69	182			36	
12.03	– · –	10			↑ · x 3 ↑· 7 ·	17					† 2ND WARNING.	70	183		10		
07			– · –	18	∶ 4 ↑ 1E 4 · 2 · 1	22		8 4	113	4	†Good Stop (GOWER).	71	190		13	40	
11	– · –	11		·	2 4 2 E1 1 ∶ · W	26	1	7 1	114			71⁵	192	8	14	41	5
14					McDERMOTT										0		
16	– · –	11			EP·	1					•Dropped short leg (EDMONDS).	72					
17½			EDMONDS	11	∶ 5 5 3(6) 4	5	1	∶ 8 1	116			73	197		4	42	
21	– · –	12			· 8 1/3 · 1	8		6/5 1 ∶ 7 1	119		5HR	74	200		5	44	
25			– · –	12	9E 4 2 · 1	10		∶ 3 3/3 3 ∶ 4 1	123	5		75	207		7	49	
29	– · –	13			5(6)2E 4 1 5 ↑/7 ∶ 2	14	2	36 3 3	125		RITCHIE'S 50: 159'	76	218		14	53	
33			– · –	13	7 6	15	1/2	∶∶∶ 4 4	130			77	225		20	54	
36	BOTHAM	17						4 1E 7 2 ↑ ∶∶ 2 · 1	136			78	227			56	
41			– · –	14	6 1E 6 1 2 1	18		6/6 · 3 ∶	139			79	232		24	57	
45	– · –	18			4 · · 2 ∶ · 1	22		7/3 ∶ 2	141			80	235		25	59	
50			EMBUREY	18	8 0	23	1/2				Ritchie changed bat.	80¹	235	9	25	59	5
51					GILBERT	RHB					(crossed)				0		
53			– · –	18				5 · 7 5 ·	146		•RO chance (GILBERT throws) – M18 to EDMONDS.	81					
56	– · –	19			∶ 2 1 · 2 x 1	5	–	6 1	147	5	M18 NB1	82	237	9	1	60	5
1·00	LUNCH										LUNCH						
1·40			EMBUREY	19				∶ 6 ∶∶ 7 7 2 1	153			83	240			63	
43	BOTHAM	20			↑ ↑ ∶ 4x · W	9	–	2↑ 7/8 2 1	155	5	†Run refused.	84	241	10	1	64	5
1·46	ALL OUT										M18 NB1		ALL	OUT			
											505 balls						

SIXTH TEST
SHEET 8

3RD DAY TIME	BOWLERS (PALMER) PAVILION END BOWLER	O.	BOWLERS (BIRD) VAUXHALL END BOWLER	O.	BATSMEN SCOREBOARD LEFT SCORING	BALLS	6s/4s	SCOREBOARD RIGHT SCORING	BALLS	6s/4s	NOTES	O.	RUNS	W.	'L' BAT	'R' BAT	EXTRAS
					HILDITCH			WOOD		LHB	56 OVERS DUE						
1·59	BOTHAM	1			.↑:⁸₁	4		×↑:₂	2			1	1		1		
2·03½			TAYLOR	1	....⁷₁	9		.	3			2	2		2		
07½	—·—	2			⁸/⁷ : ⁸ ↑₁ .2.	14		⁴⁸	4			3	6		5	1	
12			—·—	2	}	14	-	:⁴⁸/⁷.4.	8	1		3⁴	10	-	5	5	-
2·14	RAIN				}						2 OVERS LOST				R.S.P.		
24			—·—	2	}			..	10			4					
26	BOTHAM	3			↑↑ ¹⁵ ↑: .2.	18			10	-	† Hit on chest.	4⁴	12	-	7	5	-
2·29	RAIN		·												R.S.P.		
3·40	TEA										36 OVERS LOST				TEA		
5·14	BOTHAM	3			::₁	20						5					
16			TAYLOR	3				P:..:ᴳ⁴⁸₁	16		• Chance to long-leg (ELLISON).	6	13			6	
20½	—·—	4	}					ᴱˣ∴W	18	1		6²	13	1	7	6	-
21			}					WESSELS		LHB					0		
23	—·—	4	}					:....₁	4		M1	7					
26½			—·—	4	:.◌:ᴾ⁷·³₂w	27	-				(NB) NB1	8	16	2	9	0	1
31					BORDER		LHB								0		
33	—·—	5			:⁸.4₁	3	1	.↑²·↑₁	7			9	21		4	1	
38			—·—	5	⁸.₁	4		.² ↑³²/⁰⁸ ·¹ ◌·2·₁	13		(NB) NB2	10	26		5	4	2
43	—·—	6			↑²↑ ⁷⁸: ..	10					† Gooch stop (EMBURY) ‡ Edmonds hit (leg)	11					
47½			—·—	6	↑↑.⁸ᵗ ①.4.	14	2	.⁸ ¹/² .↑.₁	16		M2 NB3 1HR ‡ Hit on shoulder.	12	33		10	6	
53	—·—	7			.⁷.3	15		P²:..ᴱ¹:w₁	21		A.J.STEWART SUB (EMBURY) - 1 over.	13	37	3	13	7	2
57								WELLHAM							0		
59			ELLISON	1	:²↑₁	16		.:..₁	5			14	38		14		
6·04	—·—	8			:.×↑:. ²⁴/⁴⁸ ²4	22	3	.			† Round wkt	15	44		20		
09			—·—	2				¹⁶×. ⁸ 2·.·2.₁	11			16	48			4	
13	—·—	9			◌³/²⁸.₁	25		:↑↑ ⁶⁵₁	15		RO BUTCHER Lub (EDMONDS). (NB)	17	51		21	5	3
18½			—·—	3	}			×ᴸ∴w₁	17	-	† almost bowled. NB4	17²	51	4	21	5	3
19					}			RITCHIE			Edmonds back.				0		
21			—·—	3	}			.⁴..₁	4		M3	18					
24	TAYLOR	7			P:.⁷P.:₁	31					M4	19					
29			—·—	4				².⁶↑:.₁	10		M5	20					
32	—·—	8			¹/²2ᴸ.⁸₁	37						21	52		22		
37			—·—	5	..²ᴾ2..	43						22	54		24		
41	—·—	9						:¹ᴱ³²⁴↑·.2₁	16			23	56			2	
45			—·—	6	:..↑×.₁	49					M6	24					
49	—·—	10						⁴:..³/²⁴ ³.21₁	22		2HR	25	59			5	
53			—·—	7	⁸.₁	50		.⁴ᴾ⁸.₁	27			26	61		25	6	
58	EMBUREY	1			²↑₁	51	3	.⁵:.ᴾ₁	32	-		27	62	4	26	6	3
7·02	STUMPS										M6 NB4				STUMPS		

215

4TH DAY TIME	BOWLERS (PALMER) PAVILION END BOWLER	O.	(BIRD) VAUXHALL END BOWLER	O.	BATSMEN SCOREBOARD LEFT SCORING	BALLS	6s 4s	SCOREBOARD RIGHT SCORING	BALLS	6s 4s	AUSTRALIA 2ND INNINGS NOTES	O.	RUNS	W.	'L' BAT	'R' BAT	EXTRAS
					BORDER	51	3	RITCHIE	32	-	M6 NB4	27	62	4	26	6	3
11·00			ELLISON	8	:E9 6/7 7 4 1	55	4	: :	34		• Legside wk chance	28	67		31		
05	BOTHAM	10			: 7 4 1	58		EP ↑ X	37			29	68		32		
09			— • —	9	6 7 1	60		3 E2 4 :	41			30	69		33		
13	— • —	11			P 4 ↑ ↑ : 2 : : :	66						31	71		35		
18			— • —	10	)			E1 W	42	-		31¹	71	5	35	6	3
					(			PHILLIPS		LHB						0	
20			— • —	10	4 . .	68		E9 3 . 3	3			32	74			3	
23½	— • —	12						4B ↑↑ 7 7 8/9	9		(4B) ↑ Hit on chest via edge.	33	79			4	7
28½			— • —	11				. . ↑↑ . 4	15	1		34	83			8	
32½	— • —	13			EP 2 3↑ 4/5 . 4 : ↑	73	5	EP	16		↑ Good stop (Robinson)	35	88		40		
37½			— • —	12	9 1 : . .	77		4 5(4)	18			36	90		41	9	
41	— • —	14			1/2	78		6(4) 2 ↑ .	23			37	92		42	10	
45½			— • —	13	4 . X . . ↑ L	84	6				3HR	38	96		46		
49½	— • —	15			)			E1 W	24	1		38	96	6	46	10	7
					(			BENNETT								0	
52	— • —	15			)			2 ↑ 9 2 1	86		↑ 2 overthrows (EDMONDS)	39	100		49	1	
56			— • —	14	5(4) 1	87		: : . X 5/6	8		Border's 50: 145	40	102		50	2	
12·00	— • —	16			X 7 4 . 3	89		↑ : ? ? 1	12			41	106		53	3	
04½			— • —	15	7 4 E1 4 1 W	92	7	7/8 . 3	14			41⁵	114	7	58	6	7
08					) LAWSON							42				0	
10			— • —	15	4 . 1	1						42					
11	— • —	17						: . ↑ . ↑↑ .	20		↑ Round wkt. M7	43					
16			— • —	16	8 3 6 2 : . . 4	7	1					44	120		6		
20	TAYLOR	11			4/3	8		1 E1 E3/2 P61 : 4 ↑ . 0 .	26	1	(NB) NB 5	45	127		7	11	8
25½			— • —	17	E1 W	10	1					45²	127	8	7	11	8
26½					) McDERMOTT											0	
28½			— • —	17	↑ X 1/2 . . 2W	4	-					46	129	9	2	11	8
30					GILBERT											0	
33	— • —	12			. .			. . 5 W	29	1		46³	129	10	0	11	8
12·35	ALL OUT										M7 NB5		ALL	OUT			
	ENGLAND WON BY AN INNINGS AND 94 RUNS										284 balls		ASHES	REGAINED			

VAUXHALL END

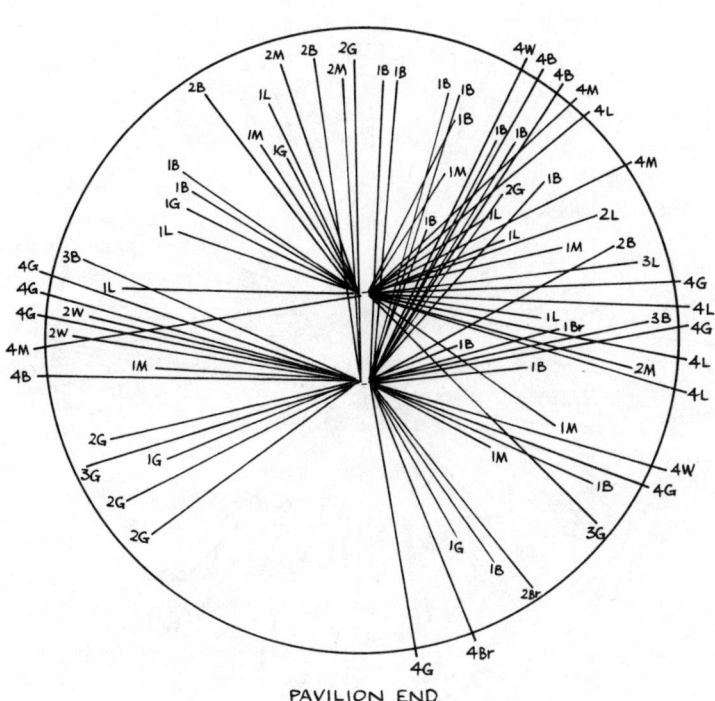

PAVILION END

BOWLER	SYMBOL	RUNS					
		1	2	3	4	6	TOTAL
BENNETT	B	15	3	2	3	-	39
BORDER	Br	1	1	-	1	-	7
GILBERT	G	4	5	2	7	-	48
LAWSON	L	6	1	1	4	-	27
McDERMOTT	M	6	3	-	3	-	24
WESSELS	W	-	2	-	2	-	12
TOTAL		32	15	5	20	-	157

D.I. GOWER at The Oval

157 RUNS
215 BALLS
337 MINUTES
(left-handed batsman)

© BILL FRINDALL 1985

SIXTH TEST
GOOCH CHART

VAUXHALL END

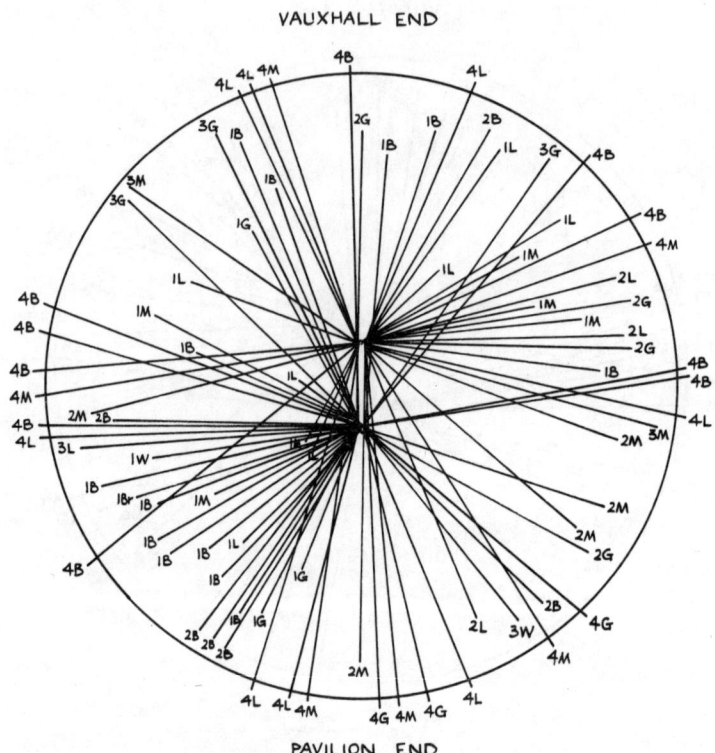

PAVILION END

BOWLER	SYMBOL	RUNS				
		1	2	3	4	6	TOTAL
BENNETT	B	13	6	-	10	-	65
BORDER	Br	1	-	-	-	-	1
GILBERT	G	3	4	3	3	-	32
LAWSON	L	7	3	1	8	-	48
McDERMOTT	M	6	5	2	6	-	46
WESSELS	W	1	-	1	-	-	4
TOTALS		31	18	7	27	-	196

G.A. GOOCH at The Oval

196 RUNS
310 BALLS
424 MINUTES

© BILL FRINDALL 1985

218

REFLECTIONS

The Ashes regained

In regaining the Ashes, which had been surrendered in Australia in 1983, England ended the series with victories by an innings at both Edgbaston and the Oval. This was a feat that had not been achieved since 1956, and one that had looked improbable earlier when England, after winning at Headingley, had experienced great difficulty in bowling Australia out at Lord's and Trent Bridge and were frustrated by the weather at Old Trafford.

Australia's batting, held together magnificently by Border until the fourth Test, was eventually found wanting, largely because in the face of large England totals, made at a brisk rate, relatively inexperienced batsmen were obliged to play a game foreign to their attacking nature and lacked the patience, self-discipline and in some cases the technique to do it.

From the moment that England broke through with the freak dismissal of Phillips on the last afternoon at Edgbaston, their bowlers and batsmen proved irresistible. Despite considerable interference from the weather, the Edgbaston Test was still won in less than four days' playing time, thus maintaining the ground's remarkable record of producing a result in each of its last eight Tests and all of them with more than a day to spare.

At the Oval, such was England's dominance that the match was over after some 90 minutes on the fourth morning, after 31 overs had been lost on the third day. The game had been sold out in advance for its first four days, which was thought to be without precedent.

For David Gower, the series was an unmitigated success. His batting, which had worried him during the one-day series to the point where suggestions that he should resign were being freely offered, regained its poise and power more or less from the moment when the selectors showed their faith in him by reappointing him at Lord's for the rest of the series.

Thereafter, he was the Gower of old, making three centuries in the series, a feat achieved previously only by Hammond, Hobbs, Leyland and Sutcliffe, and figuring in two consecutive partnerships of more than 300, which only Hutton had achieved. Moreover, as the series progressed, he looked more at ease in the handling of his side and made few, if any, errors.

The key to England's success was the consistency as a unit of the top six batsmen, who were unchanged, unprecedentedly, throughout the series and five times made totals of over 400 (on the occasion they did not, at Lord's, Australia won). It was the ability of Gower, Gooch, Robinson and Gatting to build long innings that gave England the platform for victory. Even though the contribution of Lamb and Botham was less substantial, England still scored their runs quicker than any other side in an Ashes series, which no one could have foreseen when the relative strengths and weaknesses of the sides were being assessed at the start.

Australia's fast bowlers, who were expected to be the key to the whole thing, were found wanting. True, the pre-tour disruption over South Africa, which cost them the services of Alderman, an effective bowler in English conditions, proved a setback. But even McDermott, who took 30 wickets in his first full series at the age of 20, found the day-in, day-out slog of bowling on unhelpful pitches in bleak weather too much, and he was betrayed in the end by his lack of experience. He will be lying in wait for England come the next series: nothing is more certain. Lawson, although he kept going valiantly, seemed weakened and wearied by an infection contracted early in the tour.

Thomson could not turn back the clock and was, ironically, omitted at the Oval on the one pitch that would have helped him. Nor were Australia over-blessed with spin bowling of class, a great disadvantage on the low, slow pitches that prevailed at four venues. The result was that pressure built up on batting that had always looked – Border apart – well short of England's.

They were not helped either by the weather, which tended to disrupt the tourists' efforts to find form between the Tests, or by the unfortunate habit of some English counties of fielding less than full-strength attacks against them.

Even so, after the weather had assisted Border and Phillips to save the fourth Test, there were growing fears in the English camp that the bowlers were not available to win the series, despite the efforts of the rejuvenated Botham. England's problems in that department were such that, even with the contribution of Emburey and Edmonds, who took 31 wickets between them, the lack of support for Botham suggested that Border might some-how camouflage Australia's increasingly apparent batting inadequacies.

Botham, who is now only 12 behind Lillee's record 355 Test wickets, returned after his winter's rest to bowl, at times, as fast as he ever has for

England, according to Gower, whose gradual use of him in much shorter stints was also a factor.

But after five other bowlers had fallen by the wayside, the choice of Ellison, who was injured at the start, for Edgbaston proved felicitous. Suddenly, England had a bowler who was both penetrative and accurate, and they won a Test, improbably, after much interference from the weather.

He followed his 10 wickets there with another seven at the Oval. With Taylor playing a less spectacular but still significant part, Gower finished with an attack at his disposal that, in English conditions and against these opponents, proved highly effective.

England were thus equipped to win a highly entertaining series that was played in the best of spirits and, for the most part, in front of capacity crowds.

Series Averages

England – Batting

	M	I	NO	HS	R	Avge	100	50
M.W. GATTING	6	9	3	160	527	87.83	2	3
D.I. GOWER	6	9	0	215	732	81.33	3	1
R.T. ROBINSON	6	9	1	175	490	61.25	2	1
G.A. GOOCH	6	9	0	196	487	54.11	1	2
A.J. LAMB	6	8	1	67	256	36.57	–	1
J.E. EMBUREY	6	6	2	33	130	32.50	–	–
I.T. BOTHAM	6	8	0	85	250	31.25	–	2
P.R. DOWNTON	6	7	1	54	114	19.00	–	1
P.H. EDMONDS	5	5	0	21	47	9.40	–	–
P.J.W. ALLOTT	4	5	1	12	27	6.75	–	–

Also batted: J.P. AGNEW 2*; N.G. COWANS 22*; R.M. ELLISON 3;
N.A. FOSTER 3,0; A. SIDEBOTTOM 2; L.B. TAYLOR 1*; P. WILLEY 36,3*.

England – Bowling

	O	M	R	W	Avge	Best
ELLISON	75.5	20	185	17	10.88	6–77
BOTHAM	251.4	36	855	31	27.58	5–109
EMBUREY	248.4	75	544	19	28.63	5–82
EDMONDS	225.5	59	549	15	36.60	4–40
TAYLOR	63.3	11	178	4	44.50	2–34
ALLOTT	113	22	297	5	59.40	2–74

Also bowled: AGNEW 23–2–99–0; COWANS 33–6–128–2; FOSTER 23–1–83–1;
GATTING 5–0–16–0; GOOCH 41.2–10–102–2; LAMB 1–0–10–0;
SIDEBOTTOM 18.4–3–65–1.

England – Fielding

20 – DOWNTON (19 ct, 1 st). 8 – BOTHAM, EDMONDS. 7 – LAMB. 6 – GOWER.
5 – ROBINSON. 4 – GOOCH. 3 – EMBUREY. 1 – ELLISON, TAYLOR.

*not out

Australia – Batting

	M	I	NO	HS	R	Avge	100	50
A.R. BORDER	6	11	2	196	597	66.33	2	1
G.M. RITCHIE	6	11	1	146	422	42.20	1	2
A.M.J. HILDITCH	6	11	0	119	424	38.54	1	1
W.B. PHILLIPS	6	11	1	91	350	35.00	–	2
K.C. WESSELS	6	11	0	83	368	33.45	–	3
G.M. WOOD	5	9	0	172	260	28.88	1	–
S.P. O'DONNELL	5	8	1	48	184	26.28	–	–
D.C. BOON	4	7	0	61	124	17.71	–	1
G.F. LAWSON	6	9	1	53	119	14.87	–	1
C.J. McDERMOTT	6	9	1	35	103	12.87	–	–
R.G. HOLLAND	4	5	1	10	15	3.75	–	–
J.R. THOMSON	2	4	4	28*	38	–	–	–

Also batted: M.J. BENNETT 12,11; D.R. GILBERT 1,0*;
G.R.J. MATTHEWS 4,17; D.M. WELLHAM 13,5.

Australia – Bowling

	O	M	R	W	Avge	Best
McDERMOTT	234.2	21	901	30	30.03	8–141
LAWSON	246	38	830	22	37.72	5–103
HOLLAND	172	41	465	6	77.50	5–68
O'DONNELL	145.4	31	487	6	81.16	3–37
THOMSON	56	4	275	3	91.66	2–166

Also bowled: BENNETT 32–8–111–1; BORDER 11–1–37–0; GILBERT 21–2–96–1;
MATTHEWS 9–2–21–0; RITCHIE 1–0–10–0; WESSELS 6–2–18–0.

Australia – Fielding

11 – BORDER, PHILLIPS. 4 – BOON.
3 – HILDITCH, O'DONNELL, RITCHIE, WESSELS.
2 – McDERMOTT. 1 – BENNETT, HOLLAND, THOMSON, WELLHAM, WOOD.

*not out